PHILOSOPHY

in the

RENAISSANCE

PHILOSOPHY
in the
RENAISSANCE

An Anthology

Edited by
Paul Richard Blum and James G. Snyder

The Catholic University of America Press
Washington, D.C.

Copyright © 2023
The Catholic University of America Press
All rights reserved.
The paper used in this publication meets the minimum requirements of
American National Standards for Information Science—Permanence
of Paper for Printed Library Materials, ANSI Z39.48–1984.
∞

Cataloging-in-Publication Data
is available at the Library of Congress
ISBN 9780813236209
eBook ISBN 9780813236216

Publication of this book was made possible
through support from The Center for the Humanities
at Loyola University Maryland and the Office of
Academic Affairs at Marist College.

CONTENTS

Introduction   1
Paul Richard Blum and James G. Snyder

1   Ramón Llull (1232–1316): *Felix, or the Book of Wonders*   10
Edited by Paul Richard Blum

2   George Gemistos Pletho (c. 1360–1454): *Commentary on Chaldaean Oracles*   34
Edited by Jozef Matula

3   George of Trebizond (1396–1474/75): *Comparison of Plato and Aristotle: God as the Absolutely First*   49
Edited by John Monfasani

4   Basil Bessarion (c. 1403–1472): *Against the Calumniator of Plato*   67
Edited by Eva Del Soldato

5   Lorenzo Valla (1406/7–1457): *Encomium of St. Thomas Aquinas*   82
Edited by Paul Richard Blum

6   Nicholas of Cusa (1401–1464): *Compendium*   96
Edited by Detlef Thiel

7   Leon Battista Alberti (1404–1472): *Theogenius*   102
Edited by Timothy Kircher

8   Giovanni Pico della Mirandola (1463–1494): *Spiritual Writings*   118
Edited by Victor M. Salas

Contents

9   Marsilio Ficino (1433–1499): *Letters*   136
Edited by James G. Snyder

10   Pietro Pomponazzi (1462–1525): *Exposition*   156
of Aristotle's First Book On the Parts of Animals
Edited by Tomáš Nejeschleba

11   Niccolò Machiavelli (1469–1527: *Discursus on*   169
Florentine Matters after the Death of Lorenzo
de' Medici the Younger
Edited by Mark Jurdjevic

12   Heinrich Cornelius Agrippa von Nettesheim   187
(1486–1535): *The Vanity of Arts and Sciences*
Edited by Paul Richard Blum

13   Juan Luis Vives (1493–1540): *Introduction to Wisdom*   202
Edited by Paul Richard Blum

14   Philipp Melanchthon (1497–1560): *Of Rational*   223
Ability, or Mind
Edited by Günter Frank and Gregory Graybill

15   Petrus Ramus (1515–1572): *Dialectic*   240
Edited by Robert Goulding

16   Bernardino Telesio (1509–1588): *On Mind and Wisdom*   262
Edited by Paul Richard Blum

17   Jacopo Zabarella (1533–1589): *On the Constitution*   270
of Natural Science
Edited by Per Landgren

18   Michel de Montaigne (1533–1592): *Of Experience*   280
Edited by Paul Richard Blum

19   Francesco Patrizi (1529–1597): *On History*   291
Edited by Paul Richard Blum

Contents

ix

20   Giordano Bruno (1548–1600): *On the Infinite,*   312
Universe and Worlds

Edited by Paul Richard Blum

21   Francisco Suárez (1548–1617): *On Free-Will*   333

Edited by Sydney Penner

22   Tommaso Campanella (1568–1639): *Soul, Intellect,*   350
and Body

Edited by Elisabeth Blum

List of Contributors   369
Index   373

PHILOSOPHY
in the
RENAISSANCE

INTRODUCTION

Philosophy took an interesting turn in the fifteenth and sixteenth centuries, which could not have been expected from the medieval, Scholastic point of view, and that is clearly distinct from important developments that occurred in the seventeenth and eighteenth centuries. The very discovery of the changing nature of philosophy is owed to the philosophers of the Renaissance. During this period, humanists searched for and rediscovered the philosophical writings of classical antiquity, texts that had been lost and forgotten in libraries. Once recovered and disseminated, these texts provided philosophers with a diverse array of new methods, questions, and theories that were previously unavailable to philosophers in the West. The Renaissance is thus a period of great change, experimentation, and upheaval in philosophy.

To view philosophy as inherently developing and changing over the centuries, however, has not always been a popular position to hold, for if philosophy discovers truth, and if truth is objective and unchangeable, then all of philosophy should be just one. As long as philosophy means "longing for wisdom," however —that is, philosophy is not yet truth and not always wisdom—its aim is to develop different and distinct ways towards truth and wisdom. Truth as the objective realm, in which all existence is founded, and wisdom as the habit of mind and character aiming at this realm, go well together in this human endeavor called philosophy. Consequently, philosophy cannot exist without changing and adjusting toward its aim. Renaissance intellectuals termed their era the rebirth and revival of ancient wisdom, and it is obvious that something that can be neglected and then reborn naturally and inherently changes, even if it aspires toward the unchanging.[1]

In light of these considerations, it should come as no surprise that Renaissance philosophy has remained, to this day, largely overlooked and underappreciated by historians of philosophy. The Renaissance is obstinately peripheral to the most prominent narratives about the history of philosophy and its development, narratives that stress the importance of philosophy in the periods that come immediately before and after the Renaissance, namely, medieval Scholasticism and seventeenth- and eighteenth-century philosophy and science, respectively. The Scholastics eagerly interlinked truth with revelation and authority. As a result, the idea of an unchanging philosophy as expressed in one, or very few authorities, tended to deny the reasonableness of varying approaches and therefore dismissed any philosophy that emphasized variation. On the other hand, early modern empiricism and rationalism up to the philosophy of the Enlightenment increasingly emphasized the personal research of the scientist and the fundamental subjectivity of understanding in the human mind. While this approach allows for variations, it still denied the developmental and evolutionary aspect of philosophy not validated by an ultimate goal, be that truth of facts or ideas. Modern science and philosophy believe in the virtual attainment of understanding that is conclusive, and therefore, they must deem preceding phases of research as something to be overcome and effectively negligible. As we will see in this anthology, Renaissance philosophers focused on the potential for change, improvement, recuperating lost insights, and the joy of thinking for themselves and with one another.

This anthology accompanies *Philosophers of the Renaissance,* edited

---

1. Some scholars repudiate the terms Renaissance and humanism and instead prefer chronological or vague concepts like 'early modern' or 'premodern.' See, for example, Henrik Lagerlund and Benjamin Hill, eds., *The Routledge Companion to Sixteenth-Century Philosophy* (New York: Routledge, 2017). If circumscribed and defined as done here, however, "Renaissance" and "humanism" have informative properties that go beyond negative ("pre-") or merely chronological descriptors. Cf. Christopher S. Celenza, "What Counted as Philosophy in the Italian Renaissance? The History of Philosophy, the History of Science, and Styles of Life," *Critical Inquiry* 39, no. 2 (2013): 367–401.

by Paul Richard Blum, with a collection of representative primary texts.[2] This book presents twenty-two thinkers and a great variety of philosophical themes, methods, literary styles, and personalities. Each entry was selected because it presents a central theme in the respective philosopher's thought. All entries include a brief introduction by translators and prominent scholars, as well as short bibliographies of primary and secondary sources should the reader want to learn more. The intended audience of this anthology includes specialists in the history of philosophy, as well as students of the history of philosophy. The anthology should be useful to historians of philosophy working in the Renaissance itself, as it brings together a diverse range of selections that are collected here for the first time. We also believe the book will provide historians of philosophy working in other periods, many of whom are unfamiliar with the philosophers of the fifteenth and sixteenth centuries, with an entry point to the rich and varied nature of philosophy in the Renaissance.

This book is also designed with teachers and students in mind, because it will help philosophy instructors provide their students with a more accurate and nuanced picture of the history and development of philosophy in Europe in the fifteenth and sixteenth centuries. This volume will obviously be useful to stand-alone classes in the history of Renaissance philosophy, which are admittedly few and far between. Further, the vast majority of philosophy departments require the study of medieval and early modern philosophy in their curricula, and this volume should help instructors properly contextualize the development of philosophy from, say, Aquinas to Descartes.

The collection opens with a selection from Ramón Llull, who chronologically belongs to the Middle Ages, but in the excerpt we provide, it is obvious that his thinking had evolved from Scholasticism in important ways that will resonate with many Renaissance philosophers. Llull had a lasting impact up to the Enlightenment through the development of natural theology, that is, the attempt to prove the existence and properties of God using logical arguments. The excerpt presented here combines his rational method of theology with the literary form of a dialogue cherished by humanists.

2. Paul Richard Blum, ed., *Philosophers of the Renaissance* (Washington, D.C.: The Catholic University of America Press, 2010).

4   INTRODUCTION

One may reasonably claim that modern philosophy was triggered by the presence of Byzantine scholars in Italy in the early fifteenth century.[3] Under the pressure of the Ottoman Empire, religious, political, and philosophical representatives travelled to Italy, bringing with them a renewed interest in ancient and medieval Greek culture. Georgios Gemistos Pletho published oracles that allegedly originated among the Chaldeans. In doing so, he encouraged his contemporaries to interpret non-Christian mythical sources philosophically and promoted the revival of pagan wisdom as an alternative or a complement to Christian revelation. George of Trebizond and Basil Bessarion opened a long-lasting debate over the priority of Plato vs. Aristotle in philosophy. This was a response to the leadership of Aristotelianism that emerged in thirteenth-century western scholasticism, and the debate lasted into the eighteenth century as the question of whether the two ancient Greek fathers of philosophy were favorable or detrimental to Christianity.

Lorenzo Valla and Nicholas of Cusa witnessed the revival of Greek scholarship. Valla engaged in philological and historical research into the sources of Christian wisdom and intellectual politics. He was instrumental in criticizing medieval philosophical theology, and the text presented here, *Encomium of St. Thomas Aquinas*, shows how he contextualized the authority of Thomas Aquinas. This text is also a prime example of Renaissance rhetoric. Nicholas of Cusa, who had escorted the Byzantine delegation to the Council of Ferrara-Florence, transformed the quest for philosophical theology, inspired by Llull, into speculation that if God can be known by his works, then creation is comparable to the human act of design. Comparable with Nicholas, the architect Leon Battista Alberti wrote about art and perspective; however, the dialogue chosen for this book represents the humanist genre of dialogical narrative, which aptly conveys the tensions of civic life, fortune, and the pursuit of happiness in a social context.

Giovanni Pico della Mirandola and Marsilio Ficino figure prominently in the revival of Platonic and Neoplatonic philosophy in Florence.[4] In

---

3. John Monfasani, *Byzantine Scholars in Renaissance Italy: Cardinal Bessarion and Other Émigrés: Selected Essays* (Aldershot: Variorum, 1995).

4. Rocco Rubini, *The Other Renaissance: Italian Humanism between Hegel and Heidegger* (Chicago: University of Chicago Press, 2014). We have arranged the authors by the

INTRODUCTION

the works of Pico and Ficino, philosophy becomes a culture and way of life that also aims at the health and improvement of the soul. In addition to Platonism, Pico and Ficino synthesize a wide range of philosophical sources from antiquity in their treatises. Pico is best known for his eclecticism in the collection of *900 Theses* of philosophy from all schools and for his treatise on the *Dignity of Man*. The spiritual writings selected for this anthology remind the reader of Pico's involvement in the humanist quest for union with God and dignity of spiritual life, themes that were also the driving motivation for his better-known works. Ficino is remembered today mostly for his voluminous defense of the immortality of the soul found in his *Platonic Theology*, as well as for his translations and commentaries on Plato and Plotinus. The selection in this anthology represents another feature of Renaissance philosophizing—philosophical letters. Ever since Francesco Petrarca (1304–1374), epistolary correspondence was more than plain communication; it was the mirror of the interpersonal concern for the friend, which ideally inspires speculation. Ficino wrote many shorter treatises in the form of letters to friends who are, at the same time, personal guarantors of the authenticity of the thoughts and represent the ideal audience.

Pietro Pomponazzi represents another important strain of Renaissance philosophy, namely, the rediscovery of the authentic philosophy of Aristotle, liberated from layers of Christian interpretation. With his famous treatise *On the Immortality of the Soul*, he used Aristotle to deny that the immortality of the soul independent from the body can be defended on philosophical grounds; however, he admitted that revelation and faith may be used to maintain immortality. With this approach, he opened the divide between science and religion that dominates philosophy in modernity. Engagement with a naturalistic interpretation of Aristotle, and the competing roles of science and faith, are visible in the lecture we present in this volume.

Niccolò Machiavelli is probably the best-known philosopher of the Re-

---

year of death because typically writers are most productive and influential during their later years. Pico was thirty years younger than Ficino but died five years earlier; therefore, he comes first. Moreover, Ficino appears after Pico because of his lasting impact on subsequent philosophy, but we kept the three Byzantine thinkers—Pletho, Trebizond, and Bessarion—in the order they responded to one another.

naissance. This is in large part due to his *Prince,* which is to this day still standard reading in philosophy and political theory. The *Discursus on Florentine Matters* shows his philosophy in the historic, social, and political context of Florence, which reminds the reader that sophisticated philosophical texts were, as it befits a humanist, addressed to real humans and the challenges they faced in a concrete social environment, in this case, the city state of Florence.

Magic has often repulsed readers from the serious study of some segments of Renaissance philosophy.[5] Early modern thinkers from Francis Bacon to Robert Boyle disparaged philosophical magic for its lack of empirical rigor. Heinrich Cornelius Agrippa von Nettesheim is known to have advocated magic and other occult sciences, but he was also the author of a fundamental critique of all disciplines with which humans pride themselves to dominate the world. His *Incertitude and Vanity of Sciences* contrasts human achievements and spiritual beatitude. With this treatise, Agrippa thus joins the choir of fideists and sceptics, not unlike Pomponazzi. Also catering to spiritual and religious sentiments was Juan Luis Vives. He was among the Christian writers who adapted ancient Stoicism to make the humanist case for the dignified life plausible. Wisdom requires enduring critique of the natural and societal environment with ultimate beatitude in view. Both Agrippa's and Vives's works were circulated in early English translations for consumption by an educated Christian audience; we present slightly edited versions, adapted to contemporary readers, that convey some of the early modern reception of humanism.

With Philipp Melanchthon, we enter the academic world of Lutheranism. His interpretation of Aristotle's theory of the soul remained compatible with theology, but to the medieval approaches he added concern for the individual salvation within a solid scientific context of biology, epistemology, and medicine. On the Reformed side of the denominational spectrum, we read Petrus Ramus, who taught in Paris and laid the foundations of what in modern parlance is called methodology: instead of arguing about unknowables, as metaphysics does, we need to ascertain the method and order with which reality can be classified and represented to the mind. This theory of method had the advantage of liberating from submission to

---

5. Christopher Partridge, ed., *The Occult World* (Milton Park: Routledge, 2015).

INTRODUCTION

authorities and laying the weight of intellectual certitude on the individual mind, as René Descartes will continue to do a century later. With Pomponazzi, Melanchthon, and Ramus, we have samples of university lectures of the time.

Bernardino Telesio challenged the Aristotelian approach to natural philosophy, claiming that one has to detect the internal principles of reality. The sections of his work presented in this book address the problem of cognition and wisdom. Here, Telesio appears as one of the first physicalist philosophers of mind, despite the fact that he maintained that the human mind is infused by God. With Jacopo Zabarella, who taught in Padua years after Pomponazzi, we meet another innovator of Aristotelian philosophy. He was pivotal in the buildup of the modern scientific method, which inspired Galileo. Scientific research requires the coordination of theoretical patterns and logical operations with mathematical and physical evidence.[6]

The paradigm of modern skepticism was developed in Michel de Montaigne's *Essais*, a work that from the outset refused to submit to any prescribed or preformed system of thought. The work concludes with diagnosing ignorance as the fundamental human condition. The revival of thoroughgoing skepticism, which was a philosophy of life for some in classical Greek antiquity, played a significant role in the development of early modern epistemology, and it is connected with laying the groundwork for science in the seventeenth and eighteenth centuries. Again, we present a slightly edited English translation from the early seventeenth century, this one produced by an Italian émigré from the time of Shakespeare.

Toward the end of the sixteenth century, philosophers started to reap the fruits of humanist and Renaissance innovations in philosophy. Francesco Patrizi excelled not only in anti-Aristotelianism, he also held that language is key to accurately appreciating and understanding the world of humanity. We present a chapter of his philosophy of history that combines mythology, dialogue, and narrativity. Giordano Bruno is mostly known as a devotee of Copernicus and, allegedly, a martyr of philosophical freedom. His most influential works were dialogues, each of them prefaced with a personal letter, as authors of the time were wont to do. The letter made

---

6. W. A. Wallace, *Prelude to Galileo: Essays on Medieval and Sixteenth-Century Sources of Galileo's Thought* (Dordrecht: Springer Science & Business Media, 2012).

8 INTRODUCTION

available here expounds his theory of the infinitude of the world. In the background of most authors were still versions of medieval scholasticism. Since the order of the Jesuits re-energized the power of scholastic debate, Francisco Suárez applied its method to one of the key problems of humanism and of ethics in general, that of free will and the relation between intellect and will. The volume concludes with Tommaso Campanella, best known for his *City of the Sun*, who also wrote a multivolume *Theology*; the excerpt here is a sample of his anthropology, which wavers between naturalism and spiritualism, including his most notable theory assuming that the divine Trinity is reflected in all things and in human nature.

The texts in this anthology were selected by the editors according to two criteria: they had to be representative of the individual author's philosophy, and they should be less easily available to contemporary readers of English. As mentioned, in three cases, we re-edited old translations so as to give a taste of how the early modern public would receive these philosophies; in some cases, we reprinted, with editorial improvements, existing modern translations. The majority of the texts have been translated for this anthology for the first time. We have been parsimonious with comments and bibliographies so that new readers are not scared away by the amount of existing scholarship.

The professions of the philosophers included in this volume are as varied as their methods and theories. Among the Renaissance philosophers included in this volume we find traditional academics (Pomponazzi, Melanchthon, Ramus, Zabarella, Patrizi, Suárez); more or less independent scholars (Llull, Pletho, Trebizond, Alberti, Pico, Agrippa, Vives, Telesio, Montaigne, Campanella); dependents on the support of courts and patrons (Valla, Ficino, Machiavelli, Bruno); Dominican friars (Bruno, Campanella); one Jesuit (Suárez); and two high-ranking Church officials (Bessarion, Nicholas of Cusa). Besides Italy, the regions of origin or activity were Byzantium, Germany, France, the Low Countries, Croatia, Spain, and England. From this range of backgrounds there emerges a multifaced picture of where philosophy was most at home in the Renaissance.

This anthology is a companion volume to *Philosophers of the Renaissance*, and its scope is limited to the authors originally included in that book. Readers might reasonably miss Francesco Petrarca, Coluccio Salutati, Étienne de La Boétie, Erasmus of Rotterdam, Thomas More, Leon-

INTRODUCTION

ardo da Vinci, Girolamo Fracastoro, Francisco de Vitoria, Agostino Nifo, Paracelsus, Jakob Böhme—just to name a few. However, this collection expands and complements two older anthologies of Renaissance philosophy published in 1948 and 1973.[7] If this new anthology makes scholars and students curious, encouraging them to seek out more Renaissance philosophy, it has served its purpose.

Finally, acknowledgements are in order: Besides the editors and translators mentioned in the several sections, we are indebted to Phillip Arvanitis and Kevin Kane for proofreading sections that were written by non-native speakers of English. We would also like to thank Adrien D'Aprile for his assistance finalizing this manuscript for publication. Work on this project was supported by the Center for the Humanities at Loyola University Maryland and the Office of Academic Affairs at Marist College in Poughkeepsie, New York.

—Paul Richard Blum and James G. Snyder

7. Ernst Cassirer, Paul Oskar Kristeller, and John Herman Randall, eds., *The Renaissance Philosophy of Man: Selections in Translation* (Chicago: University of Chicago Press, 1948); Leonard A. Kennedy, ed., *Renaissance Philosophy: New Translations: Lorenzo Valla (1407–1457), Paul Cortese (1456–1510), Cajetan (1469–1534), Tiberio Baccilieri (ca. 1470–1511), Juan Luis Vives (1492–1540), Peter Ramus (1515–1572)* (The Hague: Mouton, 1973).

1

RAMÓN LLULL
(1232–1316)

Felix, or the Book of Wonders

PAUL RICHARD BLUM

INTRODUCTION

Raymond Llull was a layman who engaged in multicultural and multireligious efforts during the transition from the Middle Ages to the Renaissance.[1] He was born in 1232 on the island of Mallorca and died in 1316 on a ship returning from a mission in North Africa. Mallorca, part of Catalonia, was home to Christians, Jews, and Muslims. Hence, Llull was inspired to reconcile these religions and create a common faith. To this end, Llull sought to develop a common ground of human conversation and rationality that exists among all religious peoples. This work, albeit lofty, did not exclude the use of force, however, if benevolent argument failed. Llull besieged the powers of Europe—popes, kings, and princes—to support his educational approach or else wage a crusade of unification. His own emphasis lay on information, debate, and education, and he began by developing his own skills. He sought training in Latin, hired a Muslim to teach him Arabic, and improved his mastery of the liberal arts. Many of his

---

1. The Spanish name Ramón Llull is spelled in Latin as Raimundus Lullus and in English as Raymond Lull.

writings are in Catalan, while those in Latin are of poor linguistic quality; he is said to have written in Arabic, but no work has survived.

Llull's work has theological, logical, and literary aspects. Theologically, he developed a rational approach to the mysteries of Christian doctrine. He tried to convince his readers, specifically Muslims, that the revelation of the Bible regarding the existence, power, and properties of God can be demonstrated with a logical method. For this theology, God is that toward which all categories, attributes, and effects converge into one—the level of the absolute. At the same time, God as the creator proliferates his essence into finite beings that retain divinity on a mediated and reduced level but still show marks of their divine origin. Llull was convinced that with this way of reasoning, Muslims and Christians can join peacefully. Thus, method and rationality became the basis of intercultural exchange and of inner Christian conviction. A follower of his, the Catalan Raimundus Sabundus (in Catalan: Sibiuda, died 1436), wrote the first work that circulated under the title *Theologia naturalis* (natural theology), and Michel de Montaigne wrote one of his *Essais* in defense of Sabundus (in Montaigne's French: Sebonde) because his rational theology was suspected to render revelation superfluous. In this sense, Llull inaugurated a modern strain of thought that may be termed secularism.

Llull's logic is based on the theology of the absolute God who encompasses everything that exists and is knowable in the finite and individuated world. Llull's books on logic bear the title *Art*, thus hinting at the human creativity that is active in thinking. The properties in God (named *dignitates*) were to be arranged as capital letters in circles, for instance: goodness, greatness, duration, potency, wisdom, will, virtue, truth, and glory. Internal concentric circles with the same set of properties could be turned creating propositions like: God's goodness is truth. Other circles, then, could denote derivatives of those properties in things (something is good and also true).[2]

Whereas in God any proposition is right by definition of the absolute, however, in things, such statements need to be qualified. One outcome of the system was to create statements about things derived from God, for

2. A modern illustration can be found here: "Thinking Machines—Ramon Llull and the Ars Combinatoria," http://thinkingmachines.world/.

instance: Acts of goodness are that which make good, can be made good, and are making good. These statements are based on axioms so that they become binding arguments and logically necessary, but Llull's logic goes beyond formally correct statements and aims at reconstructing relations and changes in thought and in the real world. At the same time, God is not an abstract idea, disconnected from reality, or a matter of belief; in his system, God is permanently active and creative. Llull's logic fascinated Renaissance thinkers like Nicholas of Cusa and Giordano Bruno as an improvement of the standard Aristotelian logic, so that Lullism became a common philosophical method and culminated in Gottfried Wilhelm Leibniz in the eighteenth century.

Many of Llull's works develop his logic in systematic treatises, but he also wrote a number of literary works to convey his ideas to a broader audience. The book *Felix*, excerpted here, is one that works with dialogue. As the author says, it tells "exemplary stories" about God while applying the method of interrelated properties so that the reader can understand this philosophy "by necessary reasons."

BIBLIOGRAPHY

Primary Sources

Llull, Ramón. *Doctor Illuminatus: A Ramón Llull Reader.* Edited by Anthony Bonner. Princeton: N.J.: Princeton University Press, 1993.

———. *Selected Works of Ramón Llull (1232–1316).* Edited by Anthony Bonner. 2 vols. Princeton, N.J.: Princeton University Press, 1985.

———. *The Book of the Order of Chivalry / Llibre De L'Ordre De Cavalleria / Libro De La Orden De Caballería.* IVITRA Research in Linguistics and Literature. Amsterdam: John Benjamins Publishing Company, 2015.

———. *Vita Coaetanea / A Contemporary Life / Vida Coetánea / Vida Coetània.* Edited by Antonio Cortijo Ocaña. Amsterdam: Benjamins, 2017.

Lullus, Raimundus. *Opera Latina.* Corpus Christianorum, Continuatio Mediaevalis. Turnholti: Brepols, 1975ff.

———. *Opuscula.* Edited by Erhard-Wolfram Platzeck. [Opera parva 1744–1746]. 3 vols. Hildesheim: Gerstenberg, 1971.

Secondary Sources

Austin, Amy M., and Mark D. Johnston, eds. *A Companion to Ramon Llull and Lullism.* Leiden: Brill, 2019.

Badia, Lola, Joan Santanach, and Albert Soler. *Ramon Llull as a Vernacular Writer: Communicating a New Kind of Knowledge.* Woodbridge: Tamesis, 2016.

Bonner, Anthony. *The Art and Logic of Ramon Llull: A User's Guide*. Leiden: Brill, 2007.
Lohr, Charles H. "Mathematics and the Divine: Ramon Lull." In *Mathematics and the Divine: A Historical Study*, edited by T. Koetsier and L. Bergmans, 213–28. Amsterdam: Elsevier, 2004.
———. "Ramon Lull (1232–1316): The Activity of God and the Hominization of the World." In *Philosophers of the Renaissance*, edited by Paul Richard Blum and translated by Brian McNeil, 12–22. Washington, D.C.: The Catholic University of America Press, 2010.
———. "The Arabic Background to Ramon Lull's Liber Chaos (ca 1285)." *Traditio* 55 (2000): 159–70.

Online Resources

Dambergs, Yanis. "Raymond Lull's Memory Training and Self Learning Tools." 2003. https://lullianarts.narpan.net/.
"Ramon Llull Database (Llull DB)." http://www.ub.edu/llulldb/.
"Thinking Machines—Ramon Llull and the Ars Combinatoria." http://thinkingmachines.world/.

RAMÓN LLULL

Felix, or the Book of Wonders[3]

God by virtue of your goodness, greatness, eternity, power, wisdom and will, here begins this Book of Wonders.

PROLOGUE

In a foreign land there was once a man who was sad and melancholy. He wondered greatly at how little the people of this world knew and loved God, who created this world and with great nobility and goodness gave it to men so that He would be much loved and known by them. This man wept and lamented that in this world God had so few lovers, servants, and worshipers. And in order that He be known, loved, and served, he wrote this Book of Wonders, which is divided into ten parts, namely: God, Angels, Heaven, Elements, Plants, Metals, Beasts, Man, Paradise, Hell.

---

3. Excerpted from book 1 with permission from Ramón Llull, *Selected Works of Ramón Llull (1232–1316)*, ed. Anthony Bonner (Princeton, N.J.: Princeton University Press, 1985), 659–82 (original footnotes have been omitted and new footnotes added by the editor). Typographical errors silently corrected.

This man had a son whom he loved very much and who was called Felix. He said to him: "Dear son, wisdom, charity and devotion are almost dead, and few are the men who live according to the purpose for which our Lord God created them. One no longer finds the fervor and devotion there was in the time of the Apostles and Martyrs, who were willing to languish and die for the sake of knowing and loving God. Where charity and devotion have gone is something you should wonder at. So travel through the world and wonder why men no longer love and know God. Let your whole life be one of loving and knowing God, and weep for the failings of those who are ignorant of, or do not love, God."

Felix obeyed his father, and took leave of him with God's grace and blessing. And with the teachings his father had given him, he went through woods, over hills and across plains, through deserts and towns, visiting princes and knights, in castles and cities; and he wondered at the wonders of this world, inquiring about whatever he did not understand and recounting what he knew. And he underwent hardships and dangers in order that reverence and honor be done to God.

BOOK ONE

1. Whether God Exists

After leaving his father, Felix entered a large wood where he walked for a long time, until he encountered a lovely shepherdess watching over a flock. "My friend," said Felix, "I am in great wonder at your being all alone in this wood where there are so many wild beasts who could harm you, and especially since you don't have the strength to defend your sheep from the wolves or other wild beasts."

The shepherdess replied, "Sir, God is the hope, companion and comfort of my heart, and in this wood I am beneath His protection and influence, for He helps all those who trust in Him; and since he has perfect power, wisdom and goodness, I have placed myself in His protection and company."

Felix was most pleased with what the shepherdess said about our Lord God, and he was in wonder at how much hope and wisdom she had. So he continued on his journey, but he had gone only a short way when he

Felix, or the Book of Wonders

heard the shepherdess shout and cry out very loudly. Then he saw her running after a wolf who was carrying off a lamb, and he was in wonder at her courage in chasing the wolf. While the shepherdess was chasing it, and Felix was running to help her, the wolf dropped the lamb and killed and devoured the shepherdess, and then went over to the sheep and killed many of the ewes and rams. As a result, Felix, in a state of great wonderment, began thinking about what he had seen, and he remembered what the shepherdess had said about God, in whom she had placed such trust.

While thinking about this and wondering about God, who had not helped the shepherdess, even though she had trusted in Him, Felix fell into great temptation, doubted God, and decided that God probably did not exist, for it seemed to him that if God did exist, He would have helped the shepherdess. This temptation and opinion remained with Felix throughout the day until nightfall, when he arrived at a hermitage inhabited by a holy man who had studied theology and philosophy for a long time, and who had come, with his books and wisdom, to this hermitage to contemplate and worship God. The hermit greeted Felix most pleasantly as he approached, but Felix was still so stunned that he was unable to reply; instead he threw himself at the hermit's feet and lay there a long time before he could speak. The hermit wondered at Felix's inability to speak, but by his appearance realized he had almost fainted. At the same time Felix's heart was full of wonder at the temptation into which he had fallen and how much it was tormenting him; and the more he was tempted, the more it seemed to him that God did not exist, for if He did exist, He would not have let him fall into such grievous temptation; and all the more so since he, for the love of God, had decided to travel through the world, in order to make people love Him, and know, honor, and serve Him.

"My dear friend," said the hermit, "what is the matter with you and why are you so speechless?"

"Sir," said Felix, "I wonder greatly that God abandoned me, letting me fall into such grievous temptation, and that He abandoned a shepherdess who was killed by a wolf." And then Felix told the holy man what had happened to make him doubt God's existence, and he begged the hermit to help him return to his former state of devotion and faith.

"Felix," said the hermit, "in a certain land there was a king who greatly loved justice, and over his throne he had placed a stone sculpture of a man's arm holding in its hand a sword, on the point of which was a heart made of red stone, all of which signified that the king's heart wanted to move the arm, which would move the sword, which symbolized justice. And it came to pass that, because of a large serpent, the palace was abandoned and nobody could live there. Then one day a holy man entered that palace, seeking a place to do penance and meditate upon God, and he saw the arm with the sword, and the heart which was on the sword. He wondered greatly what the arm, the sword, and the heart signified; he thought about this statue for so long, however, that he finally understood why it had been made."

"Sir," said Felix, "what is the meaning of this example you have given me?"

"Fair friend," said the hermit, "you should realize that this world exists as the occasion for good; for without occasion for good, the world would not be so beautiful a place as it is. And if God did not exist, the world would be the occasion for evil, for it would be more on the side of evil than on the side of good. And since good accords with being and evil with nonbeing, it is apparent that God is the reason the world is good, and if the world had greater evil than good the reason would be God's nonexistence; without whose existence everything there is would be in vain, and it would follow that good would exist for the sake of evil, and evil would exist by itself and be the final principle of good, and this is inconsistent; for which reason it is shown that God exists."

Felix gave a great deal of thought to what the good man told him and his soul began to gladden; with sighs and tears he said: "The shepherdess had virtue and strength of heart when she chased the wolf. If God existed, He would have helped this virtue of hers, and my soul's former virtue in loving God would not have failed me."

"Fair friend," said the hermit, "in God there is charity and justice, and since the shepherdess loved and served God and trusted in Him, He has taken her to His glory and He has given you a way to be strong against temptation and to believe in God, a thing you might not otherwise have been able to do; for a man who has taken on so lofty a task as you have must take heart. And this is why God allowed you to be tempted by the devil, so that you would become accustomed to being strong and stout of heart against temptation and vice."

After saying these words, the holy man took a stick and drew a circle around Felix and then he asked him if he thought there more necessarily existed something outside the circle than inside. While Felix was wondering at the question which had been put to him, the hermit said that greatness accorded better with being than smallness, and since that which was outside the circle was superior in greatness to that which was inside, therefore it is more necessary that there exist something larger outside the circle than inside. After giving this example, the holy man said that reason discerns and comprehends that outside the firmament there must be something, and that something is God, since that which is inside the firmament is not as large as the firmament itself, which contains everything within it. And if God were not outside the firmament, it would follow that nonbeing would be a greater thing than being, for outside the firmament there would be an infinite quantity of nonbeing, and what was inside the firmament would be finite and limited in quantity, and this is most inconsistent.

While the hermit was speaking, a large serpent passed near Felix, and Felix felt great fear and dread at the sight of it, and he wondered greatly at the hermit's lack of fear. "Dear son," said the hermit, "if God did not exist, there would be no resurrection, and the world would be eternal and would exist by itself alone, and after death mankind would be in privation and nonbeing. From which it would follow that the world existed so that people would be in nonbeing more than in being; for they would be in nonbeing without end, and in being only while living in this world. Thus, as you can see and realize yourself, if God were naught, your nature would not have been afraid of the serpent, for it would be natural to want to die, since would be the occasion for a person to enter that greater state for which he was made, that is to say, that he be forever in privation. But since your nature experienced fear of death, this shows that God exists, and that with Him just men will be in glory without end after the Resurrection."

"Sir," said Felix, "what you say makes me wonder at your not being afraid of the serpent, if by nature you prefer being to nonbeing."

"Fair friend," said the hermit, "it is so pleasant to think about and love God, that all those who understand how to love and know Him wish to see Him and bask in His glory, and they scorn the vanity of this world, which lasts so little. This is why, dear son, I have no fear of death, but rather look forward to dying and being with God. By which attitude you can see that

God exists, for if God did not exist, I would have experienced the same fear as you; which fear you experienced because you do not know how to love and understand God."

Felix was very pleased with the hermit's proof of God, and he praised and blessed God for having enlightened him with His knowledge. With contrition and tears because of his unworthiness, he submitted himself to God and confessed his sins to the holy man, praising and blessing God for having such a good meditator in this hermitage, and he hoped that many hermits had as much wisdom and love in knowing and loving our Lord God.

2. What Is God?

"Sir Hermit," said Felix, "could you tell me what God is? For I want very much to know, since with this knowledge of what God is, my will would be uplifted to love God more than I now do, because it is only natural that through enlightened understanding the will is heightened in loving something about which the understanding has knowledge."

For a long time the hermit thought over the question Felix had asked him. While the hermit was thinking how he could make Felix understand what God was, Felix wondered why the hermit was taking so long to answer the question he had asked, and he said: "Sir, a man found a precious stone which was worth a thousand sous and which he sold for one denier to a man who knew what kind of a stone it was and was able to get a thousand sous for it.[4] Therefore, sir, if you know what God is, I beg you to tell me so that I can love and know Him according to His true value. And if you do not know what God is, I am in great wonder at how you can love Him so much without knowledge, nor how for His sake you can undergo such a harsh life in this hermitage. And it seems to me that if you do not know what God is, then at the slightest opportunity you would disdain Him, as the man disdained the precious stone, about which he knew nothing, selling it for one denier, which denier he knew about, and because of His knowledge of the denier and ignorance of the value of the stone, he preferred having the denier to the stone."

"Dear son," said the hermit, "in a certain land there was once a woman

---

4. One sous was worth twelve deniers in medieval currency (*solidus* and *denarius*).

who heard a king praised for his wisdom, power, and good customs; and because of all the good things she had heard about the king, she decided to go to that land where the king ruled. When she came before the king and saw how well-ordered was his court, and saw his great power and his good administration, and when, in addition, she saw that the king was very handsome as a person, well-mannered and full of virtues, then she felt a much greater love for the king than before, when she had not yet seen the king. And you, my fair son, have already remarked how the will loves more that which is known than that which is unknown; as for me, you should realize that I came to this hermitage in order to gain knowledge of what God is, since it is something I have long wanted to know. And in order to acquire this knowledge I have studied theology and philosophy for a long time, and in this hermitage I am doing everything I can to understand and comprehend the essence of our Lord God."

The hermit said to Felix, "A king once had a wife who was very beautiful and good, and whom the king loved very much. That queen loved the king very much, and on account of this great love she was jealous of the king and of a certain damsel of his, with whom he enjoyed conversing because of her pleasant manner of speaking. Every day this queen was in great sorrow, and no matter what the king did or said, he could not cheer her up, a fact which caused him great wonder. The king tried as hard as he could to make her content, and finally when he saw that he could not make her happy, he began to suspect the queen and to think she was perhaps doing something to dishonor him.

"Dear son," said the hermit, "when the king became jealous and suspicious of his wife, then he began to love the queen less, and because of the queen, to love the damsel less. The king went for a long time without speaking to the damsel, and the queen began to cheer up, which cheer caused the king great wonder; for when he had formerly done everything he could to please her, he could not cheer her up, and now when he had stopped trying to please her, the queen loved him more than before. The king was in great wonder at the queen's odd ways, but he fell in with them and let himself be loved by the queen, so that she would be happy and content in her love.

"When men of this world take pleasure in temporal delights, and do not love them for the sake of the Creator who created them, so that with them and in them one learns to know and love Him, then God becomes estranged from such people, and because of this estrangement they can no longer have knowledge of Him, nor of the pleasure derived from this knowledge. But when a person ceases loving the delights of this world, through which delights and world a person can love God, then these delights and the world seek out that man, and give him a way in which he can love God and have knowledge of Him. And in this, fair son," said the hermit, "you can, in this world, have knowledge of what God is: namely, that God is that on account of which the world will take you further from loving God if you love the world for itself; and God is that on account of which the world exemplifies God if you love the world for the sake of knowing and loving God.

"Dear son," said the hermit, "a person has knowledge of God by saying that in Him there is nothing which lacks nobility, nor perfection of goodness, greatness, eternity, power, wisdom, will, virtue, and the other perfections existing in God; thus, when a person has acquired the knowledge that God is not something in which there is any defect, that person can have knowledge of God, who is the fulfillment of all goodness, of all greatness, all eternity, and similarly with power, wisdom, virtue, will, and the other dignities.

"Fair son," said the hermit, "a merchant had a thousand bezants,[5] and he wanted to have another thousand; and when he had two thousand, he immediately wanted more, and this way he amassed a hundred thousand bezants without feeling any satisfaction in his soul. The merchant wondered greatly at this fact, and he thought that perhaps the fulfillment of his desires lay not in money but rather in the owning of castles and estates and property, which he was determined to have and which he obtained, and yet he still felt no sense of fulfillment, for the more he bought and possessed, the more his desire to own estates and castles increased. When the merchant multiplied his wealth and saw that it still gave him no satisfaction, he thought that he would satisfy his soul by having a wife and children. He got himself wife and children and still he was not satisfied, and he wanted honors and many other things; and the more things he had, the more his soul wanted to have. The merchant was in great wonder as to how he could

5. Bezant is a medieval golden coin.

satisfy his soul with anything in this world, and he finally thought of having God in his soul. He then loved and served God with what He had given him, and he felt satisfied and fulfilled, and he desired nothing more. So you should know, fair son, that God is that which, in this world, gives satisfaction to the soul of the person who loves and serves Him with all his power.

"Through a forest where a hermit lived, a fully armed knight rode past on his horse, and he came upon the hermit picking the plants on which he subsisted in that hermitage. The knight asked the hermit what God was; and the hermit replied that God is that for which all existing things were created and ordered; and God is that which will cause the good and the wicked to rise from the dead, and will give everlasting glory to the good and punishment to the wicked; and God is that which causes it to rain, which makes plants flower and bear seed, and which gives life and sustenance to everything there is. When the hermit had satisfied the knight with regard to the question he had posed, the hermit asked the knight what a knight was. And the knight replied that a knight was a man chosen to ride on horseback to carry out justice and to protect and safeguard the king and his people so that the king could reign in such a manner that his subjects could love and know God.

"Sir," said Felix, "a knight asked a good woman, daughter of chastity, to make physical love with him, and the woman asked him what love was. The knight replied that love was that which made separate wills unite toward a common end. The woman asked the knight if this love he asked of her would unite her with God in glory when she left the life of this world. The knight felt ashamed of what he had asked the woman, and he said the following: 'For a long time I have been subject to false love and in ignorance of true love.' And he said to the woman that he realized that true love united a person with God, and separated him from treachery, lust, cowardice, and all deceit and defect. Nevertheless, he still wanted to know what love was in itself, for one thing is what love does, and another is what love is; and he therefore asked the woman to give him knowledge of what love is, since she had already given him knowledge of foolish love, which he had loved without realizing what it was. The woman was very pleased by the knight's devoutness, and she praised God for having warmed him with the fire of true love, and to God she addressed the following words: 'O Lord, true and glorious God, since, through love, You have enamored this knight, I beg of You to give him knowledge of what love is, for by Your grace and virtue I have given him knowledge of what love does, but he wishes to rise higher in his understanding of love, so that he can love all the better, and he wishes to know what love is in itself.'"

After Felix had told the hermit about the words of love between the woman and the knight, he realized that Felix was not satisfied with the knowledge he had given him of God, whose being he had expressed through God's effect on His creatures, and that Felix wanted to know what God's being was in itself and in its actions. The hermit therefore said the following words to Felix:

"There was once a philosopher who had a son he loved very much and to whom he taught philosophy for many years. When his son was very knowledgeable in the science of philosophy, his father showed him a book he had written, and he asked whether his son knew that he was a man because of the fact that he had written the book or because of the fact that he was his father. The son replied that by the book he knew that he was a man, because to man belonged the ability to write; but even more he knew his father to be a man because he had engendered a man."

After this example, the hermit told Felix that God is that to which belong actions which no one else can perform, save God alone, which actions God performs in creatures. But the way one can best know what God is in Himself, is in how God in Himself and from Himself engenders God, that is to say that God the Father engenders God who is the Son, and from the Father and the Son there issues God who is the Holy Ghost, and all three are in a single God; which God is that which is God the Father, God the Son, and God the Holy Ghost, and which is one God and not three gods. And God is that thing which is infinite, eternal, wise, volitional, virtuous, and who in Himself is the fulfillment of all goodness, all infinity, and of everything He is in Himself.

Felix was very pleased with the knowledge of God the hermit had given him, and he praised and blessed God, who had made Himself known to him; and in his soul he felt his love in loving God increase because he now understood Him better than before.

3. The Unity of God

Felix said, "In a certain land there was a king who was both very handsome and very virtuous in his habits. This king had great power in terms of men and wealth, and he was of strong constitution and noble in heart. One of his knights had a great desire for many other kings in the world to be like his king, so that there would be love and concord in the world between one king and another, and that all together they would make the world such that God would be known and loved by all people." After these words, Felix said, "Sir, I would like to know if there is only one God or if there are many; for it would be a source of great wonder to me if there were many gods, since I want to know and love one God who has every perfection, and thus, if there were many, it would naturally follow that I should desire many gods and would want to know and love many."

The hermit said, "If there is only one God, He can have every perfection, and if there were more than one, then one god would be more perfect than the others if he had in himself all those virtues that each god had in himself and for himself. It is therefore proper that one God have all the nobility, goodness, greatness, and virtue which could be in all the gods, who together could not have as much greatness as the one alone. That is to say that one God can be infinite and sovereign in goodness and in power, but if there were many gods equal to one another, each one would have to be finite and bounded by the next one, and none of them would be all-powerful in all that was. And if there were one god, infinite, powerful, and sovereign over the other gods, then all the other gods would have to obey him; and therefore it would follow that in the end there would not be more than one god.

"A foolish king wanted to be king and lord of a realm belonging to another king who was very wise and of good habits, and who held his realm in peace and justice. This wise king wanted to be king of the foolish king's realm, for it seemed to him a bad thing to have it ruled by a king without wisdom, justice, and proper administration. It came to pass that the two kings fought each other, and the wise and just king was defeated; after which the foolish king became lord of the conquered king's realm. The foolish king held these two realms amid great tribulations, because he had no wisdom; and because of his ignorance and bad habits war and poverty spread among his people and from this followed much evil."

When the hermit had spoken these words, Felix was in great wonder, and said, "Sir, according to what you say there must be many gods; for almost the entire world is in a state of tribulation and war, and there are many men in the world who are enemies of virtue and lovers of vice; some men belong to one sect and some to another; and it would therefore seem, according to what you say, either that there are many gods or that there is one god defective in wisdom, justice, goodness, power and virtue; for if there were one god who was good, virtuous, just and powerful, he would keep his people on the path of truth, and in peace and charity."

"Fair son," said the hermit, "every person bears some resemblance to God, for every person is good insofar as he is a creature and insofar as he possesses understanding and will; and the goodness he has is similar to God's goodness, since goodness, which is God, has placed a likeness of itself in man's understanding and will. And since man has some likeness to God, it is only natural that he love and know his likeness, that is, God; but since man neither knows how nor wants to use wisely his likeness to God, he acts against his own likeness and against the likeness of his God; which is why every man wants to be god when he acts against God. As a result, the confusion of those who do not love one god places the rest of the world in a state of tribulation, confusion, and error, and the God who is one has given them great liberty so they can love and know Him, in order that He may give them great glory if, freely and without constraint of will, they want to love and know Him. For God so loves His likeness in man, that He has given him the opportunity to increase this great glory by reason of the merit he might acquire in doing good works.

"A knight was out hunting, and he followed a wild boar so far that he became separated from his companions and had to spend the night in a wood. When darkness came on he was overcome with fear, and he wondered what could have caused his fear. While in this state of fear, the knight had the idea that the sun was God, because during the day he had felt no fear, which led him to think that his fear came from the absence of the sun. The next day, when the knight was returning at about midday, he met up with a squire whose father he had killed; at the sight of him the knight felt great fear, because he had offended the squire, and because he

Felix, or the Book of Wonders

was unarmed and the squire was completely armed. The knight prayed to the sun to help him against the squire, whom he saw coming, but in spite of this prayer the knight did not lose his fear; instead he grew more and more afraid as the other man drew nearer and threatened to attack him with his lance. When the squire was close enough to strike him in the chest with his lance, the knight begged for mercy and pleaded with the squire to listen to him before killing him, for he wanted to recount an experience he had had. The squire withheld his blow, and the knight recounted the fear he had felt in wood because of the absence of the sun and how he had gotten the idea that the sun was God. He added that he now knew that the sun was not God, because if it were, it would have helped him in his present fear, since it could see him. After saying this, the knight asked if he deserved death more because he had killed the squire's father, or because of his notion that the sun was God. The squire was in great wonder at the knight's question, and while he was thus wondering, trying to decide what to answer, the knight asked him another question, namely, whether he, the squire, was not guilty towards his God for hesitating to answer his question, which should be simple for a man who loved God more than his father. The squire thought for a long time about the two questions the knight had asked him, and finally he said that he should kill the knight for having killed his father; but for having not believed in God, imagining that the sun was God, he should not kill him, but rather indoctrinate and give him certitude in knowing and loving God. Then he admitted his own guilt for having taken so long to answer. After this reply, the knight said that for this guilt he needed pardoning, and furthermore since the squire had to indoctrinate him and give him knowledge of God, he should not kill him; and the knight then begged mercy for his guilt in the killing of the squire's father. They made peace with one another and agreed to love and know one God, and for a long time they were friends loving one God."

After saying these words, the hermit told Felix that the world was in tribulation and disorder because people were weak in knowledge and charity and because they held all sorts of varying opinions contrary to God. But if men agreed in knowing and loving one God, then the world would be in good condition and people would be in charity and love, and in accord over one God, like the squire and knight who were in agreement through one's pardoning the other, and through charity and knowledge.

4. The Trinity of God

"Sir Hermit," said Felix, "once, on a holy feast day called the Holy Trinity, I was present at a sermon on God's Trinity, and this sermon caused me great wonder, because the man who delivered it said that one should not try to prove that God exists in trinity; for it is preferable for people to believe in God's Trinity than for them to understand it by means of necessary reasons. I was in great wonder, sir, at these words, for if this good man was telling the truth, it follows that there is greater merit in believing in God's Trinity than in having knowledge of it, and that the will can love more through ignorance than through knowledge."

The hermit said that there was once a city with many customs which were contrary to God, lawfulness, and princely government. "These customs were privileges the people of that city had acquired, on account of which privileges the king of that city could not carry out his justice. It came to pass one day that a man of that city committed murder, and the king wanted to punish that man. But because of certain privileges he was obliged to set him free, accept the payment of a fine, and pardon him. The king was most displeased that for the sake of money or privilege he had to forsake justice, and he said to the people of that city:

"'Two sinners were praying before an altar: one prayed for God to forgive him, because he feared Him; the other begged God to have mercy on him, because he loved Him. Now you, who fly in the face of justice with your bad customs, I want you to tell me which of these two men God should most want to pardon.' The people of that city took counsel over the king's question, and they decided to tell the king that God should forgive that man who loved Him in preference to the one who feared Him. When the king heard their answer and realized that it ran counter to their wicked customs, he said, 'I am very pleased with your answer, which makes it quite clear that I should love God more than I should fear you, because by loving God I could treat you with justice; but by fearing you, I would instead be the enemy of justice.'"

After hearing the hermit's words, Felix said he wondered greatly that love could exist without fear, or fear without love.

"Fair son," said the hermit, "those who like to believe in God's Trinity and do not want to understand it, love themselves more than God; for, with the idea that there is greater merit in believing that which they do not understand, they prefer to achieve great glory through faith rather than to perceive God by means of their understanding. And this is why, fair son, fear often exists without love; that is to say, what people fear is to lose glory and to suffer punishment, and since they don't want to know and love God for His goodness and nobility, then their fear is without love."

"Sir," said Felix, "I have often wanted to ask those who are learned in our religion how God can be one in essence and yet be in trinity of persons; but for fear of not being able to understand I have hesitated to ask about the Holy Trinity, which I would like you to explain to me in words that I can understand."

The hermit said: "There was once a merchant in a certain city who had, after many years of hard work, earned a great deal of money. This merchant then became ill, both in spirit and in body. He was ill in spirit because he doubted the Holy Trinity of our Lord God, since he could not understand how God could be one in essence and yet in a trinity of persons; and since he neither understood nor knew how to believe this, he wavered in his faith, which wavering put him in a state of damnation. He was ill in body because of a fever he had, and because of the riches of this world, which he worried about and feared to lose. While the merchant was thus in great danger, he wished that he had labored as much in loving and knowing God as he had in amassing worldly wealth, which he knew could be of no help to him in this grievous trial and bodily illness. Because of how much the merchant wished that he had served God, God inspired his soul with the light of faith, by which he understood that he should not disbelieve whatever he did not understand about God's Holy Trinity; for God has given faith to man so that he may believe whatever he does not understand, since the Trinity is so lofty an object of knowledge that people who are merchants and businessmen dealing with worldly things cannot understand it."

After this, the hermit said to Felix: "Fair son, even though you cannot understand God's Holy Trinity, it is only right that you should believe it; for if it were forbidden to believe everything one could not understand, it would follow that faith were a bad thing; when faith is in fact a most noble virtue, since by faith men are on the road to salvation, because of believing that which they cannot understand. And this is why, fair son, it is enough for you to believe in the Trinity, if you cannot understand it."

"Sir," said Felix, "if I don't understand your explanations of God's Holy Trinity, I am prepared to believe and have faith. But since I want to know God because he is good, and since it is because of His goodness, rather than to achieve glory or to avoid infernal punishment, that I want to love and know Him, I would therefore like to risk trying to find a way to know and love God. Hence I beg you, sir, to tell me what you know about God's Holy Trinity."

The hermit said: "A philosopher heard about a Christian holy man who was very knowledgeable in theology and philosophy. That man lived in a hermitage where he meditated on the work God performs in Himself. One day it happened that a Jew came to that holy man and had a discussion with him about God's Holy Trinity. On that same day the philosopher visited the holy man, arriving while the Jew was arguing with him; and the holy Christian proved to the Jew that the Trinity exists in God, but the Jew could not understand it. And the reason he could not understand the Christian's arguments concerning the Holy Trinity was because the Jew disliked the proof the Christian gave him; for it is so difficult to prove the Trinity that nobody can understand it if he does not presuppose that it can be proved by necessary reasons. The philosopher understood the arguments he heard the Christian giving the Jew, and as a result he had himself baptized and became a Christian. The Jew wondered greatly at the philosopher's becoming a Christian, since he had known him before his baptism, and he said to the philosopher: 'Sir, I am in great wonder that you were so quickly converted to the Christian faith. Please tell me your reason for having been baptized, and for leaving the sect to which you used to belong.' The philosopher replied: 'For a long time now I have been trying, through philosophy, to reach a knowledge of God; and by this path I was able to arrive at a knowledge of God's work in creation, but when it came to God's work in Himself, I could find out nothing through philosophy alone. But by means of the theology the hermit used in his dispute with you, and through the philosophy I myself know and heard from him, I arrived at a knowledge of God's Trinity; which knowledge you could also attain if you presupposed the existence of Trinity, and if you were favorably disposed toward the existence of said Trinity in God, because there can be no proof of Trinity without some kind of presupposition, nor can one prove the Trinity to the obstinate understanding in a proud man's heart.'"

"Sir," Felix said to the hermit, "I well understand your words and your reason for having told me these exemplary stories. But do not hesitate to sow words of salutary benediction in me, for I am prepared to understand and to presuppose whatever you tell me about God's Holy Trinity. And I would be most pleased if I could understand it by necessary reasons, by which reasons I could eradicate forever that doubt and temptation which come to me or to others against the Trinity of our Lord God, whom I want to love, serve, honor, and know all the rest of my life."

After these words, the hermit made the sign of the cross before his face, and trusting in the help of God and the Trinity, said to Felix: "It is clear that our Lord God created everything there is for the purpose of giving people knowledge and love of Himself; and therefore, since He is one in essence and is in trinity of persons, He wanted the world to be one in essence and to be in three different things, which are sensuality, intellectuality, and animality. Sensuality refers to sensual things, that is, things which are corporal or sensible; by intellectuality we refer to what constitutes the soul of man, or that of angel; by animality we mean man, and what constitutes a union of corporal and spiritual things. These three things constitute the entire world, which is one, and yet is made up of the aforementioned things, without which the world would not have the unity it has, nor would the three things be what they are if each one were not in itself one thing and three things; that is to say, that every body is one, and yet is three things, which are matter, form and, the conjunction of matter and form in the existence of a body which is a union of matter and form. The soul also is one in essence and is three different things which constitute the soul's being: they are memory, understanding, and will, without which three things the soul could not be a single substance. An animal likewise consists of three things, which are body, spirit, and the conjunction by which the body and spirit unite and constitute a single animal, such as a man, a lion, a bird, or any of the other things that constitute a union of body and soul. And in this number of one and three lies the whole world, and everything that is created in substantial being, in order to exemplify the fact that God's substance is one and yet is in three distinct persons, that is to say, Father, Son, and Holy Ghost. If God did not exist in a unity of substance and in a trinity of persons, He would not have created everything there is in such a likeness of Himself, in order that He be known and loved by men;

30   RAMÓN LLULL

and there would have been a defect in God if men could not have known Him because of a defect in His likeness, or in the likeness of the world and of what the world contains in itself."

After the hermit had, by the example of creatures, shown God's unity and trinity to Felix, he wanted to rise even higher, and to reveal God's unity and trinity to Felix by means of God's dignities, saying: "Dear son, in God's nature there is goodness, infinity, eternity, power, wisdom, will, as well as many other dignities that are in God's essence, each one of which is God and none of which is idle. As a result, His goodness never ceases doing good, that is, producing good in itself and of itself; and by infinity, eternity, power, wisdom, will, it does good, which it begets from itself and from eternity, power, wisdom, will; which begotten good is the person of the Son, while the begetter is the person of the Father, and from the Father and the Son issues the Holy Ghost. And the very same thing goodness does, is done by immensity, eternity, power, wisdom, and will; and together the Father, the Son, and the Holy Ghost are one divine nature, one Godhead, one God. In God there is one person, the Father, source of all goodness, greatness, eternity, power, wisdom, will, for He who begets the Son and gives issue to the Holy Ghost is goodness, infinity, eternity, power, wisdom, will; and the same is true of the Son and the Holy Ghost, each of whom is goodness, infinity, eternity, power, wisdom, will. And that is why in this work God performs within Himself, one paternity, one filiation, and one procession are sufficient; and because there is infinity, eternity, there cannot be idleness, nor can there be inequality, majority or minority. If in God there were goodness which did no good, infinity which made nothing infinite, and so on for eternity, power, wisdom, and will, then in God there would be idleness of goodness, infinity, eternity, power, wisdom, and will, which idleness would be contrary to His goodness, infinity, eternity, power, wisdom, and will. Just as unity is sufficient in God, so, in this unity, one paternity, one filiation, and one spiration[6] are sufficient, because in the Father, the Son, and the Holy Ghost there is goodness, infinity, eternity, power, wisdom, will. And since the Father, with all of His goodness, infinity, eternity, power, wisdom, will, begets the Son, therefore the Son is all the goodness, infinity, eternity, power, wisdom, will of the Father; and the

6. That is, the activity of the Holy Spirit.

same follows for the Holy Ghost, which is all the goodness, infinity, eternity, power, wisdom, will of the Father and of the Son, since all of the Holy Ghost proceeds from all of the Father and from all of the Son infinitely and eternally for all of the Father and Son. It is only natural for there to exist love between a father and son, and it naturally follows that a person loves the virtue that proceeds from his remembering, understanding, and loving. Now, if a father loves a son who is begotten from his own body and from that of a woman, how much more natural for him to love even more a son begotten from himself alone, and moreover from all of himself and identical with himself. And if the soul loves the remembering, understanding, and loving that proceed from its virtue, how much more it would love them if its remembering, understanding, and loving were that virtue itself and the soul itself!"

"Fair son," said the hermit, "within your own nature you can understand and feel how you prefer being one man and not two or more men; and since you like your humanity, you like your being in three things, which are soul, body, and conjunction, without which three things you could not be one man. Now this being the case, according to that very nature by which you can feel and know what you like to be, in yourself you can understand and know what our Lord God is, He who created us to love and know Him.

"If God didn't understand or love Himself, He would not be God; and if God understands and loves Himself, then He must bonify,[7] magnify, eternalize, and empower Himself; for if He did not, then virtue, wisdom, and will would, in God, be nobler than goodness, infinity, and power, which is impossible, since in God everything is equal. As a result, goodness bonifies itself in itself and of itself: that is to say, goodness, which is the Father, begets the Son and gives issue to the Holy Ghost from itself, in itself and by itself; and the same follows for infinity, eternity and power.

"A wise man asked a philosopher which was nobler, the essence or the work of God. After thinking for a long time about the question the wise man had asked him, the philosopher said that God is as eternal as the world, and the world as eternal as God. And the reason the philosopher

---

7. Bonify: making (something) good. In this section, the hermit explains Llull's theory of the divine properties as "correlatives," namely, being mutually confirming.

said that the world was eternal, was that he attributed eternal work to God. And this is why certain philosophers have held the opinion that the world was eternal, for it did not seem to them that God, who is so noble in goodness, infinity, eternity, power, wisdom, will, could nor should be idle. But if these philosophers had known of God's work within Himself, that of the Father begetting the Son and the Holy Ghost proceeding from the Father and the Son, then they would not have held this false opinion, believing that the world had no beginning.

"Two great wise men were before a great king, and the king wanted to know which of them was wiser; and he commanded that they be asked what was the noblest thing a person could ask of God. The first wise man said it was to possess God. The other wise man said that the greatest favor one could ask of God was that He make a person's will and power be one and the same thing, with no difference between the two; for if man's will were power, he could, if he wanted to, be God. Therefore, fair son," said the hermit, "you should know that, since God is one with His power and will, He can do whatever His will wants, and His will must want as much as His power can do, for if it did not, it would be less than His power and would not be one with His power. And since His power is infinite and eternal, it is itself able to do anything, and the will must want the power, which is the Father, to beget the Son and to give issue to the Holy Ghost for all its infinity and eternity; for without such a desire, the will would not be all infinity, eternity, for the sake of goodness, wisdom, eternity, and power.

"A knight showed his son the great distance a squire had jumped. The son wondered greatly at the jump the squire had made; and the father wanted to know if his son had the discernment necessary to acquire wisdom, and he therefore asked his son why he was in such wonder at the squire's jump. 'Sir,' said the son, 'I wonder at the jump the squire made in terms of the strength of my own body, but I do not wonder, in terms of his body, which was sufficient for the jump he made.' The father was very pleased at his son's reply."

Felix told the hermit that he was satisfied with the knowledge he had gained about the Holy Trinity, in the light of God's goodness, infinity, eternity, power, wisdom, will, and about God's work in Himself by means of all of His goodness, infinity, eternity, power, wisdom, will. Felix then said to the hermit, "Sir, I greatly wonder at those philosophers who were gentiles and had great wisdom, and yet were in ignorance of the Trinity of God; but I can see that this is something about which Christian philosophers can have knowledge, and gentile philosophers not."

"Fair son," said the hermit, "the philosophers made no presuppositions based on faith in God, but only followed necessary reasons; and this is why their understanding could not rise high enough to attain God, as could that of Christian Catholic philosophers and theologians who, through faith, presupposed the existence of trinity in God from the outset. And because faith is the light of the understanding, this understanding can rise to greater heights than it could for the gentile philosophers."

2

GEORGE GEMISTOS PLETHO
(C. 1360–1454)

Commentary on Chaldaean Oracles

JOZEF MATULA

INTRODUCTION

George Gemistos Pletho was a prominent philosopher who wrote during the final years of the Byzantine Empire. Pletho was born in Constantinople, but he was active mostly in Mystras in the Peloponnese. His most comprehensive philosophical work is the *Book of Laws*, in which he maintains the hierarchical structure of intelligible reality and relates metaphysical principles with pagan gods. This work was condemned by the Orthodox Church for allegations of paganism. Pletho was also the author of a geographical treatise, an astronomical manual, a historical work on the aftermath of the battle of Mantineia, a theological treatise about the procession of the Holy Spirit, and a short treatise, *On Virtues*, that was indebted to Platonic and Stoic ethics. Pletho took part in the Byzantine delegation to the council of Ferrara-Florence in 1438 and 1439, where he presented lectures on Plato's philosophy. In his interpretation of Plato, Pletho was inspired by several ancient thinkers such as Plutarch, Numenius, Atticus, Plotinus, and Proclus. His most famous treatise, *On the Differences Between Plato and Aristotle*, opened a long debate among the Byzantines and

Italian humanists regarding the merits of the two ancient philosophers.

The *Chaldaean Oracles*, a collection of fragments and one of the most obscure ancient Greek texts and a product of Hellenistic (Alexandrian) syncretism, is the key work of Platonic theurgists. Pletho's new edition of the *Chaldaean Oracles*, called *Magian Oracles of the Magi Pupils of Zoroaster*, presents a systematically structured text.[1] This version consists of sixty Greek hexameters and is shorter than the versions possessed by the Neoplatonists and Michael Psellos. Pletho's familiarity with the *Chaldaean Oracles* comes mainly from Michael Psellos's commentary on them. Apart from that, there are two other possible influences: Pletho's reading of Persian mystics, Suhrawardi, and Pletho's early Jewish teacher Elissaios, who was a supporter of Iranian mysticism.[2] The latter became to Pletho what Ammonius Saccas had been for Plotinus.

Pletho omitted six oracles and substantially changed the order of the fragments of Psellos's commentary. Pletho went through the *Chaldaean Oracles* line by line, appended a short exegetical note to every fragment, and rearranged the order of Oracles according to his own philosophical criteria. In Psellos's collection, these Oracles were "Chaldaean oracles," but according to Pletho, they were "Magic oracles," Magi being the true followers of Zoroaster. Pletho's interest in Zoroaster is found most clearly in three of his works: *Magian Oracles of the Magi Pupils of Zoroaster*, *A Brief Explanation of the More Obscure Passages in These Texts*, and *A Summary of the Doctrines of Zoroaster and Plato*.[3] Each of these works was probably written in a different period of Pletho's life.

Pletho's admiration for Zoroaster is prominent in his *Magian Oracles of the Magi Pupils of Zoroaster*. He considered Zoroaster to be one of the

---

1. *Oracles chaldaiques. Recension de Georges Gemiste Plethon* (Μαγικὰ λόγια τῶν ἀπὸ Ζωροάστρου μάγων. Γεωργίου Γεμιστοῦ-Πλήθωνος Ἐξήγησις εἰς τὰ αὐτὰ λόγια), ed. Brigitte Tambrun-Krasker, Philosophi Byzantini (Corpus philosophorum Medii Aevi) 7 (Athens: The Academy of Athens; Paris, Librairie J. Vrin; Bruxelles, éditions Ousia, 1995). The Greek version of the name is Plethon (with final "n"); however, following Anglo-Saxon convention, we spell it Pletho.

2. Michel Tardieu, "Pléthon lecteur des Oracles," *Metis* 2 (1987): 142; Luc Brisson, "Pléthon et *les Oracles Chaldaïques*," in *Philosophie et sciences à Byzance de 1204 à 1453*, ed. Michel Cacouros and Marie-Hélène Congourdeau (Leuven: Peeters, 2006), 127–42.

3. Christopher Montague Woodhouse, *George Gemistos Plethon: The Last of the Hellenes* (Oxford: Clarendon Press, 1986), 48–61.

36 GEORGE GEMISTOS PLETHO

most important exegetes of divine matters and a singular guide to the revelation of divine mysteries. The Oracles were not assigned to Zoroaster until the edition of Pletho, who attributed the Oracles to Iranian provenience to demonstrate that the agreements between Orpheus, Pythagoras, Plato, and the *Chaldaean Oracles* come from truths spread from Zoroaster. Pletho believed that Zoroaster was the wisest and most ancient of all sages; he was convinced that Plato's philosophy is based on Pythagoras, who acquired wisdom through direct contact with the Zoroastrian Magi. Zoroaster's doctrines, such as the transmigration of souls and the relation between body and soul, are in agreement with what he considered "Platonic and Pythagorean wisdom." Pletho was influenced by Plutarch's *De Iside et Osiride* and Plato's *Seventh Letter* in his view of Zoroaster as the first to hold that a triple deity ruled over the cosmos, a doctrine that is consistent with Platonic theology. In comparison to Psellos's more comprehensive commentary, which seeks agreement between the Oracles and Christianity, Pletho returns to the ancients to confront Christianity with them. His prudent and judicious approach lead to the refutation of Psellos's concordism for ideological reasons; he interprets the *Chaldaean Oracles* in an unequivocally monistic spirit and stripped of Christian interpretation. Pletho interprets the Oracles through monistic metaphysics; the vertical emanational construction ignores the triadic structures of Neoplatonist and Christian theology. Pletho provides a philosophical explanation of these notoriously mysterious utterances, which describe in philosophical and mythical terms the journey of the soul as well as the means of its salvation. In the Oracles, Pletho saw a description of the soul's salvation that was in a sense secular.[4] The commentary seems to be closely related to his work *Book of Laws*, which is clearly not Trinitarian Christian. Pletho had to find another authority in antiquity that could obliterate the authority of the books of the Holy Bible.[5] He probably wanted to avoid debates, such as disputes concerning the Trinity, and instead establish his political reforms on a solid philosophical background. As a commentator, Pletho might have used the *Chaldaean Oracles* as a companion to a new spiritual

---

4. Brisson, "Pléthon et les *Oracles Chaldaïques*," 127.

5. Brigitte Tambrun-Krasker, "Are Psellos's and Plethon's *Chaldaean Oracles* Genuine?" in *Georgios Gemistos Plethon: The Byzantine and the Latin Renaissance*, ed. Jozef Matula and Paul Richard Blum (Olomouc: Palacký University Press, 2014), 375–89.

Commentary on Chaldaean Oracles

way that prepared the intellectual foundations of the coming new world order or the restoration of paganism.[6]

Pletho deliberately employed the style of oracles that sound obscure and remain open to various interpretations. With that, he had a profound impact on Renaissance culture through the assimilation of his thinking on the Oracles and his ideas about *philosophia perennis*. During the Renaissance, John Argyropoulos, Francesco Filelfo, Marsilio Ficino, Giovanni Pico della Mirandola, Francesco Patrizi, and Agostino Steuco relied on Pletho's edition,[7] which was re-employed by Ficino within the frameworks of *prisca theologia* and by Agostino Steuco within the framework of *philosophia perennis*.

BIBLIOGRAPHY
Primary Sources

Plethon, George Gemistos. *Oracles chaldaiques. Recension de Georges Gemiste Plethon* (Μαγικὰ λόγια τῶν ἀπὸ Ζωροάστρου μάγων. Γεωργίου Γεμιστοῦ-Πλήθωνος Ἐξήγησις εἰς τὰ αὐτὰ λόγια). Edited by Brigitte Tambrun-Krasker. Corpus philosophorum medii aevi. Athens: The Academy of Athens; Paris, Librairie J. Vrin; Bruxelles, éditions Ousia, 1995.

———. "Contre les objections de scholarios en faveur d'Aristote (réplique) (Πρὸς τὰς Σχολαρίου ὑπὲρ τοῦ Ἀριστοτέλους ἀντιλήψεις)." Edited by Bernadette Lagarde. *Byzantion* 59 (1989): 354–365, 367–507.

———. "Le 'de Differentiis' de Pléthon d'après l'autographe de La Marcienne (Περὶ ὧν Ἀριστοτέλης πρὸς Πλάτωνα διαφέρεται)." Edited by Bernadette Lagarde. *Byzantion* 43 (1973): 312–43.

———. *Contra scholarii pro Aristotele obiectiones* (Πρὸς τὰς ὑπὲρ Ἀριστοτέλους τοῦ Σχολαρίου ἀντιλήψεις). Edited by Enrico Valdo Maltese. Bibliotheca scriptorum Graecorum et Romanorum Teubneriana. Leipzig: Teubner, 1988.

———. *Traité des lois* (Πλήθωνος Νόμων συγγραφῆς τὰ σωζόμενα). Edited by Charles Alexandre. Translated by Pierre Augustin Pellissier. Paris: Librairie de Firmin Didot, 1858. Reprint, Amsterdam: Adolf M. Hakkert, 1966.

———. *Traité des vertus* (Περὶ ἀρετῶν). Edited by Brigitte Tambrun-Krasker. Corpus Philosophorum Medii Aevi, Philosophi Byzantini 3. Athens: Academy of Athens; Leiden: E. J. Brill, 1987.

---

6. Polymnia Athanassiadi, "Byzantine Commentators on the Chaldean Oracles: Psellos and Plethon," in *Byzantine Philosophy and its Ancient Sources*, ed. Katerina Ierodiakonou (Oxford: Oxford University Press, 2002), 251.

7. Michael Stausberg, *Faszination Zarathushtra: Zoroaster und die Europäische Religionsgeschichte der Frühen Neuzeit*, vol. 1 (Berlin and New York: de Gruyter, 1998), 82.

Bydén, Börje, et al. "George Gemistos (Plethon), On Aristotle's Departures from Plato 0-19: Greek Text and English Translation. Notes." In *The Aristotelian Tradition: Aristotle's Works on Logic and Metaphysics and Their Reception in the Middle Ages*, edited by Börje Bydén and Christina Thomsen Thörnqvist, 297–344. Toronto: Pontifical Institute of Mediaeval Studies, 2017.

Secondary Sources

Athanassiadi, Polymnia. "Byzantine Commentators on the Chaldaean Oracles: Psellos and Plethon." In *Byzantine Philosophy and Its Ancient Sources*, edited by Katerina Ierodiakonou. Oxford: Clarendon Press, 2002.

Boiadjiev, Tzotcho. "Der byzantinische Platonismus: Georgios Gemistos Plethon." In *Die Philosophie des Mittelalters: Byzanz, Judentum*, edited by Alexander Brungs, Georgi Kapriev, and Vilem Mudroch, 1:202–8. Grundriss der Geschichte der Philosophie. Basel: Schwabe Verlag Basel, 2019.

Brisson, Luc. "Pléthon et Les Oracles Chaldaïques." In *Philosophie et Sciences à Byzance de 1204 à 1453: Les Textes, Les Doctrines et Leur Transmission: Actes de La Table Ronde Organisée Au XXe Congrès International d'études Byzantines, Paris, 2001*, edited by Michel Cacouros and Marie-Hélène Congourdeau, 127–42. Orientalia Lovaniensia Analecta 146. Leuven: Peeters, 2006.

Hladký, Vojtěch. *The Philosophy of Gemistos Plethon: Platonism in Late Byzantium, Between Hellenism and Orthodoxy*. Farnham, Surrey; Burlington, Vt.: Ashgate Publishing, 2014.

Masai, François. *Pléthon et Le Platonisme de Mistra*. Paris: Les Belles Lettres, 1956.

Matula, Jozef, and Paul Richard Blum, eds. *Georgios Gemistos Plethon: The Byzantine and the Latin Renaissance*. Olomouc: Palacký University Press, 2014. http://www.renesancni-texty.upol.cz/soubory/publikace/Plethon_Conference_Proceedings.pdf.

Molinari, Jonathan. *Libertà e Discordia: Pletone, Bessarione, Pico della Mirandola*. Bologna: Il Mulino, 2015.

Monfasani, John. "George Gemistos Plethon and the West: Greek Emigres." In *Renaissance Encounters: Greek East and Latin West*, edited by Marina Scordilis Brownlee and Dimitri Gondicas. Medieval and Renaissance Authors and Texts 8. Leiden: Brill, 2013.

Schulz, Peter. "George Gemisthos Plethon (ca. 1360–1454), George of Trebizond (1396–1472), and Cardinal Bessarion (1403–1454): The Controversy between Platonists and Aristotelians in the Fifteenth Century." In *Philosophers of the Renaissance*, edited by Paul Richard Blum and translated by Brian McNeil, 23–32. Washington, D.C: The Catholic University of America Press, 2010.

Siniossoglou, Niketas. *Radical Platonism in Byzantium: Illumination and Utopia in Gemistos Plethon*. Cambridge Classical Studies. Cambridge: Cambridge University Press, 2011.

Stausberg, Michael. *Faszination Zarathushtra: Zoroaster und die Europäische Religionsgeschichte der Frühen Neuzeit*. 2 vols. Berlin: de Gruyter, 1998.

Tambrun, Brigitte. *Pléthon: Le retour de Platon*. Paris: Vrin, 2007.

Woodhouse, Montague Christopher. *George Gemistos Plethon: The Last of the Hellenes*. Oxford: Clarendon Press, 1986.

GEORGIOS GEMISTOS PLETHO

Commentary on Chaldaean Oracles[8]

(1) Seek the channel of the soul: where or from what rank it comes. When you have served the body, it is toward the rank from which you have flowed. You will rise up again, after joining the act to the sacred word.

The Magi disciples of Zoroaster, like many others, believe that the human soul is immortal: It came down from above to serve this mortal body, that is, for a certain time to work for it, to make it alive, and to adorn it in power and then in time return from down here to where it came from above. And that there are several places for the soul; one is wholly bright, the other is wholly dark.

Between these two places, there are some that are either half bright or half dark. Therefore, coming from the wholly bright place, the soul flowed down into this body, and if it has done its service well, it is towards the same place that it springs up again. If she did not do it well, she goes down from here to places that are worse than this one, according to how she conducted her life.

With regard to this, the oracle says, 'seek the channel of the soul,' or the way by which it happened that the soul flowed into you; from where or by which rank, clearly meaning of life. When you have served this body, you will go up again to the same rank as the one from which you flowed, manifestly by the same channel of the soul, 'joining the act to the sacred word.'

Now, what the Oracles call 'the sacred word' is that which concerns religion; as to the act, it is the religious rite. Therefore, the oracle means that besides the word, which relates to religion, use also the religious rite, for this way of guiding leads the soul back on high.

---

8. Every numbered and bold paragraph of Pletho's version of the *Chaldaean Oracles* is followed by his own commentary.

(2) Do not incline down; a precipice lies beneath the earth, drawing down along the sevenfold steps, under which is the throne of terrible necessity.

The oracle calls 'the precipice' an inclination toward corruption, evil, and misfortune, and it calls 'the earth' the earthly and mortal body. In fact, these oracles very often designate the mortal nature by earth and the divine nature by fire. The oracle designates as 'the sevenfold steps' the Fate, fixed by the planets, under which is established a certain 'terrible' and inflexible 'Necessity.' Therefore, the oracle means: do not incline yourself down toward that body which is mortal; which is subject only to the Fate fixed by the planets, it is rather part of what is not in our power. Indeed, you will be unhappy and unfortunate, if you entirely incline toward the body time and time again you will be deprived of your will by the necessity that was affixed in your body.

(3) Earthly beasts will occupy your vessel.

The 'vessel' of your soul is this mortal body; it will be inhabited by worms and beasts.

(4) Do not enlarge your fate.

Do not endeavor to enlarge your fate, or to make it bigger than is allotted; in fact, it is clear that you will not be able to do it.

(5) For nothing imperfect proceeds from the paternal principle.

Indeed, from the paternal principle—in other words, from the supreme god—nothing imperfect proceeds, that is to say, in such a way that you could perfect it. In fact, all that proceeds from there is perfect because it tends toward perfection of the whole.

(6) But the paternal intellect does not admit her will until she has come out of oblivion and says a word, inspiring the remembrance of the pure paternal watchword.

The paternal intellect—that is to say, the second god and the direct demiurge of the soul—does not admit its will until it has come out of oblivion, which the soul has suffered due to her intertwining with the body, and until it speaks a certain word. In other words, that soul has in mind some word that results from the memory of the divine paternal watchword, and that is, the injunction to pursue the good. And as soon as the soul remembers this, its demiurge becomes exceedingly rejoiced in her.

(7) You must hasten to the light and to the rays of the Father, whence the soul was sent to you, clothed in abundant intellect.

The 'light and the rays of the Father' are for the soul, its place wholly bright. From there, the soul clothed by the much abundant intellect has been sent down here; therefore, it must hasten to return to the same light.

(8) Oi, Oi! The earth laments even unto their children.

Those who do not hasten to the same light, from which their soul was sent to them, 'the earth'—that is to say, the mortal nature—laments, because they have been sent hither to adorn her. But they did not only adorn her, but also dishonored themselves by living wickedly. But in addition, the 'children' also partake of the wickedness of their parents, receiving the pernicious pedagogy that the parents give them.

(9) Those who, by drawing breath, expel the soul, are easily released.

The reasons that thrust out the soul, clearly from evil, and thus give her breath, are 'easily released.' That is to say, not difficult to free them from the oblivion that for so long held power over them.

(10) On the left side of the bed resides the font of virtue that remains entirely within and does not give up virginity.

'On the left side of your bed' there is the font of virtue or power, which remains entirely within and never gives up virginity, that is to say, of the things untouched by passion. Indeed, the power of the virtue that always resides within us cannot be lost and cannot be touched by passion, even if its activity ceases. The oracle says that the power of virtue resides on the 'left' because it wishes to place activity on the right. The 'bed' of our soul is the place underlying its various dispositions.

(11) The soul of the mortal somehow embraces God into herself; having nothing mortal in her, she is wholly intoxicated by God. She glories in the harmony in which the mortal body exists.

The human soul 'somehow embraces God into herself'; in other words, it will unite strongly with the one who is its immediate ruler by becoming similar to him as much as possible. The soul, having 'nothing mortal' in itself, 'is wholly intoxicated by God'— that is to say, is filled by divine blessings. Indeed, although it is attached to this world, even so she boasts of 'the harmony'— which is to say the union—'in which the mortal body exists.' In other words, the soul is not ashamed of the body but rather considers the harmony beneficial. The soul renders a service unto the universe, so that the mortal aspects are unified to the immortal aspects in man, and thus the universe is assembled as a single harmony.

(12) Since the soul is a luminous fire by the power of the Father, she remains immortal and is the mistress of life and contains much of what fills the hollows of the world.

The 'power of the Father,' and his intellectual power, and paternal intellect, with these words the oracles everywhere name the second god himself. He is the first of all the others that have come from the Father and supreme god. Now the oracle says that the soul is created by this 'power of the Father,' that is, in an immediate manner. The 'luminous fire,' that is, a divine and intellectual essence, 'remains immortal' by the divinity of its essence and is the mistress of life, that is to say, of herself, possessing life that cannot be cast taken away from her. For the things we have that can be taken from us, how can we be said to be masters of them? For only the use of those things is allotted to us, but of the things that cannot be taken from us, we are the masters of those. Now the soul holds, because of its own perpetuity, 'much of what fills the hollows of the world,' that is to say, of the different places in the world where she experiences in life according to what is allotted.

(13) Seek paradise.

The place of the soul, which is wholly bright.

(14) Do not contaminate the spirit and do not deepen the surface.

The Pythagorean and Platonic sages believe that the soul is a substance not absolutely separable from every body, but neither, on the contrary, is it absolutely inseparable. Instead, in one respect, it is separable, and in another inseparable. They affirm that it is potentially always separable, whereas in actuality, it is always inseparable. Actually, they propose triple forms of the soul: the first is absolutely separate from matter, and these are the supercelestial intellects. Another is absolutely inseparable and does not have an essence subsisting by itself but is dependent on matter. And when, at a certain time, matter dissolves because of the dispersing and perishing character of its nature, the consequence is the whole irrational form.

Between these two forms is posited a third, the rational soul. This soul differs, on the one hand, from the supercelestial intellects because it is always united with matter. On the other hand, the soul differs from the irrational form because it is not dependent on matter. On the contrary, matter is always dependent on it.

The soul itself has its own essence and, potentially, subsists by itself. It is indivisible, as well as the supercelestial intellects, to whom it yields the acts that are in some way related to them while it is likewise engaged in the knowledge and contemplation of beings, up to the supreme god himself. Because of that, she is imperishable.

The soul, which is this sort of form, is always united to an aethereal body as its vehicle, and the immediate contact makes it also co-immortal. But such a vehicle of the soul is not in itself inanimate, rather it is animated by the other form of soul, which is irrational, that the wise call the image of the rational soul. This image is adorned with imagination and perception. This form sees and hears absolutely everything by its totality and perceives everything thanks to those other powers attached to the soul, which are irrational.

Now, on the one hand, it is by the most excellent power of such a body, namely the imagination, that the rational soul is always united to such an entire body. On the other hand, it is by means of such a body that the human soul at some time unites with the mortal body, then the whole embryo is intermingled with all the life spirit, because of a certain kinship, since it is also a kind of spirit.

As for the souls of demons, on the one hand, they do not differ much from human souls, but they are nobler and use nobler vehicles and they cannot be mixed with mortal nature. As for the souls of the stars, these are far superior to those of the demons, and they use superior vehicles, these bodies that are so splendid by the magnitude of their active power.

It appears that the wise disciples of Zoroaster also used these doctrines on the soul before. The oracle says, 'Do not contaminate the spirit' of the soul 'and do not deepen the surface.' The oracle calls it a surface not because it is not three-dimensional body, but to highlight its very great subtlety, which the oracle calls a surface.

The oracle therefore suggests to not deepen or thicken it by adding more matter to its mass. Such a spirit of the soul is thickened by the excessive inclination of the soul toward the mortal body.

(15a) There is a portion for the image in the wholly bright place.

The oracle calls the 'image' of the soul the irrational element, which is joined to the rational element and fastened to its vehicle. It means that 'there is a portion for the image in the wholly bright place.' For the soul never casts off the vehicle that is connected to her.

(15b) And do not leave behind the dreg of matter on the precipice.

The oracle calls the mortal body 'the dreg of matter,' and it recommends not to disdain it when it lives in misery but to take care of it so long as it remains in this life, and keep it, as much as possible in good health so that it may be pure in all the things in agreement with the order of the soul.

(16) Do not tear away it, so that in going out it does not have anything.

'Do not tear away,' meaning the soul, out of the mortal body, 'so that on going out, it does not have anything.' Namely, the very fact that she drives out herself is contrary to the laws of nature.

(17) If you extend your fiery intellect to the work of piety, you will also save the flowing body.

'If you extend your divine intellect toward the work of piety,' namely toward the pious rite, 'you will also preserve the mortal body,' making it healthier by means of the rite.

(18) So from the hollows of the earth spring chthonian/subterranean dogs, which never show a true sign to mortal man.

To many initiated persons, dog-like images sometimes appear during rituals, as well as other apparitions strange in form. Now, the oracle says that these images spring forth 'from the hollows of the earth,' that is to say, from that earthly and mortal body and from the irrational passions that are innate to it. These passions are not yet sufficiently set in order by reason and images of such passions in the soul of the initiate appear as phenomena having no substance, and for this reason, do not mean anything true.

Commentary on Chaldaean Oracles

(19) **Nature persuades us that demons are pure and that the offspring of evil matter are good and useful.**

'Nature,' or natural reason, 'persuades us that the demons are pure' and that simply everything that comes from the god who is good in himself is 'good and useful,' including the 'offspring of evil matter,' namely the forms that depend on matter. The oracle says that matter is 'evil,' but not in its essence. How, indeed, would it be evil in essence when its offspring are worthy and good? But because matter is put the last among essences, and participates the least in the good, the oracle indicates by its evil nature the minimum of good in it.

And this is what the oracle means: if even the offspring of evil matter are good, in other words, those of the last essence, then even more so are the demons who rule over much because of their rational nature and by the absence of mixture with mortal nature.

(20) **Penalties are stranglers of men.**

'Penalties,' that is, the punishing demons, are 'stranglers of men;' in other words, holding them together and driving them away from vice and binding them to virtue.

(21) **Let the soul lead to the immortal depth and open all your eyes to lift upward on high.**

Let the divine 'depth lead your soul.' And 'lift up' at the same time 'all your eyes,' that is to say, your cognitive powers.

(22) **O man, cunning creation of most daring nature.**

The oracle calls man 'a cunning creation of a daring nature,' because he throws himself into great deeds.

(23) **If you speak to me many times, you will see what is said. For then, indeed, the vaulted mass of the sky does not appear; the stars do not shine. The light of the moon is hidden; the earth does not stand still, and all things are seen by lightning.**

It comes from god, the oracle says, to the initiated person: 'if you speak to me several times,' that is to say, if you call me, 'you will see what is said' everywhere, which is clearly me, whom you call. Indeed, nothing will be seen by you except by 'lightning,' that is the fire that everywhere ignites the world.

(24) Do not invoke a self-revealed image of Nature.

Do not try to see 'the self-revealed image of nature,' that is, of the nature of God, because it is not visible to your eyes. Now, the things that appear to the initiated people as lightning, fire, and all the rest, are merely symbols but not the nature of God.

(25) From all sides draw tight the reins of fire to your sincere soul.

Hold the reins of the fire that appears to you during the rite, from all sides, and course toward your 'sincere soul,' that is to say, the simple one, freed as much as possible from all evildoing.

(26) Whenever you see the formless, divine fire that shines by leaps and bounds into the depths of the whole world, then listen to the voice of fire.

When you see the divine fire without form, which shines by leaps and bounds over the world, which is to say with grace and benevolence, then listen to this voice, because it brings the truest foreknowledge.

(27) The paternal intellect has sown symbols into souls.

'The paternal intellect,' namely the direct demiurge of the essence of the soul, 'has sown the symbols into souls,' that is, the images of the intelligible forms, from which each soul always possesses in itself the reasons of beings.

(28a) Learn the intelligible because it exists outside the intellect.

'Learn the intelligible because it exists outside of your intellect,' that is, the active intellect. Indeed, even if images of the intelligible have been sown in you by the demiurge, in fact, they reside in your soul only potentially. Still, you must also search and acquire the knowledge of the intelligible.

(28b) There is indeed something intelligible, which you must understand by the flower of the intellect.

Because the supreme god is one, in the highest degree, it is not possible to conceive of him as like the other intelligible things but 'by the flower of the intellect,' that is to say, by the highest and simplest part our understanding.

Commentary on Chaldaean Oracles

(29) All things are born from the one fire.

'All things are born of one fire,' namely god.

(30) For the Father has perfected all things, and he handed them to the second intellect, which the races of men call the first.

In fact, 'the Father accomplished all things,' that is to say, the intelligible forms, because they are the ones both complete and perfect. 'He handed them over to the second god,' who comes after him, clearly to govern and direct them. So that if something is brought forward by this god, as a paradigm of his own and the rest of intelligible essence, it derives its origin from the supreme Father. 'The second god, that the people of the races of men call the first,' that is to say, all those people who assume that there is a direct demiurge of this world and that there is nothing superior to him.

(31) The *iynges*, which are thought by the Father, also think for themselves, are moved by voiceless or ineffable wills so as to have understanding.

The oracle calls *iynges* the intelligent forms; 'they are thought by the Father and they also think for themselves,' moved toward thoughts by 'voiceless or immutable wills.' Indeed, here, by the movement toward thought, the oracle does not mean a change of place or going out (discursive thought) but simply the relationship to thought. Thus, the expression by 'voiceless wills' would mean by motionless wills, because the voice implies movement. The oracle seems to mean that such forms have a relationship to the things that are immobile (i.e., not discursively), as is the case of the soul.

(32) Lo! How the world has unbending intellectual supports!

The most eminent among the intelligible forms, which introduce the immortals in the sky, the oracle calls them 'intellectual supports' of the world. Their leader, whom he thinks to be god, is the one who is second after the Father. By saying that 'the world has these unbending supports,' the oracle clearly wishes to say that it is incorruptible.

(33) The Father has snatched himself away without even confining his own fire in his intellectual power.

'The Father has taken himself out' from all other realities, without even limiting 'his own intellectual power'—that is to say, in the second god who comes after him—dividing up, his own fire, that is, his own divinity. In fact, that which is absolutely unbegotten and which exists by itself, has its divinity taken out from all other realities, is wholly incommunicable to anything else. He does not share anything of himself, not because of jealousy, but because doing so would be an utter impossibility, a contradiction.

(34) The Father does not impel fear, but he pours out persuasion.

The Father does not throw fear, but 'he pours out persuasion,' that is to say, love. Indeed, since he is absolutely good himself, he cannot be a cause of anything bad to anyone, lest he be terrifying. But since he is always the cause of good for all, he can only be loved by all. It is therefore evident that many others agree in some way with these oracles of the disciples of Zoroaster, especially the Pythagorean and Platonic sages, since those who are still followers of Zoroaster, to whom Plutarch refers, and also appear in Plato's writings, seem to be in agreement. Plutarch says that Zoroaster divided beings into three classes. And the first class of the beings is presided over by Horomazes, who is called Father by the Oracles; the last one is presided over by Ahriman, whereas Mithra presides over the middle, and it would be he who is called second intellect by the Oracles. But Horomazes has set himself triply aside from the sun, which is also called "Cyrus" in Persia; and conversely Mithra, that is to say, the one that comes after Horomazes, is doubly as great. This is quite in agreement with what Plato says: *Related to* [312e] *the King of All are all things, and for his sake they are, and of all things fair He is the cause. And related to the Second are the second things and related to the Third the third* (Plato, *Letters* II (312e1-4)). As for the three parts in which Zoroaster and Plato divided existing things, the first is eternal, the second is temporal and perpetual, and the third is mortal. Zoroaster, says Plutarch, is someone so old that he is reported to have lived five thousand years before the Trojan War.

3

GEORGE OF TREBIZOND
(1396–1474/75)

Comparison of Plato and Aristotle:
God as the Absolutely First

JOHN MONFASANI

INTRODUCTION

George of Trebizond was born in Crete in 1396 (*Trapezountios* was a common family name because of émigrés from Trebizond on the Black Sea generations earlier). He died in Rome in late 1474 or in 1475. George was brought to Venice by the patrician Francesco Barbaro in 1416 to serve as a Greek copyist, and with amazing rapidity, he mastered Latin and became one of the great teachers of rhetoric of the Italian fifteenth century. His *Rhetoricorum Libri V* of 1434 gained the status of a classic already in the Renaissance, and his small manual summarizing medieval logic for rhetorical purposes (*Isagoge Dialectica*) became a best seller in the sixteenth century. Starting in the 1440s, he also translated important Aristotelian texts into Latin. At the same time, he also succeeded in becoming a papal secretary and under Pope Nicholas V (1447–1455) a core contributor to Nicholas's grand plan to translate the Greek patristic and classical heritage into Latin, rendering not only still more works of Aristotle but also important

49

writings of Ptolemy, Plato, Eusebius of Caesarea, Cyril of Alexandria, John Chrysostom, and, earlier, Basil the Great.

George's interests, however, went beyond these typical humanist pursuits. For one thing, he greatly admired the intellectual achievements of medieval Scholasticism, especially of St. Thomas Aquinas. For another, quite early on, he plunged into medieval apocalyptic texts and eventually assumed for himself the role of an apocalyptic prophet, warning of the impending doom posed by the Turkish threat. For a third, he came to despise not only Plato as an unpatriotic and horribly immoral source of Christian heresy but also the leading Greek Platonist of the day, George Gemistos Pletho (d. 1454), as an insidious reviver of ancient hedonism. All these interests converged in his polemic with Cardinal Bessarion, a student of Pletho, and his circle in Rome.

George fired the first salvo of his attack in 1456 with his *Protectio Problematum Aristotelis*, which is both a savage assault on Theodore Gaza, a rival Greek Aristotelian translator and client of Cardinal Bessarion, and also a brilliant treatise on the art of translation. The next year he finished but did not publish until 1458 his *Comparison of the Philosophers Plato and Aristotle*, which was the first Latin work in a quarrel about the relative merits of Plato and Aristotle hitherto conducted exclusively in Greek by Byzantine scholars resident in Greece and Italy. What made George's *Comparison* explosive was that he integrated his criticism of Plato and praise of Aristotle within an apocalyptic historical vision in which immoral, hedonistic Platonism led to the corruption and downfall of the Greco-Roman Empire aided in classical times by the "second Plato" Epicurus and in medieval times by the "third Plato" Mohammed. Now these same enervating forces are attempting to subvert the Latin West through the followers of the recently deceased George Gemistos Pletho. Warning against the emergence of a "fourth Plato" (presumably meaning Bessarion, who had the possibility of becoming pope in the next conclave), George urged his Latin readers to stamp out this Platonic contagion while there was still time.

George divided the *Comparison* into three books. The first compared the contributions of the two philosophers to learning. Since the treatises of Aristotle in a wide variety of subjects had been the base texts of university education in the Latin West for centuries, while all Plato offered was a series of literary dialogues, it was easy to see who won that contest. Book

2 compared the philosophers on the content of their philosophy with the criterion of judgment being the degree to which they approached or distanced themselves from truth, that is, Christian dogma. This is the most philosophical part of the *Comparison*, as George, who knew his Aristotle well, having translated more than half of the Aristotelian corpus, argued that in accord with Christian truth Aristotle believed in an omnipotent God who created the world *ex nihilo* in a free will act of his goodness. Aristotle even understood this God to be triune without having, however, any sense of the three persons of the Trinity as revealed by Scripture. Book 3 is an unrelenting attack on Platonic hedonism, especially pederasty, running from Plato through Mohammed. The book culminates in a description of the immediate dangers posed by the neopagan Pletho and his followers to the Latin West.

Cardinal Bessarion completed his response in 1459, writing in Greek but having a Latin version printed ten years later. Bessarion answered George ponderously point by point, but omitted completely any reference to George Gemistos Pletho and his religious beliefs. Thus, as Bessarion's *Against the Slanderer of Plato* became in the course of the Renaissance and beyond the only text of this first phase of the Plato-Aristotle controversy that was read, George's apocalyptic warnings about neopagan Pletho, that were the culminating point of his book, were lost to history and only recovered in recent times.

BIBLIOGRAPHY
Primary Sources

Bessarion. *In Calumniatorem Platonis Libri IV.* Edited by Ludwig Mohler. Paderborn: Ferdinand Schöningh, 1927. Reprint, Aalen: Scientia Verlag; Paderborn: Ferdinand Schöningh, 1967.

George of Trebizond. *Comparatio Philosophorum Platonis et Aristotelis.* In John Monfasani, *Vindicatio Aristotelis. Two Works of George of Trebizond in the Plato-Aristotle Controversy of the Fifteenth Century.* Tempe, Ariz.: Medieval & Renaissance Texts & Studies, 2021.

Mohler, Ludwig, ed. *Aus Bessarions Gelehrtenkreis. Abhandlunge, Reden, Briefe.* Paderborn: Ferdinand Schöningh, 1942. Reprint, Aalen: Scientia Verlag; Paderborn: Ferdinand Schöningh, 1967.

Monfasani, John, ed. *Collectanea Trapezuntiana: Texts, Documents, and Bibliographies of George of Trebizond.* Binghamton, N.Y.: Medieval & Renaissance Texts & Studies, 1984.

Secondary Sources

Copenhaver, Brian, and Charles B. Schmitt. *Renaissance Philosophy*. Oxford: Oxford University Press, 1992.

Del Soldato, Eva. *Early Modern Aristotle: On the Making and Unmaking of Authority*. Philadelphia: University of Pennsylvania, 2020.

Hankins, James. *Plato in the Italian Renaissance*. 2 vols. Leiden: Brill, 1990.

Mohler, Ludwig. *Kardinal Bessarion als Theologe, Humanist und Staatsmann. Darstellung*. Paderborn: Ferdinand Schöningh, 1923. Reprint, Aalen: Scientia Verlag; Paderborn: Ferdinand Schöningh, 1967.

Monfasani, John. *George of Trebizond: A Biography and a Study of His Rhetoric and Logic*. Leiden: Brill, 1976.

———. "A Tale of Two Books: Bessarion's *In Calumniatorem Platonis* and George of Trebizond's *Comparatio Philosophorum Platonis et Aristotelis*." *Renaissance Studies. Journal of the Society for Renaissance Studies* 22, no. 1 (2008): 1–15.

Pontani, Anna. "Note sulla controversia platonico-aristotelica del Quattrocento." *Quaderni del Siculorum Gymnasium* 18 (1989): 99–165.

GEORGE OF TREBIZOND

Comparison of Plato and Aristotle: God as the Absolutely First[1]

CHAPTER 2

That only in matters that are necessary for salvation is it impious to disbelieve the doctors of the Church; on all other matters, it is of no consequence if you disbelieve them and even hold views contrary to theirs.

This thorny and difficult question, moreover, very much presses itself upon us not only because it entails abstruse and hidden questions on the deepest matters but also because some doctors of the Church seem to give to Plato the palm that we think rightly should be awarded to Aristotle, as we, in fact, shall show. Indeed, it would seem that we should not believe that the doctors of the Church, who, we admit, wrote under the power of divine grace, conveyed to us less than the truth about any subject. What response therefore shall we have to that? This response, name-

---

1. Translation by John Monfasani based on George of Trebizond, *Comparatio Philosophorum Platonis et Aristotelis*, ed. John Monfasani. Reprinted with permission.

Comparison of Plato and Aristotle: God as the Absolutely First 53

ly, that everyone, if they care about truth, will reject as false the assertion that the doctors of the Church spoke without grace concerning matters that pertain to the founding of the Church and that are necessary for salvation; but surely on matters that neither aid nor hinder the salvation of souls, they spoke merely as men. This is obvious from the facts themselves. For if someone were to ask some father of the Church about the squaring of the circle, whose response would seem to him that one ought more to believe, the Church father's or Archimedes's? I have no doubt that everyone would say Archimedes's.[2] If any of the holy Fathers were to discourse on the magnitude of the sun, should we prefer his arguments or those of Erasthenes or Ptolemy? In matters of this sort, I am moved by the authority of Ptolemy alone than by the authority of all the holy Fathers combined. If therefore the question is who is more expert, more erudite, and closer to the truth, Plato or Aristotle, and some doctors of the Church think it is one or the other, I am no more compelled to follow their authority in this question than I am in the previous examples. Why? Because it is impious to call into doubt all they wrote through the infusion of grace in them. For it was through the Spirit of God that they said these things. These sorts of things, however, are matters that are necessary for salvation. Whether, in fact, heaven is round, whether the [diameter of the] sun is two feet or greater,[3] whether the moon is larger than the sun or vice-versa, whether Demosthenes is closer to being the supreme orator than is Cicero, or whether Homer or Virgil is the greater poet, neither the holy Fathers nor the Church have ever made a determination nor ever will. For in such matters, they have not divinely received the grace that would make them not liable to error. For what does the question whether the moon is located behind the sun have to do with the salvation of souls? Or whether Mercury and Venus are to be located between the sun and the moon? Or whether Plato was given to virtue or to vice? Or whether Aristotle is more erudite than Plato or superior in moral virtue? Certainly nothing at all. It is obvious, consequently, that if some doctors of the Church, be they Greek or Latin, spoke on these matters, they did so not having grace infused in them but spoke as men who are liable to error, and we can piously have

2. George formulates here the argument of Galileo's famous letter to the Grand Duchess. Christina, though Galileo had a more difficult row to hoe in that he had to debunk the scientific value not only of Church Fathers such as St. Augustine but also of the Bible itself.

3. Cf. Cicero, *De Fin.*, 1.20.

an opinion on these matters different from theirs, especially because in ancient times Aristotle was poorly understood on these matters—this was because his books came to light rather late nor, apart from those he wrote on morals, could they be grasped before the time of the commentator Alexander, who, we know, flourished under the Roman Emperor Antoninus, on account of the depth of the material, which is such that one can make the case that it cannot be comprehended unless one diligently pours over all his extant books. Because therefore, as I said, Aristotle was poorly understood on these matters, while, on the other hand, Plato was familiar to everyone on account of his literary elegance and ostentatious way of speaking, it was difficult for the church fathers not to err in their judgment. For they could not grant preeminence in philosophy to an author whom they had, in fact, not read or, if they had read him, did not properly understand. Furthermore, we need to concern ourselves with the facts of the matter, not with authorities (a source that can often fail). It is on this basis that we make our comparison.

CHAPTER 3

How Book 2 is divided. And that Plato speaks in terms of one god but, in fact, worships many, while Aristotle refers everything to a single principle that is absolutely the first and not in a numerical sequence with all other things. And on the duty of a translator, on the omnipotence of God, and on the theology of Plato and Aristotle.

Having established these preliminary points, in this book, we shall first show that Aristotle thought better and more correctly concerning God than did Plato; second, that Aristotle had an inkling of the trinity of the one God, while Plato had none at all; third, that Aristotle thought the universe was produced *ex nihilo* by the will of God, while Plato, in contrast, thought it was produced from prime matter; fourth, that Aristotle expounded the truth concerning the human soul, while Plato recounted poetic fictions; fifth, that Aristotle believed that things on earth were governed by Providence, while Plato dreamt that everything was under the sway of necessity. From all this, one plainly sees that Plato is most alien to the truth and Aristotle most in accord, and that while Aristotle's writings are a tremendous help to the dogmas of the Church, Plato's are patently at war with them.

The absolute first thing Platonists say when praising their author to the sky is that he piously and learnedly attributed the whole universe to the one true God. For, they say, even if he talks about many gods, he believes nonetheless that all of them are produced by the first, the second god directly, the others indirectly; Aristotle, however, nowhere traces everything back to the first god. When they say this, they cause me and, I am sure, everyone who cares for truth to burst out in loud laughter. For the Platonists call a philosopher a man who worshiped creatures as if they were gods, who adored one first god purely verbally while in fact adoring the second god, and the tertiary gods and gods that are utterly creatures. And they are not ashamed to admit this. For, as they will publically say, and rightly so, Plato believed that many gods were produced, first by the first god, and then by the second god and the third god.[4] And if, having gone this far, he had added nothing more, since we ought always to be more inclined toward conciliating than toward attacking, I would have supposed that he was speaking in the same sort of way divine scripture sometimes uses the term "god" when speaking of men (for it is written, "I said, you are gods."[5]), especially since he adds that the second was made by the first and the third by second and thus through a certain series the others gods, not always one god making one god, but with only the second god being made by the first and the third by the second, and thence the multiplicity of gods. For it follows that if they were made, they are gods not in fact but merely nominally or by comparison since as immortals they are being compared to us mortals. Labels, however, are of no concern to a philosopher or to truth; all that matters are the facts. But now, when he worships them and thinks that we should worship them as our makers, how does he differ from those who worship snakes, those who worship bulls, those who worship cats and other monstrosities of this kind? Because he adores creatures that are nobler, does he seem to be more prudent, intelligent, and learned than those rude and stupid men? Every creature is equally distant from the First God.

4. Cf. Plato, *Timaeus*, 41a–d, 42d, 69b–c; Numenius, *Fragments*, frags. 11–13, 15–17, 19–22 [ed. des Places, 53–61].

5. Psalms 81:6.

For the distance is infinity.[6] Nor is worship and adoration due to any other than the Creator, something that even he saw.[7] But just as he thinks that the second god was made by the first, other gods by the second, and thence still other gods, so accordingly in the last book of his *Laws* he prescribes and orders that it be sanctioned in law that we are products of the celestial beings and that therefore the heavens, the sun, and the moon should be worshiped and adored as gods and our creators.[8] Nor does it make any difference if they argue that under the names of "heavens," "moon," and "sun" he understood not bodies but the intelligences that move these orbs. Yes, it is stupider to ascribe the honorific of god to bodies than to intelligences. But the impiety is the same. For in both cases, you have the worship and adoration of idols. For idolatry is the transfer of piety, hope, and adoration from the creator to the creature. What a learned man he is! He gives to natural things, that is, to bodies, the worship that is due, as philosophers are wont to say, to the one true God, and orders others to do the same!

But Aristotle wrote much more rightly, and consequently, if correctly understood, makes himself in no way an obstacle to piety. For you will not find a word in his writings that would allow one to think that he did not adore exclusively the first and supreme cause. Indeed, quite the contrary. He will be found to have shown not only that the celestial bodies are not to be adored but also that they are in a way less noble than men. For in Book 2 of the *De Generatione et Corruptione*, toward the end, where he is inquiring about the causes of these things, he says, "since we assert that nature desires what is better and that being is better than non-being and that it is impossible for being to be in all things since they are too far removed from the first principle itself, God filled the universe through the remaining mode when he made continuous generation."[9] You need note, first of all, that he asserts that all things crave the first principle (for all things desire

---

6. A firm Thomistic principle; see, among others, Thomas Aquinas, *De Veritate*, q. 2, a. 11, arg. 4; *Contra Gentiles*, III, c. 54, n. 7, and c. 57, num. 3. Nicholas of Cusa expressed the same opinion; see his *De Pace Fidei* XII (ed. Klibansky-Bascour, 36.7–9), *De Docta Ignorantia*, I, c. 4 (ed. Klibansky-Hoffmann, 11.14–16).

7. Cf. Plato, *Laws*, 4.716d; *Timaeus*, 29d–42e.

8. Cf. Plato, *Laws*, 10.899b3–d2, and *Epinomis*, 981c5–982a3; cf. also *Laws*, 4.717a–b.

9. Aristotle, *De Gen.et Corr.*, 2.336b27–32. George is quoting verbatim from his translation of the *De Gen. et Corr.*

Comparison of Plato and Aristotle: God as the Absolutely First   57

sempiternal duration so that they can be assimilated to the first principle); next, that the things closer to the first principle are individually sempiternal substances. For, he says, the things that are further removed are eternal through the remaining mode. For he posits two modes of sempiternity: one of individuals, the other of species through a succession of individuals. The things closer to the first principle are sempiternal through the first mode; those farther away through the second. "For God made continuous generation," he says, "in order to fill the universe"; that is, so that he might endow with perpetuity even all the things that are further removed in a way in which they can accept. Aristotle understood, I would argue, being close and being distant not in terms of place, but in terms of a certain property, that is, in terms of the similitude and vestige and image of the first principle impressed into things. It is not a problem that the celestial bodies are sempiternal through the first mode, but human bodies are not sempiternal at all, although the two nevertheless share the same definition in so far as they are bodies. For it is not because they are bodies that the celestial bodies achieve sempiternity but because they individually exhaust all the matter suited to them, which is something obvious from the singularity, as I would put it, of the individual celestial bodies. It is for this reason, therefore, that the first principle, who is God, made continuous generation, so that through this mode at least, namely, by means of species, since the first mode was impossible, even corruptible things here below might be sempiternal. He set forth this remaining mode with the words, "God made continuous generation."

But why, in fact, was generation made continuous, which is the very question that is germane to the issue at hand? Therefore, let the Platonists listen to him attentively and weight each of his words. "Contraries," he says, "are the causes of contraries. Hence, the first motion is not the cause of generation and corruption, but rather that motion which is through the inclined orb. For it is continuous, and there are two motions moving in it. For it is necessarily the case that if there is always going to be generation and corruption, then something always has to be in motion lest the changes themselves cease; it necessary, however, that the motions be two lest only one of the changes occurs. Motion, therefore, is the cause of the whole continuous process, but obliqueness is the cause of there being a drawing near and a receding."[10] Since generation and corruption are contraries, it is right, he says, that their causes are contraries. But the motion of the whole is one and simple. It is therefore the cause not of generation and corruption but only of the continuance of these changes. The obliqueness of the zodiac, however, through which move the sun and all the other planets, with the latter falling off a bit from the path of the sun,[11] which always passes through the middle of the oblique circle, is far and away the cause of there being a drawing near and a receding.[12] It is, however, the drawing near of the sun that is the cause of generation, and its receding the cause of corruption, with the drawing near and receding of the other planets also being causes according to the conditions of things. For they are auxiliary causes. This is why astrologers studiously pay attention to their aspect in relation to the sun so as to determine if they are still or are going forward or are regressing. If therefore the motion by which all the other spheres are borne along, is most of all the cause of the continuation of these changes, and if the obliqueness of the zodiac is the cause of these changes and of the oblique motion of the sun and the planets, it necessarily follows that the heavens were made for the sake of generation and corruption and of their continuance. Nay, in point of fact, in a certain way, Aristotle expressly proclaims that they were made for this purpose. For he says: "God made continuous generation." It is continuous, in fact, on account of the motion of the whole. This generation, he says, is caused through the motion of drawing near. Therefore, God made the motion of the whole and the motions of drawing near and receding for the sake of generation and corruption. And if this is the purpose of these motions, then it is also that of the bodies in motion to which belong these motions. Therefore, in a certain way, the heavens were made for the sake of these motions. I would add that this is also true for their movers. For in the sense that something in motion exists for the sake of generation, certainly in the exact same sense, the mover of that motion also exists for the sake of generation. And this is what Aristotle says in the *Physics*: "for we are in a certain sense the end."[13] For in an absolute sense, the first cause is the final end of everything, but

---

10. Aristotle, *De Gen. et Corr.*, 2.336a30–b4.
11. Cf. Aristotle, *Meteor.*, 1.343a23–24.
12. Aristotle, *De Gen. et Corr.*, 2.336a15–b24.
13. Aristotle, *Physics*, 2.194a35.

he says, "we are in a certain sense." For if the [celestial] motions were in an absolute sense made for the sake of generation and their continuance, the bodies in motion and their movers were made in a certain sense for the same purpose, as I have said.

Look, therefore, look, I beg of you, who adheres to Catholic truth. Is it Plato, who lapses into the evil of idolatry through impiety and ignorance and who worships the celestial bodies as if they were gods and who compels this evil by law? Or is it Aristotle, who believes, proclaims, and demonstrates that the celestial bodies are put in motion for the sake of men? For if they are put in motion for the sake of generation and its continuance, certainly they are moved for the sake of men. For obviously everything else that is generated and suffers corruptions was made for the sake of men, and there is not any of them that cannot in the final analysis be reduced to our use.

But I see that more profound issues lurk here. For he plainly says that every motion is for the sake of these celestial changes. Hence, in an absolute sense, there is an end for the sake of which these changes in celestial motions exist. If, therefore, as true piety proclaims, generation will at some time in the future stop, so, too, will the motions of the celestial bodies also necessarily cease. For the end that is their purpose is the cause of these causes. Consequently, when that purpose ceases, all the other causes must necessarily suffer the same fate as well. Yet though generation is in fact in an absolute sense the final cause of the [celestial] motions, nonetheless, it is not in an absolute sense the final cause of the celestial bodies insofar as they are bodies and substances, but only insofar as they are in motion. Hence, even in the case of the celestial bodies, man is the end, not, however, in an absolute sense but in a certain sense. But man is the end of the [celestial] movers, not absolutely insofar as they exist and are movers, but accidentally, which is something we shall shortly make clear below.

What needs to be said now is something that is utterly necessary and that convicts all the Platonists of the charge of ignorance and calumny.[14]

14. Without ever mentioning Pletho, George begins here a refutation of one point in Pletho's *De Differentiis* that will take up almost all of the remainder of this enormous chapter, namely, that Aristotle assigned his God to a sphere and therefore made him coordinate with and really no different than the other celestial movers, an absurdity, Pletho pointed out, that even the Arab Avicenna rejected (*De Differentiis*, ed. Lagarde, 322.21–323.4; Woodhouse, 193–94).

60 GEORGE OF TREBIZOND

Aristotle, they say, thinks that the first mover is the God of all things. How is that so, o you learned and holy men?

According to Aristotle continuous generation is the end that is the purpose of the motion of the first mobile sphere. For once you admit this, it follows that the activity of the first mobile, which is always to move, since in an absolute sense it exists for our sake, brings a certain happiness to the first mobile from its continuous generation of the things below. For each thing attains happiness from its end, and this is the way that an end precisely as an end certainly confers happiness. But we are the end of the celestial motions, and therefore we are the end of the [celestial] mover at least accidentally, and therefore also of the God of all, which is utterly absurd. "But what does that matter to us," the Platonists will say, "if these absurdities and non-sequiturs are consequences of your Aristotle?"[15]

These things are not consequences of what he said but of those who say these things. These consequences show that through a defect of nature, these critics are incapable of understanding anything or, alternatively, that envy has made them quite twisted. For not his own words but the fabrications of the Platonists and of those who envy him falsely seem to compel him into these absurdities. For he, in fact, calls the first mover neither the first in the absolute sense nor the first itself nor the first principle. The Platonists, however, imagine that he is thus calling the first mover the first in the absolute sense. Nor do they perceive that the first in the absolute sense, that is, the first principle and the first absolutely and without qualification, cannot be said to be the first mover if you associate the absolute first with the other movers. I say this because all these labels, when said in an absolute sense, fit the absolute first. For they are rightly attributed to it. If you ascribe them to the other firsts and if you count it with the other firsts as if they are like it, the labels do not fit. And this is the reason why Aristotle habitually spoke of the first or the first itself or the principle itself without qualification. This is similar to God being called the first principle or the first cause but not as if he is counted with the other principles and causes. This is the case because these labels do not have the same value nor the same definition when applied to the absolute first and to other firsts. For according to Aristotle, these labels are not said simply, that is, univocally, of God and of creatures, nor are they said utterly equiv-

---

15. All of this is cast in the voice of the imagined Platonist critics.

Comparison of Plato and Aristotle: God as the Absolutely First   61

ocally, but analogously. For this reason, just as God is truly said to be the first cause and first principle without the other causes and principles being counted with him, so, too, he cannot truly be said to be the first mover if counted with the other movers. For all things that exist have their existence from him; all things that live live through him; all things that move move in him. If, however, you call the first what is counted with the second and third firsts, in no way does this priority, as I would put it, fit God. For the wording stands in contradiction with itself. For what is first in this way is not absolutely and universally first but is in some sequence and belongs with the things with which it is counted. God, therefore, is in the absolute sense the first mover of all and absolutely so. For that is what God is. And if at the same time he were counted with the other movers, he would not be the first mover absolutely and universally but in an order of co-numeration with all the other movers, which is something that is utterly impossible. Since these are the facts of the matter, he is absolutely the first in an absolute and universal sense, not counted with any of the other movers, and is in no way in a place.

Let us hear what Aristotle says in Book 1 of *On the Heavens*: "Hence it is clear why there is no place or vacuum or time beyond [the last sphere]. Therefore the things beyond are not in a place ... nor is there any change in any of things that are beyond the last motion."[16] And immediately after: "On this source depends the very being and existence of everything, some more perfectly, some more imperfectly."[17] He was speaking here only incidentally of the first cause. For the subject of the passage at this point was not the first cause. Nor let anyone be disturbed by the fact that wording is in the plural, as if there are multiple first causes. For we should not be so easily swayed, especially in something so obvious that can be shown both by the very arguments he uses and by the many things he himself says about the unity of the first principle. For why should we be surprised if he spoke in this fashion? He did so because authors often use the plural in reference to a singular thing or because he usually uses everybody's common mode of speaking before he comes to a determination. Moreover, we quite well know that in his time, people indifferently spoke of multiple gods. We

---

16. Aristotle, *De Caelo*, 1.279a17–21.
17. Aristotle, *De Caelo*, 1.279a29–30.

have raised this point as if we do not have any deeper reason.[18] For the moment, we have decided to remain silent about this deeper reason. The second question [below] will make clear why. But let us return to the matter at hand.

"The things there are not in a place," he says, "because there is no place or time or any change beyond the last motion." Nor, as I believe, does he think that God is outside of the heavens in the sense that he is not inside the heavens, but rather he wanted to show that God is in no way in a place. For if you were to understand "beyond the heavens" not in this way but in terms of locality, you will necessarily be speaking in contradictions. The first cause, therefore, is in no way in a place. The first mover is in a certain way in a place. Therefore, the first mover that moves the first mobile is not the first that we are discussing here. For even if the mover of the first mobile is not in a place in the mode of bodies, it is nonetheless not in another sphere but only in the first sphere. For it is said to be in a place either because, as is said of a body, it is enclosed by the furthermost encompassing sphere or because it is here or there and not someplace else, which is the mode necessarily proper to all the intelligences besides the first. Hence, also the first mover that moves the first mobile is thus certainly in a place and cannot be said to be beyond the heavens nor beyond the first motion since it is asserted to be in this first mobile by Aristotle and everyone else. The first is, in fact, beyond the first motion and outside of the heavens. Therefore, the first mover is by its nature other than the first in an absolute sense.

Moreover, absolutely no change befalls that first that is beyond the furthermost motion and outside of the heavens. Hence, it is not moved in locomotion substantially or accidentally. The first mover in sequence, although it is not moved substantially, is nonetheless moved accidentally. For "substantially moved" is said of what is moved through a place and by its motion measures the place in which it is moved. And for this reason, only bodies are moved in locomotion. If any incorporeal thing is in a mobile body, it is, in fact, moved accidentally. But the first mover is in no other place than in the first mobile. It therefore is moved in correspondence with the motion of the first mobile. For whatever is in the first mobile, by the fact of its presence, is thus moved. Either, therefore, as the soul in the

18. Namely, that Aristotle had an inkling of the Trinity.

Comparison of Plato and Aristotle: God as the Absolutely First 63

body or as the captain in a boat or in some other way, the first mover in the sequence is moved. Therefore, this first mover is not the first itself according to Aristotle.

In addition, the first in absolute terms is even called by him the first principle, as he said in the quotation a little above, since other principles are rather far from this principle. Aristotelians even call this same principle the first cause. No one, in fact, has called the mover that is in fact incorporated into the first mobile this principle, that is, the first principle, the absolutely first cause. Consider, therefore, what follows. He adds that no one in his right mind would say that the being and life of all the other spheres and all the other motors depend upon the mover of the first mobile. In fact, the being and life of the rest, that is, all the others, save only the first, depend, as he says, on the first itself, more perfectly in the case of higher beings since they are more perfect and live more perfectly, more imperfectly, however, in the case of lower beings. Therefore, the mover of the first mobile is not the first in the absolute sense according to Aristotle, even if this shatters the Platonists.

But perhaps those who do not fully understand his argument are bothered by what he adds immediately after. For he goes on to say: "what has been said attests to the fact that this is the case because there is nothing better that will cause motion (for that thing would be more divine) nor does it have any evil nor does it want for any of the goods proper to it."[19] "Look," someone will say, "he says that there is nothing better than that which will cause motion. For if there were, this other would be more divine. There is nothing more divine, however, than that which causes motion. For this is what those words signify. Therefore, the mover of the first mobile is the supremely divine, as I would put it, according Aristotle himself, and is the best being, hence the first in absolute terms."

The solution to these and similar arguments is easily had from what has been said above. For what was said was that if the first was included in any sequence, it would share the nature of the things coordinated with it, and for that reason, this could not in any way be said of the first in absolute terms. But if, in fact, "first" is said in an absolute sense so that it is not counted or coordinated with others in any way, in this sense, "first" is

---

19. Aristotle, *De Coelo*, 1.279a33–35.

said only of the true God. Therefore, when we call matter and form first principles, we count them with all the other principles of nature. Matter and form are rightly called not only first principles but even first principles of natural things *simpliciter* [i.e., in an absolute sense]. For since *simpliciter* means universally and *per se*, if we were to say that matter and form are first principles *simpliciter* and do not add another qualification, we would fall into gross error, attributing to matter and form the power of the true God. But if you were to add "of natural things," you would have spoken rightly. For universally and *per se* matter and form are the first principles of natural things. God, however, is the first principle not only of natural things but of all things. Consequently, God is not counted with other things, nor he is said to be the first in relation to the second, but absolutely the first. Similarly, some also call the four elements the first principles of elemental bodies. They do not say, however, "first principles" without any addition. And we call letters elements and first principles, and rightly so if we immediately add "of an articulated word." Whence it is clear that the first principle is neither co-counted nor coordinated but is first absolutely in an absolute sense and universally without any qualification, that is, not in a sequence of some particular things but is the blessed God of all things. He is also similarly the first cause and the first mover not cocounted nor reduced to some sort of sequence, but truly is alone and is said to be so.

What, therefore, is disturbing people? Where are the inconsistencies? Where is the contradiction? Or where is the slightest reason for suspicion? For I see that all his statements are wonderfully consistent and square with each other. For when he said that the first with which we are concerned is not in a place and is beyond the first motion and outside of the heavens nor suffers any change and is the first cause of all other things besides itself, and is that upon which the being and life of all depend, these attributes individually and taken all together fit not the mover of the first mobile, but the first mover in the absolute sense, I would call them the description and in a certain way a definition, as much as we men can grasp it, of the true God himself. To this argument and testimony, Aristotle immediately appended this statement: "it is because there is nothing better that will cause motion." By these words, as by a sort of testimony, as he himself says, he confirmed what he said just previously. In the previous passages, he was not, in fact, speaking of the mover that is, as it were, affixed to the first mo-

Comparison of Plato and Aristotle: God as the Absolutely First 65

bile, nor about the mover that is thus someplace with the result that it is not in some other place, nor about the mover to which motion and change in some way happens, nor about the mover upon whom the being and life of all things depend, but about the mover that is beyond the first motion and is outside the heavens and that is in no way in any place. For it is not thus here so as consequently not to be there. Rather, it is similarly everywhere, incapable of suffering any change, and is that upon which the being and life of all things depend. All this attests, he says, to the fact that there is not another thing that will cause motion, that is, it is not the first mover of some mobile but is that from which everything in an absolute sense has its existence and life and movement. This is what we said and, as it were, described and defined God to be, and not another thing. For if another thing is this, it would be better and more divine. But nothing can be better or more divine than that to which these attributes apply. It therefore is the best and most divine, and not the mover of the first mobile. For not in the least degree do the enumerated attributes suit the latter.

Do you see the consistency in all these statements between themselves individually and taken all together? Do you see how in them Aristotle supremely agrees with Catholic truth? For many Fathers describing God, as it were, in human terms, say that he is that than which there is no better or more divine.[20] This is exactly what Aristotle says and in the very same words, which out of ignorance you think are inconsistent with his earlier statements. But although I think that these statements make it clear that according to Aristotle the first principle, the first cause, and the first mover of all are not the mover of the first mobile, but something far otherwise whom we call the true God, nonetheless, since it is easy to go wrong because of ambiguity, I think it worth our while to elaborate further on the issue. For we shall be removing every ambiguity if by using his very own words we can bring clarity and make distinctions in the things that seem to be an obstacle or get jumbled together as one.

In Book 12 of the *Metaphysics*, therefore, you have the following: "Hence, there is a certain middle thing which causes motion without being moved and is perpetual by essence and power. Moreover, being desirable and intelligible, it thus causes motion."[21] And to this he adds: "it

---

20. Cf. St. Anselm's proof for the existence of God in chapter 2 of the *Proslogion*.
21. Aristotle, *Metaphysics*, 12.1072a24–26.

causes motion, however, as something beloved."[22] And he concludes: "it is on this kind of principle that the heavens and nature depend."[23] Again, "it is in fact an intellect cognizing itself.... Hence, the intellect and the intelligible are identical."[24] In addition, it is even life. "For the action of this intellect," he says, "is life; that indeed is its act. Furthermore, since it is its own substance, its action is the best life and is eternal. We assert in fact that it is God, who lives and is eternal and is the best. Hence, life and eternity all at once and existing everlastingly are in God. For this is exactly God."[25] So says Aristotle.

[...]

But it is time to bring this first part [of Book 2] to an end. For it has been made abundantly clear that in his positing of the first in the absolute sense Aristotle squares perfectly with Catholic truth while Plato falls into idolatry no less than (lest I say, even more so than) the pagans.

Now we shall move on to another part [of Book 2] once we have advised the reader yet again and still yet another time that whenever Aristotle talks of the first principle or of the first of beings and of other things of this sort, it behooves us not to be immediately affected by the force of a single word but to discern what he is saying by weighing what he said before and after the passage in question, that is, whether he is speaking about God or about the first in the order of any order of things. For he understands God to be the first principle in the sense that he is utterly separated and not coordinated in any way with all other things. Hence, he attributes to the divine nature those attributes which in no way fit another nature, such as being beyond every rotation and outside of the heavens and as having its eternity be all at once and as having the existence of all things and their life be dependent upon it, and as having all motions be caused by it, just as that passage of Paul explicitly sums it up: "for in him we live and move and exist."[26] Hence, we shall easily grasp this whole argument from the attributes that follow and precede and also from the import of the surrounding words as regards whether he is talking about God or about the first in some genus of things.

22. Aristotle, *Metaphysics*, 1072b3.
23. Aristotle, *Metaphysics*, 1072b13–14.
24. Aristotle, *Metaphysics*, 1072b20–21.
25. Aristotle, *Metaphysics*, 1072b26–30.
26. Acts 17:28.

4

BASIL BESSARION
(c. 1403–1472)

Against the Calumniator of Plato

✍

EVA DEL SOLDATO

INTRODUCTION

Cardinal Basil Bessarion was one of the original intellectual forces behind the Renaissance revival of Platonism and the leader of a lively cultural circle in fifteenth-century Rome. Born in Trebizond, Bessarion arrived in Italy on the occasion of the Council of Ferrara-Florence (1438–1439), which led to an ephemeral reunification of the Greek and Roman Churches. Despite his initial diffidence, Bessarion ended up supporting the reunification wholeheartedly, becoming a Roman Church cardinal and leaving Greece for good. Over his lifetime, Bessarion assembled a library of rare texts, many of which survive today only because of the manuscripts that he collected and preserved. At his death, Bessarion left them to the city of Venice, and these books formed the original collection of the Marciana Library.

Bessarion's masterpiece, the *In calumniatorem Platonis*, is part of his overall effort to safeguard a decisive pillar of the Greek heritage: Plato, who had been for centuries the philosopher of reference in the Hellenic world. When another Greek émigré, George of Trebizond, attacked Plato in his *Comparatio phylosophorum*

Platonis et Aristotelis (1457),[1] this pitted Bessarion against George, whose work could have been fatal for the survival of Platonism in the Latin world. Already a member of Bessarion's circle, George entered into conflict with the cardinal for several reasons. He had argued with another protegé of Bessarion, Theodore Gaza, over their competing renditions of the Aristotelian *Problemata*. In that case, among other things, George had accused Gaza of being disrespectful of Scholastic translations. In a different circumstance, George opposed Bessarion's interpretation of a passage from the Gospel of John (21:22), by offering his own, infused with apocalyptic meanings. Both of these themes—the defense of Scholasticism, and an apocalyptic vision of history—were central to George's *Comparatio*. In the work, Plato and what George considered subsequent manifestations of the ancient philosopher (Epicurus, Mohamed, and a fourth unnamed Plato, possibly Gemistos Pletho[2] or Bessarion himself) are identified as the evil force behind the destruction of the Greek empire and a concrete threat to the Aristotelian Latin world itself. Bessarion needed to react against George, both to reinstate Plato's authority in the Latin world and to preserve his own position within the Roman curia.

Indeed, Bessarion's *In calumniatorem Platonis* was intended as a point-by-point response to George of Trebizond's *Comparatio*. Aware of the scarce impact that a work written in Greek would have had, in particular if contrasted with George's Latin *Comparatio*, Bessarion first translated his Greek draft of the text into Latin. Then, recognizing his own limitations as a Latin stylist, he asked a member of his circle, Niccolò Perotti, to revise it. The revised version of the text was printed in 1469, granting the *In calumniatorem* a circulation that George's *Comparatio*, available only in manuscript, would never achieve. Two more printed editions of the work—with some variations—appeared in 1503 and 1516.

The *In calumniatorem* is composed of six books. The first, second, and fourth are direct responses to the three books of George's *Comparatio* and are intended to prove Plato's wisdom, religiosity, and utility for Christianity, and finally his virtue. The third book, added for the purpose of demonstrating George's ignorance of Aristotelianism, the philosophy that he

1. See chapter 3 on Trebizond in this volume.
2. See chapter 2.

proposed as an antidote against Platonism, was in large part the product of the ingenuity of another associate of Bessarion, the Dominican Giovanni Gatti. The fifth book was an exposition of the errors made by George when translating Plato's *Laws*, which better substantiated his incapability of offering an accurate and judicious evaluation of Platonic philosophy. The sixth and final book, the *De natura et arte*, was in reality the first to be composed (around 1457) and represented the first act of the Plato-Aristotle controversy that divided George and Bessarion. In this book, Bessarion tested for the first time the argumentative strategies at play in the entirety of the *In calumniatorem*. It consisted of claiming—in the footsteps of the ancient commentator Simplicius—that Plato's and Aristotle's philosophies were compatible with one another because Plato spoke as a theologian about divine realities, while Aristotle as a *physicus* was concerned with earthly ones. With this move, Bessarion was able to avoid contrast with supporters of Aristotelian philosophy, so numerous within the Roman Church—while proving in a nonconfrontational manner the superiority of Plato to the Stagirite.

Throughout the *In calumniatorem*, using several neo-Platonic Christianizing filters, Bessarion offered translations and exegesis of Plato's texts, overturning the malicious interpretations offered by George. On the other hand, he also employed the words of Aristotelian interpreters until then scarcely known in the Latin world, such as Alexander of Aphrodisias, in order to undermine Aristotle's alleged usefulness for theology. Placing his own *comparatio* between Plato and Aristotle in a constant dialogue with the tenets of Christian religion, Bessarion was able to highlight the weaknesses of Aristotle with respect to faith, while offering Plato as a more suitable "external aid." In doing so, Bessarion was following a well-established Byzantine tradition, including Metochites and Pletho himself, yet toning down the manifest anti-Aristotelian tones of his predecessors.

Bessarion was able to transform his personal conflict with George of Trebizond into an opportunity to restore the reputation and knowledge of Plato in the Latin world, while providing Latin authors of any orientation with new material and exegetical instruments. If Marsilio Ficino will adopt and bring to extreme consequences Bessarion's Christianizing reading of Plato, Aristotelians like Pietro Pomponazzi and Francesco Vimercato will build on the characterization *in puris naturalibus* of Aristotle offered by the Greek cardinal in order to de-theologicize Peripateticism.

BIBLIOGRAPHY

Primary Sources

Bessarion. *Adversus calumniatorem Platonis*. Rome: Schweynheym and Pannartz, 1469.

———. *In Calumniatorem Platonis Libri IV*. Edited by Ludwig Mohler. Paderborn: Schöningh, 1927.

———. *De natura et arte*. In *Aus Bessarions Gelehrtenkreis: Abhandlungen, Reden, Briefe*, edited by Ludwig Mohler, 92–146. Paderborn: Schöningh, 1942.

———. *Contro il calunniatore di Platone*. Edited by Eva Del Soldato, with a bibliographical note by Ivanoe Privitera. Rome: Edizioni di Storia e Letteratura, 2014.

———. *Über Natur und Kunst*. Edited by Sergei Mariev, Monica Marchetto, and Katharina Luchner. Hamburg: Felix Meiner, 2015.

Ficino, Marsilio. *Opera omnia*. 2 vols. Basel: Petri, 1576.

George of Trebizond. *Comparatio Philosophorum Platonis et Aristotelis*. Venice: Penzio de Leuco, 1523.

———. *Vindicatio Aristotelis. Two Works of George of Trebizond in the Plato-Aristotle Controversy of the Fifteenth Century*. Edited by John Monfasani. Tempe, Ariz.: ACMRS Press, 2021.

Pomponazzi, Pietro. *Tractatus de immortalitate animae*. Bologna: Rubiera, 1516.

———. *Libri quinque de fato, de libero arbitrio et de praedestinatione*. Lugano: Thesaurus Mundi, 1957.

Vimercato, Francesco. *Commentarii in tertium librum Aristotelis de anima*. Paris: Wechel, 1543.

Secondary Sources

Charlet, Jean-Louis. "Traductions en vers latins de fragments grecs dans l'*Epitome* de N. Perotti et l'*In calumniatorem Platonis* de Bessarion," *Res Publica Litterarum* 10 (1987): 51–67.

De Keyser, Jeroen. "Perotti and Friends. Generating Rave Reviews for Bessarion's *In calumniatorem Platonis*," *Italia Medioevale e Umanistica* 52 (2011): 103–37

Del Soldato, Eva. "*Illa Litteris Graecis Abdita*: Bessarion, Plato and the Western World." In *Translatio Studiorum: Ancient, Medieval, and Modern Bearers of Intellectual History*, edited by Marco Sgarbi, 107–22. Leiden: Brill, 2012.

———. "Basil [Cardinal] Bessarion," In *The Stanford Encyclopedia of Philosophy* (Fall 2022), edited by Edward N. Zalta. https://plato.stanford.edu/archives/fall2022/entries/bessarion.

———. *Early Modern Aristotle: On the Making and Unmaking of Authority*. Philadelphia: University of Pennsylvania Press, 2020.

Hankins, James. *Plato in the Italian Renaissance*. 2 vols. Leiden: Brill, 1991.
Mariev, Sergei. "Bessarion, Cardinal." In *Encyclopedia of Renaissance Philosophy*, edited by Marco Sgarbi. Cham: Springer International Publishing, 2016. doi: 10.1007/978-3-319-02848-4_25-1.
Mariev, Sergei, ed. *Bessarion's Treasure: Editing, Translating and Interpreting Bessarion's Literary Heritage*. Berlin: De Gruyter, 2020.
Monfasani, John. *Byzantine Scholars in Renaissance Italy: Cardinal Bessarion and Other Émigré's: Selected Essays*. Aldershot: Ashgate, 1995.
———. "Cardinal Bessarion." In *Oxford Bibliographies*. Oxford: Oxford University Press, 2015. doi:10.1093/obo/9780195399301–0230.
———. *Greek Scholars Between East and West in the Fifteenth Century*. Farnham: Ashgate, 2016.
Schulz, Peter. "George Gemistos Plethon (ca. 1360–1454), George of Trebizond (1396–1472), and Cardinal Bessarion (1403–1472): The Controversy between Platonists and Aristotelians in the Fifteenth Century." In *Philosophers of the Renaissance*, edited by Paul Richard Blum and translated by Brian McNeil, 23–32. Washington, D.C.: The Catholic University of America Press, 2010.

BASIL BESSARION

Against the Calumniator of Plato

BOOK I

I. For which reason this book has been composed, and on the three slanders addressed against Plato, that is, ignorance, the conflict with our religion, and the debauchery of his behavior.

1. Not too long ago, a book came into my hands, a book which promised a complete comparison between Plato and Aristotle. I immediately devoted myself to it with pleasure, not to say avidity, and postponing all my other duties I started reading it, overtaken by an incredible desire. I hoped, in fact, to find in it an exposition or a comparison of the doctrines of the two philosophers, both those which relate to the natural realities and those which relate to the divine realities, both those which concern the moral customs and those which concern the art of disputation, which is named logic; I hoped to find in which manner these two great men agree or disagree, with which arguments this was demonstrated, if the first or the second substance has the priority, what matter and form are according to Ar-

istotle, what big and small according to Plato; I hoped to find as well how the entelechy could be harmonized with the self-movement of the soul; if some forms are separated or not and, should they be separated, if they subsist by themselves, or in the second concepts of the soul;[3] and again, how the being of beings is predicated equivocally and how univocally, so that that method of division, which Plato names enclosure of philosophy,[4] is one with the science of demonstration, or not; if this structure of the world is ingenerated and eternal, or instead generated and fleeting, or again, if it is at the same time generated and yet ingenerated and eternal, and in which sense it and the soul can be said to be generated, and in which sense ingenerated; furthermore, if God is the cause and the maker of the substance itself, or rather only of the movement of the natural things; if the heaven is to be considered the fifth of the simple bodies, or as one of the four; and again, which is to be believed the last end of man, either virtue and honesty or the contemplative science. In short, without lingering over particulars, I thought that the book was filled with these and other similar opinions of the two philosophers. After all, many of the ancients, both Greek and Latin, composed works of that kind, some preferring the arguments of Plato and some those of Aristotle, approving these and confuting those. There were also those who tried with great acumen to demonstrate the areas of agreement between the two philosophers, in particular, Simplicius among the Greeks. Among the Latins, Boethius promised to prove it; nevertheless, I do not know if he was able to achieve his goal. In fact, such a work by him has not survived until our day.[5] For all these reasons, I thought that the author of this book, earning with it the glory of posterity and offering a demonstration of his erudition and his intelligence, would have done the same, either conciliating the opinions of the two philosophers or endorsing the doctrine of only one of them, explaining the reasons which led him to believe it and had he believed Aristotle's opinions preferable, and therefore rejected Plato's, he would have justified it with a demonstration and, as convenient, with sound arguments.

3. On this debated passage, see J. Monfasani, "Greek and Latin Learning in Theodore Gaza's *Antirrhetoricon*," in *Renaissance Readings of the Corpus Aristotelicum*, ed. Marianne Pade (Copenhagen: Museum Tusculanum, 2000), 61–78.

4. Plato, *Republic* 534e. See also Epictetus, *Discourses* iii, xxvi, 15; Sextus Empiricus, *Adversus Mathematicos*, vii, 17.

5. See Boethius, *In librum De interpretatione* II (PL 64, 433d).

2. I incredibly rejoiced at similar prospects, and I read the book with unusual avidity. In fact, even though insults and offences abounded in it from the beginning, I stood them with patience, since I hoped that, keeping reading, it would have been like I have imagined it. Nevertheless, as I have finished to read the book, I can say that in the place of the treasures I hoped to find, I found—as they say—coal and, disappointed in my expectations, I have discovered nothing but accusations, offences and insults against Plato. The book was in fact filled only with these things, like ancient comedies, indeed to the extent that it overtook in this, with no doubt, every comedy ever written. Thunderstruck by such an astonishment, I was appalled by it. In fact, I would have never thought that such a work could come into the world, or that someone in all the humankind was not only unashamed to challenge so openly the truth and the common opinion of everyone, but that he even took pride in it, as if it were an extraordinary revelation, and behaving like a worthless game-cock which leaping away from the discussion—as Plato says—begun to crow, exult and look around.[6] In fact, he showers Aristotle with praises and compares him with Plato—something which cannot certainly been criticized, since Aristotle is definitely worthy of praise—but at the same time he keeps going at Plato with offences, and he curses him with insults. He admires the life of Aristotle, but also his doctrine, his erudition, his wisdom, all merits which I do not deny to the Philosopher with good reason. Yet, on the other hand, he does not only affirm that Plato is inferior to Aristotle—which would be tolerable—but also that he is ignorant, without erudition, lacking in any notion of philosophy, both natural and divine, incapable in eloquence, incompetent in the mathematics, in short unable of any respectable art, but also dishonest, intemperate, immoderate, and stained with any sort of vice.

3. He has put together all these things in three books. In the first one he compares Plato and Aristotle about erudition, without supporting his claims with any evidence but that Aristotle put in writing the precepts of the arts, while Plato never did it. In this regard, he mentions that Plato and his followers wrote and discussed on inconsistent, absurd, useless, weak, self-contradictory, frivolous, ridiculous, and childish things, and in

6. Plato, *Theaetetus* 164c.

short he considers them lacking in arguments and in any method of exposition. In the second book, he tries to demonstrate that the opinions of Aristotle agree with the excellent and very true sentences of our religion, and are even truer than them, while the opinions of Plato disagree from ours and therefore are false and alien from the truth. In the third book he defames the very virtuous, innocent, and upright life of Plato and, as he is accustomed to do, he showers him with insults and offences. What a villainy, what an infamy! Of which ham, of which parasite, of which bawd, of which dissolute man, of which wretch, guilty, pest, perfidious, deceiver, criminal, squanderer, he does not affirm that Plato lived in a more repugnant, vicious, and detestable way? What a disturbing sort of accusations, what unjust slanders, until now unprecedented! Without doubt, even if these things could be affirmed of someone, nevertheless no one would be to such extent lacking in both virtue and doctrine to dare to soil his mouth pronouncing, or to stain his hand writing things which are so bad, repugnant, guilty and infamous. But which delinquent accusation, does he not vomit on Plato? Does he not perhaps accuse him of drunkenness? Not perhaps of fornications, of adultery, of rapes, and of lying with men? Not perhaps of ingratitude, of seconding the tyranny, of violence, of thefts, of stupidity, of having proposed iniquitous laws, and of anything else horrible and repugnant can be said of thought? In fact, if you collected all the rough, brutal, cruel men of violent and bad customs who lived in the past centuries, against whom one should inveigh in the gravest and sharpest way, I ask you, which insults would have still to throw against all of them this slanderer, enemy of humankind, new Timon and second Momus?

4. As I have read these things, I am unable to not blame such an iniquitous intention of a man, and in particular of this one, who was bound to me in the past by ties of familiarity. With even more difficulty I have suffered his injury, since he appears throwing infamy not only on Plato, whose defense had not stimulated me until now, but no less on the holiest men of our religion. These men always extolled Plato and admired his doctrine and customs, as much as the affinity he has in his opinions with our faith. Therefore, [according to the adversary], they would have been either unaware that Plato was like the calumniator describes him, or they would have wanted to praise Plato falsely and against their conscience, a position which is not certainly worthy of a straight and wise man, nor of

a honest teacher.[7] In truth, what increases our indignation is the fact that the benefit our religion can get from pagan authors seems to be nullified and weakened by this slanderous accusation against Plato. And our holiest doctors actually established that against who wanted to tear down the foundations of the true faith and destroy the Christian religion with wicked arguments, the best defense lied first in using the words of the authors whom they considered wise, like arrows to counter their arrows, and in strengthening our faith through the support of those authors. Therefore, in my opinion, the holy Fathers quoted mostly Plato as an excellent testimony, and they have confirmed the faith we received through a divine inspiration with his opinion, as far as one could get from an external testimony. They followed in the first place his authority for this reason: because they knew that the palm for doctrines and customs was attributed by everyone to Plato. So, if someone despises the very important testimony of Plato, considers it useless and believes that is employed in a way which is completely alien from our religion, claiming indeed that Plato was ignorant, iniquitous, stupid, vicious and mean, how could be that this man is not going against our doctors and the advocates of the true faith, and is not declaring war to them as an arch-enemy? Or how could it be that he does not cause the biggest damage to our religion, taking away the protection of the external allies, thanks to whom, above all, we can fight and win the strength of our enemies? There is no doubt that who deprives us of such aids seems clearly to favor the adversaries of our religion and to open a passage to the enemies, so that they are enabled to desolate and devastate it, once done their assault.

5. Therefore, I have considered above all my duty to follow the authority of those holy men, and to set with great effort to honor and defend according to my possibilities the religion whose divine piety wanted me to be a member. I have also to come to the rescue of Plato, who nevertheless cannot be offended by the impudence of a tongue, because of his doctrine and the excellence of his customs, at least no more than a little cloud can obscure the blinding brightness of the sun. But I would judge extremely unjust and wrong that these things were read without any discussion, in particular by Latin-tongued men who do not have available the works of

---

7. Cf. George of Trebizond, *Comparatio* II 2, 1–13 (ed. Monfasani).

Plato, or, if they have some of them in a Latin translation, they are not used to read them. Thence, we will demonstrate the variety and the versatility of the doctrines of Plato, both through different arguments, the authority of the history and the common judgement of anybody, and through the testimony of his own works; we will show the excellence of his customs and the integrity of his life not only thanks to his public fame, but also thanks to his sentences and teachings, by which he stimulates men to live righteously and happily. In fact, though these things have already been investigated and known by the Greeks, they are still unknown to the Latins of our time. And again, though the most important learned men—both lay and churchmen—considered they have to put forward and prefer Plato to any other thinker in any subject, nevertheless the passing of time, the sloppiness and the negligence caused men to lose memory of all these things, so that very few gained knowledge of them. Accordingly, I am myself about to the established enterprise, and I will put before everyone's eyes the question through, as I said, the very words of Plato.

6. But I will speak in a simple way, the mind free of any resentment and addressed only to the truth. Nor I will take revenge of this slanderer eradicating, as they say, the evil with the evil. Indeed, I will not bring up the name of that writer, nor I will ever let understand to anyone of whom I am speaking. I will do it in the name of the ties which bound us in the past, so that he will not appear obnoxious both to our contemporaries and to our descendants. I will do it because of my custom, because I have always found awful and execrated the license to badly scold someone, but above all because this will not offer any help to those who defend Plato, nor it seems that one could obtain from our adversary an adequate revenge if I exchange mutual insults with him. After all, since he accused Plato of things which would barely appear plausible, even if referred to all the cruel and wicked men ever lived, what could be rightly said, in short, about our slanderer? Nevertheless, I will not answer singularly to the accusations raised by the adversary—this would be in fact a long, if not infinite, enterprise—but I will deal in brief only with those three which I have mentioned before: first of all I will demonstrate the wisdom and the doctrine of Plato; then the affinity of his writings with those of us Christians, and the untenability of the contrary arguments; finally the honesty of his customs and the integrity of his life.

Against the Calumniator of Plato

BOOK II

I. Plato's books are closer to the Christian religion than Aristotle's.

1. In the previous book I have demonstrated that Plato does not deserve to be esteemed less than other wise and erudite men, only because he did not leave in writing the precepts of the different disciplines. Also, I have proven that in any case he left many books, wonderfully written and offered to the benefit of those who came after him. Since in his second book the adversary claims that the philosopher closer to the truth of the Christian religion and of the Holy Church has to be considered by far wiser[8] and, accordingly, he presents Plato as much inferior to Aristotle, since the former seems instead more distant from the sentence of our doctors, whereas the latter seems greatly to agree with them, thus I will show, if I am not mistaken, the precise opposite, proving that Plato's doctrine is more in agreement with our religion than Aristotle's. But I will not do it because I think or I want to demonstrate that Plato was Christian. In fact, Plato as much Aristotle were alien from our religion, and pagans by name and by creed. For this reason the adversary praises Aristotle uselessly in this regard and, deprived of that reason which would help him to say an appearance of truth, he finds shelter in the religion, as those sentenced to death are used to do, seeking asylum behind the altars. Thus, my intention is not going all the way to show that Plato was Christian, as the adversary does for Aristotle. I will try instead to face the problem so that I will prove that, if someone wants to corroborate the truth of our religion also relying on the arguments of the pagan philosophers, he could do it through Plato's books, rather than through those by Aristotle.

II. Those who attack Plato, that among all the pagans is quoted by Christians as an authority, weaken the doctors of the Church.

1. But our adversary—seeing that the doctors of the Church, men of holy customs and deeply familiar with both our doctrine and that of the pagans, conciliate their opinions with those of Plato rather than those of

---

8. George of Trebizond, *Comparatio* II 1, 2–6 (ed. Monfasani).

Aristotle and rely almost always on Plato's testimony, whereas they barely make mention of Aristotle—has attempted in first place to disprove them and to deprive them of that admiration that everyone has toward their wisdom. Therefore, he attempts at persuading that his opinion has to be followed, rather than theirs: "In fact, everyone must believe and protect those things that our doctors wrote inspired by the divine spirit, if they concern faith and the salvation of mortals, but those which concern other matters are not to be received as they were referred by those holy men."[9] But if you think, o good man, that in those things which concern faith and true religion we must believe our doctors, and if precisely speaking of these things those holy men rely instead on Plato's words to strengthen faith and true religion, why do not you find right to believe them, when speaking of faith they show to prefer by far Plato to Aristotle? And if our saint doctors had been devoted only to God, and just had tasted, as is said, with the tip of the tongue the study of liberal arts, I would concede you that for geometrical matters we should trust a mathematician, rather than their holy simplicity, and that we should trust philosophers and experts of liberal arts rather than those, who were uncouth and ignorant, though considered excellent for the sanctity of their lives. But if those men were not only saints, but also reached the pinnacle of doctrine and wisdom, read the books of Plato and Aristotle, and carefully meditated the opinions of both philosophers—like among Greeks Basil, Gregory, Cyril, and the other Gregory, and among Latins Augustine, Boethius, and many other wise men also renowned for their knowledge of philosophy—and yet, when discussing true religion, they willingly relied on the authority of the pagan philosophers, how could you think that is better for men to follow you alone, rejecting these authors? But I, along with those who are of sound mind, will follow our saint and wise doctors, confuting you, and I will show through their sentence what I intend to demonstrate.

III. The author apologizes, because he does not intend to attack Aristotle.

1. Yet, it bothers me to be forced to write things that I would not. The iniquity of the adversary against Plato reaches such an extent, that it would

9. Cf. George of Trebizond, *Comparatio*, II 2, 3 (ed. Monfasani).

seem that I abandon my usual habit of praising Aristotle no less than Plato. But since the adversary claims and demonstrates only on the basis of his judgement that Aristotle had written of the divine nature better than Plato, having established the trinity in the divinity, while Plato would have not; that Aristotle had understood that heavens and the world were produced from nothing by the only will of God, while Plato would have posited the principle of the world in the prime matter; that Aristotle had spoken well of the soul, while Plato would have written only lies on this topic; that Aristotle had believed everything dominated and guided by the divine providence, while Plato would have subjected everything to the fate and necessity, he jabbed me with similar words to such extent, that though I try to prove the contrary, I seem to prefer Plato to Aristotle, and even to condemn this latter, that is something totally alien from my intentions. In fact, I have always spoken of Aristotle in a very honest way, and I am far from thinking something so perfidious and insolent, that is wanting to insult him while I praise Plato. I believe that they were both very wise, and I think to owe to both of them gratitude for the benefits they brought to the humankind, something that seems to be done also according to Aristotle himself. Indeed, in those books that he calls *Metaphysics*, from that part of philosophy dealing with the divine realities, he wrote: "It is not fair to be grateful only to those who left us teachings about the different doctrines in the most diligent way, but also to those that spoke about them in a superficial and light way. In fact, these too are somehow useful to us, making our habit more prompt through the exercise. And, in fact, if Timotheus had not existed, we would have not many melodies; and if Phrinis had not existed, neither Timotheus would have obtained distinction. In the same way we have to think about these who wanted to investigate the truth. We accept from them certain opinions, but in order that they were what they were, they needed others to stimulate them."[10]

2. In this comparison of the two philosophers, therefore, I do not shower one with praises and attack the other with insults and offences; that is instead what the adversary does: in fact, I worship and honor both of them. But I leave to those who can evaluate it, what is Aristotle's opinion about those things referred by the adversary, or in which way he exposed

10. Aristotle, *Metaphysics* 993b, 11–18.

these ideas. In fact, many can do this, since almost all of our Latin contemporaries are followers of the peripatetic philosophy, having studied and understood in the most diligent way what Aristotle wrote. Certainly, I will not claim that Aristotle wrote or spoke better or worse about those issues—I would fatigue uselessly on well-known matters—nor I will say anything against him, if not denying that he was a Christian, and showing that maybe the things said by Aristotle in some of those passages are not to be understood as my adversary believes, something I do not do in order to accuse Aristotle of any fault, but to highlight that the calumniator either misunderstands Aristotle, or perverts the meaning of his words. I will try instead to expose with great diligence Plato's opinions. In fact, they are unknown to almost everyone among the Latins, in part because his books are not translated into Latin, in part because those which are translated do not declare the real thought of Plato, as a result of the incapability of the translators. Rightly, we should pay particular attention to Plato's opinions on the divine realities, so that also Latins could understand how much they are close and almost akin to our religion and, on the other hand, so that they could realize how blatantly false are the arguments proposed by the adversary. I will give the best demonstration of it if I will show through the words of Plato himself the opposite of what my adversary blames. And if, in addition, I will use as a proof the authority of the doctors of our religion, and I will demonstrate that the sentences of Plato are adopted and approved by such saint mouths, the truth of my argument will shine even more, and no one will doubt that Plato thought and wrote not in the way imagined by the adversary, but how I will have demonstrated. Furthermore, after this, I will reject at the appropriate time the meaningless expositions and the light arguments of the adversary, and I will make clear how they stretch far from Aristotle's opinion and words.

3. But before doing that, I openly declare that I do not worship Plato's doctrine to the extent of approving any single aspect of it, and identifying it with the Christian truth. I do not approve, in fact, the pre-existence of the souls, nor the plurality of gods, nor the animation of the heavens and the stars, and many other things, for which the Church condemns the pagans. Instead, I have decided to expose what those two philosophers thought, and which are their respective differences. And though they are both pagans and alien from our religion, it will be nonetheless worthwhile

to declare which one of the two philosophized better and in a more convenient way with our faith, especially since I do not want to insult Aristotle, in case I conclude that Plato has to be preferred, having been pushed to weigh the two philosophers only by the iniquity of the adversary, who has not been ashamed to compare them in such a repugnant and ignominious way. In my opinion, in fact, Aristotle has to be praised both for his doctrine, that made him shine, and for his investigations, that gained him the gratitude of the humankind.

5

LORENZO VALLA
(1406/7–1457)

Encomium of St. Thomas Aquinas

PAUL RICHARD BLUM

INTRODUCTION

Lorenzo Valla was a formidable polemicist, the founder of scholarly philology, and the Renaissance humanist who turned the aspirations of the humanists into a modern way of philosophizing. Born in Rome in 1406 or 1407, he studied with Leornardo Bruni and others, became a professor of rhetoric in Pavia, and after unsuccessfully trying to work for the popes Martin V and Eugene IV, he served Alfonso of Aragon, King of Sicily and Naples (1396–1458) and a political opponent to the Roman Pontiff. In 1447, Nicholas V invited Valla to Rome, where he taught rhetoric from 1455 until his death in 1457. This success was probably owed to Nicholas of Cusa, who praised Valla's interpretation of the Bible and his skills in textual criticism.[1]

Valla's achievements were the study of Latin literary forms and style, his textual study of the Bible, the unmasking of the Donation of Constantine, a new ethics of pleasure and of free will, and a critique of the conflation of logic and metaphysics. The text

---

1. On Valla and Cusanus, cf. Paul Richard Blum, *Nicholas of Cusa on Peace, Religion, and Wisdom in Renaissance Context* (Regensburg: Roderer, 2018), 15–26.

presented here gives a specimen of his style, skill, and reasoning: the praise of Thomas Aquinas.[2] Valla had been invited to an annual lecture devoted to Thomas held at the convent of the Dominicans in Rome, Santa Maria sopra Minerva. This convent competed with the friars at San Domenico Maggiore in Naples, who advocated Thomist theology as their standard teaching, thus inaugurating what is now known as Thomism. The Romans were aware of Valla's disdain for scholasticism, so they gave the philologist the diplomatic challenge of praising Aquinas without petrifying his authority.

The debunking of the Donation of Constantine is Valla's best-known feat. The Donation was a document that confirmed the papal territory in Rome to be a gift from Emperor Constantine in Byzantium to Pope Sylvester. Valla argued that it was a forgery (or a document, produced on hindsight, intended to describe the factual position of the popes in Rome) using philological and political-theological arguments: The language of the document is newer than the still-classical Latin of the third century; more importantly, no emperor could surrender any territory voluntarily, and no pope, as the spiritual leader, could accept such a worldly donation. This linkage of linguistic with practical and religious reasoning is a signature of Valla's humanism.

In his *Elegantiae*, a study of appropriate Latin style, he demanded that language is crafted to produce conviction of the truth, and this also applies to theology. Therefore, he scrutinized the New Testament in order to disclose the true "architect" of the Gospel. In his treatise on the freedom of the will, he criticized Boethius, who, in his *Consolation of Philosophy*, had taken recourse to philosophical arguments when balancing God's infinite power and foresight with human will. Valla's probing question was "what does God's knowledge mean for me, a weak human being?" The answer is, obviously, "not much." But in raising this question, Valla inaugurated the humanist anthropocentric turn—ever since, philosophical questions are measured against the capacity of human understanding. Human freedom,

---

2. We are using the text from Salvatore I. Camporeale, *Christianity, Latinity, and Culture: Two Studies on Lorenzo Valla. With Lorenzo Valla's Encomium of Saint Thomas Aquinas*, ed. Patrick Baker and Christopher S. Celenza (Leiden: Brill, 2014). A critical edition has been published as part of the *Edizione nazionale delle opere di Lorenzo Valla: Lorenzo Valla, Encomion sancti Thome Aquinatis*, ed. Stefano Cartei (Firenze: Polistampa, 2008).

so the result, is what we hope for but cannot prove without faith in God's mercy, a line of thought appreciated by Martin Luther.

In his treatise *On Pleasure* or *The True and the False Good*, Valla turns expectations on their head: pleasure is not contrary to piety because the vision of God is the ultimate pleasure. Such breaking with conventions is also dominant in his work on logic and metaphysics; without modesty, he titled it *Repastinatio* or *Retractatio* (digging up or revising) of logic. In line with his approach to rhetoric and linguistics, he discussed the practical side of signification and understanding in logic and in meaning: the matter in question has priority over lofty abstractions. Therefore, the transcendentals, namely, "being'" and "one," "good," "true," and "thing" which in scholastic ontology were deemed convertible into one another (what *is*, is also *good*, etc.), lost their function, except for *res*—the "thing" to which speech and reasoning are referring. Thus, Valla appeared to open the door to what in modern philosophy is termed ordinary language philosophy.

BIBLIOGRAPHY

Primary Sources

Valla, Lorenzo. *Ad Alfonsum regem epistola de duobus Tarquiniis; Confutationes in Benedictum Morandum.* Edited by Francesco Lo Monaco. Firenze: Edizioni Polistampa, 2009.

———. *Collatio Novi Testamenti. Redazione inedita.* Edited by Alessandro Perosa. Firenze: Sansoni, 1970.

———. *Correspondence.* Edited by Brendan Cook. Cambridge, Mass.: Harvard University Press, 2013.

———. *De libero arbitrio.* Edited by Maria Anfossi. Firenze: Olschki, 1934. [Reprint with German translation by Eckhard Keßler, München: Fink, 1987.]

———. *De voluptate sive de vero bono / Von der Lust oder Vom wahren Guten.* Edited by Peter Michael Schenkel. Latin-German. München: Fink, 2004.

———. *Dialectical Disputations.* Edited by Brian P. Copenhaver and Lodi Nauta. 2 vols. Latin-English. Cambridge, Mass.: Harvard University Press, 2012.

———. *Emendationes quorundam locorum ex Alexandro ad Alfonsum primum Aragonum regem.* Edited by Clementina Marsico. Firenze: Polistampa, 2009.

———. *Encomion sancti Thome Aquinatis.* Edited by Stefano Cartei. Firenze: Polistampa, 2008.

———. *Epistole.* Edited by Ottavio Besomi. Patavii: Antenore, 1984.

———. "On Free Will." In *The Renaissance Philosophy of Man: Selections in Translation,* edited by Ernst Cassirer, Paul Oskar Kristeller, and John Herman Randall, Jr., translated by Charles Edward Trinkaus, 145–82. Chicago: University of Chicago Press, 1948.

———. *On Pleasure = De Voluptate*. Translated by A. Kent Hieatt and Maristella De Panizza Lorch. New York: Abaris Books, 1977.

———. *On the Donation of Constantine*. Translated by Glen W. Bowersock. Vol. 24. Cambridge, Mass.: Harvard University Press, 2008.

———. *Opera omnia, con una premessa di Eugenio Garin*. [Basileae: Henric Petri, 1540.] 2 vols. Torino: Bottega d'Erasmo, 1962.

———. *Raudensiane note*. Edited by Gian Matteo Corrias. Firenze: Polistampa, 2007.

———. *Repastinatio dialectice et philosophie*. Edited by Gianni Zippel. 2 vols. Patavii: Antenore, 1982.

———. *Sermo de mysterio eucharistie*. Edited by Clementina Marsico. Firenze: Edizioni Polistampa, 2019.

Secondary Sources

Blum, Paul Richard. "Lorenzo Valla (1406/7–1457). Humanism as Philosophy." In *Philosophers of the Renaissance*, edited by Paul Richard Blum and translated by Brian McNeil, 33–42. Washington, D.C.: The Catholic University of America Press, 2010.

———. *Nicholas of Cusa on Peace, Religion, and Wisdom in Renaissance Context*. Regensburg: Roderer, 2018.

Camporeale, Salvatore I. *Christianity, Latinity, and Culture: Two Studies on Lorenzo Valla. With Lorenzo Valla's Encomium of Saint Thomas Aquinas*. Edited by Patrick Baker and Christopher S. Celenza. Leiden: Brill, 2014.

———. *Lorenzo Valla. Umanesimo e teologia*. Firenze: Istituto nazionale di studi sul Rinascimento, 1972.

———. *Lorenzo Valla: Umanesimo, Riforma e Controriforma : Studi e Testi*. Roma: Ed. di Storia e Letteratura, 2002.

Monfasani, John. "Was Lorenzo Valla an Ordinary Language Philosopher?" *Journal of the History of Ideas* 50, no. 2 (1989): 309–23. https://doi.org/10.2307/2709737.

Nauta, Lodi. *In Defense of Common Sense: Lorenzo Valla's Humanist Critique of Scholastic Philosophy*. Cambridge, Mass.: Harvard University Press, 2009.

Regoliosi, Mariangela, ed. *Lorenzo Valla: La riforma della lingua e della logica. Atti del convegno Comitato Nazionale VI centenario della nascita di Lorenzo Valla*. 2 vols. Firenze: Polistampa, 2010.

Regoliosi, Mariangela, and Clementina Marisco, eds. *La diffusione europea del pensiero del Valla. Atti del Convegno del Comitato nazionale VI centenario della nascita di Lorenzo Valla. Prato, 3–6 dicembre 2008*. Firenze: Polistampa, 2013.

LORENZO VALLA

Encomium of St. Thomas Aquinas[3]

EXORDIUM

[1] It was customary in ancient times among the Greeks as well as the Latins for whoever was going to give a speech on some important matter, either to judges or to the people, in general to begin with a divine invocation. I think this rite was introduced by the worshipers of the true God, just like sacrifices, the offering of the first-fruits, ceremonies, and the other divine honors; and like them, it too soon passed from the true religion to false ones. Now, to accord to mortals and created things the religious worship due to immortal God, the lone creator, stands out as quite the most monstrous of all human transgressions and perhaps the chief of all evils. After this custom had reigned among both peoples for several centuries, it slowly fell into disuse, and divinities ceased to be invoked not only by those pleading bad causes, but also by those pleading good ones. Those pleading bad ones either believed that there were no gods or were afraid to invoke them—for whoever beseeches the gods beseeches them to attend to truth and justice, something the evil do not want to happen. As for those pleading good causes, in part they wanted to seem to put greater trust in their law than in the protection of the gods, in part they thought they would seem more distinguished and manlier by not continually taking refuge like women in prayers to the gods. For then, it seemed effeminate and unmanly to invoke deities, wherefore Cato says (in Sallust): "the aid of the gods is not procured with vows and womanish prayers."[4] But just as those men were wrong to cast off this most ancient custom as if banishing it from their possession, others did well to take it back into their possession and restore it intact. This they did not do, as some might think, to imitate the pagans, but rather so as not to be seen to be outdone

---

3. English translation by Patrick Baker in Salvatore I. Camporeale, *Christianity, Latinity, and Culture: Two Studies on Lorenzo Valla. With Lorenzo Valla's Encomium of Saint Thomas Aquinas*, ed. Patrick Baker and Christopher S. Celenza (Leiden: Brill, 2014), 299–315 (reprinted with permission). Subheadings and section numbers have been added by the translator.

4. Sallust, *De coniuratione Catilinae*, 52, 29.

Encomium of St. Thomas Aquinas

by them. For if the pagans gave such great honor to their false gods that they thought they should invoke them when beginning their speeches, how much more ought we bestow this honor on the true God? Therefore before beginning my praise of St Thomas Aquinas, it is my duty and my pleasure today to imitate that outstanding institution of theirs. And so, as is our custom, I invoke the most holy mother of God, the eternal virgin, greeting her with the angelic words: Ave Maria.

NARRATIVE

[2] Although all who die in the Lord are blessed and saints, nevertheless the Church expressly designates as blessed and saints those whom it recognizes either as having met death for religion, for truth, for justice, or as having achieved fame for leading a chaste and spotless life accompanied by divine signs and miracles. It uses the Greek word "martyrs" (*martyres*) for the former and the Latin one "confessors" (*confessores*) for the latter, although both terms have approximately the same meaning. For what else have martyrs done in enduring torture and meeting death than confess themselves unwilling to deny Christ? Under torture they repeatedly refused to deny Christ but rather confessed that he was the son of God. Therefore a martyr is the same as a confessor. On the other hand, what else have confessors done in living piously and writing piously than bear witness to the truth? John the Baptist was sent to bear witness to the light— that is, to the truth—and he did so no less by preaching than by meeting death.[5] Thus by acting in this way, surely confessors have shown themselves to be martyrs. For *martyr* is translated in Latin as witness (*testis*), and *martyrion* testimony (*testimonium*).

[3] Although this is the case, the Church, as I have said—at least the Latin one—has decided that only the former are to be called martyrs and honored with the privilege of that rank, because, as vigorous and brave soldiers, they are recognized by their commander for their military service and especially for their deeds in battle. The martyrs, then, who were soldiers of Christ, stood in the battle line for their commander and poured out their blood and life. The confessors were themselves also soldiers of

5. John 1:6–8.

Christ, but they merely performed military tabors (albeit great and lasting ones); and although they were prepared to undergo death for their commander, God, they did not actually undergo it or stand in the battle line. For that reason it seems that martyrs ought to have been accorded greater honor. The justice of this view notwithstanding, who could deny that there are certain confessors who not only equal but even surpass some martyrs? Divine testimony makes this clear, as we see that many confessors were much more renowned for miracles than certain martyrs.

[4] What is the point of these considerations? To show that our Thomas Aquinas, although a confessor, should not necessarily be placed below the martyrs. In my opinion, he is in no way inferior—not to look too far afield for examples—either to Peter the Dominican,[6] whose defense of the truth roused some mad peasant to kill him with a sickle, or to Thomas, bishop of Canterbury,[7] who, like the good shepherd protecting his flock, died to keep the clergy from being despoiled of its goods. That he is not inferior is further demonstrated by the following argument: although both men had the name of Thomas, our Thomas received it not by human but by divine will, since the meaning of Thomas in Hebrew is both "bottomless pit" (*abyssus*) and "twin" (*geminus*). And Thomas Aquinas truly was such a one: a kind of bottomless pit of knowledge and a twin due to the pairing of knowledge and virtue in him, both of which were without parallel and beyond belief. He was like a kind of sun, shining forth in the dazzling splendor of his learning and burning bright with the ardor of his virtues. He is to be placed among the Cherubim for the splendor of his learning, among the Seraphim for the ardor of his virtues. Of these qualities I shall now speak.

[5] But in my attempt to do so, some people seem to me to be objecting and just about throwing up their hands, crying, "What are you saying? What are you aiming at with this hyperbole of yours, which is the friend of the foolish, enemy of the prudent? Will you have no regard for the truth, for your own conscience, or for your audience, which is composed of numerous men of the greatest importance and wisdom? Are you not content to make Thomas Aquinas the equal of the martyrs and to prefer him to

6. St. Peter of Verona (St. Peter Martyr).
7. St. Thomas Becket, Archbishop of Canterbury.

Encomium of St. Thomas Aquinas

many of them? Must you raise him up to the level of the Cherubim, above whom God sits? Must you also compare him to the very Seraphim, the highest order of angels? What more will you accord to the apostle Thomas? What more to Paul the teacher of the Gentiles—that he is one of the Cherubim? What more to John the Baptist—that he is one of the Seraphim?"

[6] Let me respond that I do indeed think that all who are imbued with the knowledge of divine truths have something in common with the Cherubim, just as all who are infused with the love of God are the fellows of the Seraphim—to say nothing of Thomas, so incredibly full of knowledge and love. Still, I have been justly reproached and warned. Therefore I entreat the brothers of this order to pardon me if I relate the praises of its saint with greater temperance than I otherwise might have done, and if I do not mention all of them but focus only on those of the greatest importance. For to this august body they ought to be narrated briefly, not treated at length, lest they grow tiresome. And if I tried to praise such great and powerful virtues with words, "the day would sooner than the tale be done,"[8] as the poet says.

PROOF

[7] Justly, therefore, such a man—let me speak first about his virtues and later about his knowledge—justly was he destined to be foretold to the world before he was born, his birth prophesied, his life predicted, even his death announced. For when his mother was with child, a certain hermit, a man of God who had come precisely to bring her this news, congratulated her and told her that she would bear a son whom she would call Thomas and who would be filled with the excellence of this name. God, whenever he has resolved to give something extraordinary and new to the world, is wont to announce it with signs or prophecies. There are very many examples of this, but, for the sake of brevity, I shall be content with one from the family.

[8] In the same way the greatness of the blessed Dominic, the founder of this family, was foretold to his mother when she was pregnant. I will not say which prophecy was more extraordinary, in order to avoid (to the ex-

---

8. Virgil, *Aeneid*, I.374, trans. Dryden.

tent possible) the appearance of a contest between father and son. Let the prophecies about each man be equal, equal the merits of both their lives. Let neither be placed before the other. Let them be like two consuls, the highest of magistracies. We must honor them with equal veneration, both of them renowned for all the virtues, both for miracles without number. Although I am only here to praise one of the two, nevertheless I will join them together. First, because by setting them equal it will become all the clearer to what heights of lofty dignity I think Thomas should be raised. Second, because the rule of the Preachers is that the brothers go in twos, not singly.

[9] So then, Dominic founded the house of the Preachers; Thomas covered its floors with marble. Dominic built its walls; Thomas decorated them with the finest paintings. Dominic was the pillar of the brothers, Thomas their shining example. Dominic planted; Thomas gave water. The one shunned and resisted the honors and episcopacies bestowed upon him; the other fled nobility, wealth, kinsmen, and parents as if they were sirens. The one imitated the chastity and continence of Paul, the other the virginity of John the Evangelist. Of the one nothing was more admirable than his humility (which the Greeks more meaningfully call *tapeinophrosyne*). The other had so much humility that he was even astonished at the boasting and bragging of others; he never felt this vice in himself, as he frankly confessed to some brothers, although he still recognized his own great and numerous talents.

[10] These are the praises of their virtues. Now for the testimonies of their virtues and their rewards, the revelations, visions, and miracles which are like paradise on earth. They were so great in them that, to speak of nothing else, they saw and heard the holy Apostles Peter and Paul (either truly or in a vision), the most holy mother of God, and the Lord our Savior (either in the body or out of the body[9]). Both men were told about their imminent deaths. What is more, they prayed so heatedly that now and then they were seen levitating, God revealing the miracle to certain brothers.

[11] Finally, to complete the comparison: the one wrote the brothers' most excellent rule, the other the most outstanding and the greatest num-

9. 2 Corinthians 12:2.

Encomium of St. Thomas Aquinas

ber of books. But, you might say, it is a greater thing to have written books than a rule. Why do you say this? While Thomas devotes himself to writings, Dominic rules the provinces and, as an excellent leader, gives his peoples a Rule and law for living well. Certainly Thomas sends no more men to heaven with his writings than Dominic does with his Rule. Therefore let it be granted that virtue, glory, and miracles are equal in Dominic and Thomas, who are no more different and distinct from one another than the morning from the evening star.

REFUTATION

[12] I have spoken of Thomas's virtues and miracles briefly and simply, having made no use of exaggeration and embellishment, lest, in the short time available, I say less than the dignity of the subject requires. I believe you would now like me to say something about this saint's knowledge, which I proposed to treat second, saying whom I would set him above and whom I would call his equal.

[13] It has not escaped me that certain people who held an oration here today on the same subject not only made Thomas second to none of the doctors of the Church but also placed him above them all. They claim that they ought to consider him second to none because a certain friar of the utmost purity supposedly saw Augustine, whom they count as the greatest theologian, together with Thomas. Both were endowed with wonderful majesty, and he heard Augustine say that Thomas was his equal in glory. The reason they gave for being able to put him above everyone is that for proof in theology he used logic, metaphysics, and all philosophy, which the earlier doctors are supposed to have barely tasted with the tips of their tongues.

[14] This is a slippery and perilous place for me, not only on account of the dignity of the saint we are praising, but also because of the deep-set opinion, held by so many, that no one can become a theologian without the precepts of the dialecticians, meta physicians, and the other philosophers. What am I to do then? Shrink in fear, make an about-face, disguise what I think, and have my tongue contradict my heart? Since it was not of my own accord but at the entreaty of the brothers that I rose to speak,

and since it is not my way to remain silent, I shall not give anyone cause to think that I have not spoken my mind.

[15] I highly praise the exceptional simplicity of St. Thomas's writing; I admire his carefulness; I am amazed at the fullness, the variety, the completeness of his teachings. I add another thing, with which many people would not credit him but which he himself is supposed to have said: that he never read any book that he did not fully understand. This is something that I doubt has happened to anyone of our time: no jurist in civil law, no doctor in medicine, no philosopher in philosophy, no humanist in the reading of ancient texts, nor anyone else in the remaining arts and sciences, much less one man in all fields.

[16] But those things which they call metaphysics and modes of signifying and the like, which modern theologians regard with wonder like a newly discovered sphere or like the epicycles of the planets, I regard with no great wonder at all. Nor do I think, therefore, that it matters much whether one knows them or not. And perhaps it would be preferable not to know them, as they are like impediments to better things. This I will make clear not with my own arguments (although I could) but by citing the authority of the ancient theologians—Cyprian, Lactantius, Hilary, Ambrose, Jerome, Augustine—who were so far from treating such matters in their works that they did not even mention them.

[17] Was it because they were ignorant? How could that be possible? For if these things have a basis in our own language, those men were as Latin as can be, whereas modern theologians are nearly all barbarians. And if in Greek, the ancient theologians knew it, but these moderns of yours do not. Why, then, should they not have treated these subjects? Because they were not supposed to be treated, and perhaps they were not even supposed to be known—and this for two reasons: one having to do with their contents, the other with their words.

[18] Regarding their contents: because these subjects did not seem to lead to the knowledge of divine truths. Such also seemed to be the case to the Greek theologians Basil, Gregory, John Chrysostom, and the others of that age. They did not think that the sophisms of dialectics, the obscurities of metaphysics, or the trifles of the modes of signifying should be mixed in with sacred questions. Nor did they even lay the foundations of their disputations in philosophy, for they heeded Paul's exclamation: "not

Encomium of St. Thomas Aquinas

through philosophy and vain deceit."[10] This we know from experience as well. For what is there in philosophy? I do not mean dialectics, the whole of which lies in words; I have already spoken about it and will do so again. No, I mean moral and natural philosophy. What is there in them that is indubitable and settled except the things discovered in natural philosophy through the observations of doctors and others?

[19] Regarding their words: because the nature of Greek is different from that of Latin. This would be a rather tedious subject to discuss, and it is a question for another time. Let it suffice to have said that the Latin doctors of the Church dreaded words which the great Latin authors (who were their teachers in the language), although experts in Greek, never used, words that are continually pressed into service by modern theologians: *ens, entitas, quidditas, identitas, reale, essentiale, suum esse,* as well as those terms which are given names like *ampliari, dividi, componi,* and other such things.[11] Thus these largely worthless trifles were either not to be treated, or else they were to be disregarded, lest they lead to greater ignorance.

[20] I am not saying this to detract from modern theologians—why would I want to detract from my very own age?—but to defend the ancients, who are unjustly blamed and abused for not having theologized according to this method. Instead they devoted themselves wholly to imitating the apostle Paul, by far the prince of all theologians and the master of theologizing. His manner of speaking, his power, his majesty were such that what fell flat when spoken by others, even the Apostles, he uttered loftily; what in the mouths of others stood its ground, rushed from his into battle; and what from others shone dimly, from him seemed to flash and burn, so that it is not off the mark for him to be represented holding in his hand a sword, i.e. the word of God.[12] This is the true and, so to speak, the genuine in ode of theologizing. This is the true law of speaking and writing, and those who pursue it doubtless pursue the very best manner of speaking and theologizing. Therefore the ancients, the true disciples of Paul, should not be criticized by modem theologians or placed second to our Thomas on account of not having mixed theology with philosophy.

---

10. Colossians. 2:8.
11. Terms of scholastic ontology and logic.
12. Ephesians. 6:17.

CONCLUSION

[21] What then? Should he be their equal? I would not dare to call him the equal of them all. Yet I would prefer him, and willingly, to many whom, lest it seem of little account, I shall list by name. I set Thomas above John Cassian, whom St. Dominic is said to have been in the habit of reading as if the best doctor. I set him above Anselm, the sharpest and most refined. I set him above Bernard, a learned, sweet, eloquent, and sublime doctor. I set him above Remigius, the most learned man of his age. I set him above Bede, more learned than all of them. I set him above Isidore, whom his admirers deny is second to anyone. What should I say about the Master of the Sentences and Gratian, who deserve more to be called assiduous compilers than true authors? Likewise, I set him above all the brothers of both his order and the others (although here we are talking about modern theologians): Albert the Great, Giles, Alexander of Hales, Bonaventure, John the Scot, and the rest, who are so convinced of their own greatness that they are loath to compare themselves to the ancients.[13] Moreover, I set him above Lactantius and Boethius, although only in theology, for in other areas, there is no comparison. I say the same about Cyprian, and I add, albeit unwillingly, Hilary as well; for what, finally, is holier, more learned, more eloquent than his writings?

[22] Or is not even this enough for Thomas? How great and how praiseworthy are these men above whom I have set Thomas! Or shall we also call into question and dispute the four greatest of all, who were like a second team of evangelists? Shall we pull one of them out of that team so as to replace him with Thomas? I barely know which of them to prefer to whom, as each one had his own extraordinary gift. For although Augustine is commonly preferred to all, because he treated more theological questions and is in many respects indubitably to be preferred, nevertheless, if Ambrose's writings were compared with an equal number of Augustine's, I do not think they would be ranked second. Nor does Jerome yield in any way to Augustine's intellect; he is so much the greater in all areas of learning that Augustine seems to me like the Mediterranean, Jerome the ocean, upon

---

13. Medieval theologians Anselm of Canterbury, Bernard of Clairvaux, Remigius of Auxerre, Bede the Venerable, Peter Lombard (Master of the Sentences), Giles of Rome, and John Duns Scotus. Gratian was a jurist.

Encomium of St. Thomas Aquinas

which few of our contemporaries set sail. Gregory[14] lags far behind all in erudition, but he equals them in carefulness and diligence and is possessed of such great sweetness and holiness that he seems to speak like an angel.

[23] I am afraid to set Thomas or any of the Latins equal to any one of these men. Rather, I would compare them with the same number of Greeks: Ambrose with Basil, whose rival I see he was; Jerome with Gregory Nazianzen, whose pupil and disciple he claimed to have been; Augustine with John Chrysostom, whom he often followed in his writings and emulated in the number of his books; Gregory with Dionysius the Areopagite, because he is the first of the Latins, as far as I know, to mention him (for the works of Dionysius were unknown to the others I named, not only the Latins but the Greeks as well). Closest to these comes John Damascene, a most famous author among the Greeks, as Thomas is amongst us. It will therefore be perfectly right for John and Thomas to be paired together, and all the more so because John wrote many logical and well-nigh metaphysical works.

[24] So there will be five pairs of princes of theology resounding before the throne of God and the Lamb, in unison with the twenty-four elders. For the writers of holy things always make music in the sight of God. The first pair is Basil and Ambrose, playing the lyre; the second, Nazianzen and Jerome, playing the cithara; the third, Chrysostom and Augustine, playing the psaltery; the fourth, Dionysius and Gregory, playing the flute; the fifth, John Damascene and Thomas, playing the cymbals. And it will not be unharmonious for their number to be five now instead of four—since for musicians there are five tetrachords, not four—nor to have Thomas playing the cymbals. For as the name Thomas means "twin," and as he enjoyed playing equally in the twin tones of theology and philosophy, thus the cymbals are a double instrument emitting happy, cheerful, and pleasing music.

[25] Such is the tune of Thomas's books. With this harmony, Saint Thomas delights both the pious men who read him and the holy angels who now hear him. For he is always singing and playing before God with the other holy doctors, perpetually either praising the Lamb of God, or entreating Him that we mortals may reach the same place he has. May it be granted us by Him who lives and reigns, praised unto eternity. Amen.

14. Pope St. Gregory I ("the Great").

6

NICHOLAS OF CUSA
(1401–1464)

Compendium

❧

DETLEF THIEL

INTRODUCTION

Born 1401 in Kues, a village on the Moselle, Nicholas of Cusa, known as Cusanus, took his doctor of canon law at Padua in 1423. In his lifetime, he was seen as an important clerical politician, theologian, and philosopher. He wrote more than fifty booklets, major works, and nearly three hundred sermons. He was a member of the delegation sent in 1437 and 1438 to Constantinople to prepare for the union of the Western and Eastern churches. In 1448, he became Cardinal of San Pietro in Vincoli, Rome; in 1450, bishop of Brixen; and in 1459, curial cardinal. He lived in Rome from 1460 on and died in Todi, Umbria, in 1464.

The *Compendium,* approximately twenty-five dense pages composed in late 1463 and early 1464, is a survey of his thought. The allegory of the cosmographer (chapter 8 of 13) is often quoted and interpreted.[1] Cusanus outlines his view of the position and possibilities of the perfect animal, the human being, who has to start empirically and, having arranged the sensual data, may finally transcend all world knowledge by intellectual intuition. The

---

1. Jasper Hopkins's translation was used but modified throughout.

absolute origin and cause of the world, the form of forms, however remains inaccessible. In Cusanus's argument, the following steps can be distinguished:

1) The comparison of the five senses to five gates of a city goes back to St. Augustine, John Eriugena, St. Bonaventura, etc. Cusanus had previously referred to the senses as windows and entrances (*De mente* VIII, n. 114). If one gate stays closed, the world picture will be incomplete. Each human being is like a cosmographer, collecting as many reports from the whole world as possible. The descriptions are written down internally, presumably in a sort of abbreviated prose.

2) These data, the raw material of 'foreign' origin, are transferred to a map (*mappa*). This is not a geographical map but rather an encyclopedic diagram with graphical elements. Is Cusanus referring to collective scientific activities here, or does he want to say that everybody has to invent his own map, as an autograph, the individual world view? In any case, the map is a metaphor for human creativity.

3) When all information is codified, the description of the world is complete, and the gates are closed. This shows that Cusanus still has a finite world in view. He had earlier declared: The universe cannot be conceived of as actually or absolutely infinite (because then it would be God); and it cannot be finite, for it lacks boundaries; so it is only potentially infinite (*De docta ignorantia* II, 11, n. 156).

4) The cosmographer begins to turn his interior glance (*internum intuitum*) toward the creator of the world and contemplates some general analogies. Original creation has its formal effigy. As the image reveals the truth, the map mirrors its creator, the cosmographer. Animals are incapable to create such a map, drawn from an abundance of sensible, material signs. The map therefore has to be considered as an intellectual sign (*signum intellectuale, intelligibilis*), and the human mind as the image, the first and most perfect sign of the divine mind.

5) The cosmographer makes a final abstractive effort and concentrates on the intellectual, formal, simple signs, which are the first and nearest to the creator, whose power shines back most strongly in them. The eternal light itself, however, remains incomprehensible and invisible, even to the keenest mental vision. Such basic inaccessibility is illustrated by the quotation from John 1:5 ("The light shines forth.") and by a metaphor from

Plotinus: One and the same face appears differently in different mirrors, but it can never be fully united even with the finest mirror.

The mirror, *speculum,* has a long and rich history from Plato on. In an earlier text, Cusanus compares human beings to living mirrors that are able to straighten and clean themselves so that they can perfectly reflect the central mirror, the Logos (*De filiatione Dei* III, n. 65–67). But reflection is not identity; this onto-theological difference remains beyond any doubt. It is Cusanus's life-long idea that a certain cut-off is required, a *caesura*: the closing of the gates, the inward turn. "Our entire effort is most fervent unto the following end, viz., that we experience *in ourselves* the knowledge of truth" (*De coniecturis* II, n. 70, my emphasis). In 1450, he stated: "The human mind uses itself as a living image reflecting God, and it turns to its exemplar with all effort" (*De mente* VII, n. 106).

In sum, this chapter describes a circular movement. The universe, according to Cusanus, is the self-unfolding of the absolute unity, the self-explication of the absolute complication. Human beings find their place in this process, insofar as they are able to explore and describe the world, in order to contemplate the origin, the Creator.

BIBLIOGRAPHY
Primary Sources

Hopkins, Jasper, trans. *Nicholas of Cusa on Wisdom and Knowledge.* Minneapolis, Minn.: Banning Press, 1996. https://jasper-hopkins.info/Compendium12-2000.pdf.

Nicholas of Cusa. *Nicolai de Cusa Opera omnia.* Edited by Heidelberger Akademie der Wissenschaften. 22 vols. Lipsiae/Hamburgi: Meiner, 1932–2009. The *Compendium* appears in vol. XI 3. http://cusanus-portal.de.

———. *Selected Spiritual Writings.* Translated by H. Lawrence Bond. New York: Paulist Press, 1997.

Secondary Sources

Blum, Paul Richard. *Nicholas of Cusa on Peace, Religion, and Wisdom in Renaissance Context.* Regensburg: Roderer, 2018.

Izbicki, Thomas M., Jason Aleksander, and Donald F. Duclow, eds. *Nicholas of Cusa and Times of Transition: Essays in Honor of Gerald Christianson.* Leiden: Brill, 2019.

Thiel, Detlef. "Scientia signorum und Ars scribendi. Zur Zeichentheorie des Nikolaus von Kues." In *Scientia und ars im Hoch- und Spätmittelalter,* edited by

Ingrid Craemer-Ruegenberg and Andreas Speer, 107–25. Miscellanea Mediaevalia 22. Berlin/New York: de Gruyter, 1994.

Thiel, Detlef. "Nicholas of Cusa (1401–1464). Squaring the Circle: Politics, Piety, and Rationality." In *Philosophers of the Renaissance*, edited by Paul Richard Blum and translated by Brian McNeil, 43–56. Washington, D.C: The Catholic University of America Press, 2010.

Online Resources

"Cusanus Portal." http://cusanus-portal.de. Contains the works in Latin as well as German and English (Jasper Hopkins) translations. Also includes biographies, a bibliography, and a lexicon.

Nicholas of Cusa. *Complete Philosophical and Theological Treatises of Nicholas of Cusa*. Translated by Jasper Hopkins. 2 vols. Minneapolis: Banning, 2001. https://jasper-hopkins.info.

Haselbach, Brigitte. *Ein Kommentar zum Compendium des Nikolaus von Kues*. Zollikon: Haselbach, 2008. https://web.archive.org/web/20181016082025/http://cusanus.ch/Download/Kommentar_NvK.pdf

NICHOLAS OF CUSA
Compendium

CHAPTER 8

Therefore, a perfect animal in which there is both sense and intellect is to be considered a cosmographer owning a city with five gates, the five senses, through which messengers from all over the world enter, reporting on the entire disposition of the world, in the following order: those who bring news about the world's light and color enter through the gate of sight; those who bring news about sounds and voices—through the gate of hearing; those reporting about odors—through the gate of smell; those reporting on flavors—through the gate of taste; and those bringing news about heat, cold, and other tangible things—through the gate of touch. And the cosmographer is sitting there and writes down all reports, in order to have a description of the entire perceptible world delineated within his city. Now, if a gate to his city—say, sight—always remained closed, then because the messengers of the visible objects would have no entrance, there would be a defect in the description of the world. For the description would not make mention of the sun, the stars, light, colors, the shapes of men, of brute animals, trees, cities, and of the greater part of the world's beauty. Likewise, if the gate of hearing remained closed, the description would not contain anything about speeches, songs, melodies, and the like. The same with the rest. Therefore, the cosmographer endeavors with all his effort to keep all the gates open and to continually hear the reports of ever-new messengers and to make his description ever more true.

Finally, after he has made in his city a complete designation of the sensible world, then in order not to lose it, he brings it into a well-ordered and proportionally measured map, and he turns toward it and further dismisses the messengers, closes the gates, and transfers his inner sight toward the creator of the world, who is none of all those things about which the cosmographer has learned and recorded from the messengers, but who is the maker and cause of them all. He considers this maker to stand antecedently in relation to the whole world as he himself, as cosmographer, stands in relation to his map. And from the relation of the map to the real world, he speculates in himself, *qua* cosmographer, on the creator of the world, contemplating in his mind the truth in the image, the signified in the sign. In this speculation, he notices that no brute animal—although it seems to have a similar city, gates, and messengers—could make such a map. And, hence, he finds in himself the first and nearest sign of the creator, in which sign the creative power is reflected more than in any other known animal. For the intellectual sign is the first and most perfect sign of the creator of all things, but the sensible sign is the last. Therefore, the cosmographer withdraws himself, as best he can, from all sensible signs and turns toward intelligible and simple and formal signs.

And, being most attentive, he notices how in these intellectual signs the eternal light, inaccessible to any sharpness of mental vision, shines forth, so that he sees that the incomprehensible cannot be seen otherwise than in an incomprehensible mode of being, and that it, which is incomprehensible in terms of every comprehensible mode, is the form-of-being of all existing things. This form, while remaining incomprehensible in all existing things, shines forth in intellectual signs—as "light shines forth in darkness," which does not at all comprehend it: like a single face appearing in different polished mirrors in different ways is never inspeculated, incorporated, immateriated into any mirror (however highly polished) in such a way that both the face and the mirror could become a single com-

Compendium 101

posite, whose form would be the face and whose matter the mirror. Rather, while remaining singular in itself, the face manifests itself in different ways—just as man's intellect, while remaining singular and invisible in itself, manifests itself visibly and variously in its different arts and by means of the various products of the arts, even though in all these the intellect remains altogether unknown to any of the senses.

By means of the foregoing speculation, a contemplator arrives most delightfully at the cause, the beginning, and the end of both himself and all other things, so that he reaches a happy conclusion.

7

LEON BATTISTA ALBERTI
(1404–1472)

Theogenius

TIMOTHY KIRCHER

INTRODUCTION

The *Theogenius* is a dialogue in two books composed by the humanist polymath Leon Battista Alberti. Alberti was born in 1404 into an exiled Florentine family and eventually made his way in the world through appointments at the papal curia and from various patrons, including Leonello d'Este, to whom the dialogue is dedicated. In addition to a variety of classically inspired writings, Alberti wrote poetry and treatises on painting, sculpture, and architecture, a cartographical projection of the city of Rome, a study of ciphers, designed a self-portrait medal, and drew up plans for a number of churches in Mantua, Florence, and Rimini. His autobiography was cited in Jacob Burckhardt's famous study on the Italian Renaissance as that of the many-sided 'Renaissance man.'[1]

The generally accepted date of the dialogue's composition is around 1440, when Alberti was residing in Florence with the pa-

---

1. Jacob Burckhardt, *The Civilization of the Renaissance in Italy: An Essay*, trans. S. G. C. Middlemore (New York: Random House, 1954), 106–7. On Alberti's life, see Anthony Grafton, *Leon Battista Alberti: Master Builder of the Italian Renaissance* (Cambridge, Mass.: Harvard University Press, 2000); Caspar Pearson, *Leon Battista Alberti: The Chameleon's Eye* (London: Reaktion Books, 2022).

pal curia. At about this time, he was concluding his major vernacular dialogue *De familia* (*On the Family*), and in the following year, he began another dialogue, *Profugiorum de erumna libri* (*On Refuges from Hardships*). The *Theogenius* shares a number of philosophical concerns with these longer works: the strategies of contending with fortune and its fluctuations; the ways of voicing therapeutic consolation to someone suffering anxiety and distress; the place of classical learning in one's journey to self-understanding; and, not least, the art of translating philosophical ideas and genres into the Tuscan idiom. On this last, critical point, Alberti was also engaged in writing his *Gramatichetta*, the first vernacular grammar of its kind. The dialogue therefore appears at the apogee of his vernacular humanist project, shortly before the staging of his *Certame coronario* of October 1441, a vernacular poetry contest held in the Florentine cathedral.[2]

The dialogue opens in a bucolic setting, where Teogenio is reading and writing. His friend Microtiro comes to see him, complaining of the slander he faces in the city. Teogenio counsels him with a story about his elderly friend Genipatro, who one day encountered the rich young nobleman Tichipedo. Genipatro tells Tichipedo that he should place his happiness not in transitory pleasures and the goods of fortune but rather in the virtues of modesty and self-restraint, and in living according to nature.[3]

In the second book, Teogenio provides a commentary on the story. Humanity, he says, is prone to folly and continually marked by suffering and danger. He closes by meditating on mortality, including the pains of old age. Death should not be feared but rather accepted as an end to our suffering.

This synopsis suggests the complex scaffolding of the dialogue. Teogenio both recounts a conversation and stages his own, creating a frame within a frame. Alberti found this technique not so much among classical texts as in the structure of the *Decameron* by the fourteenth-century humanist Giovanni Boccaccio. Classical exempla appear throughout the

---

2. The edited text is found in Alberti, *Opere volgari*, ed. C. Grayson, vol. 2 (Bari: Laterza, 1966), 53–104. I have used Grayson's notes to Alberti's sources in addition to supplying my own. The italics in this translation are editorial summaries of the passages missing from these excerpts.

3. The names are playful Greek amalgams, often used by Alberti. "Teogenio" may derive from Alberti's reading of Hesiod's *Theogony* at this time, or may mean "divine mind," Microtiro ("first beginner"), Tichipedo ("child of fortune"), and Genipatro ("the father of the clan"). See Timothy Kircher, *Living Well in Renaissance Italy: The Virtues of Humanism and the Irony of Leon Battista Alberti* (Tempe, Ariz.: ACMRS, 2012), 116.

text, often placed in contrasting settings.[4] The framing permits Alberti to juxtapose Genipatro's optimism to Teogenio's pessimism, the old age of the first to the youth of second.

The theme of virtue's struggle with fortune was a favorite humanist topic: here the great percursor was Francesco Petrarch's *De remediis utriusque fortune* (*On the Two Types of Fortune, Good and Bad*). Alberti's *Theogenius* treats this subject in an innovative way. It offers resolutions that sound both Stoic and Epicurean—in fact, it presents the first vernacular translation of Lucretius's *De rerum natura*—but it refrains from any univocal, didactic philosophical statement. As a result, the philosophically minded readers cannot find clear answers from an authoritative narrator, but rather are left to their own learning and experience as the guide to enlightenment. Then again, such, perhaps, is Genipatro's lesson from his own life.

BIBLIOGRAPHY

Primary Sources

Alberti, Leon Battista. *Theogenius* in *Opere volgari*. Edited by Cecil Grayson. Vol. 2, *Rime e trattati morali*. Bari: Laterza, 1966.

Secondary Sources

Bertolini, Lucia. *Grecus sapor: Tramiti di presenze greche in Leon Battista Alberti*. Rome: Bulzoni, 1998.

Boenke, Michaela. "Leon Battista Alberti." In *Philosophers of the Renaissance*, edited by Paul Richard Blum and translated by Brian McNeil, 57–68. Washington, D.C.: The Catholic University of America Press, 2010.

Boschetto, Luca. "Ricerche sul *Theogenius* e sul *Momus* di Leon Battista Alberti." *Rinascimento* 33 (1993): 3–52.

Burckhardt, Jacob. *The Civilization of the Renaissance in Italy: An Essay*. Translated by S. G. C. Middlemore. New York: Random House, 1954.

Cannarsa, Maria Luisa. "Nota introduttiva to *Theogenius*." *Paradosso* 2 (1992): 121–26.

Ceron, Annalisa. "Leon Battista Alberti's Care of the Self as Medicine of the Mind: A First Glance at *Theogenius, Profugiorum ab erumna libri III*, and Two Related *Intercenales*." *Journal of Early Modern Studies* 4 (2015): 9–36.

4. Lucia Bertolini has noted that the 1440s were a time in which Alberti showcased his understanding of classical Greek; Mariangela Regoliosi has stressed how Alberti used one classical writer (e.g., Pliny the Elder) to counter the views of another such as Cicero. Bertolini, *Grecus sapor: Tramiti di presenze greche in Leon Battista Alberti* (Rome: Bulzoni, 1998); Regoliosi, "Per un catalogo degli *auctores* latini dell'Alberti," in *Leon Battista Alberti: La biblioteca di un umanista* (Florence: Mandragora, 2005), 105–13; 110.

Gambino, Susanna. "Alberti lettore di Lucrezio: Motivi lucreziani nel *Theogenius*." *Albertiana* 4 (2001): 69–84.
Grafton, Anthony. *Leon Battista Alberti: Master Builder of the Italian Renaissance*. Cambridge, Mass.: Harvard University Press, 2000.
Kircher, Timothy. "Landino, Alberti, and the Invention of the Neo-Vernacular." *Albertiana* 19 (2016): 29–48.
———. *Living Well in Renaissance Italy: The Virtues of Humanism and the Irony of Leon Battista Alberti*. Tempe, Ariz.: ACMRS, 2012.
Marolda, Paolo. "'Ragione' e 'follia' nel *Theogenius di L.B. Alberti*." *La rassegna della letteratura italiana* 1–2 (1981): 78–92.
McLaughlin, Martin. "Pessimismo stoico e cultura classica nel Theogenius dell'Alberti." In *Leon Battista Alberti: Actes du Congrès international "Gli Este e l'Alberti: Tempo e misura" (Ferrara, 29 · xi - 3 · xii · 2004)*, edited by Francesco Furlan and Gianni Venturi, 131–43. Vol. 1. Paris, S.I.L.B.A.; Pisa-Roma, Serra, 2010.
Pearson, Caspar. *Leon Battista Alberti: The Chameleon's Eye*. London: Reaktion Books, 2022.
Regoliosi, Mariangela. "Per un catalogo degli *auctores* latini dell'Alberti." In *Leon Battista Alberti: La biblioteca di un umanista*, edited by Roberto Cardini, Lucia Bertolini, and Mariangela Regoliosi, 105–13. Florence: Mandragora, 2005.
Tateo, Francesco. "Fortuna e felicità nel *Theogenius*." In *Leon Battista Alberti (1404–72) tra scienze e lettere. Atti del Convegno organizzato in collaborazione con la Societé Internationale Leon Battista Alberti (Parigi) e l'Istituto Italiano per gli Studi Filosofici (Napoli) Genova, 19–20 novembre 2004*, edited by Alberto Beniscelli and Francesco Furlan, 53–70. Genoa: Accademia ligure de scienze e lettere, 2005.
———. "Referenti topici e fonti del *Theogenius*." In *Alberti e la tradizione: per lo "smontaggio" dei "mosaici" albertiani. Atti del Convegno internazionale del Comitato nazionale VI centenario della nascita di Leon Battista Alberti (Arezzo, 23–24–25 settembre 2004)*, edited by Roberto Cardini and Mariangela Regoliosi, 545–59. Vol. 2. Florence: Polistampa, 2007.
Vasoli, Cesare. "L'immagine dell'uomo nel *Teogenio*." In *Leon Battista Alberti: Architettura e cultura. Atti del Convegno internazionale Mantova, 16–19 novembre 1994*, 141–62. Florence: Olschki, 1999.

LEON BATTISTA ALBERTI

Theogenius

To the Illustrious Prince, Leonello d'Este,

Lycurgus, they say, instituted in Sparta the practice that sacrifices offered to the gods should be neither lavish nor such that they could not be performed each and every day. And by this reasoning one should give to prudent princes not things prized by ignorant and common folk but rather, in particular, the thing that was always welcome to those like you, Leonello, who are worthy of being loved: one should give, in my judgment, one's very self. I do not see how one can do this without any firmer devotion than with good will matched by corresponding reverence, those very things that join us mortals with the Prince of all things, God. And I believe that to you, wise as you are, nothing could be more pleasing than to see yourself loved for your virtues. It is not hidden from me how much you value my sentiments toward you when I see your comportment toward me. And to me, this brings to mind how whenever I came to visit you, I saw myself received by you with such grace and kindness that it could only be a sign that to you Battista Alberti was most welcome. So too this little work I'm sending you will be able to show you openly—according to the way its value will seem to you—that I hold it my duty to thank you in anything I can offer.

I swear to you this much: I wrote these little books not for others but for myself, in order to console myself in my adverse fortune. And it seemed to me that I wrote in a way so that I could be understood by my fellow citizens who are not well-educated. Certainly, I knew that this work helped me and relieved my distress. And I see that these writings are requested by many, much more so than if I had written them in Latin. I would have liked to send them to you, considering your own misfortunes with the death of your father, in the sense that they were suitable to lift your spirits. But I doubted that they possessed the requisite dignity to be read by you, who are both a prince and highly educated. Yet after I showed them to you and understood that they would not displease you, it seemed to me a duty to send them to you if only to continue to show you by my little gifts that I serve you by heart and love you. And I would prize it greatly should this piece be gratifying to you, if only so that you, a most erudite person, are not among those who indict me, who say that I offend literary canons of excellence by failing to write eloquent works in Latin instead. But there will be another time to respond to this. For now, freely accept my offerings as from someone who admires your virtues in ever greater measure, and await henceforth, as much as you should ask, to receive from me similar writings and signs of affection I bring to you. I am at your command. I will communicate with you about my affairs at greater length in times to come. Hold me in your affections.

BOOK 1

Teogenio greets his friend Microtiro, who comes to see him in the woods outside the city. Microtiro complains of his adverse fortune. Teogenio tells him about his writing projects, including one concerning the fortunes of a republic, and offers him consolation in his distress. As an example of how one can contend with fortune, he begins his story about his friend Genipatro, "a man most prudent and wise in matters of living well," who encountered Tichipedo, a rich young man known to Microtiro for his calamitous misfortune.

"Genipatro and I were reading here at this spring, as it was always our custom to meet together often. Then Tichipedo came upon us while out hunting with his dogs and his large, frivolous, and impertinent retinue. He was young at the time, giddy and insolent on account of his extreme good fortune: he showed off his gems, glittering in his silk clothes, adorned with pearls and emblazoned with needle-work, and by his arrogant behavior, he displayed his presumption and his odious arrogance. He began by praising this place, swearing that this very spring was the only thing needed for his complete happiness—he certainly would move it to his splendid villa if he only could. To which Genipatro, a most prudent man, replied with a gesture most modest and replete with wondrous kindness: 'You, Tichipedo, fail to see all the joys of Teogenio that are far more pleasant and desirable than this spring. But if you're lacking nothing else, I have such authority in Teogenio's affairs that I can give you satisfaction: I permit you to take this spring along with you and place it wherever you wish.' Tichipedo responded: 'You would be generous with me without surrendering anything, since you give me something I am not able to accept.'"

"Genipatro then said, 'Our generosity would help you, should you recognize that you are not completely happy whenever you desire something you cannot possess. Take care, my good Tichipedo, that you do not lack many other things of which you are ignorant and yet are easy to possess, far more so than this charming spring, and lacking these things you can only be wretched and unhappy.' Then one of Tichipedo's retine said, 'What thing can anyone desire to be so very happy that Tichipedo does not already have? Looks, wealth, popularity—he is the most fortunate in every respect among his fellow citizens.' Here, Genipatro extended his hand in my direction and said with a smile: 'The things that Teogenio has here, as far as I may know, are those that people similar to you, even the most fortunate, do not have. Tichipedo, one who wants to be happy must be like he is, who enjoys this most pleasant spring that you so greatly desire.' 'But even more so,' I said, 'one should be like you, Genipatro, who has all the worthy and praiseworthy things.' 'And we,' said the sycophant, I think to provoke our laughter, 'who desire to be happy, should hoe these hills and callous our hands in order to be like Genipatro!'"

[...]

"Genipatro then smiled and closed his eyes awhile; then he gathered himself and said,

When I was young I was wealthy for a time and blessed by fortune not unlike your own, Tichipedo, and in this argument, I can assess something you cannot, since you don't know both ways of life. I greatly assure you that this state, in which you view me as weak, solitary, and poor, is my delight, and in my advanced age, I find more than a few comforts, surely far from small ones. I call to mind that in my case and in those of others that I have seen, there are countless examples from which I have learned neither to trust nor to bind myself to fortune's whims. I am acquainted with her instability and faithlessness; I have experienced how one who will have no dealings, no business with fortune can receive no harm from her. And what things can fortune take from us, apart from those those that you, Tichipedo, accept from her in such large measure? What harm can she do to you by taking back from you those things of hers that you should hold at no value? Thus learned and made wise through long experience with her, I taught myself to contain my will and restrain my desires. And so I was able to close any avenue between fortune and me whereby she could reclaim me and unsettle me.

In experiencing these things, being often fooled by her, and having noticed in all events her volubility and inconstancy, I had the best teacher, who can only help those who are old and have lived with great industry. And I found no little help in this advanced age of mine; whereas once a multitude of most troubling things often bothered me in my youth, now they lay no hold on me, since I am either content or free. The erotic fires have been cooled, extinguished, or removed, the torches of ambition have dimmed, the thousand cares and most burning worries that are at home and common with untested youth have quieted, and I find myself even now at my age to be honored, praised, and esteemed.... I used to indict, blame, castigate my faults, my laziness, my rash decisions, my wild desires, my feeble studies, my inconstancy. Now, happy with myself, I am grateful to be who I am: and this experience delights me the more insofar as, in order to be more satisfied and content, I improve myself day by day and become more cultured by learning and more equipped with virtues.

Theogenius 109

And these are my pleasures in which I, now old, immediately take greater and sweeter delight than those that I had when I was young, since I am without the cares and free from all anxious worry about what is coming next, whereas youthful pleasures were sweet and gratifying to the degree that I desired and anticipated them.... At this moment, I take delight in our discussion here; I take delight in reading these books by myself; I take delight in thinking and writing about these matters I discuss with you, and about others like them, and in remembering my well-spent life; and I am happy investigating on my own subtle and abstruse things. I seem to live among the gods when I search after and rediscover the ambit of the heavens and the planets and their influence upon us. Certainly, complete happiness is to live without any cares for these fallen, fragile things of fortune, and with a mind free from such corporeal contagion, and to converse with nature in solitude, having fled the strife and annoyances of the common crowd. For nature is the teacher of such marvels, and happiness is found, too, in reasoning about the whys and wherefores, the method and rules of her best, most perfect works, in recognizing and praising the father and parent of such goods. And I maintain to you still I do not rate my fortune below yours, Tichipedo, not only for these but also for many other reasons. And just as I do not rate my age lower than your youth, so I do not prefer your wealth and sway to my poverty, nor your numerous family to my solitude."

Genipatro continues his discourse, emphasizing that young people are much less prudent and experienced in handling good and bad fortune. He lists classical examples of elderly figures superior to Tichipedo in courage and virtue. He then recounts the history of those who, like himself, found virtuous contentment in material poverty, while conversely greed, he says, has fostered vice and unhappiness.

Your grandiosity and public parades, the comings and goings of many well-wishers will never be more pleasing, in my view, than my quiet solitude. Surrounding you in this throng there can only be pleaders, snitches, flatterers, wheedlers, the lustful and lightheaded, the immodest, vice-ridden, and importunate, from whom time and again you hear and entertain hateful and despicable things. In my world, there is no one who troubles me more than I would allow. I am least alone when I find myself in solitude. Expert and most eloquent men are always at my side, with whom I can consort in the evening and spend my night discoursing, this so much so that if I should take delight in amusing and festive writers, all the comic poets, Plautus, Terence, and the other comedians, Apuleius, Lucian, Martial, and similar great wits make me laugh to my heart's content. If I should like to understand useful things and to meet without trouble my domestic needs, many learned voices stand at my request, and teach me about farming, about educating children, about setting good habits and guiding my family, and the nature of friendship, and governing of the republic, all subjects of the highest and most recognized value. If I would like to know the causes and rules of the various natural occurrences I see, if I desire a way of discerning the true from the false, the good from the bad, if I am to know myself and in general to understand those things that life brings forth by which I may recognize and revere the Father, supreme and first teacher and author of such wonders, I do not lack the most blessed philosophers, among whom over time and in accordance with my inner obligations I may feel myself become not only a more learned, but also a better person. But you princes and first citizens, in your sway: what are you searching for: praise, glory, immortality? Would that you pursue true and genuine praise not with processions, not with showy spectacle, not with a great obsequious throng, but only, quite rightly, with well-merited virtue.

Genipatro develops his praise of virtue: it is always at hand to those who seek it, and always in one's possession. He seeks virtue not to win praise, or elicit envy, but only to satisfy his own sense of obligation to himself and to others. Thereby he acquires an inner peace and security, unlike those who (like Tichipedo) worry about power and prestige. Genuine happiness, he asserts, resides not on power, but in virtue. Citing classical exempla (Camillus, Aristides, and others), he notes the difficulty that the virtuous face in exercising political office, whereas demagogues more often find favor with the fickle multitude. He turns to those who pride themselves on the reach of their families, which leads him to reflect on his own experiences on his own family fortunes and losses.

I cannot but feel grief; when I missed one of them, I wished him still alive. But then when I reviewed to myself the reasons for my grief, I recognized this pain, such as it was, as nothing more than a foolish opinion, whereby I used to imagine that, the elders being gone, my cares and domestic worries would increase, nor, that without the younger ones at hand, would I be able to have the help and steady quiet I had long promised myself; and I used to greatly torment myself over the absence of my friends and those with whom I grew up and felt tied by blood and good will, those with whom, as our fortune has been shared, so I still from day to day agreeably shared my plans, my desires, my studies.

[...]

But I discovered two means of rescuing me from such foolishness. The first is time, which, as the producer of all things, is also their consumer, that through the ripeness of all things removed all bitterness, and moment by moment diminished my sadness, helping me forget my misfortune. The second remedy was like that of Mithridates, who, according to Martial use to fortify his nature by tasting poison regularly with the result that no toxin could harm him.[5] Thus in my case, the frequent funerals in my household dried up the vain tears, and consumed all my feminine foolishness, whereby we grieve over our evils, wishing to appear devoted to those who, by dying well, are well-removed from the troubles in which they left us who survive them. And so the repeated tribulations strengthened my resolve to such a degree that when earlier I was fragile and too delicate and could not hear the voice and counsels of the wisest philosophers, now, trained in adversity, I keenly heeded them, and understood these words to be the best and most wholesome advice and lessons; I understood that I should hold the deaths of my relatives, those losses that pained me so much, in no higher regard that the deaths of those that failed to affect me: of Homer, Plato, Cicero, Virgil, and the infinite number of learned men: why should not these deaths be more grievous and painful than the deaths in my family? For I could have from them beyond measure, were they still alive, the teachings for living well, the guide for every useful habit, and the joy in all my ways of thinking, much more so than any lessons from one of my kin.

BOOK 2

The book opens with Teogenio asking Microtiro how therapeutic he has found the dialogue of Genipatro. Microtiro praises Genipatro on account of his foresight about Tichipedo's fall. Teogenio then discourses on how misfortune afflicts everyone at some time in their lives, particularly in their later years.

And if Tichipedo had known complete self-restraint well-matched to the highest application, it were no wonder if fortune had smiled upon him with steady and favorable winds, fortune who by nature was always shifting and inconstant. Pliny the Elder records there was a place amidst other similar woods and islands, located in the waters near Lake Vadimo, that changed location every day.[6] Even more inconstant and shifting is fortune. What person could you name of our time, who, noted by the histories as possessing such happiness, exited this life without first suffering many types of misery?... And if we consider it carefully, perhaps we will

5. Mart. 5.76.
6. H.N. 2.209.

find no one in later years to be in the same condition as when young. Indeed, it rather seems that the highest misery is always conjoined with happiness.

Pompey's sway, Caesar's unbridled power, Cicero's eloquence, Scipio's popularity: these were capital and fatal dangers. The law of fortune is founded to overturn new things every day. Nor should one person or another be amazed if she applies her inborn treachery.... Nonetheless we should not so much blame fortune for these vicissitudes as first of all our own foolishness: we are never content with present circumstances, but always hanging between diverse expectations: we would like to equal the gods in our blessedness. Euripides denied to mortals what to the gods alone was conceded: to be allowed to remain content in perpetual happiness.[7] The natural physicists affirm, foremost among them Hippocrates, that change is to be ascribed to the human body, which constantly either grows or declines: the exact moment exactly between these two processes, they say, is very brief indeed.[8] Thus even more so for all other mortal things we surely see that there is a irremediable and fixed rule of nature that they remain always in motion, and we also see the heavens continually renew their variety in unpatterned succession.

Teogenio then describes to Microtiro not only nature's regular changes but also its "stupendous and incredible events," drawn from classical sources. Nonetheless, we should bear in mind our own humble resources and agency.

We should therefore not be amazed, little mortals as we are, the frailest of all creatures, if we suffer various disasters whenever they come, since we see entire provinces and regions subject to total devastation and destruction. And every half-wit knows that humanity, as Homer used to say, is the most fragile of all living creatures on earth.[9] The lyric poet Pindar stated that human existence is like the shadow of a dream.[10] A human being is the only one born among all the living creatures that we see to shed tears, since as soon as it enters the world it is adept first of all at crying, as if instructed by nature to intuit the miseries life will bring, or as if it is pained to see that all other animals are given by nature diverse and useful clothing, pelts, bristles, quills, plumage, feathers, scales, hides, and stony skin, and that even trees have layers of bark against the cold and useful protection against heat: yet only humanity remains weak, lying naked, in every respect helpless on its own.

You may add that from day one babies see themselves wrapped in swaddling clothes and committed to perpetual servitude, in which they then grow up and

---

7. Cf. Heracl. 608; also Ar., Ra. 1215.

8. See, for example, in the pseudo-Hippocratic Salubr. 5; Nat.Hom. 12.

9. Od. 18.130.

10. P. 8.

live out their lives. Thus not without reason they bewail their unhappiness right from the time of their birth, never ceasing their cries until they receive comfort, nor laughing until completing at least forty days of sadness. Hence they grow to maturity as if constantly battling weakness, always, in whatever respect you choose, seeking and expecting another's assistance. They can do nothing without an instructor, without training, above all without the greatest effort, which they must keep up their entire lives. In childhood, they live dejected under a school-master, and follow him throughout their youth anxious and burdened with learning the laws and institutions of their *patria*; and then, at a riper age, now placed under the rigid opinions of the common people, they suffer countless frustrations. And even when they have reached the peak of physical vitality and are adorned with manifold virtue and learning, they still, despite their bravado, fear every little crawling thing, and, while born to lord over all living things, they realize the quality of their lives and health is subject to almost the entire animal kingdom. The tiniest vermin are a nuisance; the littlest sting is lethal.

In addition to physical threats, people can die from mental and emotional shock. Classical exempla provide material about unforeseen dangers. But the greatest dangers are of our own making.

Nor does one find any creature so hated by all the others as humankind. And add to this how people harm themselves with their ambition and greed and unbridled desire to live in pleasure and vice-ridden vacuity: these things oppress mortals no less than their other misfortunes. Add the supreme foolishness that continually takes root in people's minds: namely never to rest contented or satisfied, but always to bother and bestir themselves. The other animals remain content with whatever food that nature requires, and so they follow certain inborn laws and times for taking care of their young: humanity alone, always looking into new things, afflicts itself. Malcontent with such a scope on earth, it wishes to plow across the seas and shoot itself, I believe, into outer space. It wants to plunder everything beneath the waters, in the earth, within the mountains, and push itself beyond the clouds.

[...]

O most restless and most impatient animal of any type or condition—so much so, I believe, that when nature becomes disgusted by our arrogance in striving to know all her secrets and then improve and correct her, she sometimes finds new disasters to mock us and also to put us to the test to recognize her true essence. What fools we mortals be, we who want to know when, how, by which counsel and to what end is every plan and work of God, who wish to know what matter, shape, nature, and force there be in heaven, the planets, the intelligences,

114 LEON BATTISTA ALBERTI

who want a thousand secrets to be disclosed more fully to us than to nature.... Nature hid its metals, gold, and other minerals beneath the highest mountains and in the most deserted places. We thieving little people would bring them forth to the light of day and place them under our control. She scattered the most splendid gems and in a form that, to her, the supreme teacher, appeared most fitting. We would gather them even from the farthest regions, and, chiseling them, give them new facets and form. She distinguished the trees and their fruits. We mix them with one another, splicing and joining them. She gave us rivers to quench our thirst and ordered their free and flowing course, but then we, as with the other things otherwise perfect that nature offered us, grew irritated with the springs and rivers, and thus dug, as if to nature's disgrace, deep wells. Nor satisfied with this, with such exertion, with such expense and care, humanity, alone among all creatures, grew discontented with natural water, the sweetest liquor, and discovered wine, not so much to satisfy its thirst as to vomit it forth, just as if there were no other way to pour it from its cask, since, as in other things, it could not learn the limits of drink. And for this purpose they harbor it among things they highly prize; and they like those things that often induce them into a gutter frenzy and pitch of madness. For it seems nothing pleases us except that which nature denies us; and we take delight by sweating for those things that nature in many aspects dislikes.

[...]

Fir trees have fled far from the sea, into the highest mountains; we have dragged them down as if for no other reason than to have them rot in the water. Marble lay buried in the earth: we move it to the façades of temples and over our heads. And so much are we bothered by any innate liberty of any engendered thing, that we still yearn to yoke ourselves into slavery. And for all these follies there were born and raised countless works, most certain signs and arguments of our foolishness. Add to these the little harmony humanity has with all creation, as if it swore to perform against itself the highest cruelty and inhumanity. It wishes its belly to be an open tomb for all things: herbs, plants, fruits, birds, quadrupeds, insects, worms, fish: there is nothing above or below the earth that it does not devour. Capital enemy of all it sees and does not see, humanity wishes to enslave all; enemy to its kin, enemy to itself.

The poet Plautus said that "man is a wolf to other men."[11] In which living thing do you find a greater fury than in humankind? Tigers are friends with one another, as are lions, wolves, and bears; any animal you choose, no matter how poisonously enraged, relents among its own kind. Yet people, so greatly ferocious, become le-

11. Asin. 495.

thal to all others and to themselves. And you will discover that more people die at the hands of others than for any other reason.

Teogenio upholds the examples of people who did not rejoice over their good fortune.

Similar to these most praiseworthy people, we ought never to rely on fortune in any way, for she knows and likes always to practice perfidy, she who, most deceitful, shows herself at peace only to bide time for greater war and to find the opportunity for more injurious sneak attacks; and let us furnish ourselves with a steady mind, ready to withstand her, not in the way Demipho says in Terence, always thinking of future trouble, with the consequence that one considers it a boon when less arrives than expected (something that one cannot contemplate without a certain amount of turmoil) and that it suffices to bear these troubles once they come.[12] On the contrary, we will stand inwardly prepared against fortune, having determined that neither she alone with her treachery, nor together with the worst people with all their offenses and wickedness, will ever be able to harm us much in any way. Just as Genipatro argued that the effects of fortune are powerful only to the degree we consider them to be, fortune cannot trouble us if she lays down her arms. What you little esteem will little trouble you.

And for your task, you should weigh as nothing things innately fallen, fragile, and subject to such change and adversity. And then, wherever you set your mind to it, the faithless folk—Microtiro, take this to heart—can perhaps help, but never harm. Does it seem to you an incredible assertion? You will surely see it is most true. I assure you: no one, no matter how unjust, can do you harm, and the more they practice their wickedness against you, the more they will injure themselves rather than you.

Microtiro returns to his lament over the multitude of his detractors, accusing them of disloyalty and deceit. Teogenio responds by insisting that the wicked primarily hurt themselves, whereas their attacks can only help him by inciting him to greater virtue. He should love rather than hate his enemies, and maintain an inner tranquility. His concern should be for preserving the laws and good of the patria. *Teogenio then moves to an examination of our fear of death, and our suffering in old age.*

I don't know the reason why many people cling so tightly to life, as if they have settled the score with every adversity. The verses of Juvenal, the great satiric poet:

12. Phorm. 245–46.

116   LEON BATTISTA ALBERTI

> Such are the penalties
> If you live to a ripe old age—perpetual grief,
> Black mourning, a world of sorrow, ever-recurrent
> Family bereavements to haunt your declining years.[13]

Thus the proverb, "the more one lives, the more one weeps." And clearly we see the incessant weariness in our bodies that increases with age, the countless ailments, nor will you find anyone who has lived more than a few days who does not confront some chronic and nearly constant infirmity and pain. Thus I cannot avoid blaming those who say that they cannot act without fearing their end. And who comes forward to question that all mortals must face their final day, by inborn natural necessity? The god Glaucopis, according to Homer, denied the gods the option of saving their favorites from eternal sleep and death.[14] When Socrates was told that his fellow citizens were deliberating whether he should die, he replied "Nature has many more times decided that none of them will live forever."[15] And who does not see that from the day we are born the truth of what Manilius Probus, that celestial poet, has said: we are dying almost from the moment of birth.[16] And to our first entrance into life is tied our exit at death. The most revered poet Lucretius writes these verses:

> Later, when time's dominion shakes the body,
> When limbs react in dull ungainliness,
> Then the mind limps, tongue is a babbler, mind
> is palsied, all is failure, all is loss.[17]

And Lysimachus says, in the verses of the comic poet Plautus, when one becomes old, one immediately loses sense and sensibility.[18] And that other old man in Plautus says that old age is a bad business that makes commerce in the worst things.[19] The philosophers confirm that everything that has a beginning also has a natural end, which surely applies to our life. So we ought to judge it indeed as necessary, and so also to be neither harsh nor harmful. They write that the temple of Diana

---

13. Juv. 10.243–45; English trans. by Peter Green (Juvenal, *The Sixteen Satires*, Middlesex: Penguin Books,1969), 213.

14. That is, "grey-eyed" Athena: Il. 22.177–81.

15. X., Ap. 27; supplied by Grayson.

16. Manil., Astron. 4.16: "Nascentes morimur, finisque ab origine pendet." Montaigne cites this passage in his *Essais* 1.20: "Que philosopher c'est apprendre a mourir."

17. Lucr. 3.451–54; English trans. by Rolfe Humphries (Lucretius, *The Way Things Are* [Bloomington: Indiana University Press, 1969], 99). This is considered the first vernacular translation of Lucretius's work.

18. Merc. 295.

19. Men. 758.

Theogenius

at Iasos, built at an elevation, showed the goddess with a double countenance: a sorrowful, furrowed face appeared toward those entering, a cheerful, joyous expression showed itself toward those leaving.[20] Thus perhaps, too, are our lives, which we enter with such sadness and bitterness: it is later felt most sweet by one who leaves it, an exit much like what they say about the singing swan.... And yet, such is our foolishness, it seems to us that we unavoidably strive to persevere in life for as long as we would promise ourselves, and we do not think how brief are our days on earth. Above our river here, during the very brief summer nights, little flying animals are born, which live as long as they flutter on their weak and fragile wings, and the next dawn, with rare exceptions, will find them fallen to earth and lifeless, in a space of time scarcely sufficient for us to bring a baby into this world.[21] And so compared to eternity our mortal lives in which we exist ought to seem to us so small that, even if the span of Nestor's years were fixed for us and promised by nature herself, they would have in our lives little time to upset us when we have lost them. And we fools, while thinking on this, upset ourselves about something we face as part of life's course and necessary. I lay this at the feet of our softness.

Teogenio would affirm that the soul is liberated at death from its earthly weight and prison. "Thus dying will bring such delight to those departing from life, if they will not be unwise, to the degree that they will know that by death's benefit, as Aeschylus says, they escape to freedom from a thousand evils that afflict and besiege the lives of mortals." He concludes:

And yet although death may be in itself, as they say, a necessary, not unpleasant, most useful and desirable thing, nonetheless, in light of our meager tolerance of our misfortunes, the view of Plato must always be preferred, which affirmed that as in battle so in life it is not permitted to flee the post given and assigned to you, without the consent of the supreme commander.[22] The philosopher Bias has said that the highest unhappiness is not to be able to suffer unhappiness.[23] For this reason, as Martial admonishes in that epigram in which he recounts those things that make life blessed, we should neither fear, nor desire, the last day of our lives.[24]

---

20. Cf. H.N. 36.4.12–13.

21. An image adapted from Aristotle (*History of Animals*), Cicero (*Tusculans*), and Petrarch (*Secretum*).

22. Pl. Ap. 28d.

23. D.L. 1.5. Alberti could have read this statement in Ambrogio Traversari's 1433 Latin translation.

24. *Epigr.* 10.47.13.

8

GIOVANNI PICO DELLA MIRANDOLA
(1463–1494)
Spiritual Writings

✦

VICTOR M. SALAS

INTRODUCTION

Giovanni Pico della Mirandola, born in 1463, was the son of the knight Gianfrancesco of the fief Mirandola and Concordia, hence named Prince of Concordia, often with reference to his efforts to reconcile Aristotelian and Platonic philosophy. He died in 1494 in Florence, probably poisoned for his sympathies with the reformer Girolamo Savonarola.

The following selection from Pico's *opera* reveals a deep spiritual dimension to the otherwise seemingly cantankerous and ostentatious Renaissance thinker whom modern readers have come to know. Apart from the letter to his nephew in 1492, the exact time frame of these writings is unknown and remains disputed by scholars today.[1] Because of their spiritual content, some have suggested that these works date to a later, more collected period in Pico's life that reflects the influence of the Dominican

---

1. For an overview of various scholarly positions, see Tomáš Nejeschleba, "Dignity or Misery of Man? Giovanni Pico's *Duodecalogues and their Legacy*," in *Bruniana & Campanelliana: Ricerche filosofiche e materiali storico-testuali* 24 (Pisa: Fabrizio Serra Editore, 2018), 202–4.

Spiritual Writings

friar Girolamo Savonarola.[2] A minority of scholars have gone so far as to suggest that these works are simply a forgery of Pico's nephew, Gianfrancesco.[3] Whatever the ultimate scholarly conclusion might be—should any consensus ever be possible—it is clear that the author of the following works is considerably attuned to the Christian scriptural tradition as well as the moral wisdom of antiquity. The contentious and haughty Pico of the *900 Conclusiones* and *De hominis dignitate* is here contrasted remarkably with what appears to be a serene author of keen spiritual insight, who is always mindful—perhaps because of the instruction of his own experience—of the insidious tactics that pride and lust employ to undermine the soul's happiness and union with God. They also indirectly reveal a man that has drunk deeply from the pleasures of the world only to find them tasteless. One is not surprised, then, to find Pico eager to caution others against falling prey to such empty seductions. When these spiritual writings are considered together with the more familiar works associated with his name, they enrich the reader's view of Pico and shed light on the complexity of his thought.[4]

BIBLIOGRAPHY

Primary Sources

Pico della Mirandola, Giovanni. *Opera omnia*. Basel, 1557. Reprint, Hildesheim: Georg Olms, 2005.

———. *Conclusiones Nongentae: Le novecento tesi dell'anno 1486*. Edited by Albano Biondi. Florence, Olschki, 1995.

2. See Giovanni Pico della Mirandola, *De Hominis Dignitate, Heptaplus, De Ente et Uno, e scritti vari*, ed. Eugenio Garin (Florence: Vallecchi, 1992), 45–46.

3. Stephen Farmer, *Syncretism in the West: Pico's 900 Theses (1486); the Evolution of Traditional, Religious, and Philosophical Systems: With Text, Translation, and Commentary* (Tempe, Ariz.: Medieval & Renaissance Texts & Studies, 1998), 167–68.

4. The Latin text from which this translation has been made is found in *Giovanni Pico della Mirandola Opera Omnia (1557–1573)*, vol. 1, 332–43 (Basel, 1557; reprint, Hildesheim: Georg Olms Verlag, 2005). I have done my best to make the translation as reader-friendly as possible while striving for fidelity to the text itself. Unavoidable, however, is the difficulty that preserving gender inclusivity presents. Here, the Latin "*homo*" is particularly notorious for the challenges it presents. I have chosen to translate it and its inflections as "man" entirely for stylistic reasons. "Human being" or "person" would have, unfortunately, been rather cumbersome and distracting, but imposing "man and woman" or its correlative pronouns "he and she" would likewise have perpetrated a certain degree of violence to the text. Accordingly, I beseech the reader for his or her indulgence.

———. *De Hominis Dignitate, Heptaplus, De Ente et Uno, e scritti vari*. Edited by Eugenio Garin. Florence: Vallecchi, 1992.

Secondary Soures

Allen, Michael. *Studies in the Platonism of Marsilio Ficino and Giovanni Pico*. Variorum Collected Studies. New York: Routledge, 2017.

Black, Crofton. *Pico's Heptaplus and Biblical Hermeneutics*. Leiden: Brill, 2006.

Copenhaver, Brian P. *Magic and the Dignity of Man*. Cambridge, Mass.: Belknap Press, Harvard University Press, 2019.

Dougherty, Michael. *Pico della Mirandola: New Essays*. Cambridge: Cambridge University Press, 2008.

Farmer, Stephen. *Syncretism in the West: Pico's 900 Theses (1486); the Evolution of Traditional, Religious, and Philosophical Systems: With Text, Translation, and Commentary*. Tempe, Ariz.: Medieval & Renaissance Texts & Studies, 1998.

Nejeschleba, Tomáš. "Dignity or Misery of Man? Giovanni Pico's Duodecalogues and Their Legacy." *Bruniana & Campanelliana* 24 (2018): 201–12.

GIOVANNI PICO DELLA MIRANDOLA
Spiritual Writings

I: THE TWELVE RULES OF GIOVANNI PICO DELLA MIRANDOLA, PARTLY UP-BUILDING, AND PARTLY DIRECTING A MAN IN SPIRITUAL BATTLE

1. If men view the life of virtue as difficult since it is always necessary for us to fight against the flesh, the devil, and the world, one should bear in mind that in whatever life one chooses, even if it be one according to the world, there are many adversities, sorrows, troubles, and labors that one will suffer.

2. One should bear in mind that with regard to the things of the world, the battle is longer, more painstaking, and more fruitless, in which work itself is its own end, and in which the final end is only eternal pain.

3. One should bear in mind that it is foolish to think that one can attain heaven without such a spiritual fight, just as Christ our head did not ascend into heaven except through the cross. Nor should the circumstances of the servant be better than that of the Lord.

4. One should bear in mind that this fight is not only to be endured with difficulty but also that it should be desired, even though we receive

Spiritual Writings

no reward from it and are only conformed to Christ our God and Lord. As often as you resist certain temptations that arise from the senses, think of some part of Christ's cross to which you are to be conformed. When you vex the appetites in resisting gluttony, recall that drink mixed with gall and vinegar. When you withdraw your hand from the taking of something that pleases you, think of the hands affixed to the wood of the cross for you. If you would resist pride, recall that he, who was in the form of God, accepted the form of a servant and humbled himself for you to the point of death on the cross.[5] When anger tempts you, recall that he—who was God and most righteous among all men saw himself as though a robber, and was ridiculed, spit upon, scourged, reviled, and mocked with jeers—did at no time show any sign of anger or indignation but bore everything most patiently. He reacted to everything most meekly. In such a way, pondering the aforementioned, you will discover there is no suffering that is not intended to conform you to Christ.

5. That if you would rely upon these twelve weapons, not as upon any other human remedy, but only in the power of Jesus Christ, who said: "have confidence, for I have overcome the world."[6] And in another place, "The prince of this world will be cast out."[7] Hence, we shall trust only in his power by which it is possible to conquer the world and overcome the devil. For that reason, through prayer, we should always ask him and his saints for assistance.

6. One should bear in mind that when one temptation is defeated, others should always be expected, since at all times Satan prowls about looking for someone to devour.[8] Therefore, it is always necessary to serve in alarm, as is said according to the prophets, "I will stand upon my guard."[9]

7. Not only are you not conquered by the devil, although he tempts you, but you defeat him, which occurs not only when you do not sin but also from the fact that your temptation now becomes the occasion for obtaining some good. Even if the good of some work offered to you should entice you to vainglory, immediately think of it not as your work but as

---

5. Cf. Philippians 2:6–8.
6. John 16:33.
7. John 12:31.
8. Cf. 1 Peter 5:8.
9. Habakkuk 2:1.

a favor from God. Humble and judge yourself to be ungrateful for God's benefits.

8. That when you fight, fight so as to win; then you will have perpetual peace since perhaps God will give this peace to you from his grace, and the devil will no longer return, confounded by your victory. But when you have succeeded, guard yourself as though you will soon fight, that in the fight you are always mindful of victory, and in victory always mindful of the fight.

9. When, however, much as you feel completely fortified and prepared, always flee occasions of sin since as the wise man says: "He who loves danger will perish in in it."[10]

10. That you resist temptations from the beginning and dash the infants of Babylon against the rock.[11] The rock, however, is Christ, for "the remedy is prepared too late since the malady has gained strength from long delay."[12]

11. One should bear in mind that, although the battle appears in the very conflict of temptation, it is, nevertheless, by far sweeter to overcome temptation than to go into that sin toward which temptation inclines you. And in this, many are deceived since they do not compare the sweetness of victory and the sweetness of sin. Rather, they compare the harsh battle to pleasure. Nevertheless, a man that is a tested soldier in this spiritual battle, who falls into temptation, should as many times as he is put to the test, determine what it is to conquer temptation.

12. For this reason, do not believe because you are tempted that you are forsaken by God, less pleasing to God, or of little righteousness and perfection. Remember that after Paul saw the divine essence, he suffered the temptation of the flesh, which God permitted, lest pride should tempt him. Man should bear in mind that Paul, who was a chosen vessel and carried off to the third heaven, was, however, in danger, lest he should be led to pride on account of his virtue; as he himself says, "lest the magnitude

10. Sirach 3:27.

11. The significance of this seemingly atrocious and grotesque image stems from Babylon's biblical function as a symbol for worldly ambition and temptations. See, for example, Revelation 18:21.

12. Pico seems to be quoting only part of a passage from Ovid's *Remedia Amoris*. The full passage reads, "Principiis obsta; sero medicina paratur/ Cum mala per longas convaluere moras" (lines 91–92).

of revelation should extoll me, there was given to me a thorn of my flesh, which buffets me."[13] Therefore, above all temptations, man should especially strengthen himself against the temptation of pride, since pride is the root of all evils, against which there is one remedy: to recall always that God humiliated himself for us all the way to the cross, and that death will humiliate one, even against his will, so as to become worm fodder.

II: GIOVANNI PICO DELLA MIRANDOLA'S TWELVE WEAPONS OF SPIRITUAL WARFARE, THAT A MAN SHOULD HAVE AT HAND WHEN THE DESIRE OF SIN TEMPTS HIM

1. Short and brief delight
2. The companions, fastidiousness and anxiety
3. The loss of a greater good
4. Life, a sleep and a shadow
5. A sudden and unforeseen death
6. Mistrust of impenitence
7. Eternal reward; eternal pain
8. The dignity and nature of man
9. The peace of a good mind
10. The benefits of God
11. The cross of Christ
12. The testimony of the martyrs and the example of the saints

III: GIOVANNI PICO DELLA MIRANDOLA'S ON THE TWELVE CONDITIONS OF THE LOVER

1. To love the beloved only and despise everything else for him
2. To regard he who is not with the beloved as unhappy
3. To suffer all things and to be with him, even to death
4. To adorn oneself so as to please him
5. To be with him in every way, and if not in presence, at least in thought

13. 2 Corinthians 12:7.

6. To love everything that is dear to him: all friends, house, clothes, and images

7. To long for approval and not to be able to suffer any of his dishonor

8. To think the greatest things of him, and to desire that all would likewise regard him

9. To choose also to suffer some discomfort for him and even find that discomfort sweet

10. To weep with him often, whether from sorrow if he is absent, or because of joy if he is present

11. To languish always, and always be ablaze with his desire

12. To serve him, thinking nothing of reward or recompense

We are customarily led to this, especially for three reasons. The first is when the service given is desirable of itself. Second, when that whom we serve is himself very good and lovable, as we are accustomed to say, we serve him according to his virtues. The third is that when prior to your serving him, he conferred many benefits on you. And these three reasons are in God, for whose service there is nothing newly undertaken that is not to our good either, whether with respect to the soul or to the body, since to serve him is nothing other than to tend toward him, that is, to the highest good. Similarly, he himself is the greatest, most beautiful, wisest, and has all these conditions that commonly move us to love something and to serve Him freely. He conveys the highest blessings upon us, since he created us out of nothing and through the blood of his Son redeemed us from hell.

IV: GIOVANNI PICO DELLA MIRANDOLA'S COMMENTARY ON PSALM XV

"Preserve me, Lord."

If any perfect man wishes to examine his state, he should consider whether there is the danger that his virtue is an occasion of pride. Therefore, David, speaking in the person of the just man, regarding his state, begins with, "Preserve me," which rightly considered takes away all occasion of pride. For he who can acquire something on his own can preserve it for himself. He, therefore, who asks God to conserve him in a state of virtue,

Spiritual Writings

signifies through this that not even from the beginning had he acquired virtue on his own. He, however, who remembers that virtue is conferred upon him, not properly through himself but through God's power, cannot on that account be prideful but rather more humble of heart before God, according to the Apostle's statement: "What do you have that you have not received? And if you have received it, why do you boast in it as though you had not received it?"[14] Therefore, there are two sayings that we should always be ready to say: the one is "Be merciful to me, God," when we have the recollection of sin, and the other is "Preserve me, God," when we recall his power.

"Since I hoped in you."

There is one thing that brings about our obtaining what we ask of God: namely, when we *hope* to obtain. And if we observe these two conditions— that we only ask God for those things that are beneficial to us and that for which we ask, we ask for ardently, with the firm hope that God hears us— at no time will our prayers be in vain. When, therefore, we do not obtain what we ask for, it is either on account of the fact that it is harmful to us, or we do not know what to aim at, as Christ Jesus says, "Whatever you ask for in my name, will be given to you."[15] For this name Jesus signifies the savior, and therefore nothing is sought in the name of Jesus unless it pertains to the salvation of the petitioner or because the petition is not heard. Since if we ask for good things and do not ask well, that is on account of our having little hope. He, however, who hopes with hesitation, asks coldly. And, therefore, James says, "Let him ask in faith with no hesitation."[16]

"I said to the Lord, you are my God."

After fortifying himself against pride, he begins to examine his state. The complete condition of a just person consists in this saying: "I said to the Lord, you are my God." Although that statement seems nearly common to all people, there are, however, few who can truly mean it. For if someone considers God to be the highest good, and we have that for the highest good, and only had God, though other things were lacking, we

---

14. 1 Corinthians 4:7.
15. Cf. John 14:13.
16. James 1:6.

would consider ourselves happy. But if that highest good is lacking, though we have all other things, we would consider ourselves miserable. The avaricious person, therefore, says to money, "You are my God." And so, if he lacks honor and health as well as virtue and friends but only has money, he is content. If he has all these goods that we mentioned but lacks money, he considers himself to be unhappy. The gluttonous person also says of his drunkenness; the intemperate person says of his desire; and the ambitious person says of his power or glory, "You are my God." It is seen, therefore, how few are able to say, "I have said to the Lord, you are my God." Since only he, for whom alone God suffices, is able to do this. Thus, if the kingdoms of the entire world and all the heavens and all earthly goods were offered to him, he would not, however, accept them if it would offend God but once. Therefore, the entire state of the just man consists in this saying.

"Since you do not need my good things."

He offers a reason why he says only to the Lord, "You are my God." The reason is that only God does not need our goods. Indeed, there is no creature that does not need the goods of other creatures, which are imperfect to it since, as the philosophers and theologians prove, if the imperfect creatures had not been, the superior would not have been, since the destruction of one part of the whole is the destruction of the complete whole. With the destruction, however, all the parts are destroyed. All creatures, moreover, are part of the whole of which God himself is not a part but the principle and depends upon nothing. God attains nothing from the fact that he created the world, and he would lose nothing if the whole world were annihilated. Therefore, only God does not need our goods. We should, however, be ashamed to have as God that which needs our goods, which is true of every creature. Additionally, we should not have for God, that is, for the highest good, anything except that in which the highest good consists. No creature, however, constitutes the highest good. Therefore, we should say only to the Lord, "You are my God."

"To the saints who are in His land."

After God, we should especially love those who are very much joined to God, as are the angels and blessed in heaven. Therefore, after he said to the Lord, "You are my God," he adds that God:

Spiritual Writings

"Made wonderful His desires."

That is, he has made wonderful his love and his desire with respect to his saints, who are in his land, that is, in the celestial heaven, which is said to be the land of God and land of the living. And if we truly consider how great the happiness of this land is as well as the great goodness and renown of its citizens, so much so will we consider this world's misery from which we will always want to depart so as to live in that heavenly place. We should always be mindful of these and similar things, moreover, when meditated upon, lest our meditations would be unfruitful. Yet from any meditation we should always acquire some virtue. For example, from considering the goodness of that superior land, we should acquire this virtue: that we not only meet death bravely and await our hour with patience, whether or not that death is for the sake of faith in Christ, so that we also eagerly desire to depart from this valley of miseries to reign with God and his saints in that happy land. When, therefore, the just person describes his state, which is completely made for God and things of the divine, he also despises from that exalted state the evil of men and says:

"Their infirmities are multiplied."

By infirmities, however, he means idols, and thus the Hebrew text has: for just as a good person has one God who he honors, so evil people have many gods and idols, since there are many pleasures, many vain desires, and diverse passions that they serve.[17] Therefore, also many seek pleasures, since they discover none that gives them satisfaction. Accordingly, they wander around in circles. And he adds: they make haste after—that is, after their desires—toward which they run headlong and thoughtlessly. Whence we are taught that we run no less quickly to the virtues than they run to vice. Nor do we less diligently serve our Lord himself than they who serve their lord the devil. The just person, however, considering the state of evil people, firmly proposes—just as we should always do—to follow them in no way. And he says:

"I will not gather their assembly for blood offerings,
nor remember their names upon my lips."

17. Cf. Isaiah 44.

He speaks, however, of blood offerings also since just as often as idolaters were accustomed to collect the blood of victims in order to carry out their ceremonies, so also the entire life of evil people forsakes reason and follows sensuality, which is centered upon blood. He said, however, that not only does he not wish to sacrifice to idols but he also does not wish to name them, showing through this, that not only should the perfect man abstain from illicit desires but also from those desires that are allowed so that he is more greatly carried off to heaven and free for the contemplation of divine and more pure things. But since someone might believe it to be foolish to deprive oneself of all pleasure, he adds:

"The Lord is part of my inheritance."

That is to say, do not be amazed if I relinquish everything else so as to attain God in whom, in the end, all other good things are contained. This should be the saying of any good Christian. "The Lord is a part of my inheritance." We Christians, to whom God himself has promised himself for an inheritance, should be ashamed to desire something other than him. And since it might seem to be of some presumption to dare to promise himself, he also says:

"You are He who restores my inheritance to me."

That is to say, my Lord God, I know well that since I am nothing with respect to you, I am not able to ascend to the attainment of you through my own powers. But it is you who draws me to yourself through your grace. And you are he who will give me the attainment of yourself. Then the just person considers how blessed this is that God will be his inheritance. He adds:

"The Lines fell upon me in splendid fashion."

For parts and lots were formerly divided by lines. And since there are many who, although they are called to this happiness, as are all Christians, still will not attain it inasmuch as for the sake of short pleasures, they barter it. Therefore, he adds:

"My inheritance is splendid to me."

That is to say, just as it is itself splendid, thus do I regard it splendid and all others with respect to it, like Paul said, as filth.[18] Since, however, to have

18. Cf. Philippians 3:8.

Spiritual Writings

this intellectual light, as man knows happiness is a gift given by God, he therefore adds:

"I will bless you, Lord, who grants understanding."

Moreover, man often determines to serve God according to reason, to which, however, sensuality and the flesh are repugnant. Thereupon, also a man is perfect, that not only has his soul but also his flesh carried off to God according to the saying, "My heart and my flesh exult in the living God."[19] Therefore, he adds:

"And my reins rebuke me all through the night."

It is through the reins themselves that one is most customarily inclined to concupiscence. They not only incline me to evil, but more so they rebuke me. That is, they withdraw me from sin through the night, which is to say that they themselves also afflict my very body. For affliction is often signified by the "night." Then he shows what the root of such a privation is and says:

"I always place God in my sight."

For if someone always has God before his eyes as the rule of all his actions, and in all of his actions, does not seek their usefulness, nor glory, nor pleasure, but only seeks to give satisfaction to God, only for a brief time will perfection escape him. And since he acts in such a fashion, he prospers in all things. Therefore, he says:

"He Himself is at my right hand lest I be provoked."

Then he shows how great is the just person's happiness, since his happiness will be eternal happiness in both soul and body. For which reason he adds:

"My heart is glad."

That is, my soul is happy knowing that after death heaven is prepared for it.

"And my flesh will rest in hope."

That is, although it itself is not glad, as though it will immediately accept its state after death, it nevertheless rests in the grave with this hope,

---

19. Psalm 83:3.

GIOVANNI PICO DELLA MIRANDOLA

that it will arise as immortal and most splendid on the day of judgment with its soul. And he declares this in the following verse, for since it was said that the soul will be joyful, he adds the reason:

"For the soul will not be left in hell."

And since he said that the flesh rests in hope, he adds a reason, saying:

"Nor will you give your saints over to see corruption."

Because what was corruptible will arise as incorruptible, and because Christ was the first person who entered paradise, appeared alive to us, was the first who arose, and whose resurrection is the cause of our resurrection, therefore these things of which we have spoken of the resurrection are understood principally of Christ, just as the Apostle Peter declared, and secondly about us, inasmuch as we are members of Christ, who alone sees no corruption, since his body was not corrupt in the tomb. Since, therefore, the way of living well leads us to perpetual life of the soul and body, he adds:

"You have made me to know the ways of life."

And since the complete happiness of this life consists in the bare vision and enjoyment of God, he adds:

"You will fill me with the joy of your countenance."

And since happiness will endure in eternity, he adds:

"At your right hand are delights forever."

He says, moreover, "at your right hand," since our happiness is completed in the vision and enjoyment of Christ's humanity, who, according to John, sits at the right hand in the highest majesty. This is the full reward: that we see God and him whom he sent, Jesus Christ.

V

Giovanni Pico della Mirandola to Giovanni Francesco, nephew by his brother, health be in him Who is true health

Be neither amazed, my son, nor pained or frightened, if upon your departure from me many occasions of evil should take hold of and disturb

Spiritual Writings 131

your opposite intention to live well. Rather, how great a miracle would it be if the way to heaven would be open without labor, to you alone among mortals, as though now there were no deceitful world nor evil demon, or as though, thus far, you were not in the flesh, which eagerly covets against the spirit and (unless we will shall be vigilant for our safety) makes us drunk at Circe's seductive cup and transform us into monstrous kinds of beasts.[20] But rejoice to yourself as James asserts, writing, "Rejoice, brothers, when you fall into various temptations."[21] Nor without reason, for what hope of glory is there without hope of victory? Or what place is there for victory if there is no fight? He is called to the crown who is provoked to the fight, especially to that fight in which no one can be conquered against his will, nor is some other power needed for us in order that we may conquer other than the will itself to succeed. The Christian is of great joy when victory is placed in the choice of his free will, and the rewards of every victory will be greater than all expectation.

Tell me, my dearest son, whether there is anything in this life the desire of which stirs earthly minds that will not be obtained without much labor and without enduring much indignation and miseries. The merchant regards himself as having done well if after navigating for ten years, after facing thousands of inconveniences, facing thousands of life's decisive and critical moments, he may have secured just a little gain. It is not for worldly campaigns, the miseries of which have adequately taught you and experience itself teaches, that I write you. In securing the favor of princes, in procuring the friendship of comrades, in canvassing honors, what piles of trouble, how great the anxiety, and how great the worries are. I—who contenting myself with my books, have from boyhood, learned to live always within my own condition, and (as much as possible) dwell in my own presence, sighing or standing in need of nothing outside myself—would rather learn from you how great these worries are than to teach you about them. Therefore, we will barely attain these earthly estates, inconstant, cheap and common to us and beasts, with sweat and panting. But will we be drawn, as though reluctant and as drowsy and asleep, to divine things,

---

20. The allusion here is to *The Odyssey*, book 10, lines 156–225, where the goddess Circe tricks Odysseus's men into eating and drinking, which turns them into pigs.

21. James 1:2.

which eye has not seen, nor ear heard, nor heart knew,[22] just as if without us God could not reign or those heavenly citizens be blessed? Certainly, if earthly delights presented themselves to us as easily attained, someone who refuses work might serve the world rather than serve God. But it is not less tiring to follow along on the way of God than the way of sin (whence that saying of the damned, "We tired ourselves in the way of iniquity"[23]). It cannot be but from madness to refuse to work where the work leads to reward rather than to go from work to punishment. I do not even consider, without a doubt, how great the peace and joy of the soul, when it is guilty of nothing and blushes from no guilt rather than are all the pleasures that are able to be attained or wished for in life. For what is delectable in the pleasures of the world, which make us weary in seeking them, makes us fools in acquiring them and tortures us when they are lost?

You doubt, my son, that the minds of the impious are not afflicted with constant pain. It is the Word of God, who is neither able to be deceived nor deceive. The heart of the wicked is like a raging sea that is unable to rest. For nothing gives it security, nothing gives it is safety, nothing gives it peace. Everything threatens with dread, worry, and death. Indeed, will we envy these people? Will we imitate them and forget our proper dignity, forget our country, and the heavenly Father? Since we were born in freedom, do we voluntarily make ourselves slaves to these things, being one with them in living in misery, dying in misery, and finally most miserably being thrown into eternal fire? Oh, blind human minds! Oh, blind the heart of man who does not see the clear light of all these to be truer than truth itself! Nor, however, do we do that which we know we should do, nor do we tear our heel from the filth of our desires but cling to it. Especially in these places where you pass your time, my son, (do not doubt it) in every season, innumerable hindrances will come about that (unless you are careful) throw you headlong away from the intention of living well and saintly. But among them all, it is a deadly plague to dwell day and night among those whose life is not only from all parts an allurement of sin but complete in expelling virtue and placed under the rule of the devil, under the banner of death, under the tributes of Gehenna that fight against heaven, against the Lord and against his Christ.

22. Cf. 1 Corinthians 2:9.
23. Wisdom 5:7.

Spiritual Writings

But cry out with the Prophet: "Let us shatter the fetters and cast the yoke away from ourselves."[24] For these are they who God hands over to the passions of disgrace and to reprobate senses, so as to do what is not fitting and full of all iniquity, full of hatred, murder, conflict, deceit, malice, liars, odious to God, insulting, arrogant, prideful, inventors of evil, foolish, clumsy, without feeling, without trust, without mercy. Who while they see God's justice daily, yet they do not understand, since they act in a manner worthy of death, not only those who so act but also those who consent to those actions being done.

You, therefore, my son, do not give pleasure to that which displeases virtue itself. But let the saying of the Apostle always be before your eyes: "It is more necessary to give satisfaction to God than to men,"[25] and that, "If I seek to give pleasure to men, I would not be the servant of Christ."[26] Allow a certain holy ambition to enter you and disdain those who would be teachers of your life that have more need of you as a teacher. For it is far more appropriate that they, by living well with you, should begin to be good men than that you should wish shamefully to become brutish, by joining them through abandoning your good intention. I give God as witness, sometimes amazement, and a certain torpor holds me when I begin to consider the desires of men. For I do not know whether to think it more preferable to suffer or to marvel or lament those desires or (if I would put it more clearly) consider them pure insanity. For surely, it is great madness not to believe in the Gospel, whose truth the blood of the martyrs proclaims, the voices of the apostles resound, wonders prove, reason confirms, the world testifies, the elements speak, and the demons confess. But by far greater is the madness if you do not doubt the truth of the Gospels but live as though you did not doubt that it is false. For if those words are true, that it is most difficult for the rich person, who day by day desires to accumulate wealth, to enter the reign of heaven, why do we then busy ourselves every day in heaping up riches? And if true glory is not from men but from God, why do we always depend upon the judgment of men? No one who worries about pleasing God and is in firm faith with us doubts that

24. Psalm 2:3.
25. Cf. Acts 5:29. The Vulgate passage from Acts actually reads, "We ought to obey God rather than men."
26. Galatians 1:10.

sometime in the future, the Lord will say: "Go you, wicked, into eternal fire,"[27] and, in turn, "Come blessed and possess the kingdom prepared for you from the foundation of the world."[28] Why are we afraid of nothing less than Gehenna, or than the hope of God's reign? What else can we say except that many are Christian in name but are hardly so in reality.

But you, my son, strive to enter through the narrow gate, nor act to attend to what so many do, but what the law of nature, reason itself, and what God Himself shows you to do. For neither will your glory be less if your joy is with a few, or pain lighter if you will be miserable with many. There will, however, be two special remedies available to you against the world and Satan, which are like two wings by which you will be taken away from the valley of tears: namely, alms and prayer. For what are we able to do without the help of God? And how will he help without being invoked? But he certainly will not hear you invoke him if you have not first heard the poor man who has invoked you. For neither is it fitting that God does not condemn you as a man, who as a man first looked down upon another man. It is written, "by what measure you measure, so it will be measured to you,"[29] and elsewhere, "Blessed are the merciful for they shall obtain mercy."[30]

When, however, I invite you to prayer, I do not invite you to that which consists in loquaciousness, but which in the secret recesses of your mind, in the innermost chamber of the soul, the mind itself speaks to God: and in the most lucid darkness of contemplation, not only present the mind to the Father but unite it with him by an ineffable manner that only those who have tried know. Nor do I care how long your prayer is, but only how efficacious it is, how ardent it is, rather that it be interrupted by sighs, than by a series of speeches both numerous and diffuse. If the safety of your heart is of concern to you, if you would be safe from the snares of the devil, from the storms of the world, from hostile plots, and finally if you desire to be acceptable to God and happy, let no day pass wherein you did not approach God through prayer and prostrate before him with a humble and pious affection of mind: not from the summit of your lips but from

27. Matthew 25:41.
28. Matthew 25:34.
29. Matthew 7:2.
30. Matthew 5:7.

Spiritual Writings 135

the deepest viscera, you cry out with the prophet, "You will not remember the offenses and ignorances of my youth, but according to your mercy remember me because of your goodness, Lord."[31] The spirit who intercedes for us will suggest to you what to ask from your God, as will the necessities themselves of every hour. Also sacred reading, which I ask that you always have in your hands and now put aside the nonsensical fables of the poets, will indicate to you. Nothing is more delightful to God—you are able to do nothing more useful for yourself—than if your hand were not to cease to turn through the sacred writings day and night. For hidden in that heavenly strength is a certain marvelous power, alive and effective, that is able to transform the soul of the reader (if that power would be handled in a pure and humble way).

But now I have exceeded the limits of a letter, the matter of which draws me along as well as the charity I always have with you, especially following from that hour in which I was made sure of your most holy purpose. Finally, I wish to caution you never forget these two things (about which I often spoke with you when you were here with me): that the Son of God died for you and that, even though you may live a long life, you will shortly die. These, as though twin goads—the one, indeed, of fear, the other of love—spur on your horse through the brief race course of this momentary life to the reward of eternal joy, since we should not or cannot be determined by anything other than the enjoyment of both the peace of men and infinite good without end.

Farewell and fear God.

From Ferrara
15 May 1492

31. Psalm 24:7.

9

MARSILIO FICINO
(1433–1499)

Letters

JAMES G. SNYDER

INTRODUCTION

Marsilio Ficino is one of the most important and prolific advocates of Platonism in the Renaissance. He was born in 1433 in Figline, Tuscany, and he died in 1499 in Florence. Ficino lived his whole life in the vicinity of Florence, and his writings, teachings, and correspondence were central to the rich intellectual life of the great Renaissance city. Ficino wrote many philosophical treatises over the course of his life and was a prolific translator, commentator, and letter writer. His most significant and voluminous philosophical treatise is his *Platonic Theology: On the Immortality of the Soul*, which was published in 1482. In addition to his own writings, Ficino also translated the writings of Plato and Plotinus into Latin, and he wrote extensive commentaries on both. His interpretation of Platonism was influential among philosophers for centuries on account of his treatises, translations, commentaries, and correspondence.

In addition to his treatises and commentaries, Ficino carried on a wide-ranging correspondence for decades with many contemporaries, including humanists, philosophers, royalty, and

136

heads of state. The foci of his letters were both explaining and defending his interpretation of Plato and discussing the application of Platonism to diverse theological and ethical questions and problems. His letters expound on his philosophy, and they frequently discuss the practical application of philosophy to a life well-lived. (His *Platonic Theology* and commentaries, by comparison, are much more straight-forwardly philosophical in their use of assumptions and arguments to defend his Platonism.) In these letters, Ficino touches on many of the ideas that are central to his philosophy. He maintains that God is the font of all being and goodness in the world, and he explains the privileged position that soul occupies in the hierarchy of being. For Ficino, the centrality of the human soul in this metaphysical hierarchy, and its natural inclination to the good, ensures its immortality. An important theme in his writings is the care of the soul, and he frequently discusses the steps we can take to purify ourselves. He often laments the moral and cognitive limitations that the body places on the soul and the myriad ways the body can, if not under control, prevent the soul from ascending the hierarchy of being to the divine.

Drawing on Plato's *Phaedo* and *Phaedrus*, Ficino discusses the different means by which the soul and mind can be purified of the influence of the body and argues that the soul can take two paths to God through moral and intellectual perfection, and that music and poetry can remind the soul of truth, goodness, the divine, and of the soul's divine origins. Ficino discusses the different types of divine frenzy that facilitate, in varying degrees, the soul's love of the divine. He also discusses the limitations that the intellect places on our conception of God, and how the will, driven by love, can appreciate the goodness and infinity of God, whereupon the soul achieves a state of happiness.

In his letters, Ficino engages with a wide range of philosophical schools and figures from antiquity. He references Pythagoras, Empedocles, Heraclitus, Hermes Trismegistus, and, of course, Plato, just to name a few. Here, he considers the philosophy of Epicurus and his followers, who he frequently critiques on account of their underlying materialism and denial of the immortality of the soul. Ficino was, in fact, among the first generation of philosophers with direct access to the ancient writings of Epicurean philosophers who were rediscovered by the Italian humanists. His Platonism is heavily dependent on the Neoplatonic interpretations of Plotinus and Proclus. Ficino was likely trained in fifteenth century medical traditions, and in his treatises and commentaries, he engages frequently with medieval Scholasticism, particularly the writings of Thomas Aquinas. For Ficino, the history of philosophy is central to philosophy itself.

Ficino's interpretation of Plato was influential among philosophers for centuries. It shaped the way philosophers read and engaged with the ideas of Plato and Plotinus. His *Platonic Theology* played a pivotal role in debates about the immortality of the soul in the fifteenth and sixtieth centuries, and the theory of love in his commentary on Plato's *Symposium* has been especially influential to the history of ideas. His ideas were also important to the Cambridge Platonists, a group of seventeenth-century philosophers associated with Cambridge University, and there is a growing body of evidence suggesting that Ficino's ideas and translations were influential on other early modern thinkers.

BIBLIOGRAPHY
Primary Sources

Ficino, Marsilio. *Commentaries on Plato, Volume 1:* Phaedrus *and* Ion. Edited and translated by Michael J. B. Allen. Cambridge, Mass.: Harvard University Press, 2008.

———. *The Letters of Marsilio Ficino.* 11 vols. Translated by members of the Language Department, London School of Economics. London: Shepheard-Walwyn, 1975–2020.

———. *Platonic Theology.* 6 vols. Translated by Michael J. B. Allen. Cambridge, Mass.: Harvard University Press, 2001–2006.

Secondary Sources

Albertini, Tamara. "Marsilio Ficino (1433–1499). The Aesthetic of the One in the Soul." In *Philosophers of the Renaissance,* edited by Paul Richard Blum and translated by Brian McNeil, 82–91. Washington, D.C: The Catholic University of America Press, 2010.

Allen, Michael J. B. *Plato's Third Eye: Studies in Marsilio Ficino's Metaphysics and its Sources.* Aldershot: Variorum, 1995.

———. *Synoptic Art: Marsilio Ficino on the History of Platonic Interpretation.* Florence: Olschki, 1998.

Kristeller, Paul Oskar. *The Philosophy of Marsilio Ficino.* New York: Columbia University Press, 1943.

Robichaud, Denis J.-J. *Plato's Persona: Marsilio Ficino, Renaissance Humanism, and Platonic Traditions.* Philadelphia: University of Pennsylvania Press, 2018.

Snyder, James G. "Marsilio Ficino's Critique of the Lucretian Alternative." *Journal of the History of Ideas* 72, no. 2 (2011): 165–81.

Snyder, James G., and Catherine Wilson. "Leibniz and Ficino: Life, Activity, and Matter." *Studia Leibnitiana* 49, no. 2 (2017): 243–58.

MARSILIO FICINO

Letters

LETTER 4

A Theological Dialogue between God and the Soul[1]

Marsilio Ficino to Michele Mercati of San Miniato, his beloved fellow philosopher: greetings.

We have often talked together of moral and natural philosophy, beloved Michele, and even more often of divine philosophy. I remember you used to say again and again that morals are developed through practice, natural things discovered by reason and the divine begged of God by prayer. I have also read in the works of our Plato that the divine is revealed through purity of living rather than taught by verbal instruction. When I seriously considered these things I sometimes began to feel sick at heart, for I had already come to distrust reason but still lacked faith in revelation. From this there arose an intimate conversation between the soul and God. Listen to this, if you please, although I think you may already be nearer to speaking with God than I.

God: Why do you grieve so much, my unhappy soul? O my daughter, weep no more. Behold, I, your father, am here with you. I am here, your cure and your salvation.

Soul: Oh, that my father would enter into me. If I believed such a grace could befall me, ah! I should go mad with joy. As it is, I do not see how that can come about; for if, as I thought, the creator of the world created me, his offspring, nearer to himself than his own created world, he who is

---

1. The letters are reprinted with permission from Marsilio Ficino, *The Letters of Marsilio Ficino*, 2nd ed., vol. 1 (London: Shepheard-Walwyn, 2018). Translated from the Latin by members of the Language Department of the School of Economic Science, London. We would like to thank Valery Rees for her helpful input selecting these letters.

only outside me is not my highest father. Nor could he who was only within me be my father, for my father is certainly greater than I, yet he who is contained in me must be smaller. But I do not know how anything can be both inside me and outside me at the same time. What sorely distresses me, stranger, whoever you may be, is this: that I do not wish to live without my father, yet despair of being able to find him.

GOD: Put an end to your tears, my daughter, and do not torment yourself; it is no stranger who speaks to you but one who is your very own, more familiar to you than you are to yourself. Indeed, I am both with you and within you. I am indeed with you, because I am in you; I am in you, because you are in me. If you were not in me you would not be in yourself, indeed you would not be at all. Dry those tears, my daughter, and look upon your father. Your father is the least of all things in size, just as he is the greatest of all things in excellence; and since he is very small he is within every thing, but since he is very great he is outside everything. See, I am here with you, both within and without, the greatest smallness and the smallest greatness. Behold, I say, do you not see? I fill heaven and earth, I penetrate and contain them. I fill and am not filled, for I am fullness itself. I penetrate and am not penetrated, for I am the power of penetration itself. I contain and am not contained, for I am containing itself. I, who am fullness itself, am not filled, for that would not be worthy of me. I am not penetrated lest I cease to exist, being myself existence. I am not contained lest I cease to be God, who am infinity itself. Behold, do you not see? I pass into everything unmingled, so that I may surpass all; for I am excellence itself. I excel everything without being separate, so that I am also able to enter and permeate at the same time, to enter completely and to make one, being unity itself, through which all things are made and endure, and which all things seek.

Why do you despair of finding your father, O foolish one? It is not difficult to find the place where I am; for in me are all things, out of me come all things and by me are all things sustained forever and everywhere. And with infinite power I expand through infinite space. Indeed, no place can be found where I am not; this very 'where' surely exists through me and is called 'everywhere'. Whatever anyone does anywhere, he does through my guidance and my light. Whatever anyone seeks anywhere, he seeks through my guidance and my light. There is no desiring anywhere, except for the good; there is no finding anywhere, except of the truth I am all good; I am all truth. Seek my face and you shall live. But do not move in order to touch me, for I am stillness itself. Do not be drawn in many directions in order to take hold of me; I am unity itself. Stop the movement, unify diversity, and you will surely reach me, who long ago reached you.

SOUL: How quickly you leave me, O my comforter! Why do you so suddenly leave your daughter thirsting like this? Go on, say more, continue I beg you, venerable deity. By your divine majesty, if it please you, I pray you speak more plainly. Oh may it please you! And because I know it will, tell me more plainly then what you, who are my father, are not, that I may be restored to life; and, O my father, tell me again what you are, so that I may live.

GOD: Your father is not of a physical nature, my daughter. The more you obey your father the better you are, and the more you resist the body the finer you are. It is good for you to be with your father, bad for you to be with your body. It was not some mind that fathered you, O soul; otherwise you would contemplate nothing beyond mind and you would be held in that same changing mind, and not seek an unchanging nature. It was no intellect of many parts that made you, for then you would not attain complete simplicity, and the possession of intellect itself would be sufficient for you; but as it is, you ascend by understanding and love beyond any kind of intellect, to life itself, pure existence, absolute being. And understanding is not sufficient for you unless you not only understand well but understand good itself. Without doubt only the good itself is sufficient for you, for the only reason you seek anything is because it is good.

Therefore, O soul, good is your creator; not the good body, not the good mind, not the good intellect, but good itself. Good is that which is indeed self-sufficient, infinite beyond the limits of what is beneath it, and it bestows on you infinite life, either from age to age, or at least from some beginning to the end of time. Do you desire to look on the face of good? Then look around at the whole universe, full of the light of the sun. Look at the light in the material world, full of all forms in constant movement; take away the matter, leave the rest. You have the soul, an incorporeal light that takes all shapes and is full of change. Once again, take from this the changeability, and now you have reached the intelligence of the angels, the incorporeal light, taking all shapes but unchanging. Take away from this that diversity by which any form differs from the light, and which is infused into the light from elsewhere, and then the essence of the light and of each form is the same; the light gives form to itself and through its own forms gives form to everything. That light lights without limit, because it lights by its own nature and is not stained by mixture with something else. Nor can it diminish; belonging to nothing, it shines equally through all. Its life is self-dependent, and it confers life on all, seeing that its very shadow is the light of this sun. It alone gives life to the incorporeal. It perceives everything and bestows perception, since its shadow awakens all the senses for all creatures. Finally it loves each single thing, for each single thing is especially its own.

What then is the light of the sun? It is the shadow of God. So what is God? God is the sun of the sun; the light of the sun is God in the physical world, and God is the light of the sun above the intelligences of the angels. My shadow is such, O soul, that it is the most beautiful of all physical things. What do you suppose is the nature of my light? If this is the glory of my shadow, how much greater is the glory of my light? Do you love the light everywhere above all else? Indeed, do you love the light alone? Love only me, O soul, alone the infinite light; love me, the light, boundlessly, I say; then you will shine and be infinitely delighted.

Soul: Oh wonder, surpassing wonder itself! What strange fire consumes me now? What new sun is this, and whence does it shine upon me? What is this spirit, so powerful and so sweet, which at this moment pierces and soothes my inmost heart? Whence does it come? It bites and licks, goads and tickles. What bitter sweetness is this? Who could think it? This bitter sweetness melts me through and through and disembowels me. After this even the sweetest things seem bitter to me. What sweet bitterness it is which joins together my tom fragments, making me one again, by which even the most bitter is made sweet to me? How irresistible is this will! I cannot but desire the good itself; I may avoid or postpone anything else, but not this longing for the good. How freely chosen is this, necessity; for if I want to avoid it, I shall try to do so only because the avoidance itself is good. Nothing is more freely chosen than the good; because of it I desire all things; no, rather it is good which I desire in all things everywhere and desire in such a way that I do not even wish to be capable of not desiring it. Who would think it? How full of life is that death by which I die in myself but live in God, by which I die to be dead but life for life, and live for life

Letters   143

and rejoice in joy! Oh, pleasure beyond sense! Oh delight beyond mind! Oh joy beyond understanding! I am now out of my mind, but not mindless, because I am beyond mind. Again I am in a frenzy, all too great a frenzy; yet I do not fall to the ground; I am borne upward. Now I expand in every direction and overflow but am not dispersed, because God, the unity of unities, brings me to myself, because he makes me live with himself Therefore now rejoice with me, all you whose rejoicing is God. My God has come to me, the God of the universe has embraced me. The God of gods even now enters my inmost being. Now indeed God himself nourishes me wholly, and he who created me recreates me. He who brought forth the soul, transforms it into and, turns it into God. How shall I give thanks to you, O grace of graces? Teach me yourself, O grace of graces; I pray you teach me and be my guide. May that grace be to you which is your very self, O God.

LETTER 7

On divine frenzy

Marsilio Ficino to Peregrino Agli: greetings.

On November 29th my father, Ficino the doctor, brought to me at Figline two letters from you, one in verse and the other in prose. Having read these, I heartily congratulate our age for producing a young man whose name and fame may render it illustrious.

Indeed, my dearest Peregrino, when I consider your age and those things which come from you every day, I not only rejoice but much marvel at such great gifts in a friend. I do not know which of the ancients whose memory we respect, not to mention men of our own time, achieved so much at your age. This I ascribe not just to study and technique, but much more to divine frenzy. Without this, say Democritus and Plato, no man has ever been great. The powerful emotion and burning desire which your writings express prove, as I have said, that you are inspired and inwardly possessed by that frenzy; and this power, which is manifested in external movements, the ancient philosophers maintained was the most potent proof that the divine force dwelt in our souls. But since I have mentioned this frenzy, I shall relate the opinion of our Plato about it in a few words, with that brevity which a letter demands; so that you may easily understand what it is, how many kinds of it there are, and which god is responsible for each. I am sure that this description will not only please you, but also be of the very greatest use to you. Plato considers, as Pythagoras, Empedocles, and Heraclitus maintained earlier, that our soul, before it descended into bodies, dwelt in the abodes of heaven where, as Socrates says in the *Phaedrus*, it was nourished and rejoiced in the contemplation of youth.

Those philosophers I have just mentioned had learnt from Mercurius Trismegistus, the wisest of all the Egyptians, that God is the supreme source and light within whom shine the models of all things, which they call ideas. Thus, they believed, it followed that the soul, in steadfastly contemplating the eternal mind of God, also beholds with greater clarity the natures of all things. So, according to Plato, the soul saw justice itself, wisdom, harmony, and the marvelous beauty of the divine nature. And sometimes he calls all these natures 'ideas', sometimes 'divine essences', and sometimes 'first natures which exist in the eternal mind of God'. The minds of men, while they are there, are well nourished with perfect knowledge. But souls are depressed into bodies through thinking about and desiring earthly things. Then those who were previously fed on ambrosia and nectar, that is the perfect knowledge and bliss of God, in their descent are said to drink continuously of the river Lethe, that is forgetfulness of the divine. They do not fly back to heaven, whence they fell by weight of their earthly thoughts, until they begin to contemplate once more those divine natures which they have forgotten. The divine philosopher considers we achieve this through two virtues, one relating to moral conduct and the other to contemplation; one he names with a common term 'Justice', and the other 'wisdom'. For this reason, he says, souls fly hack to heaven on two wings, meaning, as I understand it, these virtues; and likewise Socrates teaches in *Phaedo* that we acquire these by the two parts of philosophy; namely the active and the contemplative. Hence, he says of again in *Phaedrus* that only the mind of a philosopher regains wings. On recovery of these wings, the soul is separated from the body by their power. Filled with God, it strives with all its might to reach the heavens, and thither it is drawn. Plato calls this drawing away and striving 'divine frenzy', and he divides it into four parts. He thinks that men never remember the divine unless they are stirred by its shadows or images as they may be described, which are perceived by the bodily senses.

Paul and Dionysius, the wisest of Christian theologians, affirm that the invisible things of God are understood from what has been made and is to be seen here, but Plato says that the wisdom of men is the image of divine wisdom. He thinks that the harmony which we make with musical instruments and voices is the image of divine harmony, and that the symmetry and comeliness that arise from the perfect union of the parts and members of the body are an image of divine beauty.

Since wisdom is present in no man, or at any rate in very few, and cannot be perceived by bodily sense, it follows that images of divine wisdom are very rare amongst us, hidden from our senses and totally ignored. Because of this, Socrates says in *Phaedrus* that the image of wisdom may not be seen at all by the eyes, because if it were it would deeply arouse that marvelous love of the divine wisdom of which it is an image.

But we do indeed perceive the reflection of divine beauty with our eyes and mark the resonance of divine harmony with our ears-those bodily senses which Plato considers the most perceptive of all. Thus when the soul has received through the physical senses those images which are within material objects, we remember what we knew before when we existed outside the prison of the body. The soul is fired by this memory and, shaking its wings, by degrees purges itself from contact with the body and its filth and becomes wholly possessed by divine frenzy. From the two senses I have just mentioned two kinds of frenzy are aroused. Regaining the memory of the true and divine beauty by the appearance of beauty that the eyes perceive, we desire the former with a secret and unutterable ardor of the mind. This Plato calls 'divine love', which he defines as the desire to return again to the contemplation of divine beauty; a desire arising from the sight of its physical likeness. Moreover, it is necessary for him who is so moved not only to desire that supernal beauty but also wholly to delight in its appearance which is revealed to his eyes. For Nature has so ordained that he who seeks anything should also delight in its image; but Plato holds it the mark of a dull mind and corrupt state if a man desires no more than the shadows of that beauty nor looks for anything beyond the form his eyes can see. For he believes that such a man is afflicted with the kind of love that is the companion of wantonness and lust. And he defines as irrational and heedless the love of that pleasure in physical form which is enjoyed by the senses.

Elsewhere he describes this love as the ardent desire of a soul which in a way is dead in its own body, while alive in another. He then says that the soul of a lover leads its life in another body. This the Epicureans follow when they say that love is a union of small particles, which they call atoms, made to penetrate the person from whom the images of beauty have been taken. Plato says that this kind of love is born of human sickness and is full of trouble and anxiety, and that it arises in those men whose mind is so covered over with darkness that it dwells on nothing exalted, nothing outstanding, nothing beyond the weak and transient image of this little body. It does not look up to the heavens, for in its black prison it is shuttered by night. But when those whose spirit is drawn away and freed from the clay of the body first see form and grace in any one, they rejoice, as at the reflection of divine beauty. But those people should at once recall to memory that divine beauty, which they should honor and desire above all; as it is by a burning desire for this beauty that they may be drawn to the heavens. This first attempt at flight Plato calls divine ecstasy and frenzy. I have already written enough about that frenzy which, I have said, arises through the eyes.

But the soul receives the sweetest harmonies and numbers through the ears, and by these echoes is reminded and aroused to the divine music which may be heard by the more subtle and penetrating sense of mind. According to the followers of Plato, divine music is twofold. One kind, they say, exists entirely in the eternal mind of God. The second is in the motions and order of the heavens, by which the heavenly spheres and their orbits make a marvelous harmony. In both of these our soul took part before it was imprisoned in our bodies. But it uses the ears as messengers, as though they were chinks in this darkness. By the ears, as I have already said, the soul receives the echoes of that incomparable music, by which it is led back to the deep and silent memory of the harmony which it previously enjoyed. The whole soul then kindles with desire to fly back to its rightful home, so that it may enjoy that true music again. It realizes that as long as it is enclosed in the dark abode of the body it can in no way reach that music. It therefore strives wholeheartedly to imitate it, because it cannot here enjoy its possession. Now with men this imitation is twofold. Some imitate the celestial music by harmony of voice and the sounds of various instruments, and these we call superficial and vulgar musicians. But some, who imitate the divine and heavenly harmony with deeper and sounder judgment, render a sense of its inner reason and knowledge into verse, feet and numbers. It is these who, inspired by the divine spirit, give forth with full voice the most solemn and glorious song. Plato calls this solemn music and poetry the most effective imitation of the celestial harmony. For the more superficial kind which I have just mentioned does no more than soothe with the sweetness of the voice, but poetry does what is also proper to divine harmony. It expresses with fire the most profound and, as a poet would say, prophetic meanings, in the numbers of voice and movement. Thus not only does it delight the ear, but brings to the mind the finest nourishment, most like the food of the gods; and so seems to come very close to God. In Plato's view, this poetic frenzy springs from the Muses; but he considers both the man and his poetry worthless who approaches the doors of poetry without the call of the Muses, in the hope that he will become a good poet by technique. He thinks that those poets who are possessed by divine inspiration and power often utter such supreme words when inspired by the Muses, that afterwards, when the rapture has left them, they themselves scarcely understand what they have uttered.

And, as I believe, the divine Plato considers that the Muses should be understood as divine songs; thus they say 'melody' and 'muse' take their name from 'song'. Hence divine men are inspired by divine beings and song to imitate them by employing the modes and meters of poetry. When Plato deals with the motion of the spheres in the *Republic*, he says that one siren is established within each orbit; meaning, as one Platonist says, that by the movement of the spheres song is offered to the gods. For 'siren' rightly means in Greek 'singing in honor of God'. And the ancient theologians maintained that the nine Muses were the musical songs of the eight spheres, and in addition the one great harmony arising from all the others.

Therefore, poetry springs from divine frenzy, frenzy from the Muses, and the Muses from Jove. The followers of Plato repeatedly call the soul of the whole universe Jove, who inwardly nourishes heaven and earth, the loving seas, the moon's shining orb, the stars and sun. Permeating every limb, he moves the whole mass and mingles with its vast substance. It is thus that the heavenly spheres are set in motion and governed by Jove, the

148 MARSILIO FICINO

spirit and mind of the whole universe, and that from him also arise the musical songs of these spheres, which are called the Muses. As that illustrious Platonist says, Jove is the origin of the Muses; all things are full of Jove, and that spirit which is called Jove is everywhere; he enlivens and fulfils all things. And as Alexander Milesius, the Pythagorean, says, 'touching the heavens as though they were a lyre, he creates this celestial harmony.' The divine prophet Orpheus says, 'Jove is first, Jove is last, Jove is the head, Jove is the center. The universe is born of Jove, Jove is the foundation of the earth and of the star-bearing heavens. Jove appears as man, yet he is the spotless bride. Jove is the breath and form of all things, Jove is the source of the ocean, Jove is the movement in the undying fire, Jove is the sun and moon, Jove, the King and Prince of all. Hiding his light, he has shed it afresh from his blissful heart, manifesting his purpose.' We may understand from this that all bodies are full of Jove; he contains and nourishes them, so that truly it is said that whatever you see and wherever you move is Jove.

After these follow the remaining kinds of divine frenzy, which Plato considers are twofold. One is centered in the mysteries, and the other, which he calls prophecy, concerns future events. The first, he says, is a powerful stirring of the soul, in perfecting what relates to the worship of the gods, religious observance, purification, and sacred ceremonies. But the tendency of mind which falsely imitates that frenzy he calls superstition. He considers the last kind of frenzy, in which he includes prophecy, to be nothing other than foreknowledge inspired by the divine spirit, which we properly call divination and prophecy. If the soul is fired in the act of divination he calls it frenzy; that is, when the mind, withdrawn from the body, is moved by divine rapture. But if someone foresees future events by human ingenuity rather than by divine inspiration, he thinks that this should be named foresight or inference. From all this it is now clear that there are four kinds of divine frenzy: love, poetry, the mysteries, and prophecy. That common and completely insane love is a false copy of divine love; superficial music, of poetry; superstition, of the mysteries; and prediction, of prophecy. According to Plato, Socrates attributes the first kind of frenzy to Venus, the second to the Muses, the third to Dionysius, and the last to Apollo.

I have chosen to describe at greater length the frenzy belonging to divine love and poetry for two reasons: first, because I know you are strongly moved by both of these; and second, so that you will remember that what is written by you comes not from you but from Jove and the Muses, with whose spirit and divinity you are filled. For this reason, my Pellegrino, you will act justly and rightly if you acknowledge, as I believe you do already, that the author and cause of what is best and greatest is not you, nor indeed any other man, but immortal God.

Farewell, and be sure that nothing is dearer to me than you are.

1st December 1457
Figline.

LETTER 115

What happiness is; that it has degrees; that it is eternal

Marsilio Ficino to the magnanimous Lorenzo de' Medici: greetings.

At Careggi recently, when you and I had discussed at length many aspects of happiness, we eventually arrived through reason at the same conclusion. You then perceptively discovered fresh proofs why happiness lies in the action of will rather than the action of intellect. You wanted to set down that discussion in verse, and wished me to do so in prose. You have just fulfilled your duty with an elegant poem and so, God willing, I will now carry out my task as briefly as possible.

There are reckoned to be three kinds of human good. These are of course the benefits of fortune, of the body and of the soul. The benefits of fortune consist in wealth, honor, favor and power. And so to begin at the beginning; wealth is not the highest good, as Midas believed, for it is sought and acquired not for its own sake but for the convenience of the body and soul. Nor are honor and favor the highest good, as Augustus used to say, since they are at the discretion of another and are often not experienced by us; and very often, they are bestowed or withdrawn irrespective of merit. Nor is power the highest good, as Caesar maintained, since the more people we control, the more acutely are we harassed by worries, the more dangers we are subject to, the more men and the more business we have to serve, and the more enemies we have.

The benefits of the body consist in strength, health and beauty.

Strength and health are not the supreme good, as Milo of Crotona seemed to think, for we are cast down by the most trifling discomforts; nor is beauty, so much honored by Herillus the Sceptic. No one, however beautiful, could live content in this alone, and beauty is a benefit for others rather than for the beautiful themselves.

Some benefits belong to the irrational and others to the rational part of the soul. The benefits of the irrational part are the keenness of the senses and their enjoyment. Aristippus thought that the highest good lay in both of these. We believe that happiness lies in neither; not in keenness of sense, for in this we are surpassed by many animals and a keen sense generally disgusts as often as it delights; nor does the highest good consist in the enjoyment of the senses, for this is preceded by longing, accompanied by doubt and followed by regret. One short pleasure is purchased by much prolonged pain. And the intensity of this kind of pleasure lasts only as long as the demands of the body; consider how drink is sweet only as long as one is thirsty. But every demand of the body is a kind of annoyance. Sensual pleasure, therefore, because it is frequently mixed with its opposite, that is pain, is neither pure nor true, nor does it satisfy. And if anyone says that there are some sensual pleasures which do not spring from the demands of the body, I reply that these are so weak that no one finds any happiness in them. Indeed, let no one venture to ascribe happiness to that state which consists of the keenness and delight of the senses, since this state is false, fleeting and anxious. Trifling amusements do not satisfy the soul, which by natural inclination seeks finer things.

Some good qualities of the rational part of the soul arc said to be natural, such as a keen intellect, memory and a bold and ready will. Happiness is not in these, for used well they are indeed good, but badly used they arc evil. Other good qualities of the rational part of the soul, such as the moral and reflective virtues, are acquired. Is happiness found in moral conduct, as the Stoics and Cynics believe? Certainly not, for the practice of moral virtues such as moderation and endurance is full of toil and difficulty. We will not find the goal we seek in toil, but in rest, for we are endlessly busy to enjoy leisure, and wage war to live in peace. Besides, right conduct is never sought for its own sake but put to use, like a medicine, for cleansing and calming the mind. Neither is Epicurean peace the ultimate goal. For the

Letters 151

use of a still mind is the contemplation of truth, as the use of a clear sky is to admit sunlight.

Does happiness then reside in the virtues of reflection, such as the contemplation of truth? Certainly, it does. But there is, so to speak, contemplation of different kinds: sub-celestial, celestial and super-celestial. Democritus set as his goal the first of these. Anaxagoras was not satisfied with this, because the celestial is higher than the sub-celestial, but he was willing to be content in the contemplation of the celestial for, he said, he was born to contemplate that, and heaven was his homeland. But Aristotle disagreed with this because the consideration of the super-celestial seemed to him altogether more deserving. He thought happiness consisted in the highest activity of the highest power directed to the highest purpose. The soul trapped in a body is able to consider these things in one way, and the soul which is free in another. Aristotle believed that man in the first state is happy, but our Plato denied this, since consideration of the divine in this life is always mixed with uncertainty of intellect and unsteadiness of will. So, according to Plato, true happiness is the property of the soul which, when freed from the body, contemplates the divine. Both angels and God are accounted divine. Avicenna and Al Ghazzali seem to maintain that the soul will be happy in contemplating angels. The Platonists refute this for two reasons. The first is that it is the nature of our intellect to look for the cause of things, and then the cause beyond this cause. For this reason, the search of the intellect never ceases, except it discovers the cause behind which there is no cause, but is itself the cause of causes, and that is God alone. The second reason is that the desire of the will cannot be satisfied by any good so long as we think that some other good remains beyond; therefore it is only satisfied with that good beyond which there is no other. What else is this but God? Therefore in God alone may the search of the intellect and the desire of the will come to rest. The happiness of man therefore consists in God alone, from which it follows that nothing can rest except in its own cause. And since God alone is the real cause of the soul it rests in God alone. But we discussed these things more fully in the *Theology of the Immortality of Soul*.

However, there are two activities of the soul in its relationship to God, for it sees God through the intellect and it rejoices in the knowledge of Him through will. Plato calls the vision ambrosia, the joy, nectar, and the

MARSILIO FICINO

intellect and will, twin wings by which we may fly back to God, as though to our father and homeland. This is why, he says, when pure souls ascend to heaven they feed at the divine table on ambrosia and nectar.

In that happiness the joy surpasses the vision. For as we find more merit with God in this life by loving Him than by searching for Him, so the reward in the next life is greater for loving than searching. We find far more merit by loving than by searching for many reasons. First, because no one in this life truly knows God. But a man truly loves God, no matter how he understands Him, if he despises everything else for His sake. Second, just as it is worse to hate God than to be ignorant of Him, so it is better to love Him than to know Him. Third, we may make ill use of the knowledge of God, for instance through pride. We cannot misuse the love for Him. Fourth, the man who looks for God pays Him no tribute, but he who loves Him yields to God both himself and all he possesses. So it is that God gives Himself to the lover rather than the investigator. Fifth, in investigating God, we take a long time to make very little progress, but by loving Him we make much progress in a very short time. The reason love unites the mind with God more swiftly, closely and firmly than cognition is that the power of cognition lies mainly in making distinctions but the power of love lies in union. Sixth, by loving God, not only do I experience greater joy than by seeking Him out, but we are made better people. For these reasons we may conclude that the reward of loving is greater than that of human enquiry.

It befits the lover to enjoy and rejoice in the beloved for that is the aim of love, but it befits the seeker to see. Thus joy in a happy man surpasses vision. Besides we desire to see in order to rejoice; we do not seek to rejoice in order to see. We can find the cause for our desire to see, but we cannot find the cause for our desire to rejoice, other than the very joy itself, as though it is desired for its own sake. We do not desire simply to see, but to see those things that make us rejoice, in a way that makes us rejoice. Nature herself never rejects any joy, but she sometimes rejects cognition, and indeed she rejects life too if she thinks that it will be very burdensome; so that delight is not only the seasoning of cognition but also of life itself. When this is removed everything seems tasteless. Joy is richer than cognition, for not every man that knows rejoices, but those who rejoice necessarily know. Just as nature considers it worse to suffer misery

Letters 153

than ignorance, so it is better to rejoice than to know. And just as nature always and everywhere avoids pain on its own account and everything connected with it as being the greatest evil, so she pursues pleasure on its own account, and other things connected with it, as being the I highest good. Since the power of cognition, as l have said before, lies mainly in making distinctions, but the power of love lies in union, we are united more closely with God through the joy of love than through cognition, for joy transforms us into beloved God. Just as it is not the man who sees the good, but he who desires it, that becomes good, so likewise the soul becomes divine, not by considering God but by loving Him; as timber becomes fire because it draws heat, not light, from the flame. Hence, since the soul is not goodness itself what is good for it must be sought outside its own nature. It follows that a turn of the will, so that will is directed towards what is outside, is more truly based on goodness itself than an intellectual concept which remains something purely internal. For the intellect grasps the object by a kind of imagery, but will strives to transfer itself to its object by natural impulse. Desire, which is wide-ranging and continual, is rooted in being since all created things are always desiring something. Cognition acts through images that are received; it is the property of few beings and is intermittent. Therefore the enjoyment of goodness is more substantial through the medium of desire than through the vision of cognition.

If God were to separate the mind from the will and keep the two apart, the mind might seem to retain its previous form, for it would still be a form of reason; but the will might change its form since it would be a desire lacking the power to choose, a property of reason. But the mind would not enjoy any further good at all; it would be like a creature without taste; nothing would please it; it would find nothing good, nor would it be agreeable to itself or anything else. But will would continue to enjoy to the full some goodness of its own. Therefore enjoyment of the highest good seems to be the property of will rather than intellect. The end of movement, that is happiness, rightly pertains to will, since that is the aim of movement at its outset. The intellect, understanding things, not so much through their nature but rather through its own, seems to draw things towards itself and for that reason it cannot really be said to move the soul. Since will desires to perceive things as they are in themselves, it draws the soul to things outside itself; and therefore it is will that is the origin of movement. Moreover the end of all movement is outside the soul but is finally connected to the soul as form. Through will the soul greatly rejoices in this end, for the labourer is worthy of his hire. The concern and impulse to attain the good and to avoid evil are based on desire. The will receives a greater reward from God than the intellect, not only because it enjoys Him more fully, but also because the discovery of happiness belongs to will. The more ardently a man loves, the happier he becomes in that he approaches the very substance of happiness itself. What shall we add to this? Since far more people can love God ardently than can know him clearly, the way of love is safer to mankind and far more suitable for the infinite good, which wishes to impart itself to as many as possible.

So it is through will that happiness is attained. Again, what more? Free movement is the property of reasonable beings, and because it is free a man may therefore advance beyond any finite limit whatever, to achieve all that he deserves, so that he can rise above the bliss of many of the angels; indeed, we can rise above them by loving and rejoicing rather than by apprehending. Therefore, by cognising God, we reduce His size to the capacity and understanding of our mind; but by loving Him we enlarge our mind to the immeasurable breadth of divine goodness. By the first we bring God down to our own scale, by the second we raise ourselves to God. For our cognition is measured by our capacity to understand; but we love Him not only as far as we perceive Him but also as far as we may conceive His divine goodness extending beyond what we can clearly see. When dimly and feebly we look into the depth of God's infinity, our love burns warmly and eagerly and so does our joy. Vision is not the measure of joy as some believe, for he who sees little may love much and vice versa.

Finally, the highest good for the soul is what satisfies it, but it is not really satisfied with its own vision of God. For the vision perceived by the eyes of the soul is a created thing and limited by degrees of perfection, just as the soul is. Yet the soul is never satisfied with any created or finite good. So vision is not the highest good. The soul is satisfied by the God who is seen, rather than by the seeing of Him. The enjoyment of the good in sensual perception arises not because the good moves sense but because sense is reflected, turned towards and diffused in the good which is presented to it. This spiritual turning and diffusion is delight, as we explained in our book on delight. Thus, even for the mind which has been separated from

Letters

the body, so to speak, the enjoyment of God does not primarily arise because God reveals Himself to the mind, which in any case is an act of God rather than our own, but it arises because the mind turns to God, and this is joy.

It should not be thought that the soul turns to the vision of God to rest in that, but turns rather to the God who is seen; it desires the vision for what is seen which becomes joined to the soul as form. In the according to its measure of goodness, in infinite goodness it finds infinite rest. But if the soul, even while involved in the movement of the body, chooses the happiness that is free from all change, it will do so far more when it is beyond movement. Nor can the lower parts of the soul divert the higher ones from this state, since the lower will yield to the higher forever, when the soul turns toward the infinite existence of God.

Lastly, if ever the soul had to be separated from this state, either the soul would not realize it, in which case being ignorant of God it could not be happy; or else it would know, in which case it could not be happy either, for it would be sick and afraid. Therefore, he who once finds happiness in God finds it forever. Read happily, happy Lorenzo, what your Marsilio Ficino has written here about happiness, much of which you discovered yourself. The subject is treated briefly here as befits a letter, but more thoroughly in the books on *Love* and on *Theology*.

The end. Praise be to God.

Farewell.

10

PIETRO POMPONAZZI
(1462–1525)

Exposition of Aristotle's First Book On the Parts of Animals

TOMÁŠ NEJESCHLEBA

INTRODUCTION

Pietro Pomponazzi is widely considered the most important proponent of Renaissance Aristotelianism.[1] Born in Mantua, he studied philosophy and medicine in Padua, which was a bastion of Aristotelianism in the fifteenth and sixteenth centuries. After obtaining his doctoral degree, Pomponazzi taught natural philosophy first in Padua, then shortly thereafter in Ferrara, finally residing in Bologna from 1512 until his death. Pomponazzi became a popular and respected teacher as an interpreter of Aristotle and had many students and supporters.

Pomponazzi's writings focus heavily on natural philosophy, which included his doctrine on the soul. He commented on Aris-

---

1. Jill Kraye, "Pietro Pomponazzi (1462–1525): Secular Aristotelianism in the Renaissance," in *Philosophers of the Renaissance*, ed. Paul Richard Blum (Washington, D.C.: The Catholic University of America Press, 2010), 92–115; José Manuel García Valverde, "Pietro Pomponazzi," in *Encyclopedia of Renaissance Philosophy*, ed. Marco Sgarbi (Cham: Springer, 2017); and Paul Oskar Kristeller, *Eight Philosophers of the Italian Renaissance* (Stanford, Calif.: Stanford University Press, 1964).

Exposition of Aristotle's First Book On the Parts of Animals   157

totle's book *On the Soul* at the end of the fifteenth century, and his *Treatise on the Immortality of the Soul*, published in 1516,[2] caused wide controversy. This work seemingly contradicted a declaration of the V. Lateran council, from 1513, which forbade the teaching of mortality, including Alexander of Aphrodisias's materialistic interpretation of Aristotle. Alexander of Aphrodisias argued for the unity of the human soul, called "monopsychism," which was the Averroist interpretation of Aristotle. In the treatise, Pomponazzi analyzes the positions of Averroes, Plato, Thomas Aquinas, and Alexander of Aphrodisias with respect to two methodological criteria: firstly, a pure philosophical solution, that is, without any reference to revelation, and secondly, conformity with Aristotle's thought. According to Pomponazzi, both criteria are fulfilled in Alexander's view, which considered the human soul as individual and mortal, since the activity of the rational soul is bound with imagination and senses, which cease in unison with the death of the body. Thus, Alexander's position seems to be the most probable. Pomponazzi concludes that the immortality of the soul is a neutral problem and not solvable by means of philosophy. It is an article of faith, and Pomponazzi's approach thus entails fideism.

A real battle for the soul was initiated.[3] Many contemporary scholars were involved in it,[4] and Pomponazzi had to write his defense and his *Apologia*.[5] The accusation of heresy also played a role in the controversy. Though Pomponazzi was never condemned, the affair led him to hold off from publishing his other main writings. Therefore, his other substantial texts—the books *De incantationibus* and *De fato, libero arbitrio et de praedestinatione*—were published posthumously.[6] In these, Pomponazzi

2. Pietro Pomponazzi, "On the Immortality of the Soul," in *The Renaissance Philosophy of Man*, ed. Ernst Cassirer, Paul Oskar Kristeller, and John Herman Randall Jr., trans. William Henry Hay (Chicago: University of Chicago Press, 1948), 280–386.

3. Martin L. Pine, *Pietro Pomponazzi: Radical Philosopher of the Renaissance* (Padova: Antenore, 1986).

4. Cf., for example, Gasparo Contarini, *De immortalitate animae / On the Immortality of the Soul*, ed. Paul Richard Blum (Nordhausen: Traugott Bautz, 2020). Cf. Paul Richard Blum, "The Immortality of the Soul," in *The Cambridge Companion to Renaissance Philosophy*, ed. James Hankins (Cambridge: Cambridge University Press, 2007), 211–33.

5. Pietro Pomponazzi, *Tractatus acutissimi utillimi & mere peripatetici* (Venetiis: Arte & sumptibus heredum O. Scoti, 1525); Pietro Pomponazzi, *Tutti i trattati peripatetici*, ed. Francesco Paolo Raimondi and José Manuel García Valverde (Milano: Bompiani, 2013).

6. Pietro Pomponazzi, *Opera: De naturalium effectuum admirandorum causis, seu, De incantationibus liber; item De fato, libero arbitrio, praedestinatione, providentia Dei, libri V.* (Basileae: Ex officina Henricpetrina, 1567).

uses the same approach to philosophy as in *De immortalitate*, wherein the connection of the intellect to the imagination and the senses is emphasized. In his naturalistic approach, the subject of natural philosophy is the body, potentially perceived by senses. Thus, natural philosophy must be based on the sensory cognition of primary qualities.

With respect to this methodology, in *De incantationibus*, Pomponazzi strives to achieve a natural explanation of all events that are wrongly assessed as miracles. Each phenomenon viewed as allegedly supernatural has, in reality, natural causes within a deterministic cosmos, which was ordered by God, who as the prime mover is the first cause. A supernatural miracle would be a violation of the order established by God. In such a cosmos, any free decision is the illusion, says Pomponazzi in *De fato*. Each act, even human acts, must have its cause. A certain cause can be identified in every choice, and choices thus cannot be considered free. Although Pomponazzi presents himself as Aristotelian philosopher in *De immortalitate*, he rather follows Stoicism than Aristotelianism here. Both *De incantationibus* and *De fato*, however, end with fideism, stressing the opposition of reason and faith. The separation of philosophy from theology is considered the most important result of Pomponazzi's teaching and comprises a crucial part of his legacy.

Pomponazzi's *Exposition* of Aristotle's *De partibus animalium* from 1521 is the first Renaissance commentary of this zoological writing.[7] In the eighth lecture of the first book, Pomponazzi deals with the issue of natural philosophy and surprisingly criticizes Aristotle's approach as inconsistent. In this text, Pomponazzi also touches on the topic of the immortality of the soul and a strict distinction between truths of faith and philosophy.

BIBLIOGRAPHY

Primary Sources

Contarini, Gasparo. *De immortalitate animae / On the Immortality of the Soul*. Edited by Paul Richard Blum. Nordhausen: Traugott Bautz, 2020.

Pomponazzi, Pietro. *Expositio super primo et secundo De partibus animalium*. Edited by Stefano Perfetti. Firenze: Leo S. Olschki editore, 2004.

7. Pietro Pomponazzi, *Expositio super primo et secundo De partibus animalium*, ed. Stefano Perfetti (Firenze: Leo S. Olschki editore, 2004).

———. "On the Immortality of the Soul." In *The Renaissance Philosophy of Man*, edited by Ernst Cassirer, Paul Oskar Kristeller, and John Herman Randall Jr., translated by William Henry Hay, 280–386. Chicago: University of Chicago Press, 1948.

———. *Tractatus acutissimi utillimi & mere peripatetici*. Venetiis: Arte & sumptibus heredum O. Scoti, 1525.

———. *Tutti i trattati peripatetici*. Edited by Francesco Paolo Raimondi and José Manuel García Valverde. Milano: Bompiani, 2013.

———. *Opera: De naturalium effectuum admirandorum causis, seu, De incantationibus liber; item De fato, libero arbitrio, praedestinatione, providentia Dei, libri V*. Basileae: Ex officina Henricpetrina, 1567.

Secondary Sources

Blum, Paul Richard. "The Immortality of the Soul." In *The Cambridge Companion to Renaissance Philosophy*, edited by James Hankins, 211–33. Cambridge: Cambridge University Press, 2007.

Kraye, Jill. "Pietro Pomponazzi (1462–1525): Secular Aristotelianism in the Renaissance." In *Philosophers of the Renaissance*, edited by Paul Richard Blum and translated by Brian McNeil, 92–115. Washington, D.C.: The Catholic University of America Press, 2010.

Kristeller, Paul Oskar. *Eight Philosophers of the Italian Renaissance*. Stanford, Calif.: Stanford University Press, 1964.

Pine, Martin L. *Pietro Pomponazzi: Radical Philosopher of the Renaissance*. Padova: Antenore, 1986.

Valverde, José Manuel García. "Pietro Pomponazzi." In *Encyclopedia of Renaissance Philosophy*, edited by Marco Sgarbi. Cham: Springer, 2017.

PIETRO POMPONAZZI

Exposition of Aristotle's First Book On the Parts of Animals[8]

LECTURE 8

In the previous lecture, Aristotle asked whether the work of the natural philosopher is to examine all types of the soul. Aristotle responded that the natural philosopher should not examine the intellective soul, that is, the mind. He seems to ground his proof of this on three arguments.

---

8. Pietro Pomponazzi, *Expositio super primo et secundo De partibus animalium*, ed. Stefano Perfetti (Firenze: Leo S. Olschki editore, 2004), 41–49.

The first argument was as follows: If the natural philosopher would examine the intellective soul, he would examine intelligible things. However, since the natural philosopher examines also sensible things, he would examine both the intelligible and the sensible. But everything that exists is either sensible or intelligible. Therefore, the natural philosopher would examine everything. Then other sciences would be superfluous, and natural science alone would be sufficient.[9]

The second argument was as follows: The natural philosopher examines the form that is a principle of a motion. There are three kinds of motion: in quantity, in quality, and locomotion. But the intellective soul is not the principle of any of these motions. Thus, the natural philosopher does not examine the intellective soul.

The third argument follows. The natural philosopher should not examine things separated from matter. But the intellective soul is separated from matter. The major premise is proved, so that the natural philosopher examines only things in which there is an efficient and a final cause. However, things separated from matter do not have an efficient or a final cause, since they are eternal.

It seems that this was Aristotle's opinion in the previous lecture.

Dear gentlemen. This issue is the most important. Everything depends on it, since there is nothing better than to know whether our soul is mortal or immortal. But this issue is very difficult.

I have two doubts concerning this issue. The first doubt concerns the conclusion, the second concerns Aristotle's reasoning. Therefore, my first argument will be the proof that Aristotle's conclusion is false. Then I will prove that Aristotle's reasoning is fallacious.

In respect of the first doubt, the conclusion seems to be false, that is that the natural philosopher does not examine the intellective soul. The book *On the Soul* deals with the intellective soul, and this book deals with natural philosophy and is ranked among books on natural philosophy. From this reason Avicenna calls the book *On the Soul*, which he wrote, the sixth book of natural philosophy.

---

9. Michael Ephesius, *In Libros De partibus animalium, De animalium motione, De animalia incessu Commentaria*, ed. Michael Hayduck (Berlin: Georg Reimer, 1904), 7, lines 2–5. Cf. Latin translation of Dominicus Monthesaurus, Michael Ephesius, *Scholia, id est, Brevis sed erudita atque utilis interpretatio in IIII. Libros Aristotelis De partibus animalium* (Basileae: per Petrum Pernam, 1559), 20.

Exposition of Aristotle's First Book On the Parts of Animals   161

Do you say that among books *On the Soul,* which Aristotle wrote, the first two deal with natural philosophy and the third does not? Then I respond that you are not correct in saying so, since Aristotle is not in the habit of making such a mixture, that is, mixing together natural science and metaphysics. For, apart from the books *On the Soul,* Aristotle examines many issues about the soul, for instance, in the book *On Sense and the Sensible,* in the book *On Life and Death,* etc. All three books in *On the Soul* deal with natural philosophy, but in the third book of *On the Soul,* he deals with the intellective soul. Therefore, the opinion that the natural philosopher does not examine the intellective soul is false.

Moreover, in the second book of *The Physics,*[10] Aristotle asks which forms are reached by the musings of natural philosophy and where its limit is. He says that the natural philosopher examines everything except the human soul, and the Commentator states that the thoughts of natural philosophy stop at the last material and the first separated thing.[11] But this is the intellective soul, which is on the boundary and in between the material and the separated. This is why he says that the intellective soul was created on the horizon of the eternity.[12]

Until this point, the argument has been supported by authority. Now, it will be shown through reason that Aristotle's conclusion is false.

The first argument: Since the natural philosopher should examine everything that concerns physical and sensible matter, and the intellective soul is related to physical matter, the natural philosopher can therefore study the intellective soul. The major premise is known from many places (in Aristotle's works) and is accepted by everybody. The minor premise is obvious from the definition of the soul. That is to say, that the soul is the "act of a physical organic body, having life in potentiality."[13] It is clear that the physical is put in the definition. Therefore, the natural philosopher should study the intellective soul.

The same thing is apparent from another definition of the soul that

---

10. Aristotle, *Phys.* II, 2, 194b9–15.

11. Averroes, *Commentarium in Libros Physicorum,*" in *Aristotelis Opera cum Averrois Commentariis,* vol. IV (Venetiis: Apud Iunctas, 1562; reprint, Frankfurt am Main: Minerva, 1962), comm. 26, f59r A-D.

12. *Liber de Causis,* ed. Adriaan Pattin, *Tijdschrift Voor Filosofie* 28 (1966): 90–203; 138, lines 80–82.

13. Aristotle, *De an.* II, 1, 412a28.

reads: "the soul is the principle of vegetative, sensitive, intellective powers, and of locomotion."[14] It seems, therefore, that the soul is the principle of a kind of motion.

Moreover, the natural philosopher should study everything that is moving and is moved. The intellective soul is moving and is moved; therefore, it is a subject of natural philosophy. The major premise is apparent from the second book of *The Physics*, where it is said that everything that is moving and is moved is studied in physics.[15] The minor premise is obvious, since the intellective soul seems to be transforming continuously. We begin to know, we begin to want, and we are continuously transformed from ignorance to knowledge. Sometimes, we seem to know something; sometimes, we seem to not know the same thing. Sometimes, we are of a certain opinion, sometimes of another. Therefore, our intellect seems to be transforming continuously. Therefore, it seems to be moving and moved.

Moreover, the study of natural philosophy must be conducted wherever one can find an efficient cause and a final cause, and where something truly new can be found. One can find an efficient cause, a final cause, and something new in the intellective soul. It is proved by Aristotle, who states that the agent intellect makes what is known in potentiality known in actuality. There are new things in the soul, since sometimes we forget, and sometimes, something casts back to our mind.

Therefore, Aristotle's conclusion seems to be false. That is all on the first doubt.

Concerning the second doubt, Aristotle's reasoning seems to be fallacious. Firstly, let's have a look at the first argument, where it is said that, if the natural philosopher were to deal with the intellective soul, then other sciences would be superfluous and only natural science would be sufficient. If the argument was not made by Aristotle, it would be ridiculous, since it contains multiple errors. Firstly, Aristotle's argument is based upon the notion that if the natural philosopher were to study the intellective soul, and consequently he would have to deal with an intelligible object, then he would have to examine everything that is intelligible. This is a completely false notion. Although he would study an intelligible thing, it

14. Aristotle, *De an.* II, 2, 413b11–13.
15. Aristotle, *Phys.* II, 7, 198a27–28.

Exposition of Aristotle's First Book On the Parts of Animals 163

does not mean that he would examine *all* intelligible things and in all possible ways. If I think about you, it does not mean that I think about you in all possible ways. Even if we admit that he would have to study all intelligible things, Aristotle's argument still seems to be mistaken. I can ask Aristotle whether the intellective soul is studied by someone. Surely Aristotle must agree that the intellective soul is studied by someone. Then, since he neglects that it is studied by a natural philosopher, he must say that it is studied by a metaphysician. Now we proceed as follows: The intellective soul is studied by a metaphysician; therefore, natural philosophy is superfluous. At the beginning of the proof, I say that metaphysics deals with all intelligible things, ergo, it deals with the intellective soul. If this argument is not valid against Aristotle, then Aristotle's argument is also not valid. If Aristotle's argument is valid, then my argument against Aristotle is also valid. This is the end of the proof.

Furthermore, Aristotle states, that "while examining the senses he examines sensible things, and while examining the intellect he examines intelligible things."[16] From this statement, he deduces that other sciences concerning intelligible things are superfluous because the natural philosopher examines the intellective soul. Therefore, what he wants to say is: If the natural philosopher examines the intellective soul, other sciences that deal with intelligible things are superfluous. In spite of this, he does not conclude that other sciences that deal with sensible things are superfluous, since mathematics deals with sensible things and medicine deals with sensible things, and these are not superfluous. Why did Aristotle not conclude that the other sciences are superfluous, since the natural philosopher examines sensible things similarly, as he did with sciences on intelligible things? Aristotle's first argument, therefore, seems to be groundless and extremely erroneous.

Also, Aristotle's second argument seems to be wrong. The argument was as follows. The natural philosopher deals with the soul, which is a principle of motion. The intellective soul, however, is not a principle of motion, since it is not a principle of motion with respect to quantity, quality, or locomotion. Therefore, the natural philosopher does not study the intellective soul. Quantitative motion is incremental motion, qualitative mo-

16. Aristotle, *De part. an.* I, 1, 641b1–4.

tion pertains to the sensitive soul, and locomotion pertains to the soul as far as it is moved with respect to a place.

However, there is another question. When Aristotle stated that motion with respect to quantity pertains to the sensitive soul and that the sensitive soul is the principle of alteration, it means either alteration with respect to corruption or alteration with respect to perfection. When it is said that the sensitive soul is the principle of an alteration with respect to corruption, it is not true, since senses as senses do not heat or cool. For this reason, the sensitive soul is the principle of an alteration with respect to perfection. Furthermore, the intellective soul is the principle of an alteration with respect to perfection. For Aristotle in the third book *On the Soul* states that the intellect is perfected in a similar way to the senses.[17] Ergo, the intellect is perfected in a similar way to the senses, and since the senses are the subject of study in physics, therefore, the intellect also has to be a subject of study in physics. Moreover, in the third book *On the Soul*, Aristotle determines the principle of locomotion and states that the intellect and will are the principle of motion with respect to places.[18] How could Aristotle in this book say the contrary?

Aristotle's third argument seems to be no less defective. The argument was as follows. The natural philosopher should not examine things separated from matter. The intellective soul is separated from matter. Therefore, the natural philosopher should not examine the intellective soul. I state that Aristotle was right in saying that the natural philosopher does not examine things separated from matter. The intellective soul, however, is not completely separated from matter, since it cannot be separated from a body. Were it separated from matter, it would have some operations without a body. Aristotle, nevertheless, states the contrary, since no man remains after death.[19] A man does not have an intellection without a phantasma.[20] The argument, thus, seems to be false.

So, it has been proved that all three of Aristotle's arguments are false.

I would like to be a pupil in this field and have someone who would

---

17. Aristotle, *De an.* III, 2, 429b29–430a2. Cf. Averroes, *Commentarium Magnum in Aristotelis De Anima libros*, ed. F. Stuart Crawford, Corpus Commentariorum Averrois in Aristotelem (Cambridge, Mass.: The Medieval Academy of America, 1953), III, 14, 428–33.

18. Aristotle, *De an.* III, 10, passim.

19. Aristotle, *De an.* III, 5, 430a24.

20. An image in the mind derived from sense perception.

Exposition of Aristotle's First Book On the Parts of Animals 165

teach me. When I was a young man, I used to express my opinions thoughtlessly, and I thought that I knew everything. But now, as an old man, I do not know what to say, and the same thing happens to me as did to St. Peter, who told Christ with great boldness: "I will never disown you even if I have to die with you."[21] Later, after he had disowned him three times, Christ said to him: "Peter, do you believe in me?" He shrugged, because he remembered that he had disowned him.[22] It happens to me. When I was younger, oh, oh, I was so learned. I risked my own skin and now, surrendered lying on my back, I do not know what to say. I believe that the arguments I raised against Aristotle will persuade you if you have listened to me carefully.

Avicenna, Albert the Great, and the Commentator [Averroes] wrote about this book of *On the Parts of Animals*. Avicenna, however, did not write about this first book; he wrote only on three books. The Commentator wrote a paraphrase,[23] and he confirms this explicitly in the corresponding part. He states that the natural philosopher should examine the intellective soul, since the natural philosopher should examine the principle of a motion. This is the soul; therefore, the natural philosopher examines the intellective soul. Albert says that the task of natural philosophy is not to examine intelligences, but its task is to examine well the human intellective soul, according to its essence and perfection. Therefore, Albert says, when Aristotle states that the natural philosopher does not examine the intellective soul, he meant the soul of intelligences, not the human soul.[24] You can see that there is no problem if this position is true. On the other hand, we have to say that the available text is false, since the words do not sound that way.

However, I will show you, that their exposition, that is, that of the Commentator and Albert the Great, is not convenient. Alberto, the lord of Carpi, employed a Greek who interpreted this book of *On the Parts of Animals*; this man was called Michael of Ephesos. I had the book sent to

21. Matthew 26:35.

22. John 21:17.

23. Averroes, *Paraphrasis de Partibus Animalium*, in *Aristotelis Opera cum Averrois Commentariis*, vol. VI (Venetiis: Apud Iunctas, 1592; reprint, Frankfurt am Main: Minerva, 1962), f121rD.

24. Albertus Magnus, *De Animalibus Libri XXVI;*, ed. Hermann Stadler, vol. 1, *Beiträge zur Geschichte der Philosophie des Mittelalters* (Münster: Aschendorff, 1916), XI, tr. 1, c. 3, 774–75.

me, and I asked a certain man from Carpi to bring it to me. That part of the book was translated for me by people who know Greek. They told me that this Greek interpreter does not add anything and does not shatter Aristotle's words with respect to the interpretation of Theodor Gaza. Now you can see the difficulty of the issue.

So, what can I say? I confess that I am perplexed and would like to have someone who could teach me. For Aristotle in the second book of *Rhetoric* and Plato in *The Republic* state that young men are ambitious and profess to know everything but old men do not do it because they singed their feathers.[25] And I am an old man.

It is usually said that the being of the intellective soul is two-fold, that is, separated and complex, and that the unity of the agent and the possible intellect is not natural. All of this seems to me to be nonsense, since I have never seen Aristotle speaking about the other world, and Aristotle denies that the intellective soul would have a principle of a motion.

So, what shall we say?[26]

Strabo reports that Aristotle's books were distorted because someone put them on the ground, and they lay there for many years. Therefore, by the time that they were found, they had been gnawed at.[27] This is why one person says this and another one that. Everyone interpreted them in his own way since they could not clearly grasp what he said because of the corruption of the text.

I, however, can say two things about this issue. One thing is clear: I do not know and I am perplexed. The second thing I can say, although I say it unwillingly and I also touched upon it earlier, is that in my opinion, Aristotle did not consider the intellective soul to be immortal but mortal, generable, and corruptible. Aristotle considered it similar to other souls, since he stated in the previous lecture that the intellect or the mind is not in any animal.[28] Therefore, I think that Aristotle was of the opinion that the soul is mortal. Even Scotus was of the same opinion with respect to Aristotle's thought. Our intellect is some kind of sense, and the word intellect is used

25. Cf. Aristotle, *Rhet.* II, 12–13, 1389b13–17; Plato, *Rep.* I, 329a2–9.
26. Note by the scribe: "He curses, swears, and says it is the pen's fault."
27. Strabo, *The Geography of Strabo*, ed. Horace Leonard Jones and J. R. Sitlington Sterrett (London: Heinemann; Cambridge, Mass.: Harvard University Press, 1960), XIII, 1, 54.
28. Aristotle, *De part. an.* I, 1, 641b8.

Exposition of Aristotle's First Book On the Parts of Animals 167

metaphorically. For Aristotle states that the intellect or the mind is not in any animal if we are speaking about the true intellect. Our intellect is not the true intellect,[29] but the intellect of intelligences is the true intellect. Their intellection, according to Aristotle, does not have a beginning but exists due to their substances, and there is no alteration in them. For according to theologians, only in God is nothing new. Our intellect in Aristotle's opinion is mortal and is not the true intellect but is only analogous to it, since the true intellect is not in any animal.

If you say: "Oh, why then does Aristotle say in the third book *On the Soul* that there is a true intellect?" I respond that not everything should be revealed to ordinary people.[30] This is my answer.

I say: In my opinion, it is a heresy to insist that every intellect is mortal. I am ready to suffer death for my defense of the immortality of the intellect. But it is not evil to state what Aristotle's opinion is. According to Aristotle, our soul is not the true intellect, since he insists that the intellect and the mind are not in any animal. Therefore, it is easy to solve the issue if we hold this position.

But there are two arguments that have to be answered. Firstly, if the natural philosopher were to study the intellective soul, he would also have to study intelligible things, so the other sciences would be superfluous.

One can add to this argument another one: If the natural philosopher were to study the intellective soul and intelligible things, then only metaphysics would be superfluous and not all sciences. This is the interpretation of Michael of Ephesos.[31] However, in our text, it says that: "all sciences would be superfluous," and Albert and the old wording of the text say the same thing.[32]

A different response is: then all sciences would be superfluous, because mathematics was not called a science in the classical era but an introductory discipline, as Plato says in the sixth book of *The Republic*.[33] But natural

---

29. Cf. Pietro Pomponazzi, *On the Immortality of the Soul*, in *The Renaissance Philosophy of Man*, ed. Ernst Cassirer, Paul Oskar Kristeller, and John Herman Jr. Randall, trans. William Henry Hay (Chicago: University of Chicago Press, 1948), chap. 9, 325.

30. Cf. Pietro Pomponazzi, *Opera: De naturalium effectuum admirandorum causis, seu, De incantationibus liber...* (Basileae: Ex officina Henricpetrina, 1567), XII, 242–43.

31. Ephesius, *In libros De partibus animalium Commentaria*, 7, lines 4–5.

32. Aristotle, *De part. an.* I, 1, 641a35–36. Cf. Albertus Magnus, *De Animalibus Libri XXV*, XI, tr. 1, c. 3, 774, 23–24.

33. Plato, *Rep.* VII, 522a-527d.

168   PIETRO POMPONAZZI

philosophy, metaphysics, and some other disciplines together with them are sciences.

Another response is: Here Aristotle does not speak in a determinative way but in an argumentative way.

Secondly, this argument has not yet been answered: He says that there is neither an efficient cause nor a final cause in things separated from matter.[34] But in science, one has to search for an efficient cause, etc.

This argument does not seem to be true, since an efficient and a final cause seem to be subjects of metaphysics. In the twelfth book of *Metaphysics*, he states that God only moves as (the object of) love and desire.[35] How can one say that things separated from matter lack an efficient and a final cause? In the first book of *The Physics*, he says that metaphysics deals with three causes, natural philosophy with four causes, mathematics with one, etc.[36]

Moreover, you should know that what Michael of Ephesos understood as "things separated from matter" are mathematical objects.[37] Natural philosophy should not deal with mathematical objects, since mathematical objects do not have an efficient or final cause, as is said in the second book of *The Physics*.[38] If it is as Michael of Ephesos says, we do not have an argument. The issue is hard to assess, since according to Theodor's interpretation, Michael's exposition is not good, because Aristotle says: "one can add, a thing separated from matter,"[39] where "one can add" lies beyond this argument. Ergo, if it is a different argument, one speaks about the same issue. Moreover, it seems that it would not fit (with Aristotle's other views) if he were to say it only about mathematics. Thus, if we follow Theodor's text, what will we say? I say that there is neither an efficient nor a final cause in divine things, only untruly and equivocally speaking. The true efficient and true final cause can be discovered in natural things. This is what I have to say about this issue.

On the feast of St. Lucia 1521

---

34. Aristotle, *De part. an.* I, 1, 641b13.
35. Aristotle, *Met.* XII, 7, 1072b3.
36. Averroes, *Commentarium in Libros Physicorum*, comm. 1, f. 6rB-C.
37. Ephesius, *In libros De partibus animalium Commentaria*, 7, lines 17–19.
38. Aristotle, *Phys.* II, 2.
39. Aristotle, *De part. an.* I, 1, 641b10.

11

NICCOLÒ MACHIAVELLI
(1469–1527)

Discursus on Florentine Matters after the Death of Lorenzo de' Medici the Younger

MARK JURDJEVIC

INTRODUCTION

In Niccolò Machiavelli's *Discourse on Florentine Affairs* of 1519, one of his lesser known texts, we encounter Machiavelli engaged in the causes he valued above all else–actively participating in the politics of his city and championing a strong and stable republican government in Florence.[1] In this respect, the text stands in striking contrast to the *Prince* and the *Discourses on Livy*. The former is his most infamous and widely read work of political theory, and the latter his most substantial. Those texts were written in a context of political ostracization that followed his professional downfall and consequently display wide-ranging intellectual and historical interests that reflect more the scholar's study than the active political arena that provides the context for Machiavelli's *Discourse on Florentine Affairs*.

Machiavelli had served the Florentine Republic in several im-

---

1. On this text's relationship to his earlier writings, see Mark Jurdjevic, *A Great and Wretched City: Promise and Failure in Machiavelli's Florentine Political Thought* (Cambridge, Mass.: Harvard University Press, 2014), 53–80.

170 NICCOLÒ MACHIAVELLI

portant capacities from 1498 until its collapse in 1512: as secretary to the city's powerful war council, the Ten of Liberty and Peace, as a diplomat to Europe's bellicose monarchs vying for domination of the Italian peninsula, and as the architect of the city's controversial project to re-establish a citizen militia. These political activities came to a crushing halt in 1512 when a Spanish army toppled the republic and restored to power the exiled Medici family, the de facto rulers of the city for much of the fifteenth century. The Medici family viewed Machiavelli with considerable suspicion, owing to his close relationship with Piero Soderini, the lifetime Standard Bearer of Justice and chief official of the republic, and to his role as head of the Florentine militia. After the discovery of an anti-Medici conspiracy in which Machiavelli's name was involved, he was arrested and tortured.[2] In his ensuing political isolation, he wrote his two most famous works of political theory, profound works of political imagination through which he mentally transcended his dismal reality in Florence.

By 1520, however, he had regained his standing with the Medici family and had finally received what he had fruitlessly sought to accomplish by dedicating the *Prince* to the Medici: political employment by the ruling family and re-engagement with pressing issues in Florentine politics.[3] The text presented here, the *Discourse on Florentine Affairs*, was the first fruit of his long-awaited rapprochement. The death of Lorenzo de' Medici, the duke of Urbino and presumptive center of Medici power in Florence, left the family leadership in the hands of two ecclesiastics, Pope Leo X (Giovanni de' Medici) and Cardinal Giulio de' Medici (the future Clement VII), both of whom lacked legitimate offspring. As a result, Giulio commissioned a number of constitutional proposals from members of their circle, Machiavelli included, and asked them to outline how best to integrate Medici power in Florence in ways that might avoid the destabilizing resentments that had led to the family's expulsion in 1494. However staggering his talents as a man of letters, Machiavelli always prioritized the value of active political engagement over abstract reflection, so the request

---

2. On Machiavelli's professional career, see the recent biography by Robert Black, *Machiavelli* (London: Routledge, 2013), 30–72.

3. On Machiavelli's complex relationship to the Medici family, see John M. Najemy, "Machiavelli and the Medici: The Lessons of Florentine History," *Renaissance Quarterly* 35, no. 4 (1982): 551–76.

for him to outline the best form of government for his beloved native city could not have been more welcome.[4]

His constitutional proposal reveals some of Machiavelli's long-standing political convictions, as well as some innovative aspects not evident in his earlier writings. As Heinrich C. Kuhn observed in the companion to this volume, we see his recurring admiration and lofty praise for that those who successfully reform states—Machiavelli's true heroes—and his populist conviction that the people should have and will always wisely use veto power over legislation created in councils dominated by nobles and wealthy elites.[5] We also see some new elements. When reflecting on the lessons of ancient Greek and Roman examples in the *Prince* and the *Discourses*, Machiavelli always analyzed society in terms of two groups: the people and the nobles. But when called upon to create an ideal government for Florence, a mercantile republic with relatively high degrees of social mobility, he analyzed society in terms of three groups: the people, the middle ranks, and the nobles. And whereas in the *Prince* and the *Discourses* he had categorically characterized aristocrats and their culture of violent entitlement as the chief obstacle to a stable government, here he acknowledged that no stable government could exist without granting the city's elite a privileged role consistent with their ambitious and proud self-image. But the most provocative and revealing statement that he made to the city's ruling family was to prepare for their own obsolescence. Machiavelli argued that princely government, even if cloaked in the discreet shadow rule that the fifteenth-century Medici had shrewdly deployed, could never last in Florence because of its stubborn tradition of republican liberty. He urged his audience of a Medici pope and cardinal to establish a government that would function as a quasi-monarchy while these ecclesiastics lived but that would upon their deaths revert to a fully-functioning and inclusive republic with no trace of Medici domination.

---

4. On this theme in Machiavelli's writings, see Mark Jurdjevic and Meredith K. Ray, eds. and trans., *Machiavelli: Political, Literary, and Historical Writings* (Philadelphia: University of Pennsylvania Press, 2019).

5. Heinrich C. Kuhn, "Niccolò Machiavelli (1469–1527): A Good State for Bad People," in *Philosophers of the Renaissance*, ed. Paul Richard Blum and trans. Brian McNeil (Washington, D.C.: The Catholic University of America Press, 2010), 116–17; on Machiavelli's populism more broadly, see John P. McCormick, *Machiavellian Democracy* (Cambridge: Cambridge University Press, 2011).

BIBLIOGRAPHY

Primary Sources

Machiavelli, Niccolò. *The Chief Works and Others*. Translated by Allan Gilbert. 3 vols. Durham, N.C.: Duke University Press, 1989.

———. *Machiavelli and His Friends: Their Personal Correspondence*. Translated by James Atkinson and David Sices. DeKalb: Northern Illinois University Press, 1996.

———. *L'arte della guerra. Scritti politici minori*. Edited by Giorgio Masi, Jean-Jacques Marchand, and Denis Fachard. Rome: Salerno editrice, 2001.

———. *Discorsi sopra la prima deca di Tito Livio*. Edited by Francesco Bausi. Rome: Salerno editrice, 2001.

———. *Legazioni, commissarie, scritti di governo*. 7 vols. Edited by Jean-Jacques Marchand, Denis Fachard, Emmanuele Cutinelli-Rèndina, Matteo Melera-Morettini, and Andrea Guidi. Rome: Salerno editrice, 2002–2012.

———. *Il principe*. Edited by Mario Martelli. Rome: Salerno editrice, 2006.

———. *The Essential Writings of Machiavelli*. Translated by Peter Constantine. New York: Random House, 2007.

———. *Opere storiche*. Edited by Alessandro Montevecchi and Carlo Varotti. Rome: Salerno editrice, 2011.

———. *Scritti in poesia e in prosa*. Edited by A. Corsaro, P. Cosentino, E. Cutinelli-Rèndina, F. Grazzini, and N. Marcelli. Rome: Salerno editrice, 2013.

———. *Teatro: Andria, Mandragola, Clizia*. Edited by Pasquale Stoppelli. Rome: Salerno editrice, 2017.

———. *Machiavelli: Political, Literary, and Historical Writings*. Edited and translated by Mark Jurdjevic and Meredith K. Ray. Philadelphia: University of Pennsylvania Press, 2019.

Secondary Sources

Bausi, Francesco. *Machiavelli*. Rome: Salerno editrice, 2005.

Black, Robert. *Machiavelli: A Biography*. London: Routledge, 2014.

Bock, Gisela, Quentin Skinner, and Maurizio Viroli, eds. *Machiavelli and Republicanism*. Cambridge: Cambridge University Press, 1990.

Guidi, Andrea. *Un segretario militante: politica, diplomazia, e armi nel cancelliere Machiavelli*.

Bologna: Il Mulino, 2009.

Hankins, James. *Virtue Politics: Soulcraft and Statecraft in Renaissance Italy*. Cambridge, Mass.: Harvard University Press, 2019.

Jurdjevic, Mark. *A Great and Wretched City: Promise and Failure in Machiavelli's Florentine Political Thought*. Cambridge, Mass.: Harvard University Press, 2014.

Kuhn, Heinrich. "Niccolò Macchiavelli (1469–1527): A Good State for Bad People." In *Philosophers of the Renaissance*, edited by Paul Richard Blum and translated by Brian McNeil, 116–23. Washington, D.C.: The Catholic University of America Press, 2010.

McCormick, John P. *Machiavellian Democracy*. Cambridge: Cambridge University Press, 2011.

———. *Reading Machiavelli: Scandalous Books, Suspect Engagements, and the Virtue of Populist Politics*. Princeton, N.J.: Princeton University Press, 2018.

Najemy, John M. *Between Friends: Discourses of Desire in the Machiavelli-Vettori Letters of 1513–1515*. Princeton, N.J.: Princeton University Press, 1993.

Najemy, John, ed. *The Cambridge Companion to Machiavelli*. Cambridge: Cambridge University Press, 2010.

Pedullà, Gabriele. *Machiavelli in Tumult: The* Discourses on Livy *and the Origins of Political Conflictualism*. Cambridge: Cambridge University Press, 2018.

Pocock, J. G. A. *The Machiavellian Moment: Florentine Political Thought and the Atlantic Republican Tradition*. Princeton, N.J.: Princeton University Press, 2003.

Skinner, Quentin. *Machiavelli: A Very Short Introduction*. Oxford: Oxford University Press, 2000.

✣

NICCOLÒ MACHIAVELLI

Discursus on Florentine Matters after the Death of Lorenzo de' Medici the Younger[6]

Florence's governments have often changed their forms because the state has never been either a proper republic or principate. One cannot call a principate stable when the will of a single individual is deliberated over and confirmed by the consent of many. Neither can one consider a republic sustainable when those whose satisfaction is necessary to avoid its ruin remain unsatisfied. The truth of this is borne out by the kinds of states that the city has established since 1393. Commencing with the kinds of reforms enacted by Messer Maso degli Albizzi at that time, we see a republic governed by aristocrats that was so defective that it endured barely forty years. Indeed, it would have lasted even fewer years if not for the unity generated by the wars with the Visconti of Milan.

Among its defects was the fact that scrutinies for office were estab-

---

6. This translation is by John P. McCormick and was first published in *Florentine Political Writings from Petrarch to Machiavelli*, ed. Mark Jurdjevic, Natasha Piano, and John P. McCormick (Philadelphia: University of Pennsylvania Press, 2019), 213–23. Reprinted with permission.

lished too far in advance, which permitted rampant fraud and produced poor appointments. Since men are variable and prone to corruption, individuals who initially may have been truly worthy when deemed eligible to hold office, later may no longer be so when they are actually appointed to office. Additionally, great men never sufficiently feared punishment for engaging in the formation of sects, which is always the ruin of a state. Furthermore, the Signoria, which enjoyed too little reputation and too much authority, could execute and despoil citizens without appeal, and could too readily call the people to a *parlamento*. As a result, whenever a reputed citizen managed to control or circumvent it, the Signoria became less the state's defender and more the instrument of its failures. Alternatively, as already noted, it enjoyed a low reputation because it contained unworthy men, as well as many who were too young; also, its terms were excessively short, and it dealt with matters of little genuine gravity.

That state was disordered in yet another not insignificant way: it elevated the reputation of private men over public ones, which diminished the authority and reputation of the magistrates in a manner that is contrary to all civil orders. In addition to these disorders, there was another one as important as all the rest combined: the people did not play their appropriate part in the state. All of these factors contributed to infinite disorders such that, as noted, if external wars had not kept the state together, it would have come to ruin much sooner than it actually did.

Then came Cosimo's state, which inclined more toward a principate than a republic. It endured longer than the previous state for two reasons: firstly, it was established with the favor of the people; and, secondly, it was governed by two especially prudent men, Cosimo and his grandson, Lorenzo. Still, a certain weakness inhered in the fact that large numbers had to deliberate over plans that Cosimo wished to enact, such that he often incurred the danger of failure. This resulted in frequent *parliamenti* and many exiles under this state, and, eventually, during the accident of King Charles's invasion, it collapsed.

Immediately thereafter, the city resolved to restore the form of a republic, but unfortunately not in a mode that would ensure durability: the orders that were instituted failed to satisfy the humors of all kinds of the citizens; moreover, the state proved incapable of meting out appropriate punishments. Indeed, it was so flawed and so far removed from the mod-

Discursus on Florentine Matters

el of a true republic that a life-tenured Gonfalonier, had he been wise and wicked, could have readily become prince; had he been weak and righteous, he could be readily expelled, with the ruin of the entire state ensuing. It would take far too long to elaborate all the reasons for this, so I will mention only one: the Gonfalonier was surrounded by no one who could, if the former were good, defend him, and if he were wicked, curb and correct him.

These governments were all deficient because every attempt to reform them was aimed not at the satisfaction of the common good, but rather to benefit and render secure only those parties who initiated the reforms. Such security always proved elusive, however, because there ever remained another malcontented party, which invariably proved to be an exceedingly useful instrument for those who wished to pursue further innovations of the state.

There is only left to consider the state from 1512 to the present time, its deficiencies and strengths—but since it is a recent and familiar matter, and thus well-known by everyone, I will omit a discussion of it. More pressing is the fact that the Duke's recent death necessitates a full consideration of new modes of government. In order to demonstrate my loyalty to Your Holiness, I believe that I ought not err by failing to express my thoughts. Firstly, I will convey the opinions that I have heard others express, and then I will present my own—if I err at all in this regard, I trust that Your Holiness will absolve me for being more loving than prudent.

Some insist that no more reliable form of government could be ordered than that which prevailed in the times of Cosimo and Lorenzo; others prefer a government more widely inclusive. Those who prefer a government reminiscent of Cosimo's say that all things return easily to their nature. They say that Florentine citizens naturally honor your house, enjoy the graces that it has bestowed upon them, love the things that they have always loved, and that they have become accustomed to maintaining a certain habit for sixty years. Thus, on this view, Florentines can do nothing else than follow the previous ways and return to their former spirits. Furthermore, they believe that it is only a few who adhere to an opposite way of thinking and who engage in contrary habits, and thus that the latter can be easily eliminated. Beyond these reasons, they invoke necessity, arguing that Florence cannot function without a head. Since it must have one, they conjecture, it might as well come from a house that tends to be adored; rather than, either absent a head, confusion befall the city, or, turning to an alternate head, settle for someone less reputable and less pleasing to everyone.

One could respond to this opinion with the observation that such a state would risk the danger of being weak. If Cosimo's state suffered in those times from the many deficiencies outlined above, they would be doubled in the present. After all, now the city, the citizens and the times are quite different from what they were then, such that presently it would be impossible to create a state similar to that previous one that could endure in Florence. Firstly, that state had the universality as a friend, while this one incurs its enmity. Those citizens had never in their lifetimes enjoyed in Florence a state more inclusive of the universality than that one. These citizens remember one that they consider more civil and with which they were more contented. In Italy back then, there was neither an army nor a power that the Florentines with their arms could not repel, despite often standing alone. Now, with Spain and France here, we must be friends with one of them, whom, should they be vanquished, leave Florence prey to the victor—a situation that never would have transpired before.

Previously, citizens as a matter of course paid heavy taxes; presently, through either incapacity or bad habits, they are no longer inclined to do so—and efforts to re-habituate them in this respect prove to be odious and dangerous affairs. The Medici who governed in those times were born and reared among fellow citizens such that they governed with familiarity and thus gained grace from the latter. Since they have now become so great as to transcend the bounds of civility, such familiarity, and thus such grace, is no longer possible. Consequently, given how much men and times have changed, nothing could be more delusional than the belief that now an old form could be imposed upon qualitatively different matter. If back then, as I stated above, the Medici were in danger of losing the state every ten years, now they would certainly lose it. Furthermore, no one should believe it to be true that men readily return to an old and familiar way of life. They may do so when they consider the old ways more pleasant than the new, but when they like it less, they can only return to it under compulsion; and they will endure it only so long as that compulsion persists.

Additionally, it may be true that Florence cannot function without a head, and that among various private heads it would surely love one from the House of Medici over more than any other. Yet, if it were to choose between a private and a public head, it would always find the public head, whatever House he came from, more preferable to the private one.

Some say that it is impossible to lose the state without an external assault, believing furthermore that in such circumstances there is always time to befriend the invading enemy. But this is grievous self-deception: usually friendship is not necessarily forged with the most powerful adversary but merely with the one that happens to be attacking you at that particular moment, or with the one that your spirit or imagination inclines you to love. It can easily happen then that your friend loses, leaving his fate to the discretion of the winner; at which time, the latter may decide against coming to an accord with you, either because you were tardy in seeking it to begin with, or because you have incurred his hatred as a result of your friendship with his enemy.

For instance, both Duke Ludovico of Milan and King Frederick of Naples were eager to form an accord with King Louis XII of France, and both lost their states as a result of their failures to do so—such are the countless factors that often impede efforts to obtain treaties. All things considered then, one cannot call this kind of state either secure or stable because too many things may prove a source of unpredictability. Therefore, it should not be pleasing to Your Holiness or to your friends.

Regarding those who desire a government more widely inclusive than this one: I say that if it is not expanded in a way that results in a well-ordered republic, then that widening will quickly ruin it. If such persons explained quite specifically what it is that they want, then I would respond to them with greater specificity; but if they continue to speak in generalities, I can only address them generally. I would like the following answer to suffice for now: apropos Cosimo's state, it must be said that no state is stable that is not a true principate or a true republic, because all the governments between these two are deficient. The reason could not be clearer: the principate's one path toward demise proceeds in the direction of a republic, while, likewise, a declining republic tends in the direction of a principate. Yet, those states in between incline toward not one but two possible paths to their demise, either toward a principality or a republic—in this resides their instability. Therefore, Your Holiness, if you wish to provide Florence with a stable state, one both worthy of your glory and compatible with your friends' well-being, you should order either a true principate or a true republic, with each of their respectively appropriate qualities. All other accomplishments will prove futile and excessively brief.

I will refrain from discussing a principate in any detail, due to the difficulty in establishing one here, and the absence of any instrument to make it possible. Furthermore, Your Holiness must understand that in all cities where there is widespread equality among citizens, only with maximum difficulty can a principate be established; and in those where there is widespread inequality, a republic cannot be ordered at all. For instance, in order to found a republic in Milan, where there is extensive inequality among citizens, it would be necessary to eliminate the entire nobility, and reduce everyone to equality. Because so many there live in an extravagant fashion, laws are insufficient to constrain them; rather they require a vigorous voice and overweening power to control them.

Alternatively, to establish a principate in Florence, where there is great equality, it would be necessary to institute significant inequality: one would have to elevate nobles with great castles and villas, who would defend the prince with arms and attendants by suppressing the entire city and province. A prince acting alone without a supporting nobility could not maintain a principate; he would require there to be between himself and the universality an intermediary that acts as his auxiliary in ruling. As we see in France, the gentlemen control the people, the princes control the gentlemen, and the King controls the princes.

In short, to establish a principate in a city where a republic would be more appropriate requires efforts arduous, inhumane and unworthy of anyone wishing to be deemed merciful and good. Therefore, I will forego any further discussion of a principate and speak only of a republic. Indeed, Florence is very eager to take on such a form, and Your Holiness is very much inclined to provide it—you delay in doing so only in the hopes of maintaining your authority and your friends' security in Florence. I have devised a way to make both things possible. Thus, I want Your Holiness to understand my thinking, so that, if any good inheres within it, you can make use of it, and furthermore appreciate just how much I wish to serve you. For you will see that in this republic of mine your authority not only endures but increases, and that your friends remain honored and secure;

Discursus on Florentine Matters

alternately, the universality will have manifest reasons to be content with it. I pray, with the greatest reverence, that Your Holiness neither blame nor praise my *discorso* without reading it in its entirety. Moreover, I pray that you not be alarmed by certain alterations in the magistracies, because where things are poorly ordered, the less of the old that is retained, the less of the bad likewise remains.

Those who order a republic must take account of the three different qualities of men who comprise all cities, that is, the first, the middle and the last. And although Florence is characterized by the equality noted before, still an elevated spirit motivates some citizens who think themselves entitled to maintain preeminence over others. When ordering a republic, it is necessary to satisfy these men—indeed, the previous state was ruined for no other reason than failing to provide them such satisfaction. This simply cannot be accomplished unless majesty is bestowed upon the highest ranks of the republic, a majesty that is sustained in their persons.

It will be impossible to confer such majesty upon the first ranks of the Florentine state without changing the present configurations of Signoria and the Colleges. Due to the manner in which such offices are created presently, men of gravity and reputation seldom sit in them, and the state's majesty is either diminished entirely, displaced elsewhere or entrusted to private men—which contravenes all political order. This must be corrected in a way that satisfies the highest ambitions within the city. Here is such a way.

Annul the Signoria, the Eight of Practica, and the Twelve Good Men, and, in order to enhance the government's majesty, replace them with sixty-five men of forty-plus years of age (fifty-three from the major guilds and twelve from the minor ones). They should remain within government for the duration of their lives in the following mode: Create from among them a Gonfalonier of Justice for a two- or three-year term (if a life-termed one is deemed undesirable); divide the remaining sixty-four citizens in half, with each set of thirty-two governing alongside the Gonfalonier in alternating years as ordered below in perpetuity. These all together will be called the Signoria.

Each year's thirty-two should be divided into four parts of eight members, each of which should preside with the Gonfalonier for three months in the palace, assuming the magistracy with the usual ceremonies, conducting all the affairs of the Signoria as it does today. Then, along with their companions among the alternate thirty-two, they will have all the authority of and the capacity to conduct policy presently associated with the combined Signoria, Eight of Practica and the Colleges, which were annulled above. This, as I have written, will be the first head and first organ of the state. This order, if considered well, manifestly bestows majesty and reputation unto the head of the state; for men of gravity and authority will always, quite obviously, fill the highest ranks of the city. There will henceforth be no further need of conferring on public matters with private men, which, as noted, is always pernicious for republics; from now on, the thirty-two who, in any particular year, do not sit in the magistracy, will provide requisite advice and counsel. And Your Holiness, as I will explain, may elect to this rank all of your friends and confidants. But now let us consider the second rank of the state.

As I said before, I believe that there are three qualities of men, and, therefore, it is necessary to have three types of rank in a republic, but no more. Hence, you would do well to clear up the confusion of councils that have long confounded the city. These were instituted not because they served a civil way of life, but because they fed the appetite for office of ever more citizens, improving the city's health not a bit but providing instead opportunities for sects to corrupt it.

If, therefore, I am attempting to erect a republic comprised of three groups then it seems to me that the Seventy, the One Hundred, the Council of the People and the Council of the Commune should be annulled. These should be replaced with a Council of the Two Hundred, comprised of forty-year-olds, forty of whom should come from the minor guilds, and one hundred and sixty of whom should come from the major ones—none of these may also be eligible for the Signoria. These two hundred should serve for life and be called the Select Council.

This Council, in tandem with the reconfigured Signoria, should have all the authority and responsibilities presently enjoyed by the councils we are explicitly annulling. Your Holiness may appoint this second rank of the state, just as you may appoint the first. To accomplish this, and to maintain, regulate and supervise these new orders (and those still to be described), and for the security of your authority and of Your Holiness's friends, I recommend the following: Your Holiness and the Most Rever-

Discursus on Florentine Matters

end Cardinal de'Medici must retain, through the Balìa, as much authority during the length of both your lives as does the whole Florentine people. To this end, the Eight of Guardia and the Balìa ought to be established whenever you deem them to be needed. Moreover, for the state's security and that of Your Holiness's friends, the infantry should be ordered by dividing it into two bands, over which should be appointed, through Your Holiness's authority, two commissioners, respectively.

We see from the matters discussed above that we have satisfied two qualities of men and confirmed your own authority over the city and your friends' security within it; arms and criminal justice are placed in your hands, the laws abide in your breast, and all the heads of the state belong to you. It remains now to satisfy the third and last rank of men, which is the entire universality of the citizens; these will never be satisfied unless their authority is restored or if such a restoration is promised to them—anyone who believes otherwise is quite unwise. Since, to do so all at once would serve neither your friends' security nor the maintenance of Your Holiness's authority, it will be necessary partly to restore it and partly to promise to restore it fully such that the universality enjoys complete confidence of actually gaining it back.

Therefore, I think that it is necessary to reopen the Great Council, with a quorum of one thousand or at least six-hundred citizens, to distribute all the offices and magistracies as it did before—except for the aforementioned Sixty-Five, the Two Hundred and the Eight of Balìa, which, during the life of Your Holiness and of the Cardinal, you would continue to select. And so that your friends would be certain, when the Council is to make a selection, that their names have been placed in the bags, Your Holiness will appoint eight *accoppiatori,* who may secretly select or reject anyone they like. In order for the universal to believe that those ultimately selected for office were actually drawn from the bags, the Council must be allowed to choose and send two citizen scrutinizers to observe the placement of names in the bags.

No stable republic can ever be established without satisfying the universal. And if the Great Hall is not reopened, never will the universality of Florentine citizens be satisfied. Reopening this room and rendering to the universal this distribution is simply necessary to have a Florentine Republic. Be sure of this, Your Holiness: whoever thinks about seizing the state from you will above all other things plan on reopening it. Therefore, it is better to reopen it under terms and with modes that are safe, and thus remove from your enemies the opportunity of reopening it to your dismay and your friends' destruction and ruin.

By ordering the state in this manner, if Your Holiness and the Most Reverend Monsignor were immortal, it would be unnecessary to do anything else. However, you must at some point pass on, and yet you desire to leave behind a perfect republic fortified with all requisite parts, observed and recognized by all to be so. Thus, so that the universal may be content with it (through what is both delivered to them and promised to them), the following additions must also be ordered.

The Sixteen Gonfaloniers of the Companies of the People should be created in the same mode and for the same duration as they presently are. They may be selected through your own authority or by the Great Council, whichever pleases you more. The divieto should be increased only so that the magistracy will be spread more widely throughout the city, and, to the same end, none of the Sixty-Five citizens may be deemed eligible to hold it. Once the Sixteen have been created, four Provosts should be selected by lottery from among them to serve for one month; thus, all of the Gonfaloniers will have served as Provosts by the end of their tenure. From these four, one should be selected to reside for one week in the Palace with the nine presiding Signori, such that by the end of the month all four will have resided there. The sitting Signori residing in the Palace are permitted to do nothing in the absence of the Provost. The latter need not necessarily speak but merely serve as a witness of the Signori's actions. The Provost may with good cause impede their proceedings and demand that these be discussed by the entire Thirty-Two as a whole.

Likewise, in such circumstances, the Thirty-Two will not be permitted to deliberate anything except in the presence of two Provosts. The latter possess no authority other than the ability to put a stop to deliberations among the Thirty-Two and appeal them to the Select Council. In a similar manner, this Council, that of the Two-Hundred, is forbidden from doing anything without at least six of the Sixteen, among which there must be two Provosts, being present. The Six are empowered to do no more than—when three of them concur—demand that a matter be transferred from the Select Council to the Great Council. The latter council may not gather together without twelve Gonfaloniers present, among which there must be three Provosts, all of whom may participate like any other citizen within the Great Council.

This ordering of these Colleges is necessary beyond the lives of Your Holiness and the Most Reverend Monsignor for the following reasons. Firstly, if the Signoria or the Select Council fail to deliberate properly on account of disunion, or if they act against the common good out of malice, someone will be available to suspend their authority and confer it upon another Council. After all, it is not a good thing for one magistracy or council to undermine the public good when another is available to advance it properly. It is also good that citizens who hold the state in their hands should have others who watch them, and who can either deter them from engaging in bad behavior, or deprive them of their authority when they are using it badly.

Secondly, in abolishing the present Signoria and depriving the universality of the people the possibility of becoming Signori, it is necessary to compensate them with a rank commensurate with the one that has been taken away. In this manner, the magistracy of the Provosts is greater, more honorable and more useful to the republic. Moreover, for now it would be best to select the Gonfaloniers ordinarily, so that the city begins to conform to its proper orders; however, they will not be allowed to exercise their office without Your Holiness' permission—in fact, you might put them to use in reporting on certain actions pertinent to your authority and your state.

Beyond this, in order to establish a perfect republic beyond the lifetimes of Your Holiness and the Most Reverend Monsignor, so that it is not lacking in any regard, it will be necessary to order appeals from decisions rendered by the Eight of Guardia and the Balìa. An appellate body, composed of thirty citizens selected from the bags of the Two Hundred and the Sixty-Five combined, would be empowered to call both complainants and the accused within a specified time-frame. No one would be allowed, during your lifetimes, to avail themselves of this appellate body without your permission.

Such appeals are necessary in republics because bodies comprised few citizens seldom exhibit the fortitude to punish great men; therefore, to achieve such a result many citizens should participate in these judgments, and do so in secret, so that they cannot be blamed individually for outcomes. These appeals will also prove serviceable in your lifetime, as the Eight will be encouraged to judge cases expeditiously and justly; that is, they will judge rightly out of fear that you would subsequently allow an appeal to proceed. To avoid the prospect of too many appeals, these may be limited exclusively to instances of fraud in the amount of at least fifty ducats, and applied only to instances of violence entailing broken bones, spilled blood and damages exceeding at least fifty ducats.

Let us consider all these orders to constitute a republic, which, absent your authority, lacks nothing necessary that has been disputed and discoursed at length above. However, during the lives of Your Holiness and the Most Reverend Monsignor it remains a monarchy, for you command over the arms, you command over criminal justice and you hold the laws close to your breast. I know not what more one could desire for a city. You will see no reason why those among your friends, who are good and wish to live with what they have, should have cause to fear, since Your Holiness will retain so much authority and they will sit in the first ranks of government. Also it is inconceivable that the universality of citizens themselves would not be content as a significant part of the state has been distributed to them and that little by little more will fall into their hands. Sometimes Your Holiness might consider permitting the Great Council to fill open slots among the Sixty-Five and the Two Hundred, while you yourself would continue to do so when circumstances require it. Therefore, I am sure that in a short time, through the authority of Your Holiness, who would control everything, that this present state would be converted into the other kind, and likewise the other into this kind, such that they would each become the same, all within one body, with the city's peace and Your Holiness's perpetual fame resulting. Always your own authority would address whatever defects might become apparent over time.

I believe that the greatest honor earned by men is that which is voluntarily bestowed upon them by their patria. I believe that the greatest good that men achieve, and that which is most favored by God, is that which they provide to their patria. Moreover, no man is exalted for his actions more than those who reform republics and principates through laws and institutions; after those who became gods, these were the most lauded. Since there have been few with the occasion to do so, and even fewer with

Discursus on Florentine Matters

the ability to do so, small indeed is the number who have done so. So highly esteemed is this glory by those who singularly pursue it that those who have been unable to found a republic in fact have done so in writing, such as Aristotle, Plato and many others. They wished to show the world that if, like Solon and Lycurgus, they could not found a civil way of life, they were prevented from putting it into practice not through lack of knowledge but through lack of ability.

Heaven, therefore, gives to a man no greater gift, nor shows him no more glorious path than this. Hence, among the infinite felicitudes that God has bestowed upon your House and upon the person of Your Holiness, this is by far the greatest: to give you both the power and the matter to make yourself immortal, and, consequently, to far surpass the glory of your father and grandfather. Consider well, Your Holiness, that by maintaining the city of Florence on present terms the slightest accident may bring forth a thousand dangers; even before they arrive, Your Holiness must confront a thousand inconveniences that would be excruciating for any man—just how excruciating, the Most Reverend Lord Cardinal, who has been in Florence these past months, can confirm. These inconveniences come in part from many citizens who are presumptuous and insufferable, and in part from many who, feeling as though they do not live securely at present, demand only that order be brought to government. Some say in this regard that the government should be rendered more widely inclusive, while others say it should be rendered more narrowly restrictive—with neither coming to particulars regarding the mode of doing either because everyone is confused. While they feel that they enjoy little security under the present mode of living, they know not how to improve the situation; moreover, anyone who might know, they refuse to trust. Such widespread confusion is enough to confound even the most well-regulated brain.

To escape these troubles, then, there are only two ways: either retire from giving audiences, and discourage men from requesting them, even in the customary way, or refrain from speaking when not asked to do so, as did the late, illustrious Duke; or, order the state in a mode through which it will administer itself, such that Your Holiness need only keep half of an eye upon it. Of these two modes, the latter liberates you from many dangers and inconveniences; the former liberates you only from inconveniences. Regarding the dangers that you incur if matters stand as they do presently, I will offer a prediction. When accidents supervene while the city has failed to be reordered comprehensively, one or another thing, or both things simultaneously, will ensue: a head will be set up hastily and tumultuously, one who will defend the state exclusively with arms and violence; or, one party will rush to reopen the Great Hall, and will pounce upon the other as prey.

God forbid that either of these two things should happen; but please consider, Your Holiness, how many dead, how many exiles, how many extortions would result if they do. It would make even a cruel man, let alone a merciful one like Your Holiness, die of sorrow. There is simply no other way to escape these evils than to provide the city with orders through which it can stand firm. This will always be so when everyone plays a part in such orders, when everyone knows what he must do and in whom he can trust; and when no citizen of whatever rank, either out of fear for themselves or out of naked ambition, desires to undertake an innovation.

12

HEINRICH CORNELIUS AGRIPPA VON NETTESHEIM (1486–1535)

The Vanity of Arts and Sciences

PAUL RICHARD BLUM

INTRODUCTION

Heinrich Cornelius, commonly known as Agrippa von Nettesheim, was born in Cologne in 1486. After his initial studies of liberal arts in Cologne, he became an itinerant scholar, traveling through France, England, Italy, Switzerland, Germany, and Belgium. He held positions as a lawyer and as a physician. He died in Grenoble in 1535.[1]

Agrippa is best known for his *De occulta philosophia*, an encyclopedia of all sciences associated with magic. He finished its first version in 1510 but had it printed only in 1531 after a number of inauthentic manuscripts had begun circulating. The aim of Agrippa's text is to study the liberal arts disciplines so as to make explicit the hidden parallels that exist between cosmic and human processes. For Agrippa, human observers must first admit these commonalities if they hope to obtain true knowledge about the universe in order to subdue its occult powers to human design.

---

1. Andrea Strazzoni, "Agrippa, Heinrich Cornelius," in *Encyclopedia of Renaissance Philosophy*, ed. Marco Sgarbi (Cham: Springer International Publishing, 2016), 1–4, https://doi.org/10.1007/978-3-319-02848-4_547-1.

188 HEINRICH CORNELIUS AGRIPPA VON NETTESHEIM

Francis Bacon (1561–1626) pursued the same goal in his *New Organum* (1620), leaving aside everything that was merely spiritual. Agrippa's inspirations were Neoplatonism, Hermeticism, Kabbalah, and related theoretical frameworks that were highly respected among Renaissance philosophers like Marsilio Ficino (1433–1499) and remained so among scholars in the seventeenth and eighteenth centuries. During the same time, he wrote the *De vanitate scientiarum*, which was first published in Antwerp in 1530.[2]

The full title of the book reveals its program: "Speech on the uncertainty and vacuity [or: vainness] of disciplines and arts and the excellence of the Word of God." Human conceit is compared with divine revelation: futility of human endeavor in the face of God's superiority. Between the opening and the concluding chapters, which we present here, the author works through 101 fields of human knowledge and activity, which—for the scope of the attack—are worth listing:

Writing, grammar, poetry, history, rhetoric, logic, sophistry, Lullian art, art of memory, mathematics in general, arithmetic, geomancy, aleatoric, Pythagorean lot, more arithmetic, music, dancing, sword fight, stage acting, debating, geometry, optics, painting, plastic art, optics, world geography, architecture, metallurgy, astronomy, astrological prediction, divination in general, physiognomics, face reading, hand reading, geomantics, divination from stars, interpreting lightnings, dream reading, frenzy, magic in general, natural magic, mathematical magic, poison magic, earth and corps reading, theurgic, cabala, illusion, natural philosophy, principles, world, soul, metaphysics, ethics, politics, religion in general, images, temples, feasts, ceremonies, church offices, monastic orders, prostitution, fornication, begging, economy in general, personal economy, court economy, court nobility, common courtiers, court women, commerce, stewardship, agriculture, cattle holding, fishing, hunting, more on agriculture, military, nobility, heraldics, medicine in general, medical practice, pharmacy, chirurgy, anatomy, veterinary, dietetics, cooking, alchemy, right and law, canon law, attorneyship, notary, jurisprudence, inquisition, scholastic theology, the Word of God, masters of sciences.

It is not easy to divide the list into consistent blocks of disciplines, but it is visible that standard academic fields are alongside those with obscure

---

2. Heinrich Cornelius Agrippa von Nettesheim, *De incertitudine et vanitate scientiarum et artium atque excellentia Verbi Dei declamatio* (Antverpiae: Graphaeus, 1530). On the Neoplatonic context, see Daniele Conti, "Religione naturale e salvezza universale. Appunti sulla fortuna di Ficino e una nota su Agrippa e Camillo Renato," *Rinascimento seconda serie* 57 (2017): 231–85.

The Vanity of Arts and Sciences 189

activities and social behavior. The book concludes with a praise of the ass, a literary figure popular since *The Golden Ass* by Apuleius in the second century and resurrected as a means of satire in the Renaissance.[3]

The question of the meaning of this work may be addressed from this conclusion: Whatever Agrippa has to say about knowledge and science, it definitely has a satirical ring. Not only is the body of the work an instructive survey of all manner of knowledge, science, and human behavior, including courts, prostitution, and fishing; even in the two chapters presented here, the irony should not be lost on the reader that in those few pages, over thirty references can be made. (And the editor does not claim to have identified all sources.) The vanity of scholarship is presented through mustering much learning. On the surface, the book *On Occult Philosophy* appears to take its subject seriously, and yet, Agrippa was working on both books contemporaneously. If the occult sciences purport to provide the key to mastering the world, *On the Uncertainty* cautions against hubris. It is indicative that Michel de Montaigne in his *Essais* (III 9) elaborated on the theme of vanity in that same double meaning of hubris and skepticism; to him, as to Agrippa, scholarship is morally worthless and needs to be met with intellectual skepticism.[4]

BIBLIOGRAPHY

Primary Sources

Agrippa von Nettesheim, Heinrich Cornelius. *De incertitudine et vanitate scientiarum et artium atque excellentia Verbi Dei declamatio*. Antverpiae: Graphaeus, 1530.

Agrippa von Nettesheim, Heinrich Cornelius. *The vanity of arts and sciences by Henry Cornelius Agrippa ...* London: Everingham, Bentley, and Brown, 1694.

Ficino, Marsilio. *Opera omnia*. Edited by Paul Oskar Kristeller. 2 vols. [Basel 1576] Torino: Bottega d'Erasmo, 1983.

Pico della Mirandola, Giovanni Francesco. *Examen vanitatis doctrinae gentium et veritatis Christianae disciplinae*. [Mirandulae]: Maciochius, 1520.

Sanchez, Francisco. *That nothing is known = Quod nihil scitur*. Edited by Doug-

---

3. Cf. Nuccio Ordine, *Giordano Bruno and the Philosophy of the Ass* (New Haven, Conn.: Yale University Press, 1996).

4. Nicolas Correard, "'Qui addit scientiam, addit et laborem' (Ecc. I, 18): La vanité de savoir dans la littérature sério-comique de la Renaissance," *Études Épistémè. Revue de littérature et de civilisation (XVIe—XVIIIe siècles)* 22 (September 1, 2012), https://doi.org/10.4000/episteme.361.

las F. S. Thomson and Elaine Limbrick. Cambridge: Cambridge University Press, 1988.
Theophrastus. *On First Principles: (Known as His Metaphysics): Greek Text and Medieval Arabic Translation.* Edited by Dimitri Gutas. Translated by Bartolomeo da Messina. Leiden: Brill, 2010.
Victor, Sextus Aurelius. *Book on the Emperors.* Translated by H. W. Bird. Liverpool: Liverpool University Press, 1994.

Secondary Sources

Conti, Daniele. "Religione naturale e salvezza universale. Appunti sulla fortuna di Ficino e una nota su Agrippa e Camillo Renato." *Rinascimento* Seconda serie 57 (2017): 231–85.
Correard, Nicolas. "'Qui addit scientiam, addit et laborem' (Ecc. I, 18): La vanité de savoir dans la littérature sério-comique de la Renaissance." *Études Épistémè. Revue de littérature et de civilisation (XVIe—XVIIIe siècles)* 22 (September 1, 2012). https://doi.org/10.4000/episteme.361.
Hanegraaff, Wouter J. "Heinrich Cornelius Agrippa." In *The Occult World*, edited by Christopher Partridge. Milton Park: Routledge, 2015, 92–98.
Müller-Jahncke, Wolf-Dieter, and Paul Richard Blum. "Agrippa von Nettesheim (1486–1535): Philosophical Magic, Empiricism, and Skepticism." In *Philosophers of the Renaissance*, edited by Paul Richard Blum and translated by Brian McNeil, 124–32. Washington,. D.C.: The Catholic University of America Press, 2010.
Ordine, Nuccio. *Giordano Bruno and the Philosophy of the Ass.* New Haven, Conn.: Yale University Press, 1996.
Poel, Marc van der. *Cornelius Agrippa: The Humanist Theologian and His Declamations.* Leiden: Brill, 1997.
Strazzoni, Andrea. "Agrippa, Heinrich Cornelius." In *Encyclopedia of Renaissance Philosophy*, edited by Marco Sgarbi, 1–4. Cham: Springer International Publishing, 2016. https://doi.org/10.1007/978-3-319-02848-4_547-1.

HEINRICH CORNELIUS AGRIPPA VON NETTESHEIM

The Vanity of Arts and Sciences

Dedication[5]
Of the gods, none that Momus never plucks.
Of the heroes, Hercules chases all the monsters.
Of the demons, Pluto the king of the underworld berates all shadows.

5. This poem, without title and author, precedes or follows the table of contents in the Latin editions from the first one (1530) on; it is missing in English versions.

The Vanity of Arts and Sciences

Of the philosophers, Democritus ridicules all,
While Heraclitus bewails them.
Nothing knows Pyrrho.
To know all Aristotle vaunts.
Everything Diogenes despises.
None spares Agrippa,
Despises, knows, bewails, ridicules, berates, chases, plucks them all,
He is the philosopher, demon, hero, God and all.

OF THE INCERTAINTY AND VANITY OF WORLDLY ARTS AND SCIENCES[6]

Of the Sciences in General

It is an old opinion—and the concurring and unanimous judgment almost of all philosophers—that every science adds so much of a sublime nature to man himself. According to the capacity and worth of every person, science enables people to translate themselves beyond the limits of humanity and even to the celestial seats of the blessed. From hence have proceeded those various and innumerable encomiums of the sciences, whereby everyone has endeavored, in accurate and long orations, to prefer and, as it were, to extol beyond the heavens themselves those arts and mysteries wherein with continual labor he has exercised the strength and vigor of his ingenuity or invention.

But I, persuaded by reasons of another nature, do verily believe that there is nothing more pernicious, nothing more destructive to the well-being of men and the salvation of our souls, than the arts and sciences themselves. And therefore, quite contrary to what has been hitherto practiced, my opinion is that these arts and sciences are so far from being to be extolled with such high applause and esteem but, rather, that they are, for the most part, to be dispraised and vilified, and that, indeed, there is none which does not merit just cause of reproof and censure, nor any one which of itself deserves any praise or commendation, unless what it may borrow from the ingenuity and virtue of the first possessor. Despite this, I would ask you to take this opinion of mine in that modesty, which may imagine

---

6. Heinrich Cornelius Agrippa von Nettesheim, *The Vanity of Arts and Sciences by Henry Cornelius Agrippa* ... (London: Everingham, Bentley, and Brown, 1694), chap. 1 and "The Conclusion of the Work," 1–9, 364–68. Anonymous translation from the Latin edited by Jan Beran.

that I neither intend to reprehend those who believe the contrary nor that I endeavor to arrogate anything particular to myself above others. Therefore, I shall entreat you to suspend your censure of me for differing in this one thing from all others, so long as you find me laying an auspicious foundation of proof, not upon vulgar arguments drawn from the superficies and outside of things but upon the most firm reasons deduced from the most hidden bowels of secret knowledge. And this not in the sharp stile of Demosthenes or Chrysippus, which may not so well beseem a professor of Christianity but would rather show me to be a vain pursuer of flattery and ostentation, while I endeavor to varnish my speech with the focuses of eloquence.[7]

For to speak properly, not rhetorically, and to intend the truth of the matter, not the ornament of language, is the duty of one professing Sacred Literature. For the seat of truth is not in the tongue but in the heart. Neither is it of importance what language we use in the relation of truth, seeing that falsehood wants only eloquence and the trappings of words, whereby to insinuate itself into the minds of men. But the language of truth, as Euripides writes, is plain and simple,[8] not seeking the graces of art or painted flourishes. Therefore, if this great work of ours, undertaken without any flowers of eloquence (which in the series of our discourse we have not so much slighted as condemned), does prove offensive to your more delicate ears, we entreat you to bear it with the same patience as one of the Roman Emperors made use of when he stood still with his whole army to hear the tittle-tattle of an impertinent woman and with the same humor that King Archelaus[9] was wont to hear persons that were hoarse and of an unpleasant utterance, that thereby afterwards he might take more delight in the pleasing sounds of eloquent rhetoricians and tuneful voices. Remember that saying of Theophrastus, that the most illiterate were able to speak in the presence of the most elegant persons, while they spoke nothing but truth and reason.[10]

And now that I may no longer keep you in suspense through what

---

7. On rhetoric and theology, see Marc van der Poel, *Cornelius Agrippa: The Humanist Theologian and His Declamations* (Leiden: Brill, 1997). See in the appendix sections condemned by the Sorbonne in 1531.

8. Euripides, *Phoenissae* 469.

9. Latin: Archesilaus. The reference is unclear.

10. A negative example in Theophrastus, *Characters*, 7: "The Talker" or "Loquacity."

The Vanity of Arts and Sciences

tracts and byways, as it were, I have used to hint out this opinion of mine, it is time that I declare unto you. But first, I must admonish you that all sciences are as evil as good and that they bring us no other advantage to excel as deities more than what the Serpent of old promised when he said, "You shall be as Gods, knowing good and evil."[11] Let him therefore glory in this Serpent, who boasts himself in knowledge. We read this heresy of the Ophites[12] not a little unbecomingly to have done, who worshiped a serpent among the rest of their superstitions, as being the creature that first introduced the knowledge of virtue into Paradise. This agrees with that Platonic fable that feigns that one Theutus, being offended with mankind, was the first raiser of that devil called the sciences, not less hurtful than profitable, as Thamus, King of Egypt, wisely discourses writing of the inventors of arts and letters.[13] Hence, most grammarians expound and interpret the word *daemons* as much as to say artists.

But leaving these fables to their poets and philosophers, suppose there were no other inventors of arts than men themselves, yet were they the sons of the worst generation, even the sons of Cain, of whom it is truly said, "The sons of this world are wiser than the sons of light in this generation." If men were therefore the inventors of arts, is it not said, "Every man is a liar," "neither is there one that does good?"[14]

But grant on the other side that there may be some good men. Yet follows it not that the sciences themselves have anything of virtue, anything of truth in them, but what they reap and borrow from the inventors and possessors thereof? For if they light upon any evil person, they are hurtful, as: a perverse grammarian, an ostentatious poet, a lying historian, a flattering rhetorician, a litigious logician, a turbulent sophist, a loquacious Lullist,[15] a fortunetelling arithmetician, a lascivious musician, an impudent dancing-master, a boasting geometrician, a wandering cosmographer, a pernicious architect, a pirate-navigator, a fallacious astrologer, a wicked

11. Genesis 3:5.

12. A gnostic sect. See, for instance, Hippolytus, *Refutation of All Heresies,* bk. 5, chap. 6.

13. Plato, *Phaedrus* 274c-d.

14. Luke 16:8; Psalm 115:2; Psalm 13:1.

15. Follower of Raymond Lull (1232–1316). Agrippa had published a commentary *In artem brevem Raymundi Lullii commentaria* (Cologne, 1533), reprinted in his *Opera* in 1578, immediately after this *De vanitate.* All the disciplines mentioned here are also treated in the main text of this work and—if related to occultism—in *De occulta philosophia.*

magician, a perfidious cabalist, a dreaming naturalist, a wonder-feigning metaphysician, a morose ethicist, a treacherous politician, a tyrannical prince, an oppressing magistrate, a seditious people, a schismatic priest, a superstitious monk, a prodigal husband, a bargain-breaking merchant, a stealing customs officer, a slothful peasant, a careless shepherd, an envious fisherman, a bawling hunter, a plundering soldier, an exacting landlord, a murderous physician, a poisoning apothecary, a glutton-cook, a deceitful alchemist, a juggling lawyer, a perfidious notary, a bribe-taking judge, and a heretical and seducing divine. So, there is nothing more ominous than art and knowledge guarded with impiety, seeing that every man will become a ready inventor and a learned author of evil things.

If it light upon a person that is not so evil as foolish, there is nothing more insolent or dogmatic, having besides its own headstrong obstinacy the authority of learning and the weapons of argument to defend its own fury. While other fools lack it, they are tamer and quietly mad. As Plato said of rhetorician, "That the more simple and illiterate he is, the more he will take upon him to make speeches, imitate all things, and think himself not unworthy of any undertaking."[16] So that there is nothing more deadly than to be, as it were, rationally mad. If good and just men were the possessors of knowledge, then arts and sciences may probably become useful to the public weal, though they render their possessors no happier. For it is not, as Porphyrius and Iamblichus report, "That Happiness consists in the multitude of arts or heaps of words."[17] Happiness gains no increment from the quality of reasons and words. For should that be true, they that were most loaded with sciences would be happiest and those that wanted them would be unhappy altogether, hence it would come to pass that philosophers would be happier than divines.

For true beatitude consists not in the knowledge of good things but in good life, not in understanding but in living understandingly. Neither is it great learning but good will that joins men to God. Nor do outward arts avail to happiness, only as conditional means and not the causes of completing our happiness, unless assisted with a life answerable to the nature of those good things we profess. Therefore, Cicero says in his *Ora-*

16. Plato, *Republic* III, 397a.

17. Porphyrius, *De abstinentia animalium*, cap. 2; Marsilio Ficino, *Opera omnia*, ed. Paul Oskar Kristeller, vol. 2 [Basel 1576] (Torino: Bottega d'Erasmo, 1983), 1932.

The Vanity of Arts and Sciences   195

tion for Archias: "Experience tells us that nature without learning is more diligent in the pursuit of praise and virtue than learning without natural inclination."[18] It shall not then be needed (as the followers of Averroes contend) so violently to labor to season our minds with the so long, so tedious, so difficult, so unattainable learning of all sorts of sciences, which Aristotle confesses to be a common felicity and easy to be attained to by labor and diligence, but only to give ourselves to what is more easy and common to all, namely, the contemplation of the most noble object of all things, God.[19] This common act of contemplation is so easy to all men and is not obtained by syllogism and demonstration but by belief and adoration.

Where is, then, the great felicity of enjoying the sciences? Where is the praise and beatitude of the wise philosophers that make so much noise in the school, sounding with the encomiums of those men whose souls perhaps in the meantime are at that instant suffering the torments of hell? This Saint Augustine saw and feared while he exclaims with St. Paul, "The unlearned rise, and take heaven by force, while we with all our knowledge, are cast down into hell."[20] So that, if we may be bold to confess the truth, the tradition of all sciences are so dangerous and inconstant that it is far safer to be ignorant than to know: Adam had never been ejected out of Paradise had not the serpent been his master to teach him good and evil. And Saint Paul would have them thrown out of the church who would know more than they ought.[21] Socrates, when he had dived into the secrets of all sorts of science, was adjudged by the Oracle to be the wisest among many, when he had publicly professed that he knew nothing.[22]

The knowledge of all sciences is so difficult, if I may not say impossible, that the age of man will not suffice to learn the perfection of one art as it ought to be, which Ecclesiastes seems to intimate where he says, "Then I beheld the whole work of God that man cannot find out the work that is wrought under the Sun; wherefore man labors to seek it and cannot find it; yes, and though the wise man may think to know it, he cannot find it."[23]

18. Cicero, *Pro Archia* 7.15:2.
19. Cf. Aristotle, *Nicomachean Ethics* X, esp. chaps. 9–10, 1178 b 33 ff. Compare also Thomas Aquinas, *Sententia libri Ethicorum*, lib 10, lects. 13–14.
20. Augustine, *Confessions* 8.8.19.
21. Romans 1:18–32.
22. Plato, *Apology* 21a-b.
23. Ecclesiastes 8:17.

196 HEINRICH CORNELIUS AGRIPPA VON NETTESHEIM

Nothing can happen more pestilential to man than knowledge. This is that true plague that invades all mankind with so much confusion that it subverts all innocence subjecting us to so many clouds of sin and error and at length to death. This is the true pest that has subverted the whole and all human race at once, driven out all innocence, exposed us to so many sins and to death; it has extinguished the light of faith, casting our souls into profound darkness, and condemning the truth has mounted error to the highest throne. Therefore, in my opinion, neither is Valentinian the Emperor to be dispraised, who is reported to be such an open enemy of learning, nor is Licinius to be accounted blameworthy, who affirmed learning to be the poison and bane of the commonwealth; even Cicero, the abundant fount of letters, is reported by Valerius to have eventually despised the letters.[24]

But such is the large freeness and free largeness of truth as can be apprehended by no contemplations of science, by no judgment of sense how quick so ever, by no evident proof, no syllogistic demonstration, no human discourse of reason, but only by faith.[25] Aristotle, in his book of *Second Resolutions*, accounts him who is endowed with it [faith] to be in a better condition than him who is endowed with knowledge.[26] Expounding these words, Philoponus said, faith is to be better disposed as more knowing by faith than by demonstration, which is done by the cause. Therefore, says Theophrastus in his *Book of Supernaturals*, "As to so far, we may discern by the cause, taking our beginnings from the senses; but after we have passed the extremes and first principles, we can go no farther, either because we know not the cause or through the defect of our weak understanding."[27] Plato in his *Timaeus* said, "That our abilities will not reach to the explanation of those things, but commands to believe those that delivered them

---

24. Valentinianus, Ammianus Marcellinus, *Rerum gestarum* 30.10:8; Licinius: cf. Sextus Aurelius Victor, *Book on the Emperors*, trans. H. W. Bird (Liverpool: Liverpool University Press, 1994), 41, 49; Cicero: Valerius Maximus, *Facta et dicta memorabilia* 8.13 (ext).1.

25. The Protestant formula regarding salvation of the soul: *sola fide*, rather than through works.

26. Aristoteles, *Posterior Analytics* 1, 72 a 33. Cf. Thomas Aquinas, *Expositio Posteriorum*, lib. 1 l. 6 n. 5. The Latin and the English text refer to *Prior Analytics*.

27. Theophrastus, *On First Principles: (Known As His Metaphysics): Greek Text and Medieval Arabic Translation*, ed. Dimitri Gutas, trans. Bartolomeo da Messina (Leiden: Brill, 2010), 20b, 240.

The Vanity of Arts and Sciences

before, though they speak without any necessity of demonstration."[28] For the Academic philosophers were in high esteem, for affirming that nothing could be affirmed. There were also the Pyrrhonists and many others who were of the same opinion, namely, that nothing could be affirmed.[29]

So that knowledge has nothing super-excellent above belief, especially where the integrity of the author directs the free will of believing. Hence that Pythagorical answer of "He has said it,"[30] and that vulgar proverb of the Peripatetics, "We are to believe every man expert in his art."[31] Thus, we believe the grammarian as to the signification of words. The logician believes the parts of speech delivered by the grammarian. The rhetorician takes for granted his forms of argument from the logician. The poet borrows his measures from the musician. The geometrician takes his proportions from the arithmetician, and upon both these, the astrologer pins his sleeve. Supernaturalists use the conjectures of naturalists, and every artist rightly trusts to the method and rules of another, for every science has certain principles that must be believed and can be by no means demonstrated; if any one denies them, those philosophers will straight cry out: he is not to be disputed withal as a denier of principles, or else they will deliver him over to the rack of his own experience, such that if one should deny fire to be hot, let him be thrown into the fire and then resolve the question. So that philosophers are forced to become executioners, compelling men to believe that by force that they cannot teach by reason.

To a commonwealth, there can be nothing more pernicious than learning and science. If some happen to exceed the rest in these, all things are carried out by their determination as taking upon them to be most knowing; relying on the simplicity and inexperience of the multitude, they appropriate all authority to themselves, which is often the occasion of the

---

28. Plato, *Timaeus* 40d.

29. In the short version "that nothing is known," it became a book title for Francisco Sanches (or Sanchez; 1581): Francisco Sanchez, *That nothing is known = Quod nihil scitur*, eds. Douglas F. S. Thomson and Elaine Limbrick (Cambridge: Cambridge University Press, 1988). A list of ancient sceptics, including Pyrrho and the Academy, in Giovanni Francesco Pico della Mirandola, *Examen vanitatis doctrinae gentium et veritatis Christianae disciplinae* ([Mirandulae]: Maciochius, 1520), bk. 1, chap. 4.

30. Cicero, *De natura deorum* 1:10: "Ipse dixit," the argument from authority. In Ficino, *Opera omnia*, vol. 1, 77 (end of *De Christiana religione*, transferred to Christ).

31. Known as a juridical maxim.

changing of a republic into an oligarchy, which dividing into factions is at length easily oppressed by single tyranny. Never any man in the world was ever known to attain this without knowledge, without learning, without literature. Only Sulla the Dictator, who, an illiterate person, invaded and obtained the supreme government, to whose ignorance the commonwealth was yet so far beholden that it was the occasion that of his own accord, he quit his great command.[32]

Furthermore, all sciences are but the opinions and decrees of private men, both those that are of use and those that are pernicious, as well those that are wholesome, as those that are pestiferous, as well the bad, as the good, never being perfect but both doubtful, full of error and contention. And that this is evident we shall make appear by taking a survey and making a particular inspection into every particular science.

The Conclusion of the Work

You, therefore, Asses[33] who are now with your children under the command of Christ by means of his Apostles and messengers and readers of true wisdom in his holy Gospel: Being freed from the fogs and mists of flesh and blood, if you desire to attain to this divine and true wisdom—not of the "tree of the knowledge of good and evil" but of the *tree of life*—then set aside the traditions of men and every inquiry and discourse of flesh and blood, whether it concern reason, consideration of causes or effects, conversing now not with the schools of philosophers and sophists but with your own selves. For the notions of all things are trusted within your own breasts, which—as the Academics confess—the scriptures themselves do testify seeing that God created all things as "very good," that is to say, in the best degree they could consist. He, therefore, as he created the trees full of fruit, so he created our souls, which are like rational trees, full of Forms and Ideas, though through the sin of our first parents all things were concealed, and oblivion took place, the mother of ignorance.

But you who can remove the veil from your understandings, who are wrapped up in the darkness of ignorance, vomit up that Lethean Drench, which has made you drunk with forgetfulness. Awake in the true light, you

32. Plutarch, *Parallel lives*, Sulla 5:5–6, on his rough character and violent success.
33. The preceding chapter contains "A praise of the Ass," a literary trope since antiquity.

The Vanity of Arts and Sciences

who are drowned in the sleep of irrationality, and then forthwith with an open countenance you shall pass from light to light. For "you are anointed," as Saint John says, "by the Holy Ghost and know all things." And again, "There is no necessity that you should be taught by any, because his anointing instructs you in all things."[34] For he alone is that which gives language and wisdom. David, Isaiah, Ezekiel, Jeremiah, Daniel, John Baptist, and many other prophets and Apostles were never bred up in learning, but out of shepherds, peasants, and fools became thoroughly learned in all things. Solomon in a dream of one night was replenished with the knowledge of all things, both sublunary and celestial, and with so much prudence in the administration of government that there was never any prince equal to him. Yet all these were mortal men, as you are, and sinners. You will say, perhaps, that this has happened to a very few, and those:

> A few whom equal Jove
> Would signalize by his transcending love;
> Or such whose ardent zeal divinely fired
> With constant motion to the stars aspired.[35]

However, do not despair. The hand of God is not shortened to them that call upon him, that give a true obedience to his will. Anthony and the Barbarian Christian servant gained the full knowledge of divine things by the help of three days prayer, as Saint Augustine testifies.[36] But you, who cannot, like the prophets, like the Apostles, like those other holy men, behold those things with a clear and unclouded intellect, may procure understanding from them who have beheld these things with a clear sight.

There is also another way remaining as Saint Jerome says to Ruffinus, that what the Spirit has suggested to the prophets and Apostles should be sought by you with diligent study; I mean the study of that learning that is delivered in the Bible, being the most sacred oracles of the true God and received by the church with an unanimous consent.[37] They are not of such things as have been invented by the wit of men, for they do not enlighten but darken the understanding. And therefore, we must have recourse to Moses, to Solomon, to the Prophets, to the Evangelists, to the Apostles,

---

34. 1 Johannes 2:20 and 27.
35. Virgil, *Aeneis* VI 129–130.
36. Augustinus, *De doctrina Christiana*, Prolgus 4.
37. Perhaps Hieronymus, *Epistolae* 3 (ad Rufinum monachum), in PL 23, 334.

who, shining with all sorts of learning, wisdom, manners, languages, oracles, prophecies, miracles, and holiness, have spoken of heavenly things from God himself, of inferior things above men, delivering all the things of God and secrets of nature distinctly and clearly to us. For all the secrets of God and Nature, all manner of customs and laws, all understanding of things past, present, and to come are fairly taught in the books of the Holy Scripture.

Whither do you therefore run headlong? Why do you seek knowledge of them who, having spent all their days in searching, have lost all their time and labor being unable to attain to any thing of certain truth? Fools and wicked men who, not regarding the gifts of the Holy Ghost, strive to learn from lying philosophers and doctors of error those things that you ought to receive from Christ and the Holy Ghost! Think you to draw knowledge from the ignorance of Socrates, or light out of the darkness of Anaxagoras, or virtue of the wells of Democritus, and wisdom out of the madness of Empedocles? Think you to have piety out of Diogenes's tub, or sense out of the stupidity of Carneades, or wisdom from impious Aristotle or perfidious Averroes, or faith out of the superstition of the Platonists? You are in error, being deceived by them who were themselves deceived.

But recall yourselves: You who are desirous of the truth, descend from the clouds of men's traditions and adhere to the true light. Behold, a voice from heaven, a voice speaking from above and showing more apparent than the sun that you are enemies to yourselves and delay the receiving of wisdom. Hear the oracle of Baruch: "God is," says he, "and no other shall be compared to him. He has found out all manner of learning, and has taught it to Jacob's son and to Israel his beloved, giving laws and precepts and ordaining sacrifices."[38] After this, he was seen upon the earth, conversed with men, was made flesh, teaching us plainly with his own mouth what was mysteriously delivered in the law and by the Prophets. And that you may not think the scriptures relate only to divine, and not natural things, hear what the wise man witnesses of himself:

He has given the true knowledge of those things that are, that I might know the situation of the earth's compass, the virtues of the elements, the beginning, ending, middle, and revolution of the times, the course of the year, the influence of

38. Cf. Baruch 3:35–37.

The Vanity of Arts and Sciences

the stars, the nature of animals, sympathy and antipathy of creatures, the force of winds, thought of men, difference of plants, and the virtues of roots. In brief, I have learned whatever things are hidden and concealed, for the Artificer of all things has taught me wisdom.[39]

The divine wisdom fails in nothing, nothing escapes it, there is no addition to it, for it comprehends all things. Know, therefore, that there needs no long study but humility of spirit and pureness of heart, not the sumptuous furniture of books but a pure understanding made fit for the truth as the lock is for the key. For the number of books hinders the learner, and he who follows many authors errs with many. All things are contained and taught in the only volume of the Bible, but only with the proviso that they are not to be understood but by those who are enlightened. For, to others, they are only parables and riddles, sealed up with many seals. Pray then to the Lord God in faith, doubtful of nothing, that the Lamb of the tribe of Judah may come and open his sealed book;[40] it is the Lamb who is "only holy and true, who alone has the key" of wisdom and knowledge, who "opens and no man shuts, and shuts and no man opens."[41] This is Jesus Christ, the Word, the Son of God the Father, the wisdom that makes godlike,[42] the true teacher, made man like unto us that he might make us Children of God, like himself, blessed to all eternity.

But lest I should declaim beyond my hourglass, let this be the end of our discourse.

39. Wisdom 7:17–21.
40. Apocalypse 6:1.
41. Apocalypse 3:7; Isaiah 22:22.
42. Latin: *et sapientia Deificans*, missing in the English: a Neoplatonic formula of spiritual ascent.

13

JUAN LUIS VIVES
(1493–1540)

Introduction to Wisdom

PAUL RICHARD BLUM

INTRODUCTION

Juan Luis Vives was born in Valencia, Spain, to a Jewish family who had converted to Christianity. Because of the persecution of "conversos," he left Spain for good and studied at various colleges in Paris. In 1519, he taught at the University of Louvain, living most of the time in Bruges (now Belgium), from where he traveled repeatedly to England, among other places to Oxford, where he befriended the humanists Thomas Linacre and Thomas More. Under the influence of Erasmus of Rotterdam (1466–1536), Vives continued spreading humanist ideals of language, logic, and ethics.

Vives' *Introduction to Wisdom*, first published in 1524 in Latin, was one of his most popular works and was published in the English translation of Richard Morison in 1540 (anonymous) and 1544 (with the translator's name).[1] In republishing the beginning

---

1. Juan Luis Vives, *Introductio ad sapientiam. Eiusdem Satellitium siue symbola. Eiusdem Epistolae duae de ratione studii puerilis* (Lovanii: apud Petrum Martinum Alostensem, 1524); we are using idem: *Introductio ad sapientiam. Satellitium siue symbola. Epistolae duae de ratione studii puerilis. Tria capita addita initio Suetoni Tranquilli* (Parisiis: Colinaeus, 1527); Juan Luis Vives,

Introduction to Wisdom 203

of this work in this anthology using the old translation, we draw attention to the content as it was available to the public of Tudor England, which includes the most prominent English writers, from Thomas More to William Shakespeare.

Vives offers an exhortation to leading the life of wisdom, and in doing so, he amalgamates Christian tradition with Stoic ethics. As a result, we read advice premised on humanity's ambiguity about materiality versus spirituality, animalistic needs versus intellectual aspirations. Without elaborating on it, Vives exposes the paradox of human life between pure intellectuality and physical conditions. At the same time, he suggests that the human mind, while being entangled in corporeality, can and must be nourished both physically and educationally. In that, he presages both Juan Huarte's physicalist notion of the human mind and Ignatius of Loyola, who, in his *Spiritual Exercises*, proposed conscious and purposeful direction of the human intellectual talents.[2] This humanist effort to find an approach to human understanding in Christian context culminated in René Descartes and his theory of the passions of the soul. One component that is peculiar to Vives's humanist perspective is his including the surrounding world in the discussion of wisdom: in addition to body and mind, there are "things *extra hominem*" that nevertheless shape life; among these are not only material goods but also "power, nobility, honor, dignity" and their contraries, that is, all the values that are beyond the self and depend on social interaction. Here, we see the Stoic influence, which modifies any potential mind-body dualism.

We are presenting here the 1540 translation with careful modernization, in which we changed only those words and syntactical structures that are unintelligible to the present-day reader.[3] This may help reading

---

An Introduction to Wysedome (Londini: Bertheletus, 1540); and Juan Luis Vives, *An Introduction to Vvysedome, Made by Ludouicus Viues, and Translated in to Englyshe by Rycharde Morysine* [Richard Morison] (Londini: Bertheletus, 1544). A transcription in modern typeface of the latter edition is available at Juan Luis Vives, "An Introduction to Vvysedome, Made by Ludouicus Viues, and Translated in to Englyshe by Rycharde Morysine," accessed December 1, 2019, https://quod.lib.umich.edu/e/eebo/a14530.0001.001/1: A14530.0001.001:3.3?view=toc.

2. Cf. Paul Richard Blum, "Psychology and Culture of the Intellect: Ignatius of Loyola and Antonio Possevino," in *Cognitive Psychology in Early Jesuit Scholasticism*, ed. Daniel Heider (Neunkirchen-Seelscheid: Editiones Scholasticae, 2016), 12–37.

3. Thanks to Kevin Kane for transcribing and editing. A modern retranslation with a valuable introduction is available in Juan Luis Vives, *Vives' Introduction to Wisdom: A*

204   JUAN LUIS VIVES

Vives's advice (which otherwise might sound commonplace) critically, with a view on sixteenth-century intellectual frameworks. In addition to that, Morison's translation is not faithful to Vives's style of aphorisms and maxims; frequently, he elaborated on the argument in an effort to make it plausible, and occasionally he left passages out or combined two into one.[4] In the Latin editions, the sections were numbered, but not so in the English. Our selection presents the equivalent of the first 201 statements covering the introduction, division of things, definition and price of things, body, mind, and erudition. What follows elaborates on specifics, namely, virtue and passions, religion, charity, conviviality, language, human interaction, and behavior toward oneself.

BIBLIOGRAPHY

Primary Sources

Vives, Juan Luis. "A Fable of Man." In *The Renaissance Philosophy of Man: Selections in Translation*, edited by Ernst Cassirer, Paul Oskar Kristeller, and John Herman Randall, Jr., and translated by Nancy Lenkeith, 383–93. Chicago: University of Chicago Press, 1948.

———. *An Introduction to Vvysedome, Made by Ludouicus Viues, and Translated in to Englyshe by Rycharde Morysine.* Londini: Bertheletus, 1544.

———. "An Introduction to Vvysedome, Made by Ludouicus Viues, and Translated in to Englyshe by Rycharde Morysine." Accessed December 1, 2019. https://quod.lib.umich.edu/e/eebo/a14530.0001.001/1:A14530.0001.001:3.3?view=toc.

———. *An Introduction to Wysedome.* Londini: Bertheletus, 1540.

———. *In Pseudodialecticos: A Critical Edition.* Edited by Charles Fantazzi. Leiden: Brill, 1979.

———. *Introductio ad sapientiam. Satellitium siue symbola. Epistolae duae de ratione studii puerilis. Tria capita addita initio Suetoni Tranquilli.* Parisiis: Colinaeus, 1527.

———. *Introductio ad sapientiam. Eiusdem Satellitium siue symbola. Eiusdem Epistolae duae de ratione studii puerilis.* Lovanii: apud Petrum Martinum Alostensem, 1524.

———. *Juan Luis Vives against the Pseudodialecticians.* Edited and translated by Rita Guerlac. Dordrecht: Reidel, 1979.

———. *On Assistance to the Poor.* Translated by Alice Tobriner [Originally 1971]. Toronto: University of Toronto Press, 1999.

Renaissance Textbook, trans. Marian Leona Tobriner (New York: Teachers College Press, 1968).

4. Tracey A. Sowerby, *Renaissance and Reform in Tudor England: The Careers of Sir Richard Morison* (Oxford: University Press, 2010), 35–39.

———. *On Education*. Translated by Foster Watson [Originally 1913]. Cambridge: Cambridge University Press, 2015.
———. *Selected Works of Juan Luis Vives*. Edited by Constantinus Matheeussen, Charles Fantazzi, and E. George. 12 vols. Leiden: Brill, 1987ff.
———. *The Education of a Christian Woman: A Sixteenth-Century Manual*. Edited and translated by Charles Fantazzi. Chicago: University of Chicago Press, 2000.
———. *The Origins of Modern Welfare: Juan Luis Vives, De Subventione Pauperum, and City of Ypres, Forma Subventionis Pauperum*. Translated by Paul Spicker. Oxford: Peter Lang, 2010.
———. *Vives' Introduction to Wisdom: A Renaissance Textbook*. Translated by Marian Leona Tobriner. New York: Teachers College Press, 1968.

Secondary Sources

Andersson, D. C. "Juan Luis Vives (1492/93–1540). A Pious Eclectic." In *Philosophers of the Renaissance*, edited by Paul Richard Blum and translated by Brian McNeil, 133–47. Washington, D.C.: The Catholic University of America Press, 2010.
Casini, Lorenzo. "Juan Luis Vives [Joannes Ludovicus Vives]." In *The Stanford Encyclopedia of Philosophy*, edited by Edward N. Zalta, Spring 2017. Stanford, Calif.: Metaphysics Research Lab, Stanford University, 2017. https://plato.stanford.edu/archives/spr2017/entries/vives/.
———. "Vives, Juan Luis." In *Encyclopedia of Renaissance Philosophy*, edited by Marco Sgarbi, 1–10. Cham: Springer International Publishing, 2016. https://doi.org/10.1007/978-3-319-02848-4_694-1.
Fantazzi, Charles, ed. *A Companion to Juan Luis Vives*. Leiden: Brill, 2008.
Sowerby, Tracey A. *Renaissance and Reform in Tudor England: The Careers of Sir Richard Morison*. Oxford: University Press, 2010.
Vilarroig, Jaime, ed. *En busca del humanismo perdido: Estudios sobre la obra de Juan Luis Vives*. Granada: Editorial Comares, 2017.

JUAN LUIS VIVES

Introduction to Wisdom

True and real wisdom is, corrupt affectation set aside, truly to judge of things. We hope to esteem everything to be as it is, neither coveting the vile, as though they were precious, nor refuting precious, as though they were of no price, nor giving dispraise to things worthy of praise, nor commending things worthy of discommendation. For from this spring, all error runs into men's minds.

There is nothing more hurtful in man's life than this corrupt judgment: to not esteem everything as it ought to be, and at such price as it is worth.

The opinions and common persuasions of the people are pernicious, because for the most part, they judge all things most fondly.

Certainly, the vulgar people are a great schoolmaster of great errors.

There is nothing to which we ought to give more study than he who gives himself to knowledge and wisdom despite the judgment of the rude multitude.

First, let him suspect as many things as the multitude with great assent and consent does approve until he has examined them after those men's rule who make virtue a measure to try all matters by.

Let every man, even from his childhood, use to have right opinions of all things, which shall grow and increase as his age does.

Let every man desire upright things and flee the crooked, choose the good, and refute the evil. This use and custom shall turn well-doing almost into nature and work so that none but those who are compelled and found to be weaker in combat shall be brought to do evil.

The best kind of life is (as soon as you can) to be chosen: custom shall make this as it is best for you, so within a short space to be most pleasant.

All the rest of our life hangs upon our upbringing when we were children.

Therefore, the first step by which men climb unto wisdom is that which so many ancient writers speak of *se ipsum nosce*: "Every man ought to know himself."[5]

A DIVISION OF SUCH THINGS AS ARE PERTAINING UNTO MEN

Man is constituted and made of body and mind: the body we have of the earth and those elements that we feel and touch, like unto the bodies of beasts.

The mind we have given to us from heaven, like unto angels, like to God himself: by this part, man is esteemed man, and as great wise men

---

5. Motto of the Oracle in Delphi, often repeated.

think, they alone are to be taken for men who in this have their just portion.

There shall be in the body, as belonging unto it, beauty, health, integrity of members, strength, lightness, delectation, and their contraries: sickness, lack of limbs, weakness, sloth, sorrow, and other as well commodities and incommodities of the body; there shall be commodities of the mind, such as learning and virtue, and their contraries, such as rudeness and vice.

There shall be certain things not given to all men but to a few; these shall be called "things *extra hominem*"—as they are outside the nature of man, such as riches, power, nobility, honor, dignity, neediness, ignobility, vile estimation, shame, obscureness, and hatred.

A DEFINITION OF THINGS AND THEIR PRICE

The queen and princess of all things most high is virtue unto whom all others serve as handmaids to their mistresses: they do as by duty what they are commanded. I call virtue a reverent love toward God and man, a right service and worshipping of God, a right love toward man: love I say, not ending in words but joined with earnest will to do good. Other things, if they are referred to this virtue, that is, if they are taught, kept, and spent for her sake and at her command, they cannot seem evil. Nor so they that call riches or other goods, thought so of them as now the rude people do, which have so corrupted the true and native significations of things, that many of them have lost their right estimation and are changed upside-down. For we must understand where, when, and how far these things are good.

We may not esteem riches above their value, or judge that precious stones, metals, royal palaces, or gorgeous implements of the home are riches, or to be rich those who have these but, rather, that riches is to not want such things that are necessarily required to man's life.

True glory is to be well spoken of for virtue's sake.

True honor is to be had in veneration for some great virtue.

The grace that men obtain of princes or other people should be a favor borne to them for their amiable virtues and qualities worthy of love.

Dignity is either a right opinion that one man has of the other for virtue's sake or else a certain beauty of some inward virtue, outwardly expressed before the eyes of men.

Power and reign is to have many who you may succor and aid in right and honesty.

He is to be reckoned noble who is known by some excellent act to be noble, or else comes of an ancient stock and shows himself to be virtuous and have worthy qualities, like his parents.

A right gentleman is he who nature has fashioned and set as in a standing for the reception of virtue.

Health is a temperate habit of the body, whereby the mind both keeps her strength and exercises her power.

Beauty stands in such lineaments, shape, and portraiture of the body and does show a beautiful mind dwells therein.

Strength and valiance suffice to accomplish the exercises of virtue without weariness.

Pleasure is a pure, sound, whole, and continual delectation, which is taken only of those things that belong to the mind.

If a man does discuss and reason these things aforementioned to be otherwise, that is, after the mind and judgment of the ignorant people, he shall find them to be things worthy for men, things vain, and also very hurtful.

First, all outward things should be either referred to the body or to the mind, as riches are to maintenance of our life, as honor bears witness to our virtue and well-doing.

The body itself is nothing else but a cover and a thing bound to serve the soul, whereunto both nature, reason, and comeliness command that said body to be subject as a brute thing, so that death, an earthly thing, can never truly harm a man because of the divine nature within him.

Furthermore, learning is sought for and lodged in the mind for this intent, that we may thereby know both sin and eschew it, and know virtue, and attain it.

If learning does not do this in him who has it, she leaves her whole duty undone.

What other thing is our life but a certain pilgrimage, beset on every side with so many dangerous chances, where the end thereof is every hour hanging over it so that it often times falls upon most light occasions?

Therefore, it is a great folly to do anything that is foul or filthy, for the love of uncertain life, as who should say you are sure to live long after your naughty doing?

As it is in a journey, so is it in men's life: the lighter and less burden a man carries, the easier and pleasanter his journey is.

Moreover, the nature of man is such and so ordained that it needs very few things. In so much that, if a man will more closely behold this thing, doubtless he cannot but utterly condemn as mad folk those who so greedily and so carefully accumulate goods upon goods, whereas so little is sufficient.

His saying was pretty and quick that thus expresses riches: *sunt brevis vitae longum viaticum*, that is: they are great and a long purveyance for a little and short life.[6]

Therefore, riches, possessions, and apparel ought to be prepared only for our necessary use, which is not helped by immeasurable riches but rather oppressed, as ships overladen with too great a freight.

Gold itself, if you use it not, differs very little from clay, save that the custody thereof does put you to more unquietness, causing you, for your mind is set thereon, to neglect such things as ought to be regarded above all other.

Money brings men into a kind of idolatry, as often for it, other things are left aside (I mean godly reverence and cleanliness), which are the great, chief, and first in nature. How many deceits, guiles, and snares are lain for riches? How many and sundry ways do they come to nothing? And into how many vices do they, when they tarry, drive men, draw men, drown men?

What other thing is gay apparel but instruments to strike up a dance of pride?

Necessity first invented the profitable garment; debauchery and riches found the precious, which vanity fashioned into her trick. Great contention is in variety of apparel, which has taught men many superfluous and hurtful things by reason that they seek to be honored, even for that which plainly declares their infirmity, folly, and weakness.

---

6. Common place, for instance, in Cassiodorus, *De artibus ac disciplinis*, 570: De definitionibus.

Hereby, it comes to pass that this part of riches, such as gorgeous buildings, goodly household stuff, precious stones, and other such ornaments is rather for bragging and to lure other men's eyes than for the use and profit of those that possess them.

What other thing is nobility now but a chance to be borne of this or that gentle blood and an opinion grafted upon the foolishness of rude and unlearned people, which often times is gotten by robbery and similar ways?

True and perfect nobility springs from virtue. Therefore, it is great madness for any man to boast of one's parents being nothing himself, dishonoring their noble acts with his lewd doings.

Truly, we are all made of like elements and have all one God, Father to us all, yet to despise the birth or stock of any man is to criticize God because he is the author of every man's nativity.

What other thing is power than a fair burden, wherein if man knew what troubles and cares lie hidden, how great a sea of evil every day overruns the small sweetness of it, then there would be no man so ambitious nor so greedy of honor who would not flee from power as a grievous misery. He would, as that king said, not stoop to take up a royal crown if it lay before him on the ground.

How odious a thing is it to govern evil men? How much more if you be evil yourself?

Honor, if it springs not of virtue, is falsely given and wrongfully taken. Neither can it fully delight you, whereas your conscience denies you to serve it. Again, if it does arise of virtue, virtue teaches you to refuse it. For that which is done for desire of honor ought not to be called or taken for virtue. Honor must follow well-doing and is not to be craved of the well-doers.

How can dignities be called dignities when they chance to most unworthy persons, ensnared by deceit, by craving for money, and such other naughty means, especially where they be given by the arbitration of the rude multitude, a beast of many heads that does nothing as reason and right judgment would? And what thing is glory other than, as he said, a vain blast that fills fools' ears? And as honor and dignity are rather in him who gives them than in him who receives them, so glory brings little or nothing to whom it is given unto. Certainly, they both are uncertain, wandering and soon gone very like the multitude, their parent, which in the space of a day both highly praises and deeply dispraises the same man. We see, therefore, that honor commonly fastest flies from him that most seeks it and goes to them that least regard it, agreeing in this point with the nature and condition of the variable people, who oftentimes flee from whom they ought soonest to follow. I need not say that this honor and dignity arise of causes sometimes foolish, sometimes very naughty. Oftentimes, he advances that can play well at tennis; oftentimes he waxes honorable that leaves honesty, spending his patrimony upon trinkets, minstrels, and scoffers.

But beware, that is to say, robbery without punishment is a great announcer of men to honor—such is the madness of foolish people.

Let every man descend down into himself and there secretly think well upon this matter, and then he shall find how little comes to him by fame, by rumors, by worship, but rather by such honor as the people give him, wherein many now know much glory.

What difference is between the highest king, that is, and the lowest slave, when they both be asleep?

What is beauty in the body, truly a well-colored skin? If the inward parts could be seen, what filthiness would be discovered even in the most beautiful body?

The fairest body is nothing else but a dunghill covered by white and purple.

What does beauty or pretty features of the body avail, if the mind is unclean and if there be as the Greek writer says: *in hospicio pulchro, hospes deformis,* that is to say, a foul guest in a fair host.

For what purpose does strength of the body serve? What things most great and fitting for man are not gotten by strength of the body but by the gifts of wit? Our strength, be it ever so great, can in no way be equal with the strength of a bull or an elephant; it is reason, it is wit, it is policy whereby we overcome them.

I need tell no man that beauty, strength, agility, and other gifts of the body shortly vanish away as flowers do.

And aches, a small fever alone, brings oftentimes a very strong champion to death's door and soon shakes away his fresh color, his beauty, and his strength.

And although sickness or other mischance come not to them, for all them of necessity through age, which ever creeps on, must needs decay.

No man, therefore, of right can count such outward things, as so suddenly depart away from him to other men, to be his; no man can reckon things of the body to be his, which flee away so fast, and so soon depart.

What will you now say when those things, which so many do highly desire, be occasions of great vices as of insolent arrogance, of lustfulness, of fierceness, of envy, of pure hatred, of strife, of debate, of battle, murder, and manslaughter?

The delectation of the body is vile and beastly, as the body itself is, and beasts be more often moved and have more pleasure and longer also than men. This pleasure not only overwhelms the body with many diseases, bringing great damage and loss of goods, but also wounds the mind with sorrowful repentance and dulls the wit, which is much extenuated, abated, and broken through the delicate cherishing of the body. Finally, there follows irksomeness of itself and hatred of all virtue.

It is not lawful for any man to use such pleasures openly. For as they are much unbecoming to the nobleness of the man's mind, so is there none so far past all grace but he who abashes to use them in presence of many witnesses. No, because they engender ignominy and shame, such as who use them are driven to seek darkness and secret corners.

And furthermore, these fleeting, short, and soon passing pleasures may neither by any means be returned and kept, neither do they come pure but are with some bitterness intermingled. Therefore, judge not after the consent of the common people the greatest evil to be poverty, ignobility, imprisonment, nakedness, worldly shame, deformity of body, sickness, and imbecility; rather, think vices and their affinities as foolishness, ignorance, amassed dullness, and lack of brain the greatest evils, and their contraries: knowledge, quickness of wit, and sobriety of mind, to be great virtues.

If you have either gifts of fortune or of the body, they shall much profit you if you bestow them virtuously. But if they help to set out vice, they will necessarily do much hurt. If you have neither the one nor the other, do not seek them with loss of honesty, for that would be like buying a little clay with a great sum of gold or to change health for painful sickness.

There can be no greater advantage to the soul than the increase of godliness, no greater gains to the body than to know how to use the state present and to be content with it, how simple so ever it be.

And albeit we ought to do nothing to the intent that we would prefer men should tickle us with fond praises, yet we must labor to keep our good name always unspotted, for the regard thereof keeps us oftentimes from much naughtiness and also is a good example to stir others to well doing.

And hereof comes that old precept of great wise men: "Thou shalt no evil do, nor any thing that belongs thereto." If we cannot attain to this, well, we must be content that in our conscience we know our selves devoid of secret grudge and unquietness. For when men's nature be so corrupt that they count virtue to be vice, then we must be content that God alone approves our inward and outward acts, though men allow neither.

It is easy to turn either the incommodities of the body or the mischances of fortune to our profit and those of evils to make them good, if you suffer them patiently, and the less that they serve you, the more you endure to follow virtue. Virtues oftentimes have been exceedingly increased by hurts of the body and loss of goods.

OF THE BODY

And for as much as in our pilgrimage we bear a soul enclosed within our body, great treasure in fictile vessels, we may not utterly refuse and cast always all regard and respect to the body. Yet we must so entreat and order the same that it may not take itself to be a master or a fellow but rather a servant. The body is not fed for his own sake but the soul's sake.

The more cherishing that the carcass has, the less is the soul looked upon. The more delicately the body is handled, the more stubbornly it wrestles against the mind and casts it off, as a horse too well cherished uses to casts off his rider. The huge burden of the body sorely oppresses the mind, fatness, and overmuch cherishing of the belly diminishes and dulls the quickness of wit.

Food, sleep, all manner of exercise, and all the whole governance of the body must be used for the health thereof and must not be set upon pleasure and delicacy. Thus, it may better serve the mind and not wax wanton through too much pampering. Yet, it must not fall into decay for lack of strength and nourishment.

There is nothing that does so much debilitate the lively power, the quick vigor of the mind, and also the strength of the body as does voluptuousness. For as all the strength of the body and mind is established and made hardy with exercise and moderate labor, so by idleness and wanton pleasure their powers are weakened, and their strengths fade and fall away.

Clean keeping of the body (delicate meals and drink laid apart) does greatly both maintain health of the body and much comfort their wit.

You shall wash your hands and your face often with cold water and dry them again with a fair towel.

You shall often clean those places of your body out of which filthiness comes from your inward parts, as your head, your ears, your nostrils, your eyes, your arm holes, and your other secret places that nature hides and honestly scarcely would have named. Let your feet be kept clean and warm.

Among all the parts of your body, keep the nape of your neck from cold.

Eat not by and by after you rise, and eat little before dinner; breakfast is given to assuage the gnawing and complaints of a young stomach or to comfort nature and not to fill the belly. Therefore, three or four morsels of bread are sufficient without any drink or with a little, and that very small. For such is no less wholesome unto the wit than as it is to the body.

Accustom yourself at dinner and supper to feed but on one manner of meal. If your substance will suffer you, let it be such as is most wholesome, fine, and of least grossness. Eat but of one although there be many dishes, and if you be at your own table, suffer not many to come upon it. Variety of meats is very hurtful, yet the diversity of sauces is much worse.

Clean and pure diet, agreeable to temperate and chaste minds, is a great saver in a household, and that alone shows us how few things we have need of.

Let us do notable offence either in hope of gain or in trust thereby replenish our bellies with dainty delectables and far-sought dishes.

We shall do well if we not only content ourselves with such things as we have but also do depart with some of them to such people as have need for relief.

Our lord himself gives us an example of this when, after he has feasted a multitude of people, suffered not such bread and fish as was left to be lost.

Nature teaches us things necessary, which be but few and soon prepared. Foolishness has invented things superfluous that are without

Introduction to Wisdom

number and hard to come by. If you give necessaries unto nature, she is delighted to become strong as with things fit for her, but if you give her superfluous things, she is weakened and afflicted as with goblets not agreeing unto her diet.

As necessaries do not suffice where foolishness craves, so do superfluous things overwhelm rather than satisfy where appetites are to be served.

Your drink shall be that natural liquor prepared of God indifferent to all living creatures, which is pure and clean water, or else, a single beer or wine combined with the said water is sufficient.

There is nothing that can more hurt the bodies of young men than hot meals and hot drinks, for they inflame their livers and set on fire their entrails. And hereby men's minds are made hot, angry, proud, impudent, and are thence so carried with rashness that, as they were mad, they crave to accomplish all their lusts regardless of how filthy.

Drink not after supper or, if thirst moves you, take some moist or cold thing, or a little quantity of drink and that of the smallest quantity.

Between that and your going to bed, let it be at the least half an hour.

When you want to refresh your mind with any pastime, consider how short time is given to man's life, think it unlawful to spend this time in games, in feasting, or in other childish toys—follies if you properly name them.

The course of your life is but short, I say, although it were every wit devoted to ordering and adorning your mind.

Think not that we be made by God to gaming, to trifles, but rather we are sent to be occupied in sage matters as to attain unto moderation, modesty, temperance, religion, and all other kinds of virtue.

Heal not the sickness of your body with the disease of mind. Better it is that it be sick than the mind not whole.

Exercises of body shall not be too great but led with a certain regard of health, wherein we must follow the counsels of expert and cunning physicians so far as you shall not transcend the limits of honesty or bid us do any filthy thing against God's law.

Also, in pastimes and the refreshing of the mind, see there be some remembrance of virtue all the way.

Banish all arrogance, contention, quarrelling, envy, and covetousness.

For what reason, or rather foolishness, is it to unquiet your mind, while you study to delight it? You do as wisely as they that put gall into that honey, which they want to make most sweet.

Sleep must be taken as a certain medicine, and so much only as is sufficient to refresh the body, for immoderate sleep brings the body to many hurtful humors and much hinders the quickness of the mind.

The time that is spent in sleep is scarce to be counted any part of life. *Vita enim vigilia est*, life is a watch or a waking.

OF THE MIND

There be two parts in the soul: the one that understands, remembers, and savors things as they are, using reason, judgment, and wit is called *mens*, that is, "The Mind," the superior part, by which alone we are known to be men, made like unto God, far passing all other living creatures.

The other part, which is called will, is devoid of reason, brute, fierce, cruel, more like a beast than a man, wherein dwell these motions that are named either affections or perturbations: arrogance, envy, malice, ire, fear, sorrow, desire never satisfied, and vain joy. This is called the inferior and viler part, whereby we little or nothing differ from beasts. In this, we go far from God who is without all sickness and affections.

This is the order of nature that wisdom governs all things and that all creatures that we see obey unto man, and that in man, the body be obedient to the soul, and the soul unto God.

If anything breaks this order, it is offensive.

As it is, therefore, a point of treason that such lewd perturbations, as are afore said, should rage, rebel, and take upon them the rule of the whole man, contemptuously despising the authority of the mind, so it is extreme folly of your mind to be slave unto fond affections and to serve the vile carcass at a nod, without regard for the express law of God.

ON ERUDITION[7]

Therefore, as strength of intelligence is given to the mind to weigh everything and to know what is good to be done and what to be left undone,

7. This subtitle, taken from the Latin, is missing in the English version.

so is will of so great a power that there is nothing in the mind that is not forced to obey will, if the mind is in conflict; and will yields no part of her right to her adversary.

Wit is exercised with many and diverse feats, much sharpened and instructed with long experiences of sundry matters, whereby it may exactly know the natures and values of all things and so teach man's will what is good to be followed and what contrarywise to be eschewed. Such crafts must, therefore, be shunned that fight against virtue, that is, all crafts that work by vain conjectures, as palm reading, pyromancy, necromancy, hydromancy, and astrology, wherein much pestilent vanity lies hidden, invented by the devil, our deceitful enemy, for they intreat and profess these things that God has reserved unto himself alone, that is to say, the knowledge of things to come. We may not seek to know the mastery and the secrets of God, being far from our knowledge, and such as God would not want man to meddle withal.

He that searches the greatness of God's mastery shall be oppressed and overwhelmed with his exultant glory. Therefore, Paul bids us to be not wiser than it becomes us but to be moderately wise, saying that he saw things not to be spoken that no man can utter. Also, Solomon says: "You shall not inquire of things above your capacity, neither of things above your strength but content yourself with the knowledge of those, that God has commanded thee: think always upon them, never bring to curious in searching of his works."

All arts invented by the devil must be refused and forsaken by us, with whom, as with the enemies of God, we may in no way be conversant or have anything to do. It is not expedient for us to know the opinions either of philosophers or heretics contrary to our profession, lest that subtle and crafty merchant, the devil, cast some scrupulous doubt into our ears, which may much toss us and perchance bring us into destruction.

Authors that write wantonly and whereby may spring occasion of hurt must not be touched, lest any filthiness remain in the mind through the reading of them.

Evil communication often corrupts good manners.

Other erudition is sincere and fruitful, so that it be applied to its right mark, that is, to virtue, and well-doing.

There is a divine knowledge given of God, wherein all treasures of science and wisdom are lain about, and this is the very true light of man's mind.

All other learnings, compared unto this, are very dark and childish trifles.

Yet they be read for this intent: that our light by comparing the one with the other may shine and appear more bright. Furthermore, that we may use the said learnings as testimonies of men against them, who can little better abide the divine scripture than sore eyes can the brightness of the sun. And whereas we shall see such excellent virtues in gentiles, we may well be put in remembrance how much becomes a true disciple of our master Christ, who is by reason he knows this light, charged upon no small bond, to live accordingly unto God's commandment. Besides those things, they give us much knowledge of how we should live here together in this world, the experience whereof we lack oftentimes.

We be framed and fashioned by these three things: knowledge, wit, and memory; and the diligence, which we use to the attaining of them, is called study.

Wit is quickened by exercise and memory increased by diligent telling and occupying thereof. Delightful handling weakens them both: good health confirms and makes them strong; idleness and daily ease puts them to flight. Use and exercise sets them at hand and ever in a readiness.

Whether you read or hear anything, do it with attention and effectiveness; let not your mind wander but contain it to be there and to do that thing that is in hand, and none other.

If it is to go astray or swerve aside, call it again, as it were, with a little whistle; defer all cogitations that may bring you from that what you have in hand and defer them until some other time, remembering with yourself that you lose both time and labor if you be not attentive upon such things as you do read and hear.

Be not abashed to learn and ask such things, as you know not; for as much as noble clerks and great men have not been ashamed thereof but, rather, blush because you are ignorant and not willing to learn.

Boast not of yourself to have knowledge of those things wherein you are ignorant, but rather inquire and learn of such people as you suppose do understand them.

If you would like to be taken as a learned man, endeavor yourself that you so be, for there is no other way more compendious or nearer there unto, as you can by no other means more easily obtain to be esteemed an honest man than if you so be in true deed. Finally, labor always to be even such a one, indeed, as you desire to appear unto men, or else you desire it all in vain.

False things faint and fall away by process of time, and time strengthens the truth.

Simulation does not last long.

Follow your master always, do not run at any time before him; believe him, do not resist him.

Love him and take him as your father, thinking everything, whatever he says, to be very true and sure.

Beware that you do not offend wherein you, being culpable, were twice or thrice reformed; fall not the fourth time so that your amendment and reformation may seem to have profited you.

It becomes you chiefly to have those things in remembrance that have in times past deceived you, lest you are in like manner by them seduced again.

It is naturally given to all men to err, but to no man to persevere and continue therein, except he be unwise and a very naughty person.

Learn and understand that there is no sense whereby we be better or more speedily instructed and taught than by hearing, as there is nothing easier than to hear many things, so there is nothing more profitable.

Hear not light trifles, things to be laughed at, but rather the earnest, the wise, and the weighty.

They be both learned with like pain and labor, albeit the commodity that rises of the one is far unlike the other.

Seek not to speak many words to make a long answer but rather see you spend your words in time and let them in their place.

Adjoin such company to you at dinner and supper as can both make you merry with their pleasant and learned communication and also make you rise wiser than when you sat down.

Suffer not such scoffers, small feasts, foolish and filthy talkers, triflers, drinkers, filthy and shameless lurkers, belly guts, and such others, apt either by their words or deeds to cause lewd laughter, to sit at your table; neither have any delight in them but rather seek your pastime of such, which will with feat, wit, and learned talk make you merry. Keep not only your mouth from foul and impudent communication but also your ears, being as a man should say windows of the mind, remembering ever that old saying of the Apostle: Naughty communication oftentimes corrupts good manners.[8]

Give diligent ear what every man says, whether it be at the table or anywhere, for so doing, you will learn of the wise to make yourself better, and of the foolish to be more aware and circumspect, following always what the wise approve, eschewing that which the foolish commend. And if you perceive anything taken of the wise sort to be spoken quickly, gravely, learnedly, wittily, comely, bear in mind that you may when you shall have occasion use the same.

You shall have always at hand a paper book, wherein you shall write such notable things as you read yourself or hear of other men worthy to be noted, be it some exquisite sentence or word, fitting familiar speech, that you may have it ready when time requires.

Study not so much to gather words as to understand the proper signification of them, rehearsing and teaching such things as you have read or heard partly to your students in Latin, partly in the vernacular to other unlearned persons. Trying always to rehearse and teach them with no less grace than you have heard and read the same before, for thus doing, you shall exercise both your wit and your tongue.

Your style must also be exercised that is the best master of clean and eloquent speech.

Write and write again, making every second day or at least every third day an epistle unto some man that knows how to answer thereunto again. How be it, you shall show it first unto your master, there to be reformed, before you presume to send the same, noting and bearing well in mind such facts as he shall correct, so that you may not miss in them or any like in time to come.

After a meal, as when you have dined or supped, breathe for a space before you go to your study, and sit down in some place, where you may talk and hear some pleasant communication or play at some such game, whereby you may not chafe or much encumber your body.

8. 1 Corinthians 15:33.

Introduction to Wisdom

After supper, walk with some merry company that is learned, which may make the walk merrier with his communication and whose words and sentences you may follow with honesty.

Between supper and bed, drink not in any way, for there is nothing more pernicious, both to the body and the memory, and also the wit. Therefore, if you shall at any time constrain yourself to drink, do not go to rest under the space of half an hour after, at the least.

You shall not neglect your memory nor suffer it to decay through idleness, for it rejoices above all things to be set to work and increases not a little thereby. Exercise it daily with some worthy business.

The more often you commit things in her to her custody, the better and more faithful will she keep them. And contrarily, the more seldom, the more unreliable you shall find her.

When you have put anything to her keeping, suffer it to rest in her hands for a season, and within a while after, require it of her again as a thing left for a time in her custody.

If you wish to learn anything perfectly, read it with attention four or five times over night and go to bed, and when you rise the next morning, ask a reckoning of your memory for that thing you did deliver to her custody the evening before.

You must beware of surfeits, of rawness in the stomach, and especially of cold in your neck.

As too much wine weakens the sinews of man, so it kills his memory.

It should be very well if you would a little before you go to rest call to your remembrance all such things as you have seen, read, heard, or done all day before.

And if you have behaved yourself worthily to your commendation, you should rejoice in knowing it to come of God, purposing to continue in like goodness; on the other side, if you have done anything filthily, outrageously, childishly, fondly, or worthy of rebuke, forget not to ascribe it to your own lewdness and to be sorry therefore, never willing to do any like trespass again.

If you have heard or read any fitting, grave, or godly sentence, forget it not.

And if you have seen any commendable thing, follow it and shun the contrary. Let no day escape you without reading, hearing, or writing somewhat that may increase your knowledge, your judgment, or your living.

When you prepare yourself to bed, read or hear something worthy of memory and let it be such that your dreaming of it may take both pleasure and profit, so that even by night visions, you may learn to amend your life.

There is no end appointed unto the study of wisdom in this world, but it must be ended together with life.

It behooves man to rehearse these three things with himself all the time of his life, that is to say, how he may think well, say well, and act well.

All arrogance must be secluded from studies. For all that, which even the best learned man alive knows, is very little or nothing in comparison to the infinite things that he is ignorant in.

The knowledge of man is slender, a marvelous small thing, and that very obscure and uncertain; our minds being tied and bound in the prison of this body are oppressed with great darkness in so much that hard it is for our wits to enter even into a mean knowledge of things.

Furthermore, arrogance much encumbers the profit of studies, for many might have come to wisdom if only they had not thought themselves there already.

Also contention, ambition, detraction, and vain desire of Glory must be eschewed. For we follow studies for this cause especially so that we may by their help be delivered from the cruel dominion of the said vices.

Nothing can be imagined more pleasant than the knowledge of many things, few or none more fruitful than the intelligence of virtue.

Studies be of such efficacy and strength that they temper prosperity, mitigate adversity, keep down the hasty and rash emotions of youth, delight and comfort crooked and painful age, while being with us at home, abroad, in public and private business, when we are alone, when we may be accompanied in idleness, in labors, and never absent, but always ready to help and aid us.

As erudition is the most right and most wholesome food of the mind, so is it a thing unfitting that the body should have his nourishment but the soul being kept hungry, from whence springs out plentifully all delectation and prefect pleasures; as among these, the one brings in another, and those that be present do renew them of the past, so they never depart, nor make any many wary, when he has the most of them.

14

PHILIPP MELANCHTHON
(1497–1560)

Of Rational Ability, or Mind

GÜNTER FRANK AND GREGORY GRAYBILL

INTRODUCTION

Philipp Schwarzerd was born on February 16, 1497, in the town of Bretten in the German region of Palatinate. At eleven years old, he attended Latin school in Pforzheim, learning Greek, Latin, and Hebrew. The famous humanist and Hebrew scholar Johannes Reuchlin supported his young relative and gave him the humanist name Melanchthon (the Greek translation of Schwarzerd). On October 14, 1509, he enrolled at the University of Heidelberg, graduating three years later with a bachelor of *artes liberales*. Melanchthon continued his studies at the University of Türingen, and on January 25, 1514, he graduated as *magister artium*. Melanchthon received an invitation, relayed through Reuchlin, to fill the newly established Greek chair at the University of Wittenberg.

With that appointment, a diverse academic field opened up to him. At the same time, he came within the sphere of influence of Martin Luther and his theological Reformation ideas. From 1521 to 1536, Melanchthon worked as a church Reformer in the Electorate of Saxony. Melanchthon (ultimately unsuccessfully) took over the role of the leading commissioner at the Diets and theological disputes in Speyer and Marburg (1529), as well as in Augsburg (1530). Moreover, he wrote important Evangelical confessions of faith, like the first confessional document, "Confessio Augustana," in 1530. Besides numerous theological writings, Melanchthon wrote about almost all philosophical disciplines of his time. His Greek (1518 and 1520) and Latin (1525) Grammars have often been reprinted. His "Rhetorics," which had its origin in Tübingen, was revised in 1521 until its final version in 1531. Melanchthon handed down through his own paraphrases and commentaries the corpus of Aristotelian writings that belonged to the most important fields. It was crucial for this teaching tradition that Melanchthon removed the burden of the theological problem of a fusion of theology and philosophy by dividing law and gospel, which he did to secure the autonomy of revelation theology and soteriology. Aristotle's *Ethics* had been revised from 1529 onward and was edited several times until it eventually took shape in the large tractates "Philosophiae moralis epitome" (Compendium of Moral Philosophy, 1538) and "Ethicae doctrinae elementa" (Basic Concepts of Moral Doctrine, 1550).

Melanchthon's interest in Aristotle's *Physics* first led to the short "Commentarius de anima" (Commentary on the Soul) in 1540, which was completely revised and published in the "Liber de anima" (Book on the Soul) in 1553. In 1549 Melanchthon published the textbook "Initia doctrinae physicae" (Basic Concepts of the Doctrine of Nature), about Aristotelian philosophy of nature, together with Paul Eber. His writings about Cicero's texts and other classical authors are numerous, and he was devoted to these all of his life.

With Luther's death in 1546, Melanchthon became increasingly involved in internal Protestant teaching disputes, which, in addition to his university duties, occupied the last period of his life. Melanchthon died on April 19, 1560, as a result of a feverish cold that he had caught on a journey from Leipzig.

The following selection is part of Melanchthon's commentary on Aristotle's anthropology (*De anima*). This commentary arose from lectures given at the University of Wittenberg. Even though the commentary is close to Aristotle's *De anima*, it combines a variety of perspectives on anthropology: the organic composition of human being, medicine, epistemology, knowledge of God, the doctrine of human being as image of God, as well as the immortality of the human soul. Melanchthon's textbook became one of his most influential books, not only at Protestant universities of the following three centuries. About forty editions are known to be in existence, printed at various places throughout Europe.

BIBLIOGRAPHY

Primary Sources

Melanchthon, Philippus. *Opera quae supersunt omnia*. Edited by Carolus Gottlieb Bretschneider, 137–49. Corpus Reformatorum 13. Halle: C.A. Schwetschke, 1846. Reprint, New York: Johnson, 1963.

Melanchthons Werke in Auswahl. Vol. 3. Edited by Richard Nürnberger, 326–39. Gütersloh: Gerd Mohn, 1969.

Keen, Ralph, ed. and trans. *A Melanchthon Reader*. New York: Peter Lang, 1988.

Secondary Sources

Bihlmaier, Sandra. "Anthropologie." In *Philipp Melanchthon. Der Reformator zwischen Glauben und Wissen. Ein Handbuch,* edited by Günter Frank, 483–94. Berlin: DeGruyter, 2017.

De Angelis, Simone. *Anthropologien: Genese und Konfiguration einer Wissenschaft vom Menschen in der frühen Neuzeit*. Berlin: DeGruyter, 2010.

Frank, Günter. "Philipp Melanchthons 'Liber de anima' und die Etablierung der frühneuzeitlichen Anthropologie." In *Humanismus und Wittenberger Reformation*, edited by Michael Beyer and Günther Wartenberg, 313–26. Leipzig: Evangelische Verlagsanstalt, 1996.

———. "Philipp Melanchthon (1497–1560): Reformer and Philosopher." In *Philosophers of the Renaissance*, edited by Paul Richard Blum and translated by Brian McNeil, 148–62. Washington, D.C: The Catholic University of America Press, 2010.

———. "Melanchthon, Philipp." In *Encyclopedia of Renaissance Philosophy*, edited by Marco Sgarbi, 1–15. Cham: Springer International Publishing, 2016. https://doi.org/10.1007/978-3-319-02848-4_274-1.

———. "'Deus vult aliquas esse certas notitias…' Epistemological Discussions in the Philosophy of the Early Modern Period." *JEMS* 8, no. 1 (2019): 25–59.

Kusukawa, Sachiko. "Between 'De anima' and 'Dialectics': a Prolegomenon to Philippo-Ramism." In *Sapientiam Amemus: Humanismus und Aristotelismus in der Renaissance*, edited by Paul Richard Blum, Constance Blackwell, and Charles Lohr, 127–39. Munich: Wilhelm Finck, 1997.

Salatowsky, Sacha. *De Anima: Die Rezeption der aristotelischen Psychologie im 16. und 17. Jahrhundert*. Amsterdam: Grüner, 2006.

Stiening, Gideon. "Deus vult aliquas esse certas notitias: Philipp Melanchthon, Rudolph Goclenius und das Theorem der *notitiae naturales* in der Psychologie des 16. Jahrhunderts." In *Melanchthon und die Marburger Professoren, Vol. 2 (1527–1627)*, edited by Barbara Bauer, 757–88. Marburg: Universitätsbibliothek, 1999.

Wels, Volkhard. "Melanchthons Anthropologie zwischen Theologie, Medizin und Astrologie." In *Religion und Naturwissenschaften im 16. und 17. Jahrhundert*, edited by Kaspar von Greyertz et al., 51–85. Gütersloh: Gütersloher Verlagshaus, 2010.

PHILIPP MELANCHTHON

Of Rational Ability, or Mind[1]

Even if the nature of things cannot be penetrated by the human mind, God still wants it to be contemplated by human beings, so that in it we may consider the evidences which show both that God exists and what he is like. And the order of everything else in nature, beyond the human mind, shows that this world does not exist by accident, but that its maker is a wise artisan, who with amazing intentionality positioned bodies, heaven, earth, air, water and the heavenly movements—and distributed power to things as they came into existence.

But just as human beings were made so that the notion of God may shine in them, and so that God may communicate his wisdom and goodness to them, so he wanted the human mind to be the clearest testimony of himself. Such light has been implanted, by which we can recognize God; and notions are implanted that distinguish the honorable from the shameful. And so that this distinction may be clear and definite, an avenger has been given to us. Dread torments proceed in an unalterable sequence, condemning sin and utterly annihilating the sinner. This shows what God is like and what sort of judge and avenger he is. It is impossible for notions of numbers and other things, and the distinction between what is honorable and what is shameful, to arise from brute nature or to come about by

---

1. This translation of *De anima* by Günter Frank and Gregory Graybill is based on the Latin edition, *Corpus Reformatorum. Philippi Melanthonis Opera quae supersunt omnia*, ed. Carolus Gottlieb Bretschneider, vol. 13 (Halle/S.: C.A. Schwetschke, 1846, 137–49; reprint, New York: Johnson, 1963); *Melanchthons Werke in Auswahl*, 2nd ed., ed. Richard Nürnberger, vol. 3 (Gütersloh: Mohn, 1969), 326–39. For an earlier English translation in its entirety, see *De anima*, ed. and trans. Ralph Keen, *A Melanchthon Reader* (New York: Peter Lang, 1988), 239–89.

Of Rational Ability, or Mind

accident. Therefore, the mind is a wise architect. And since we do understand numbers, and the distinction between the honorable and the shameful shines unchangeably in human minds, thus we find out that human nature is destroyed by the avenger God when it violates that order. Such then is God, that he wants this order and these notions to be the rays of divine wisdom.

But this light would shine more clearly in us if human nature were not so weak. Nevertheless, some sparks remain—for example, there is no doubt about numbers. Indeed, the judgment upon iniquity after the transgression so tenaciously remains, that the guilty have been destroyed by their anguished consciences.

Since, therefore, in this part of a person, the testimonies of God shine so brightly, clearly distinguishing humanity from the beasts, and being a guide to life; it must diligently be considered how much ability it has. The fount of all the arts is in this [rational] power. Hence knowledge of it is necessary for the judgment of many things.

But even though this mirror of God cannot show as much as mirrors for our bodies made from glass and lead, still our actions reveal that there is such a power in us, and we discern what it is like in that eternal light. Now let us consider and discern the actions that distinguish us from beasts. They are testimonies of God, they regulate life, and they bring forth all honorable arts.

We have spoken above about the powers which are called organic, i.e., which exercise their own force through bodily organs, and, since they can be seen even in beasts, teaching about them is less obscure. But it is agreed that in human beings there is another superior power, because we have actions which beasts cannot imitate. People count, understand not only individual things but even general things, have innate notions, reason about things far removed from each other, build up the arts, evaluate their own reasons, both detect and correct errors, have what are called reflex actions, discern the honorable from the shameful, and deliberate on the basis of extended reasoning. We do not hold these things in common with the beasts, as we do with the actions of the senses, with seeing and hearing—in which the beasts are superior to us, as with the sharp eyes of the eagle or the scenting ability of the vulture.

There is then a uniquely human rational power, as they call it, which is the highest force of the human spirit. And they usually call this power inorganic. For even though in this life the inner senses both serve and present objects—nevertheless, when the spirit apart from its body has certain actions and movements of its own it is called inorganic.

This highest part has two powers, which I call intellect and will.[2] That is, I retain the customary terms and divisions. Augustine, in order to show the image of God in the soul, named three powers: memory, intellect, and will.[3] I shall speak later of the image of God. But even though it will become clearer later, still it is necessary to distinguish intellect and will, or the powers of cognition and desire. Still now, youths should be advised of the usefulness of this distinction from the beginning [of their education].[4] It is necessary to know that the one thing is a notion and the other a series of appetites, as Pompey had a notion of Julius which remained the same before war and in war. But while before there was benevolence in the will, later hatred was ignited. There are thus diverse things—a notion and an affection, and other seats in one way or another have to be constituted. These indeed are shown in the organs to have been connected to the soul. The inner senses are connected with[5] the cognitive power, while the heart is connected with the earnest power of the will. Thus the notion of Julius is in the brain, but goodwill and hatred are in the heart.

Consider this distinction and what Paul says in the first chapter of his letter to the Romans [1:18], where he says that truth is held captive in injustice. It is an obscure speech to those unaware of this doctrine of the distinction of powers. But he calls truth the true notions of God and of law. These rays of God's wisdom shine in the cognitive power, as the notion of Julius in Pompey. But neither in the will nor in the heart are the emotions and ardors in accord with the law of God. In order that this can be understood in some way it is necessary to examine human nature and its various powers.

And here the solution of the arguments is taken up:

Natural things are the most possible for that nature to which they belong.

2. Voluntas.
3. *De trinitatae* 10.13.
4. in vestibulo.
5. cum + abl. = "with."

Of Rational Ability, or Mind

The best law is that which is in accord with nature.

Therefore the best law is possible.

The first response to the major premise is that natural things are possible for a sound nature, but not for a corrupted one.

Then when it is objected in turn that notions of law are born in us even in this corrupted nature, we say that this distinction of powers is to be examined. A notion of law is born in us in the cognitive power, just like the comprehension of numbers. But proud defiance lurks in the will and heart.

Now the extent of our infirmity is to be deplored when we discern such a separation between the two kindred highest powers. In this case God's plan must be considered, why he wished the notion of law to remain in us, and what sort of liberty exists in the will. The notion remains in order to provide evidence of God, and to disclose sin. It also remains to be a guide to external discipline, for this degree of liberty endures. Reason is able to rule the locomotive power which activates external actions. Yet an avenger of sins remains in the heart, a terrible anguish of judgment in the cognitive power that follows a transgression. For God wants the distinction between the honorable and the shameful to be observed and for nature to be destroyed by law, as if overcome by the sentence of an eternal judge. The doctrine of these most important things would be much clearer if the power and the actions of individual powers were examined in their proper order. And since in this field of examination, there can be considered to be two parts of human nature, it is necessary and very useful to compare natural philosophy with the doctrine of the church.

I add the explanation of the other argument:

Natural things are unchangeable.

The divine laws, which are set before everyone in the Decalogue, were altered so that many gods were invented with horrible furor against the first tablet, and against the second tablet pacts of adultery among the Lacedaemonians were permitted, and among many peoples the murders of gladiators were allowed.

Thus those divine laws are not natural.

Response: I deny the minor premise. For those laws were not altered, because they remain a part of cognition. For just as the notion of numbers always shines in the human mind, so does the true notion that one true God is to be invoked. Many gods are not to be invented. Innocent people are not to be killed for sport. Roving lusts are not to be approved. But even though in this mental murk, this light glimmers less clearly in human minds; nevertheless, it cannot entirely be extinguished. For that reason wise men like Xenophon, Aristotle and Cicero disapproved of a multitude of gods.

But here let us recognize and deplore our weakness, because the will and the heart rush into foul sins, even against the judgment of the cognitive power, as Medea says: "I see the better things and I approve, but I follow the worse."[6]

The will accepted the murders of the gladiators among the Romans, against the judgment of the mind. For the will is able to resist right judgment.

Here is to be added that devils impel hearts and implant furors in minds, so that the darkness in the cognitive part actually obscures judgment. Thus many are furious, and those who are incited by furors are cruel to themselves and their loved ones, as Heracles killed his wife and children. Likewise, in the story of the Xanthi, the mother hanged herself from the ceiling with her son hanging from her neck and holding a torch which set the house on fire. And on the bank of the Alba before the Saxon war a mother maddened in childbirth killed two babies she had just given birth to. Similarly, some time ago in Basel a husband transfixed his pregnant wife with a sword, and then threw himself head first from the top of the house.

Not even on account of these deeds is the natural light completely extinguished in these people, and it is even less so in other sane ones. But the devils violently compel a nature separated from God. Such examples warn us to ask for guidance from the Son of God, who came to destroy the works of the devil, lest the light of judgment be obscured in us and our hearts be impelled to rush ruinously against the will of God. For this reason even in our daily prayer we say: "Lead us not into temptation."[7] And the Lord says, "Pray, so that you do not enter into temptation."[8]

The explanation of these and similar arguments about the most serious matters shows the usefulness of the doctrine. And many other things

6. Ovid, *Met.* 7:21–2.
7. Matthew 6:13.
8. Mark 14:38.

will follow, which bring some light to understanding the teaching of the church. As when the Son of God is called the Word, that he is the image of the eternal Father, and when the distinction between word and spirit is shown, it is useful to recognize the distinction of the powers. Thus I return to the precepts.

WHAT IS INTELLECT?

Intellect is the power that recognizes, records, judges, and makes rational arguments about individual and universal things, according to certain innate notions born in us, or about the principles of the great arts, having self-reflection by which it discerns and judges its own actions, and is able to correct errors.

This definition shows the distinction between senses and the intellect, and between the cognitions of brutes and people.

There are three differences:

First. Sense pertains to individual things; it neither apprehends nor connects

universals.

Second. Sense has no innate notions. Hence cattle are unable to count.

Third. No senses and no beasts have self-reflection. Bees construct amazing works but do not judge their own construction.

WHAT ARE THE ACTIONS OF THE INTELLECT?

These words usually enumerate three actions: apprehension of simple things, connection and division, and discourse. If these appellations seem obscure, then reckon them like this:

Recognition of simple things,
Counting,
Connection and division,
Reasoning,
Memory, and

Judgment, which along with the general norms which are called criteria, recognizes true propositions and properly-coherent consequences,

PHILIPP MELANCHTHON

and rejects both false propositions and incoherent parts of arguments. It is necessary to add those distinctions.

Now sense and intellect are commonly distinguished with these words: Sense is of single things, and intellect is of universals. That statement is certainly not to be understood exclusively, as if intellect were just of universals. For although sense apprehends only individual objects, the intellect nevertheless discerns, composes, divides and judges *both* the singular *and* the universal. One can clearly see the confirmation of this view of ours in counting, which is most characteristic of this highest power of intellect—*not* of sense—since counting proceeds from units and individuals to the many. Yes, and the human mind is designed to recognize one God, as the divine law says: "Love the Lord your God. Likewise, love your neighbor."[9] Therefore it is necessary for the mind to be able to discern individual things. Thus the stupid and fatuous interpretation of those who imagine that the intellect is only of universals is to be rejected.

WHAT IS THE OBJECT OF THE INTELLECT?

Everything that exists, insofar as it is observable,[10] that is, God and the entire universe of things, is the object of the intellect, for the recognition of which we were made. As the divine law clearly states: "Love the Lord your God," etc. This light was brighter before the corruption of human nature—afterwards, darkness descended. Now we understand God and the natural spirits and the substance of bodies less clearly, though to some degree we still recognize them *a posteriori*, dimly and tenuously.

Thus while we do not recognize all things in the same way, still it is rightly said that everything that exists, insofar as it is observable,[11] is the object of the intellect—that is, God and the entire universe of things, because we were created to observe all these things.

But even though not all cognition arises in the human mind from sense, as numbers and many principles do, still the senses were so created that likenesses of external things are transmitted to the intellect, there to be envoys to the mind and witnesses of experience. Indeed, they excite the

9. Matthew 22:37–9, in paraphrase.
10. Ens quam late patet.
11. Ens quam late patet.

intellect to the observation of things which are external to it, and considering them, it constructs, divides, seeks universals, judges, observes criteria, and corrects errors.

Of this external object exciting the intellect in this weakness of ours, it is rightly said that the object is all things that are perceived by the senses. For from this the intellect proceeds by its own power to other things—it proceeds from signs to causes, from accidents to some sort of recognition of substances. Let us be content with this moderate declaration in a question which is surrounded by many labyrinths.

IS IT TRUE THAT SOME NOTIONS ARE BORN WITHIN US?

It is an old dispute between the Aristotelians and the Platonists whether certain notions are born in our minds. But it is simpler and more correct to maintain the view that some notions in the human mind are innate with us—such as numbers, recognition of order and proportion, and the understanding of the logical conclusion of a syllogism. Other examples include the principles of geometry, physics, and ethics.

I also embrace this view because when Paul discusses notions, he expressly says that the law is written in human hearts.[12] Thus, just as there is light in the eyes by which vision takes place, so in the mind there is a certain light by which we count, recognize the principles of the arts, and discern integrity from depravity. It is rightly said that this light is the notions sprinkled in our minds by divine influence, and we realize what kind of light it is when we grasp God as its archetype. Meanwhile, considered from afar, we must nevertheless recognize that these eternal notions are shining testimonies of God and of providence, spread among people by the wondrous counsel of God. For it is clear that it is not by accident that this eternal and unchanging wisdom, the concept of numbers, and the distinction between integrity and depravity endure throughout the whole human race.

Now even if God imprinted many traces in the architecture of the entire universe by which he wishes to make his existence known, and if these

12. Romans 2:15.

traces show that this world does not exist by accident, but that there is a mind who is wise, good, just, true, chaste and free—an architect;[13] nevertheless, this reasoning cannot occur unless many notions already blaze in our minds, such as the distinction of unity and multiplicity, the distinction between a wise and good nature and a brute and evil nature, and many other things. No indeed, among these, some notion of God also has to blaze in us, so that we can apply these signs to the notion [of him].

But I do not wish to dispute this any more fully; rather I pray to God the Maker himself that after the darkness that has come into us on account of sin, he will again ignite the notions he has given so that they may become clearer and stronger.

Let us not be disturbed by the common saying, "Nothing is in the intellect unless it was first in the senses." For unless that is understood properly, it is completely absurd. For universal notions and judgment were not previously in the senses.

But it must be said that the intellect is moved and excited by the action of the senses and individual objects, and then it proceeds to thinking about universals and making judgments.

WHAT IS A NOTION?

A notion signifies at one time an action and at another time a habit, that is, a certain lasting light,[14] I might say, in the mind, which we use when we wish, just as art is a lasting light. But let us speak of action. A notion is a mental action through which one looks at a thing, as if forming an image of the thing contemplated. Nor are these images or ideas anything other than *actus intelligendi*. Nor can any clearer description be given of this extraordinary action than that it is the formation of an image.

But it is now often said that the intellect is intimately joined to the inner senses. After the outer sense receives the *species sensibiles*, as when the eyes see a lion or a deer, they transmit it to the inner senses. There, cerebral and spiritual motions form thoughts, which are the images of the things considered or seen. In the same way we paint mental images, like someone

---

13. *Architectatricem* is Melanchthon's translation of Plato's δημιουγός. See *Timaios* 29a, 1–3; 29d, 5–30a, 4; 31c, 1–32c, 6.

14. *Lumen durabile*, literally "a durable light."

thinking about his parents forms their images by his own action. An architect thinking of a house forms an image of it and judges it. This can only be said to a great extent when we ask what a notion is. By his amazing plan God wanted notions to be images, since he wanted shadows in us to indicate something of himself. The eternal Father considering himself begets his Son by thought, who is the image of the eternal Father. But of these meanings we shall speak further below.

Now I will recite the commonly-used appellations. A notion is called intuitive when cognition of a present object is received by the sense and the mind at the same time, so that it is almost a single event, as when the mind and the eyes simultaneously see a picture on a wall. And since this level of notion is the clearest, antiquity said that intuitive notions were like definitions. For example, a clearer definition of absinth cannot be given than to perceive the color and shape with the eyes and taste the flavor with the tongue.

A notion is called abstractive when we think of absence, as when we think of absent friends. For memory is like a storeroom in the brain in which figures of image, formed by thought, are imprinted, and the mind can see them whenever it wants. Essentially, memory in a rational soul is inorganic. But there are abstractive notions of universals, and of thoughts, and of other things which are not immediately grasped by sense.

Now this consideration pertains to dialecticians, where thought proceeds from the prior, the posterior, the causes, and from the effects of signs.

ANOTHER DIVISION OF THE INTELLECT

In order to interpret certain common words, another division must be added, which distinguishes the speculative and practical intellects. But it must be known that this division does not signify diverse powers but a single intellectual power revolving around diverse objects—in some respects, around perceptible things, and other respects around considerations about actions, as the eyes discern color and shape. Many more such differences of objects can be added, as in the mechanical intellect in an architect. I have briefly written about this, so that younger students may consider the variety of terms and interpret them correctly.

The word "reason" is used in various ways. Sometimes it signifies both the part of the governing intellect and the obedient will, and the part restraining contrary impulses. Thus the Platonists call the two combined powers—the properly judging intellect and the obedient will—"hegemonic."[15] And most Aristotelians call the governing notion *logos*,[16] as he says in the first book of the *Ethics*. Reason urges us to the best things, that is, to a natural notion, which is the ray of divine wisdom implanted in the human mind. Sometimes it does not signify a power, but an argument. For example, "So I wish, thus I order." That is will instead of reason. Of this difference ample descriptions have been passed down by many, which nevertheless can be easily distinguished if one bears in mind that the uses of the word differ.

Conscience is the entire argument—either judgment in the mind or of the cognitive power by which we approve of things done rightly and disapprove of sins, and because of that judgment in the divinely established order, tranquility of the heart follows upon right actions, and anguish of the heart upon sins, punishing and destroying the agent of the sin.

For human nature was created by God so that it may both conform to God and live—not so that it may be extinguished by anguish. Whereby if one is conformed to God, and the heart is conformed with right judgment, then it shall be delighted with doing good both before and after the fact.

Now, in fact, in this depraved state the heart before sinning burns with its own flames in conflict with right judgment, and does not fear evil. For it is the true justice of God[17] to destroy the disobedient nature, and therefore he ordained this order so that a tormenting anguish punishes and destroys criminals after their deeds. Even if this anguish is blunted for a while in bad people, it can still eventually become severe and extinguish them, because the law is the judgment of God. Also, in addition to the natural pain comes an overwhelming terror, by which God himself like a lightning bolt crushes the sources, as it is said in the Psalm:[18] "In your anger you will throw them into confusion. Fill their faces with disgrace!" And, "Like a lion, he ground all my bones to dust."[19] Thus it must be known that the

---

15. ἡγεμονικόν.
16. Λόγος.
17. Iustitiae Dei.
18. Psalm 82:16 in the Latin Vulgate—Psalm 83:16 in modern English versions.
19. Isaiah 38:13.

Of Rational Ability, or Mind

causes of anguish are many, for some are certainly of the order of nature, and in others God actually pours forth his own unmediated anger, as in the case of Judas and the like. It is indeed useful to consider the causes of anguish in conscience.

Theologians use the word *synteresis* (conscience), by which they understand a notion of law that is born with us, which they therefore call *synteresis* (conscience) since even in a wicked person an admonition remains, indicating what is right and what is the judgment of God. And some distinguish these terms by saying that in a practical syllogism the conscience provides the minor term and the conclusion, while the major [term] is the very *synteresis*; although Saul, however wicked, still reasoned thus: "God gets horribly angry at murderers who kill the innocent, and in turn drags such murderers off to punishment. I have killed many innocent priests. Therefore God is angry at me and will punish me."[20] In such a syllogism they call the major premise the *synteresis* and conscience is truly the minor premise and the conclusion. Paul calls the whole syllogism conscience. I have inserted this brief consideration about these terms, about which others stir up many strange questions—which can be easily judged from these initial examinations.

OF THE ACTIVE AND PASSIVE INTELLECT

Although there are great controversies about the active and passive intellect,[21] nevertheless, if we adopt a distinction from actions, the explanation is simple and clear.

The unimpaired eyes of most persons, when they look upon something, see it equally. But minds, even when they seek the same thing, do not all find it equally. They are able to understand discoveries when they are proclaimed, but nobody except the Creator can provide the reason for dust storms or the movements of the spheres. Other craftsmen understand and approve of what they find.

Thus Aristotle distinguishes two offices of the intellect, for there are more offices of the intellect than of the eyes, which receive so many single objects but do not reason at all. But when it receives objects, the intellect

---

20. See 1 Samuel 22, esp. v. 18.
21. de intellectu agente et patiente.

238 PHILIPP MELANCHTHON

composes, divides, considers, and judges. In this type of reckoning one thing is ascertained from another. This is the inventor intellect, and as the poet says, the agent or the one who does right.

Another function is then to understand what is discovered, to recognize it, and, as it were, to receive its lessons. From this function the passive intellect is named. Aristotle saw, in all life, in the arts, in public and private counsels, in strategies, in poetry, and in eloquence, that some people are more insightful than others. These are more effective at discovery, while others understand their findings and think about them. Thus Themistocles persuaded the citizens of the abandoned city to board ships, and did better than others with his productive intellect,[22] though they understood and approved the plan.

Hannibal, when he was cut off by Fabius, made his exit with amazing skill. He bound lit twigs to the horns of bulls to throw the Roman army off course. This had not come randomly to his mind, even though others understood and approved the idea.

When Alexander on his way to Asia was warned that the statue of Orpheus was sweating, and that it seemed to be some kind of bleak omen, Alexander said the opposite—that the omen pleased him, because it would make him a great subject of poets. Others understood the urbanity of this saying, who, despite much thought, had not invented it themselves.

Moreover, since it gives great dignity to all parts of life, that is, the correct discovery either of counsel or of doctrine, and since it governs the greatest affairs, Aristotle rightly adorns this inventor intellect with fullest praises.

As light aids the eyes, so he says that the passive intellect is aided by the inventor intellect. For it is necessary for us to find the plans ourselves or to use those invented and proclaimed by others.

He says this to abstract from the phantasms of objects. That is, it quickly gathers objects, seeks signs, the causes or effects of signs, and makes comparisons and allusions. Then it chooses the most suitable course. For example, Demades said that when Alexander was dead his army was like the Cyclops with his eye gouged out, yet it made the fastest assembly of

---

22. Melanchthon apparently intends "productive intellect" (*intellectu faciente*) as a synonym for "inventor intellect" (*intellectu agente*).

any great army that had lost its leader, like the great body of the Cyclops with an eye missing.

Additionally, Aristotle says that this inventor intellect is like an art with a material, as an artisan forms and polishes a material, and a teacher forms and teaches a student.

He also adds that it is separate, not mixed, nor punishable by injury or apathy, which some have interpreted as immortality. Nor do I disagree. And I want this to be understood of immortality, especially since Aristotle says elsewhere, "The mind enters from without."[23] For these are his words in the second book *On Generation*: "It remains that the mind alone comes from without and is alone divine."[24] For it occurred to him to view the mind as a sort of heavenly torch that gives light to the brain. However, its qualities, or how it vanishes,[25] he does not explain in the books that we have.

But whatever Aristotle's view was about the productive and passive intellects, we have surely distinguished their actions correctly, between discovering and accepting precepts. Since the distinctions of these actions are clear, I am content with this popular explanation, which can be understood, and leads the reader to considering the different actions of the intellect. The inventor intellect was far more insightful in Archimedes than in any other ordinary architect.

I have seen the explanations of others who think they are more subtle, but they are empty dreams and cannot be understood.

But while Averroes' idea of becoming like God is derided and perhaps alien from Aristotle, still, if it is skillfully understood it is not absurd. For when he says that the productive intellect is God himself causing excellent motions in people, he is really saying that excellent and beautiful thoughts are revealed and guided by God himself. As Solomon says, "As the eye sees, and the ear hears, God does both."[26] And Cicero truly says, "There is no excellent virtue without divine inspiration."[27] God persuaded Scipio of the plan of moving into Africa, even though Fabius and the other elders disagreed.

23. Mens extrinsecus accedit.
24. *De gen. animalium* 736b:27–28.
25. *quo avolet*, lit. "to whither it flies away."
26. Proverbs 20:12.
27. De nat. deor. 2:167.

15

PETRUS RAMUS
(1515–1572)

Dialectic

ROBERT GOULDING

INTRODUCTION

Petrus Ramus (or Pierre de la Ramée) came from fairly humble circumstances in Northern France. He matriculated at the University of Paris at age twelve, supporting himself as a servant to a rich student. He graduated with a master of arts in 1536, qualifying him to teach at the university, where he spent practically the whole of his life.[1] He was primarily a "dialectician," teaching and writing on logic. This was not the formal logic of his medieval predecessors and many of his colleagues at the university; rather, he embraced the humanist version of logic or dialectic, which emphasized the persuasive purpose of argumentation and drew a rather uncertain line between logical and rhetorical argument. Centered around "topics" or commonplaces, the first part of Ramus's applied logic concerned the discovery of arguments; the second part of his dialectic (taking the place of the more traditional logic of propositions and syllogisms) was "judgement," which arranged the fruits of invention into a persuasive form.

---

1. There are two book-length intellectual biographies of Ramus. Waddington (1855) is rich with primary material but tends to be a little uncritical of its subject; Ong (1958), on the other hand, tends to be far too critical.

Dialectic

Beyond dialectic, his interests covered the whole range of learning. Two of his earliest publications, the *Dialecticae institutiones* (*Education in dialectic*) of 1543 and its companion work, the *Aristotelicae animadversiones* (*Aristotelian observations*), attacked Aristotle's philosophy so savagely that he was banned from teaching philosophy at the university by royal edict. During this time, Ramus began to develop an interest in mathematics, which caught his interest both for its logical rigor and practical applications. His mathematical textbooks would be very influential over the next half-century in European schools and universities.

In 1551, with the help of powerful patronage, Ramus regained the right to teach philosophy. Now in the Collège Royal, Ramus styled himself Professor of Philosophy and Eloquence, thereby indicating his intention to continue a style of teaching that helped bring about his earlier censure: he taught philosophy and dialectic not from philosophical texts but from classical works favored by humanists, and in genres such as poetry, oratory, and history. He became a powerful figure within the Collège, eventually its dean, and as a teacher, he drew hundreds of students to his famously brilliant and controversial lectures. He also began to build up a formidable international reputation, through his incessant publication of his own works, including his extraordinarily successful *Dialectic* and the stream of other publications that his protégés in the Collège produced, especially on ancient mathematics and sciences.

Ramus's name is particularly associated with "method," which should not be confused with modern notions of scientific method. Ramus had very little to say about how one can discover *new* knowledge; rather, he was concerned with the best way to arrange and present existing knowledge. Method, as he described it, was the third part of judgement, after propositions and syllogisms: having judged the truth of statements, method was the next step of arranging entire discrete propositions and arguments into an *art*, disposing them from the most general to the most particular in accordance with nature and the best working of the human mind. In Ramus's hands and those of his followers, method was used to refashion every art and science into a form particularly suited for beginners in the subject. The student who grasped an art through the regimented method, marching from general to particular, could then effectively use the arguments in different orders, effacing the logical connections in order to sway others more subtly in discourse—a negation of method that Ramus called the "method of prudence."

The French Wars of Religion, starting in the early 1560s, marked the beginning of a tumultuous time for Ramus, whose recent conversion to Protestantism was an open secret. Several times he was forced to leave Paris because of anti-Protestant unrest. In 1562 he took refuge at the royal palace of Fontainebleau, preparing for publication his lecture notes on mathematics, physics, and metaphysics. In 1568, he was forced to leave France altogether. His travels through Germany and Switzerland laid the seeds for the growth of Ramism as a pedagogical and philosophical movement beyond France in the late sixteenth century.

In August 1572, Ramus was brutally murdered by a Catholic mob in the St. Bartholomew's Day massacre. His death led him to be considered a religious martyr in Protestant Europe, contributing greatly to the spread of Ramism in continental Europe, England, and New England.

BIBLIOGRAPHY
Primary Sources

Ramus, Petrus. "That There Is but One Method of Establishing a Science." In *Renaissance Philosophy: New Translations*, edited by Leonard A. Kennedy, 109–14. The Hague: Mouton, 1973.

———. *Arguments in Rhetoric against Quintilian: Translation and Text of Peter Ramus's Rhetoricae Distinctiones in Quintilianum (1549)*. Edited by James J. Murphy. Translated by Carole E. Newlands. DeKalb: Northern Illinois University Press, 1986.

———. *Dialecticae institutiones*. Paris, 1543. Reprinted with an introduction by W. Risse. Stuttgart-Bad Cannstatt: Frommann-Holzboog, 1964.

———. *Dialecticae libri duo* [1572; Latin-German]. Edited by Sebastian Lalla. Stuttgart: Frommann-Holzboog, 2011.

———. *Dialecticae libri duo, Audomari Talaei praelectionibus illustrati*. Edited by Omer Talon. Coloniae: Iacobi, 1566.

———. *Dialecticae libri duo, Audomari Talaei praelectionibus illustrati*. Edited by Omer Talon. Parisiis: Wechel, 1566.

———. *Peter Ramus's Attack on Cicero: Text and Translation of Ramus's Brutinae Quaestiones*. Edited by James J. Murphy. Translated by Carole E. Newlands. Davis, Calif.: Hermagoras Press, 1992.

———. *Scholae in liberales artes*. Basel, 1569. Reprinted with an introduction by W. J. Ong. Hildesheim, New York: G. Olms, 1970.

———. *Scholarum mathematicarum, libri unus et triginta*. Basel: Episcopius, 1569.

———. *The Logike of the Moste Excellent Philosopher P. Ramus, Martyr.* Edited by Catherine M. Dunn. Translated by Roland MacIlmaine. Renaissance Editions 3. Northridge, Calif.: San Fernando Valley State College, 1969.

Talon, Omer. *Academia.* Paris: Matthäus David, 1550.

Secondary Sources

Gilbert, Neal Ward. *Renaissance Concepts of Method.* New York: Columbia University Press, 1960.

Goulding, Robert. *Defending Hypatia: Ramus, Savile, and the Renaissance Rediscovery of Mathematical History.* Dordrecht: Springer, 2010.

Kusukawa, Sachiko. "Petrus Ramus (1515–1572): Method and Reform." In *Philosophers of the Renaissance,* edited by Paul Richard Blum and translated by Brian McNeil, 163–67. Washington, D.C.: The Catholic University of America Press, 2010.

Meerhoff, Kees. "'Beauty and the Beast': Nature, Logic and Literature in Ramus." In *The Influence of Petrus Ramus: Studies in Sixteenth and Seventeenth Century Philosophy and Science,* edited by Mordechai Feingold, Joseph S. Freedman, and Wolfgang Rother, 200–214. Schwabe Philosophica 1. Basel: Schwabe and Co. AG, 2001.

Ong, W. J. *Ramus: Method and the Decay of Dialogue: From the Art of Discourse to the Art of Reason.* Cambridge, Mass.: Harvard University Press, 1958.

Sellberg, Erland. "Petrus Ramus." In *The Stanford Encyclopedia of Philosophy,* edited by Edward N. Zalta. Stanford, Calif.: Metaphysics Research Lab, Stanford University, 2016. https://plato.stanford.edu/entries/ramus.

Sharratt, P. "Peter Ramus and the Reform of the University: The Divorce of Philosophy and Eloquence?" In *French Renaissance Studies, 1540–70: Humanism and the Encyclopedia,* edited by P. Sharratt, 4–20. Edinburgh: Edinburgh University Press, 1976.

Reiss, Timothy J. *Knowledge, Discovery and Imagination in Early Modern Europe: The Rise of Aesthetic Rationalism.* Cambridge: Cambridge University Press, 1997.

Waddington, Charles. *Ramus: Sa vie, ses écrits et ses opinions.* Paris: Meyrueis, 1855.

PETRUS RAMUS

Dialectic

WHAT IS DIALECTIC?

Ramus's famous dialectic went through many editions and appeared in several markedly different versions over the course of his life. This extract is taken from the opening pages of the first printed edition of his Dialecticae institutiones (*Education in dialectic*) *of 1543 (fols 5v–8v), one of the works that led to his ban from teaching philosophy.*

Dialectic, like any of the other arts, consists of nature, theory (*doctrina*), and practice. Nature shows the beginning of discoursing. Once a start has been made, theory instructs through proper and commensurable guidance. And once the pupil has been instructed by the art, practice draws him into operation and perfects him. These are the three books necessary both for the performance and the praise of any art. God engraved the first in our minds with eternal letters. A diligent observer of nature copied out that writing and fashioned the second book as a replica of those eternal signs. The third is taken up by hands and tongues—however much and however abundantly they wish. And so, from these three parts of dialectic, the first (the highest in dignity) and the third (taking second place in our praise) are within ourselves—one innate, the other a matter of will. Only the second (for which there is really very little room left) is taken on from outside, from teachers. And so, if anyone wants to acquire this power, he already has almost everything he needs.

Now, natural dialectic (that is, talent, reason, mind, the image of God the Father of all, light that rivals the blessed and eternal light) is proper to man and is born with him. And so, as soon as a man is born, a kind of innate, natural zeal compels him to put reason to work. One man will feel an immediate, more powerful force; another, one that comes later and less strongly. All men share in reason, just as all stars have a share in light. But, as some rays are clearer and more brilliant than others, so, too, do some men stand out in talent and excel by nature. This is the origin of discoursing; this is nature's education. If anyone were able to make out and grasp its course, and—with nature as his trusted guide—to walk wisely upon the path laid out for him, then he would create the most beautiful art and theory. And so, this is where we must work ceaselessly, this is where we must bend all our minds' thought: to seeing what nature herself provides and applying that in disputation.

To see the power of nature more easily, choose from all of the thousands of men living, not those who excel in their natural wit and judgement but (so that nature's generosity to men will seem even more admirable) some rustic and uneducated vineyard workers. They should never have heard of the art of discoursing—no, not even a rumor of it. Ask them about the fertility of the coming year and the abundance of the crop, ask them how much wine there will be; then, from their minds, as if from mirrors, an image of nature will be reflected. Listen to what these interpreters of nature will do. First, they will (I think) silently think out an account (*ratio*) and will find an argument that can answer the question. Then, when they have thought about it enough, they will express their thought— not randomly but methodically (*via et ratione*)[2] divided and arranged, in just the same way, perhaps, as some answered me when I tried this out and asked these questions. There is no hope (they said to me) for fertility in such an unsettled summer: sometimes wind, sometimes storms, sometimes rain, but hardly ever any sun. Most every day of this summer has been damp and cold; it is hardly possible to hope for anything good from it. Now, suppose that these same men were taken out of France to some foreign country and you asked them, "What is Paris?": they would broadly but accurately circumscribe the location of the city between the lands of the Celts and the Belgians, and they would run through its parts one by one: that the university is where the schools are, that the island is where the forum and the palace are, and that there is another part of the city where the merchants and every kind of craftsman live. Now, suppose they were to be seized by a greater desire for learning, just like those ancient, untaught philosophers and mountain shepherd, the poets; then they would exhibit the same skill thinking about the whole universe, but at an even higher level of excellence if they were to set out in order the things that are known and marvel at them, and then desire to find out the Author of so great a work. And so, when there is an opportunity for disputation, nature arouses in our minds two kinds of motion: the subtle and acute motions toward finding the truth of any doubtful matter, and the prudent and restrained motions toward expressing this truth, putting it in order according to the type and number of the things, and judging it. This is the sure observation of nature, from which theory ought never to depart but should follow like a god. It will seem to have performed its task outstandingly if it can imitate the prudence of nature.

2. Before Ramus started using the term *methodus*, this was his usual locution for methodical (in his sense) arrangement of ideas.

246 PETRUS RAMUS

And so [art] examines all the parts of nature and all the properties of its parts, with the kind of care with which Apelles observed Alexander before he painted him. In the same way, it will observe those rules built into human minds and innate to them; and having also seen that they are engraved onto the very similar tablet of nature, [art] will draw together an image and set it before those who are discoursing for them to imitate. Thus, in this (so to speak) artificial mirror, nature can contemplate the dignity of its form, and if it is marred by any spot, it can wipe it away. And this is how art, which started out as a student of nature, becomes in a certain way her mistress. For there is no nature, however firm or constant, that cannot become firmer and more constant through knowing itself and cataloguing its powers. Moreover, there is none so weak and lazy that it cannot become sharper and livelier by the help of art.

But let us now discuss this student and mistress, and let us include the rules and counsels of nature among the precepts of art. We have said enough about nature; now we must consider art, the second part of our division. To make surer progress in portraying art, let us always keep its living exemplar before our eyes. And just as our Apelles tried to represent the head of Alexander through the likeness of his painted head, and so too with his arms and all his other members—in the same way, we should try to copy most accurately and imitate with our brushstrokes the virtues, members, and features of natural dialectic.

And so, the art of dialectic is the theory of discoursing (*doctrina disserendi*). Its living force is in nature; art consists of guidance, advice, and rules to act in such a way that nature itself may act fully and uncorrupted. Thus, art teaches the correct laws of nature (*rectas naturae leges*) and does not concern itself with showing how one can err in discourse by following paths easily taken.[3]

Discourse or disputation involves a question—whatever question is proposed. And it is to this that the entire power of this art is directed. For there should not be disputation—nor even *can* there be—about a matter that is clear and obvious. On the other hand, if a matter is in doubt, it can only be proven through discourse. Thus, a "question" is an utterance that inquires into and investigates some matter of doubt.

3. That is, there is no place in a textbook of logic for the discussion of fallacies.

Such a question is the following, which should be posed by us when considering any examples of dialectical teaching: whether man is dialectical. Through this question, it will be easier to know how dialectic should be used in all other matters of doubt. There are two parts to the question: one that precedes and one that follows. The former is called the minor part, the latter the major. In our question, "man" will be the minor part, "dialectical" the major. This is how a question should be divided up and separated in order to apply the theory to it with ease (as you will soon understand).

And so, when a question has been put forward, we use the guidance of theory to explicate it. The parts of theory are framed according to the model of living truth found in the human being—we must continue to keep Apelles in mind. And so there are two parts, discovery [*inventio*] and judgement, because precisely the same number of parts are found in humans. But there everything is alive; here, in theory, we have only imitated representations. Thus, artificial discovery will be the theory of discovering, by means of which any question can be considered and explained. (It should be noted that discovery is a part of theory, not the whole of it. However, because the proper words do not exist, I am forced to use inappropriate ones, and to apply to the part a term which refers to the whole.)

THE NATURE OF METHOD

The second part of dialectic, judgement, assesses the truth of the statements and syllogistic arguments that are thought up through discovery and then arranges those statements and arguments into the best possible order. The latter is the "method" with which Ramus's name is so closely associated. The text is from his dialectic in its final form, the Dialecticae libri duo of 1566, 232–57.

Method, and first of all, method of teaching: Method is a kind of arrangement, whereby knowledge of many things is put in order: the first in the first place, the second in the second, the third in the third, and so forth. The word really refers to every discipline and subject of argument, but it is more properly used to mean a shortcut. Method is either method of teaching (*methodus doctrinae*) or method of prudence. By the method of teaching, the entirely more evident and absolutely better-known thing is put first. So, for instance, causes are more evident and better known than their effects. For the same reason, the tokens that stand for them: for example, general and universal before special and singular.[4] This method is a counterpart in the genre of judgement to the necessary enunciation [of propositions] and the proper conclusion of syllogisms. And so, although in all genuine arts all the rules are general and universal, still they are distinguished in levels: insofar as any one of them is more general, precisely to that extent will it precede. The most general will be the first in place and order, because it is the first in clarity and conception (*lumine et notitia*). The subalterns follow next, because they are next in clarity; the better known of them will be put first, and the lesser known will be placed beneath them. And in last place will be located the instances (*exempla*), which are the most specific things.

This is the one and only method in those arts that have been passed down to us in a good state. In this and only this method does one proceed from antecedents that are completely and absolutely more clear and better known, so as to clarify and illuminate consequents that are obscure and unknown. How is that, you may ask. This artful method is like a kind of long golden chain, as Homer described. Its links are those levels, which hang from each other in just the same way, and all of them are conjoined with each other so ingeniously that not one of them can be moved without the entire series and linkage of things falling apart.

But I would like to use a familiar example, just so that the whole concept may be made more familiar. Suppose that all the definitions, divisions, and rules of grammar have been discovered, and each and every one of them has been judged to be true. Then suppose that all of these facts are written down on individual slips of paper, and then they are all thrown together and mixed up in an urn, just like in a raffle. So here is my question: what part of dialectic would teach me how to arrange these mixed-up rules and restore them to order? First of all, there is no need of discovery, since everything has already been discovered. Each and every statement has been examined and assessed, so there is no need of first judgement (for propositions), nor of second judgement (for syllogisms), since all of the

---

4. Note that Ramus tends to conflate the multiple ways in which one thing can be "prior" to another: causes before effects, universals before individuals, wholes before parts.

Dialectic

disagreements over individual matters in this field of knowledge have been debated and decided upon. All that remains is the method of teaching. And so, by the light of artful method, dialectic will pick out the definition of grammar (that is, the most general token of all) in this urn and will set it in the first place: Grammar is the art of speaking well. Then it will search out the division of grammar in the same urn and will set it in second place: there are two parts of grammar, etymology and syntax. Then, in that same urn, it will pull out the definition of the first part and join it in third place to its predecessors. And so, by defining and dividing, it will descend all the way to the most specific instances and will set them in last place. And then it will do the same for the second part [i.e., syntax]. By this route, we ourselves have tried to set out the precepts of grammar and dialectic, putting the most general in first place, subalterns in the middle, and most specific at the bottom.

And the application of this method is not limited to the matter of the arts and sciences but can be used for any subject that we want to learn easily and clearly.

[...]

The method of nature and of learning are the same thing. It is easy to explain what it is but very difficult to use and practice it—nor can one do so casually. For no one can properly make use of the method unless he already knows how to use the places of discovery and first and second judgement. Moreover, it is a bigger job, and a much harder one, to divide and arrange things with this artful method than it is to discover things well or to judge propositions or syllogisms well. And there can be no doubt that an art is made much more excellent through method than it had been either in the places of discovery, or in propositions, or in syllogisms. One can see that by considering the astonishing example of all the arts and sciences in which very many things have been cleverly discovered and perfectly judged according to first and second judgement, but few of those same things have been carefully assessed and arranged by means of this artful method.

There follows the method of prudence, in which the first things are not those that are completely and absolutely better known but those that are definitely more appropriate and plausible for the student and for leading him where we want him to go. The orators called it "prudential arrangement" because it has more to do with human prudence than with the art and the precepts of a discipline. One might say that method of learning is the judgement of knowledge (*scientia*), while the method of prudence is the judgement of opinion; though this method, when used by philosophers, poets, and orators, also looks somewhat like the syllogism. Under this head we can classify *crypsis*—that is, concealed and indirect insinuation. It is almost possible to describe it with a rule: begin in the middle, do not set out at the beginning where you are going, do not explain the parts of your plan nor set out at length the reasons and antecedents, and proceed mainly by simile and metaphor. Now, if the person you are addressing is imprudent, you should proceed directly [i.e., using the method of teaching], for it is very easy to win over intellects of that kind. But if he is clever and astute, don't go in a straight line, revealing the arguments one by one, but change it up, mix in unrelated subjects, consider the contrary, put up some resistance to yourself, make out that you don't really care, use colloquial or slang terms, rush through it, get angry or argumentative, and speak very frankly and boldly, so that your opponent gets all confused and asks himself, "where on earth is this all going?" And then finally say whatever it is that you wanted to state in conclusion. Socrates used these tactics against the sophists who did not want to be taught by him.

[...]

All that said, we now understand how the method of prudence was taught and used by philosophers, poets, and orators, and we can learn from their precepts and examples just how powerful this prudence is. But we will learn much more from the daily business of men, in which clever insinuation is easily the most important thing if you want to persuade someone who is unwilling. And so, if the entryway to the artful and true path is closed off, dialectic will make for itself another path, using the powers of wit and prudence. It will summon the aid of custom and common use since it is deprived of the protection of theory; because it cannot hew to a straight course, it will alter its sailing and, with whatever wind its sails can catch, will bring the boat to port safe and unharmed. And just as the Spartans were once praised for covert attacks, so too will dialectic be praised—or rather will be praised infinitely more fully—when it uses such skill to win over the consent of a rebellious and recalcitrant mind.

Dialectic

APPLYING RAMIST LOGIC TO
NATURAL PHILOSOPHY

In these extracts from the preface to his lectures on natural philosophy (Scholae physicae), Ramus sets out his intention to subject the text of the Physics and natural philosophy itself to his three "laws of method," which he had derived from Aristotle's own Posterior analytics *I.4; in other words, Aristotle (as Ramus interpreted him) would be used to criticize Aristotle. This passage provides a good introduction to those laws themselves. This text is from Ramus's final, revised edition of the preface in the 1569* Scholae in liberales artes.

We must examine Aristotle's *Physics* using exactly the same tools with which we have already examined other arts. We must keep before our eyes those logical laws concerning the material and form of a [liberal] art: that is, that all material should be *kata pantos, kath'auto,* and *kath'olou prôton* (universally true, essentially true, and as general as possible).

The first (*kata pantos*) is the Law of Truth, which requires that no fact should be included in an art unless it is completely and necessarily true. And so, not only falsehoods but even things that are only contingently true will be excluded.

By the second law (*kath'auto*), we are further admonished that any element of an art should be not only completely and necessarily true, but should be homogeneous and as it were a member of the same body. So there should be nothing geometrical in arithmetic, nor should there be any arithmetic in geometry. Otherwise, the geometry in arithmetic would be unarithmetical, and the arithmetic in geometry would be ungeometrical. (In just the same way, any logic in physics would be unphysical, while any physics in logic would be unlogical.) For the same reason, even true refutations of a false error must be removed from an art, since they teach only how to avoid lack of knowledge without teaching knowledge. This is the Law of Justice, which most justly adjudicates the bounds of the arts and allots to each its own.

By the third and final law (*kath'olou prôton*), it is ordained that the precepts of an art should not only be completely and necessarily true and homogeneous but also essentially reciprocal in its parts. A general concept should not be allotted to a species, nor a specific one to a genus; the general must be expounded generally, the specific specifically. If you were to teach that lines perpendicular [to the same line] do not meet, that the three angles of an equilateral triangle are equal to two right angles, or were to explain ratio in terms of number and [geometrical] magnitude, then you would be assigning a general attribute to a species, since parallelism applies also to oblique lines, equality to two right angles applies to all triangles, and ratio applies to all things. Or if you were to teach the equality to two right angles with respect to a figure in general, then you would attribute a specific attribute to a genus, and so you would also be teaching sophistically. This third law is the Law of Wisdom. These three laws comprise the intuitive judgement of principles and of statements that are clear in themselves; this has nothing to do with the syllogistic judgement of uncertain statements. It [i.e., the Law of Wisdom] is the only law that concerns the artful and methodical arrangement and form of statements that have been judged either intuitively or syllogistically, requiring that things that are absolutely better known and clearer should come first [i.e., Ramus's "method"]. Although it can be stated in very few words, it has the greatest utility and effect of all the laws.

So these are Aristotle's logical laws concerning the material and form of the arts. They are common to all times, places and people, and no exceptions for reasons of plan, intention, or occasion can be admitted. You would be breaking the laws of grammar somewhat if you were to pronounce a long syllable as short, and your error would be corrected by the whistles of the audience. But the laws of dialectic, which are the kings and queens of all other learning—if you were to break these even in the smallest degree, how much worse would be the offense, and how could it be borne at all? *This* is the mistress of infinite error: when an opinion is adopted many centuries ago, quite in contravention of the universal laws of establishing doctrine and then girded with all the various privileges bestowed by academic or public authority and heaped up with the kinds of extraordinary honor and respect by which Aristotle's *Physics* (like his other works) is esteemed. But I hope that I will find in the city of logic judges who consider the universal laws of their city to be greater than any loophole through which sophism has taken root, however hallowed by time, and who hold their laws more inviolable than any sense of privilege, however widely approved.

Dialectic

Now, if you were to consult with an architect about the building of a palace and you asked him what instruments he would use to make a survey, he would bring out (I guess) a rule, plumb, and square. Likewise, if someone should ask me what tools I am going to trust when I assess the whole Aristotelian system of the world, I should bring out as instruments those Aristotelian laws that concern the matter and form of an art.[5] For the philosophy of Aristotle is a kind of library of all the philosophers who came before him, their opinions piled up in various places rather than subjected to judgement and spoiled and corrupted by the moths and worms of Apellicon[6] (as I've said elsewhere). And so, on any matter, we must compare all the relevant passages of Aristotle and then apply a selection that conforms to those universal laws. For there is no philosophical opinion so celebrated that something contradicting it cannot also be found somewhere in Aristotle. So, what more authoritative or excellent judge and interpreter could we find for an Aristotelian dispute than the Aristotelian laws themselves—that is, the most careful and weighty judgements that Aristotle himself made?

Therefore, all you philosophers, whoever you are who will read, hear, and understand my words, raise up your spirits through the God of nature (since nature is the subject under discussion)!

Most scholars, even those who are piously religious (which really astonishes me), have so great an opinion of this philosopher that they would sooner have doubts about Moses or Christ than about Aristotle! But if they would just put aside for a moment their fierce loyalty and strive to be unbiased in their judgement, then they will see that the books of the *Physics* are very different from their opinions of them. Then they will be a little more fair, a little more tractable. You see, if someone were to be picked up and carried off to the highest point in the universe, and from there were to take in entirely the earth and sky and everything contained by them, and if he were then to turn back to Aristotle's eight books of physics, he would find mentioned there not one single natural thing, only logical conundrums: about causes and principles in the first two books, about effects of causes

---

5. That is, the three laws of method above, the first two of which concern the matter of the art and the third, the form.

6. Apellicon of Teos (d. 84 BC), who badly edited Aristotle's worm-eaten manuscripts.

and motion in the third and fifth, about the underlying place and the accompanying time in the fourth, and about the infinite in part of the third and the whole of the sixth. Finally, he would find the seventh and eighth books devoted to certain horrifying monsters of eternity—not only irrelevant to liberal learning but inimical to true faith and piety. But Christian men somehow or other manage to stomach Aristotle's commentators defending his impious fictions (*commenta*) and mocking Moses as an Egyptian fantasist, or calling Christians uneducated fools or crazed zealots. Yet our predecessors did not revere Aristotle as though he were some second Jove (as our crazed commentators do) but exposed his lies with their own clear and convincing arguments.[7] Now I have decided not just to use those same arguments against Aristotle but also to engage in this philosophical battle with the weapons of logic, mathematics, and physics: that is, to fight a philosophical war with the arms of philosophy. I hope that those who engage in—and judge—this controversy will at last change their minds and pledge their immortal gratitude to me.

WHERE DOES MATHEMATICAL KNOWLEDGE COME FROM?

Ramus's 1567 Prooemium mathematicum (*Paris, 1567*), *later incorporated into the beginning of his* Scholae mathematicae *of 1569, was the first substantial Renaissance work on the history and philosophy of mathematics. The first selection (from book II, 44–45 of the* Scholae mathematicae*) forms part of his long defense of the utility and practicality of mathematics, for which he calls in Plato and Aristotle as his witnesses. And in the second selection (from book III, 82–84 of the* Scholae mathematicae*), as part of his critique of both Euclid and his commentator Proclus, Ramus considers the nature and origin of "mathematicals," by which he means both the art of mathematics and mathematical objects. Ramus considered himself to be a Platonist, but only by dint of a reading of Plato that focused on the more "Socratic" and practical minded side of Plato, dismissing Platonic metaphysics as a fabrication of the Pythagoreans and the later Academy.*

---

7. Ramus is referring to the Neoplatonic commentators on Aristotle, which he studied carefully during his exile in Fontainebleau.

Dialectic

We will argue for a two-fold utility [in mathematics]: for contemplation and for action. Earlier in my account, Pythagoras, Plato, Xenocrates, and Aristotle all placed the foundations and elements of learning the arts of natural philosophy and politics in mathematics. So, let us defend Pythagoras, Plato, Xenocrates, and Aristotle from the slanders of simple-minded idiots, and let us teach that the mathematical arts are the foundations and elements of natural and political philosophy: those who are ignorant of such principles will never have a firm grasp on the knowledge of natural or moral matters. Let Plato be heard, then, and his Academy be upheld. Let him teach how mathematics is the first step on the path to learning and understanding. For Plato indicates that the whole genus of mathematicals, both arithmetical and geometrical, is drawn from the senses when he uses terms like "attracting," "impelling," "awakening," "arousing," or "turning" the "intellect," "reasoning," "contemplation," or "truth." All of that is above all *logical*. For, out of all of the arts, mathematics has been singularly zealous for truth and especially logical. It makes judgements not on the authority of any plausible or approved persons but on the necessity of the arguments. It compels the mind to stay among things themselves. No school has ever held to a more uncompromising logic than mathematics. If you want to see the colors before you clearly, you must keep the eyes of the body open and clear and turned in the right direction. And likewise, if you want to grasp intelligibles, you must keep your mind alert and attentive through the exercise of reason and turned in the right direction. And mathematics, in fact, arouses and exercises the mind and, more than all other arts, strengthens and supports human judgement.

But here is where some Pythagoreans and degenerate Platonists dream up the fantastic notion of *aphairesis*,[8] and there are some passages in Aristotle, too, on the same subject. But the same philosopher refutes those statements in other contradictory and more powerful passages. *Metaphysics* 13.2–3, in fact, completely undermines that kind of *aphairesis*, making abstraction common to all arts. In the arts, general *facts* (only) are expounded, having been inducted and abstracted from individual instances. But that theory of mathematical abstraction is called a "fabrication."[9]

---

8. The term used to mean mathematical abstraction, but which Ramus uses more generally to mean the separation and reification of an abstract idea from its concrete origin.

9. Aristotle, *Metaphysics* 13.2 (1076b1).

And so, when you hear Plato say that mathematicals are "attracting," "impelling," "awakening," "arousing," or "turning," or when Aristotle says that they have been "abstracted," you must not understand that as some sort of sophistic shadow of a fairytale, whereby mathematicals are hidden away somewhere, like in the intermundane spaces of Democritus, but as a logical action of the mind by which the demonstration of the truth is made more pure and precise.

Thus, the blind Stoic teacher of Cicero, Diodorus, was able to perform the duties of a geometer (incredible though it seems), instructing his students which line to draw, from what point to what point, as Cicero says in the *Tusculan Disputations* V. Likewise, Didymus of Alexandria[10] was blinded from a tender age, and for that reason was completely ignorant of letters, yet he showed everyone a miracle—himself—by mastering dialectic and geometry (which of all arts requires sight), according to Jerome in his catalogue of ecclesiastical authors. The more penetrating insight of the mind flourished in those blinded bodies, and the less they could use the perception of the eyes, the more they relied on the mind. So I have no argument with the claim that mathematics can wake us up from our slumbers, like an alarm clock in the morning, but I do insist that by this brilliant light, the eyes of the mind are opened, stimulated, and directed, so that they can see and understand all other things.[11]

[...]

In the first place, there is the question of the origin of mathematicals. In [his *Commentary on the first book of Euclid's* Elements] II.4 and 6, Proclus argues against Plato and Aristotle at great length, denying that the mathematical arts were either observed or discovered by humans with the aid of the senses; instead, he argues, they were ungenerated and implanted by nature on the grounds that no precise and irrefutable reason or demonstration can arise from the senses, and that sensible things are posterior to intelligibles, and that the mind is nobler and more excellent than sensation. Pythagoras was the greatest philosopher, as I made clear before, but just as with Plato and Aristotle, Pythagoras was not always Pythago-

---

10. A fourth-century theologian.

11. That is, mathematics is not an end in itself, nor an innate knowledge of objects of its own, but a tool to better understand *other* things.

Dialectic 257

ras. He made up the *metempsychosis* of immortal souls from bodies to other bodies. From that doctrine, many absurdities followed, including Proclus's statement above. So, in I.2, Proclus (again at great length) rehearses the dreams of the Pythagoreans and thereby concludes that the mind is the author and parent of the mathematical genus because it received from the divine mind a taste of the species of all things, not just of mathematicals. And so the mathematicals are more ancient than the particular forms in our minds, and it is not the case (as Aristotle thought) that the human mind is a blank slate. Rather, it is painted and adorned with mathematical notions (*rationes*)—in fact, by its own nature, painting and adorning *itself* with all these forms. But really, these arguments of Proclus are pretty feeble and are refuted first in the *Analytics* and then more extensively in the *Metaphysics*, where I have written at length following the opinion of both Plato and Aristotle that "the faculty of perceiving all things was given to the mind by God and nature, just as the faculty of discerning all colors was given to the eye; but the faculty of perceiving the forms of all thing was *not* given to the mind, just as the eye was not given the faculty of perceiving the *species* of colors."

Pythagoras, it seems to me, went too far by exaggerating that mental faculty in us for perceiving knowledge (*disciplina*). But it has to be said that Aristotle perhaps too readily dismissed it. After all, Aristotle himself talks of natural virtues and natural logic, attributing to our minds not so much the faculties of the virtues and the arts but the beginnings and seeds, so to speak, of them. Thus, the mind is not a completely blank slate but is naturally strewn with some shadings and tracings. And so I can forgive the Pythagoreans a little for their statements about the immortality of the soul and their overly zealous promotion of this divine faculty. But I reject Proclus's refutation [of Aristotle and Plato], because he spurns Plato and Aristotle's justification of a better and more correct position.

But Proclus introduced (in I.15) yet another argument on this subject, connecting the origin of the name [of mathematics] to Pythagorean *anamnesis*, or recollection. Concerning the very names "mathematics" and "mathematicals," he asks: from where shall we say did the ancients get this name to apply to these disciplines, and what was a plausible reason for their doing so? He answers that this name was not invented by the common people (as most names are) but was applied by the Pythagoreans from

258 PETRUS RAMUS

the notion of recollection—because everything that is considered "learning" is in fact remembering, but especially that which is called *mathesis*, which is the recollection of eternal concepts in the mind, and so, in particular, it was called "mathematics," inasmuch as it assembles concepts so that they can be remembered. That's what Proclus says, and it is about as convincing as what he had to say about the origin of mathematics. No one (at least so far) has ever found this "remembering" so fruitful that they can use it to learn any art without study and hard work. The name was chosen [for mathematics] not because of some excellence in its origin but just because the name happened to fit it. For many centuries, the mathematical arts were the *only* arts. The rudiments of grammar are attributed to Aristotle and his pupil Theophrastus, Corax and Tisias first made a start of rhetoric, Plato attributes the origin of logic to Prometheus, while Aristotle attributes it to the Zeno, who argued with Socrates in Plato's *Parmenides*. In his logical *Organon*, Aristotle also claims logic for himself (however falsely), just as in his *Rhetoric* he lays claim to invention and action. And so in times more ancient than those, the mathematical disciplines were the *only* disciplines taught to boys in school, and so they were called by the name of the whole genus: *mathemata*, or disciplines.... But what need for many arguments to dispute [Proclus's] position? The whole of his first book of mathematical demonstrations[12] is filled with ample examples of industry, labor, and diligence—examples that are not only contrary to Proclus but chosen with the authority of Proclus himself!—and that book leaves no doubt that the mathematical arts come into the mind through the senses, induction, and experience; they are not inborn in our minds, nor are they stimulated by some fortunate recollection. They are, in other words, immigrants, not natives. And so Proclus ought to allow himself to be led away from the Pythagorean school to the Academy and Lyceum, and he should embrace the philosophy of Plato and Aristotle on this matter. There is nothing here [i.e., in the "Pythagorean" philosophy] that is *kata pantos*, nothing *kath'auto*, nothing *kath'olou prôton*: the laws laid down by mathematics itself forbid such ideas.

---

12. This is a confusing way to refer to the second book of the prologue to Proclus's *Commentary* on Euclid, where Proclus sets out the history of mathematics.

Dialectic

THE FREEDOM TO PHILOSOPHIZE

The preface to Cicero's Academica *(1550) was published while Ramus was under his ban from teaching philosophy and was issued under the name of his collaborator, Omer Talon. This section of the preface, defending Ramus against his detractors and passionately claiming the right to philosophical freedom (while drifting into the first person), is very likely from Ramus's own pen. The text is from Audomarus Talaeus,* Academia *(Paris, 1550), 15–16, 23–24.*

Some Aristotelians share the vanity of the same error [the Pythagoreans' exaggerated deference to their master]; they defer so much to their master that they treat him like a kind of god and consider it to be almost the same thing to contradict Aristotle as it would be to contradict nature, truth, or God himself. Hence, when my brother Petrus Ramus spoke against the doctrine of the Aristotelians—in a manner that was very customary and that every age had approved—two men[13] got so angry and worked up, judging that anyone who criticized Aristotle was trying to throw the arts into confusion, was overturning divine and human law, was destroying the freedom of human judgement, and (in short) was banishing the sun itself from the cosmos. Puffed up with an Aristotelian spirit, they proclaimed that so great a crime had to be expiated by fire. There is proof of their enormous stupidity (because it would be scarcely believable if it were not attested and confessed in writing) in the pamphlets written against the *Aristotelicae animadversiones* and distributed through the whole world, publishing and proclaiming that sentence.... But why should I single out these two Aristotelians, when that whole clan is the same? In fact, why should I rehearse this extraordinary history, unlike anything ever witnessed by the human race? Grammarians, rhetoricians, mathematicians, and philosophers have always had total freedom to speak and write against other grammarians, rhetoricians, mathematicians, and philosophers. And because that freedom has always seemed essential for the advancement of any art, all philosophers (especially Aristotle) have valued it highly and have recommended it in their teachings. But because Petrus Ramus, in his *Aristotelicae animadversiones*, had dared to poke the slumbering Aristotelians, good God, I shudder to recall what happened.

---

13. Antonio de Gouveia and Joachim de Perion.

Lest the Aristotelians, enraged again, hunt me down too, I take refuge in the Academy—the Academy that is not proud or violent but, on the contrary, tolerant (*facilis*) and benign. The Academy is so far from getting enraged with those who contradict it, that, in fact, it welcomes as allies the very people who zealously try to deny it the right of free inquiry.

Henceforth, this should be the absolutely settled rule laid down for common sense, to anyone who wants to judge rightly and dependably about all matters. When you buy or procure the things that are essential for the needs and comfort of the body, you take such care, never buying anything without great discrimination, even if the merchant swears up and down to you that the goods he has for sale are the very best. And so don't you think you should exert yourself even more, and give even more careful thought to examining and choosing the commodities of the mind that the philosophers are trying to sell us? As Horace puts it,

The man who has not the skill to match with Sidonian purple the fleeces that drink up Aquinum's dye, will not suffer surer loss or one closer to his heart than he who shall fail to distinguish false from true. [*Epistles* I.10.26–29]

These philosophers are the merchants and salesmen of wisdom. So, if there is something in Plato's sayings and writings that is useful and applicable for me, I'll take it. If something in Epicurus's garden shows itself to be good, I won't reject it. If Aristotle is selling something better (to any extent and in any way), I'll buy it. If Zeno's wares are a better buy than Aristotle's, I'll leave behind Aristotle and go into Zeno's shop. If everything on sale in the philosophers' stores is vain and useless, I just won't buy anything; on the other hand, I also won't put an end to my search for the very best, guided always by Horace's well-known advice and teaching:

What is right and seemly is my study and pursuit, and to that I am wholly given. Do you ask, perchance, who is my chief, in what home I take shelter? I am not bound over to swear as any master dictates; wherever the storm drives me, I turn in for comfort. Now I become all action, and plunge into the tide of civil life, stern champion and follower of true Virtue; now I slip back stealthily into the rules of Aristippus, and would bend the world to myself, not myself to the world. [*Epistles* I.1.11, 13–19]

This is the characteristic and genuine liberty of the Academics, or of true men (I consider those to mean the same thing): to be compelled to

Dialectic 261

obey the philosophical laws and regulations of no other man; moderation, in interposing no judgement of his own in uncertain matters; prudence, in weighing up the causes of things and expressing what he thinks can be said on any doctrine, relying on no one else's authority; and wisdom, in cherishing Truth alone as a goddess in every facet of life—and valuing her more than the testimony of all the philosophers.

16

BERNARDINO TELESIO
(1509–1588)

On Mind and Wisdom

🙚

PAUL RICHARD BLUM

INTRODUCTION

Bernardino Telesio was born in 1509 in the southern Italian province of Calabria in the town Cosenza. At a young age, he moved to northern Italy and studied at the university of Padua; however, he did not obtain a degree. He was connected with literary and church circles in Rome and elsewhere and also with heterodox followers of Juan de Valdés (1490–1541). In 1563, he completed a draft of a treatise that he published in 1565 as *On Nature according to its Own Principles (De natura iuxta propria principia)*.[1] In 1568, Telesio was accused of denying the immortality of the soul, which prompted some rephrasing in subsequent editions.[2] From this time until his death, he was the leader of a circle of colleagues, the Accademia Cosentina, in his native town Cosenza, while keeping contact with nobility in Naples. He died in Cosenza in 1588.

1. The translation below is based on the 1976 edition by Luigi De Franco (see bibliography). A new *Edizione Nazionale delle Opere di Bernardino Telesio* began publication by Aragno in 2006. The series *Telesiana* offers reprints of original editions with commentaries.
2. Luca Addante, "Telesio, Bernardino."

On Mind and Wisdom 263

Telesio is known to have prepared the way to modern scientific research while distancing his philosophy from traditional patterns of the Aristotelian and Platonic traditions, as well as from Galen's medical approach. He claimed to study nature's "very own principles," but the question for modern readers remains what, exactly, that entails. The excerpts provided here document the fact that Telesio focused precisely on the intersection of 'objective' reality and the working of the mind. First of all, he terms the human power of understanding 'spirit.' In traditional philosophy, spirit meant a nonmaterial substance, and as such, something that cannot be embodied but has, on the other hand, access to the transcendent reality (be that the divine, the Platonic Form, or else).

As we see in the text below, spirit in Telesio's work is that physical power of humans to intuit external reality. This way of understanding nature entails the coincidence of truth entering the mind and the mind determining the truth of it. Therefore, we read Telesio repeating the process of sensing and judging. The human 'spirit' not only perceives impressions, it even appropriates them and forms its judgment about reality. The human mind is, thus, neither only receptive nor only creative—it is both. Thus, it is empowered to understand nature as such.

As an alternative to any Platonizing conception of intellect, which would describe sense perception as a 'trigger' to recall innate ideas, Telesio describes understanding as 'inserted' by God into the human body and mind. Only because of its being the universal faculty is it able to judge particulars. The universality of this faculty is termed wisdom (*sapientia*), which embeds the individual human spirit in the real universal wisdom that—paying tribute to theological specifications—is described as the instantiation of the divine mind in the human mind. With this theory that inspired Tommaso Campanella, Telesio preemptively bridges what later would become the competition between sensualism/empiricism—as in Francis Bacon (1561–1626) and John Locke (1632–1704)—and rationalism as in René Descartes (1596–1650). The apparently pedantic style of his writing expresses his labor in presenting a theory of understanding reality that avoids the pitfalls of the preceding tradition.

BIBLIOGRAPHY

Primary Sources

Telesio, Bernardino. *De natura iuxta propria principia. Liber primus et secundus.* Edited by Alessandro Ottaviani. Torino: Aragno, 2006.

———. *De rerum natura = Intorno alla natura [libri I–VI].* Edited and translated by Luigi De Franco. 2 vols. Cosenza: Casa del libro, 1965.

———. *De rerum natura: libri VII–VIII–IX.* Edited and translated by Luigi De Franco. Firenze: La Nuova Italia, 1976.

———. *La natura secondo i suoi principi* [lib. 1 e 2]. Edited and translated by Roberto Bondì. Latin-Italian. Firenze: La Nuova Italia, 1999.

———. *Varii de naturalibus rebus libelli.* Edited by Luigi De Franco. Firenze: La Nuova Italia, 1981.

———. *Telesiana.* Edited by Roberto Bondì et al. Reprints of original editions with commentaries. 5 vols. Roma: Carocci, 2011–2014.

Secondary Sources

Addante, Luca, "Telesio, Bernardino," Dizionario Biografico degli Italiani—Volume 95, 2019, http://www.treccani.it//enciclopedia/bernardinotelesio_(Dizionario-Biografico).

Boenke, Michaela. "Bernardino Telesio." In *The Stanford Encyclopedia of Philosophy*, edited by Edward N. Zalta. Stanford, Calif.: Metaphysics Research Lab, Stanford University, 2018. https://plato.stanford.edu/archives/win2018/entries/telesio/.

———. *Körper, Spiritus, Geist: Psychologie vor Descartes.* München: Wilhelm Fink Verlag, 2005.

Bondì, Roberto. *Il primo dei moderni. Filosofia e scienza in Bernardino Telesio.* Roma: Edizioni di Storia e Letteratura, 2018.

———. "'Spiritus' e 'anima' in Bernardino Telesio." *Giornale critico della filosofia italiana* 72, no. 3 (1993): 405–17.

Bondì, Roberto, ed. *Bernardino Telesio y la nueva imagen de la naturaleza en el Renacimento.* Madrid: Siruela, 2013.

Garber, Daniel. "Telesio among the Novatores: Telesio's Reception in the Seventeenth Century." In *Early Modern Philosophers and the Renaissance Legacy*, edited by Cecilia Muratori and Gianni Paganini, 119–33. Cham: Springer Verlag, 2016.

Mocchi, Giuliana, Sandra Plastina, and Emilio Sergio, eds. *Bernardino Telesio: Tra filosofia naturale e scienza moderna.* Pisa: Serra, 2012.

Omodeo, Pietro Daniel, ed. *Bernardino Telesio and the Natural Sciences in the Renaissance.* Leiden: Brill, 2019.

Pupo, Spartaco. *L'anima immortale in Telesio: Per una storia delle interpretazioni.* Cosenza: Pellegrini, 1999.

Sergio, Emilio. "Bernardino Telesio 1509–1588." Galleria dell'Accademia Cosentina, 2014. http://www.iliesi.cnr.it/ATC/htm/accos/Bernardino_Telesio.html.

———. "Telesio, Bernardino." In *Encyclopedia of Renaissance Philosophy*, edited by Marco Sgarbi, 1–6. Cham: Springer International Publishing, 2018. https://doi.org/10.1007/978-3-319-02848-4_267-2.

Sirri, Raffaele. *Le opere e i giorni d'un filosofo: Bernardino Telesio*. Napoli: Istituto italiano per gli studi filosofici, 2006.

Spruit, Leen. "Bernardino Telesio on Spirit, Sense, and Imagination." In *Image, Imagination, and Cognition. Medieval and Early Modern Theory and Practice*, edited by Christoph Lüthy et al., 94–116. Leiden: Brill, 2018.

BERNARDINO TELESIO

On Mind and Wisdom[3]

This spirit senses the similarity and diversity of the things that it senses; it senses as one the things that do the same and as different those that do different acts.

Since the spirit suffers and is moved by all things, it also perceives their similitude and dissimilarity. That is to say, spirit perceives and judges all those things as one and the same that do the same to it and by which it suffers the same but as diverse those that act diverse and from which it suffers diverse things. Therefore, the spirit perceives as one and the same everything, and it judges everything to be throughout one that does the same thing and from which it suffers the same, even if it resides in very many different things. On the contrary, whatever does diverse things and from which it suffers diversely, the spirit perceives as different and judges them to be different, although they are inherent in one thing. Consequently, what the spirit suffers from all fires being moved by the same movements, all that it perceives to be one and declares to be one; likewise, all snows to be one snow, while suffering from all of them and being moved from all of them by the same movement. On the other hand, if the spirit has suffered diverse things from one man in diverse movements, it neither senses nor judges it to be one but to be composed of various things.

---

3. Bernardino Telesio, *De rerum natura = Intorno alla natura* [*libri I–VI*], ed. and trans. Luigi De Franco, 2 vols. (Cosenza: Casa del libro, 1965); Bernardino Telesio, *De rerum natura: libri VII–VIII–IX*, ed. and trans. Luigi De Franco (Firenze: La Nuova Italia, 1976). Excerpts are from bk. VIII, chap. 1, 160–62, and bk. IX, chap. 6, 358–66.

The spirit senses and judges as one not only those things that are similar to themselves and do wholly and throughout to the spirit in the same way the same things; it also declares to be one and the same those things that in some ways differ among themselves, provided they conform somehow. For, whatever does the same and from which it suffers the same, by that the spirit suffers through the same movement. Therefore, when it sees any number of humans, albeit different in many ways, it senses them as one man and judges them to be one. Namely, they are congruent and conform, and the spirit suffers from them insofar as they are humans, that is, composed of the same parts and gifted with the same powers to operate and to suffer, and they are gifted with the same ability to sense and to move. The spirit perceives the similitude that inheres all humans, separate from whatever is in them as single men. Likewise, with horses and lions (even horses and lions and humans), the spirit senses all of them and judges them as one and the same, although very much distant from each other because they are similar and congruent in being animals. The spirit attributes to animal—as common to man, horse, and lion—everything that it senses to be inherent to all and to occur to all. The spirit gathers and combines into one, and declares to be one, everything that it senses as throughout similar in many—separate from what it perceives to be different in them. When the spirit senses diverse things in one being, then it senses them to be diverse and judges them to be diverse, while what inheres or occurs to similar beings, all that it attributes to their common nature. It attributes everything to man and judges everything to belong to humans that which it senses to inhere in all humans and to occur to all humans, but not what belongs to individuals, separate from others; rather, it attributes to individuals only what it senses to be inherent in them and what appears to be peculiar to them.

ON WISDOM

Cognition—of all other beings and animals but also of the spirit itself and of the body, in which it is implanted and without which it cannot be preserved—is desired and necessary for the spirit in order to meet with their various powers and conditions its own needs and those of the body—not only in the present but also in the future. Furthermore, the

On Mind and Wisdom 267

spirit is by nature all-knowing (like the heaven). That is, it is able to contemplate all things and sense their nature and powers. Moreover, since it is perfected and permanently made one by the substance that is inserted by God, it is incited and empowered to cognize not only all other things but God himself and of divine beings. Necessarily, the spirit is made wise about not only other things but also about God and divine beings, namely, about its parent and its own artisan and kindred substances (who would deny that?). However, as though sent into exile and thrown into prison and darkness and, hence, deprived of contemplation of things and made unknowing of all things, it strives most anxiously to be restored to its own nature and perfection, and as long as it has not yet achieved it, the spirit suffers and is tormented and dislikes itself. The spirit strives and works to know not only what somehow relates to its conservation and that it is apt in a way to sense, but also what apparently contributes nothing to that and also what exceeds by far its acumen and what the spirit by itself and without being incited by the substance that is inserted by God cannot contemplate nor even desire, that is, the substance, working, and beatitude of God and the other divine beings.

Evidently, wisdom is intelligence that determines the nature and power of everything in that it fully perceives and at the same time fully penetrates. Therefore, it may understand which things and which of their powers are good and appropriate for the present purpose and which powers, in order to become good, should be intensified or reduced and in which way this should be done. It may distinguish the differences of all other things and of those of the same kind and first of all of the spirits, and it foresees future outcomes of many things and the future acts of humans. (For, nothing happens otherwise than what their nature requires and has been observed to happen; nor do humans act any other actions than what their constitution promises and they are known to do.) Furthermore, this wisdom determines (and, by God, first and foremost) which substance of God is to be contemplated—but in no way using reason—what occurs always in the same way. Wisdom is certainly able to explain, and explains throughout, that all the world and what it contains is founded by the most wise and most potent and the best creator. However, these creations of God cannot be contemplated in their integrity and magnitude but on a much smaller level, which is far remote from contemplating other things;

all the more, when it contemplates His lightning, it [wisdom] is clouded and blinded more than anyone who has seen the light of the sun and the sun itself. That wisdom is intelligence and true and highest which states that God himself and his substance and conditions are not to be understood with reason like the other things but rather, disregarding reason, by contemplating them in the sacred and divine scriptures and in God's very own words. It also resolves to care not (as reason does) for the momentary benefit that submits to many dangers and abounds with persistent miseries and is not at all great, but for beatitude that is eternal and certain, pure and most high, and to find also a way to achieve it.

It is characteristic of the spirit (as stated), especially as being perfected by the substance inserted by God, to contemplate and cognize all things. The following makes this most clear: the uppermost desire to contemplate and sense all things, even if knowing them does not offer any advantage and we may not be allowed to contemplate and sense them; the delight enjoyed contemplating and understanding those highest things; the pain that afflicts the spirit when deprived of it; and the reverence, adoration, and love toward the wise and the disdain for the unwise. For, when we desire wealth and power, we rejoice and jubilate when we achieve them, and we respect the rich and powerful; however, when we strive for wisdom and achieve it, we are pleased with ourselves in a more noble way. When we are outdone in wealth and power (even if that is our fault), we all very much despise and dislike ourselves, being in no way made more or less wise about ourselves; the rich and powerful we praise and respect only as long as we hope for some benefit from them, but we never love them. On the other hand, we venerate the wise, even if already passed from life, like divine beings, and follow them with the greatest love because we contemplate in them the perfection of the spirit and of ourselves.

It is not the case what the Aristotelians say: some things are always or are made the same way, whereas other things are neither perpetually the same nor do they come about the same way; or, some things are made by nature, and their course cannot be changed or bent by us, but other things are being done by us and are in our command. Therefore, [they erroneously conclude] that cognition of these appears to assumes a different potential, namely either one and the same capability and knowing that works in the same way with things that are fully perceived or with similitude in

On Mind and Wisdom

things that are not fully observed; likewise, (they don't see) that in crafts that treat different matter and with different tools but nevertheless with the same power of the spirit and throughout with the same skill. Wisdom is intelligence that contemplates the natures of all things, and things that are dealt with for the conservation of the spirit regarding the operations that are to be set up need to be treated and done correctly so that the character of other things as well as the spirit is evident. It is plainly evident that said wisdom is not a particular but a universal power. The remaining species or parts are all on the whole wisdom; however, not of all things but particular and specific powers and wholly specific powers of those things with which singular powers deal, and none of them is of itself and separate from the others perfected and absolute. It would be totally unknown and unclear if it would happen that any of them manifests its proper powers, but it remains controversial which kinship and similitude it has with the others and what it shares with them.

Hence appears why also the ancients all deemed that wise is the one who is good and endowed with all virtues. Hence, wisdom not only provides the highest good to the spirit but also renders it similar to the divine beings and even to God himself (as far as it may). For, someone who ignores that God is the most wise and the principal of the virtues (that we may know to be inherent in God) is wisdom, which contemplates the building of the world and of the character of all things as well as of the animals, can be seen as not only wicked and wild but also foolish.

To the substance that is inserted into both the universal body and the true spirit and which (as has been said) was deprived of contemplation by the overpowering shadows of the body and the forces of things, wisdom offers the things that can be contemplated, somewhat solicits this operation to do its own work, and restores it to its proper nature and proper perfection.

17

JACOPO ZABARELLA
(1533–1589)

On the Constitution of Natural Science

PER LANDGREN

INTRODUCTION[1]

The University of Padua was the most prestigious of all European universities during the sixteenth century.[2] Jacopo Zabarella (also Jacobus or Giacomo) was a dominant teacher of logic and natural philosophy. His authority as a magisterial interpreter of Aristotle was undisputed and his influence pervasive.[3] When he died on October 15, 1589, he had a rock-solid academic reputation. He earned even greater fame, however, by way of his posthumous and voluminous publications.

Skilled in Latin as well as classical Greek from his childhood, and with a humanist education in an open-minded scholastic and Aristotelian institution, Zabarella completed his doctor-

---

1. My sincere thanks go to Richard Blum, James Snyder, and Howard Hotson for improvements to this introduction.
2. Paul F. Grendler, *The Universities of the Italian Renaissance* (Baltimore: Johns Hopkins University Press, 2002), 37.
3. See, for example, William A. Wallace, "Zabarella, Jacopo," in *Encyclopedia of the Renaissance*, vol. 6, ed. Paul F. Grendler (New York: Charles Scribner's Sons, 1999), 337–39; Charles B. Schmitt, "Zabarella, Jacopo," in *Dictionary of Scientific Biography*, vol. 14, ed. C. C. Gillispie (New York: Scribner, 1981), 580–82.

ate in June 1553. In 1564, he got the principal chair in logic, and in 1569, he was awarded an extraordinary professorship in natural philosophy. In 1578, Zabarella published his *Opera logica* (*Logical Works*), which became his most successful work in terms of impact and influence. After fifteen years as professor in natural philosophy, Zabarella published his introductory work on the subject, *De naturalis scientiae constitutione*, in which he argues for an order of the subdisciplines, which corresponds to what he found to be the natural order in the works of Aristotle. He also delineates a didactic sequence and an epistemic structure of the disciplines in natural science. Two chapters from this work are presented here. Posthumously, two massive works in natural philosophy were published: in 1590, *De rebus naturalibus*, and in 1602, the Frankfurt edition of a commentary on Aristotle's *Physica* and a few shorter works.

While reading the following two chapters, it is important to bear in mind that Zabarella follows Aristotle in holding that all things belong to two genera, necessary things, and contingent things. Out of these genera, two kinds of disciplines arise. The first kind is about necessary things and generates absolute knowledge, *scientia*. These are called *scientiae*, sciences, such as metaphysics, mathematics, and natural philosophy. The second kind is about contingent things, those that are dependent on us. These are practical disciplines, such as ethics, economics, and politics, and they are called *prudentia*.[4]

In the beginning of *De naturalis scientiae constitutione*, in chapter 6, Zabarella defines natural philosophy as a contemplative science about natural bodies. The goal is complete knowledge, which consists of two kinds, namely knowledge of the subject's principles and accidents.[5]

The concept of contemplative science can easily be misunderstood as a kind of armchair philosophy with no interest in experiential knowledge. That is not, however, what Zabarella means. Knowledge about principles is certainly rational, but knowledge about accidents is experiential, and induction from particulars and their accidental characteristics is the

---

4. Jacques Zabarella, "De rerum ac disciplinarum divisione," in *La nature de la logique*, Livre I, Cap. II, 38-45.

5. Giacomo Zabarella, "De naturalis scientiae constitutione," in *De rebus naturalibus*, ed. José Manuel García Valverde, vol. 1 (Leiden: Brill, 2016), 71.

way, the *methodus*, for an Aristotelian to acquire knowledge of the principles.[6]

In chapter 32 of the same work, we are told that historical works contain things that can be learned by experience and the senses without knowledge of causes, since causes belong to natural science.[7] Here, he asserts that the books about "history of animals" are preparations for the scientific books about animals. The reason is that the former books deliver accidental or factual knowledge that something is, *quod ita sit*, but the books that follow declare the causes of that factual knowledge, *propter quid*.[8] *Historia* conveys here etymologically the Greek concept of something that "has been seen" and therefore is known by experience.[9] Experiential or factual knowledge is the province of natural history.[10] But *historia naturalis* belongs only to natural philosophy in so far as it delivers *historiae* in inductive generalizations, that is, certain knowledge, to be used in syllogisms and explained philosophically, that is to say, causally.[11]

Strictly speaking, it is therefore misguided to search for the development of empiricism and experimentalism in early modern natural *philosophy*, as many have done since Randall's pioneering study of the development of scientific method in Padua.[12] In the Aristotelian paradigm of Zabarella, at least, the province of experiential knowledge was not natural philosophy but natural history.

---

6. See, for example, Jacobus Zabarella, "In duos Aristotelis libros posteriores analyticos commentarii," Liber primus, Caput XV, in *Opera logica* (Cologne, 1597; reprint, Hildesheim: Olms, 1966), 887–91.

7. Zabarella, "De naturalis scientiae constitutione," 154.

8. Zabarella, "De naturalis scientiae constitutione," 154.

9. See, for example, Bruno Snell, *Die Ausdrücke für den Begriff des Wissens in der vorplatonischen Philosophie* (Berlin: Weidmannsche Buchhandlung, 1924). According to Snell, "historia" means, when it first occurs in Herodot, "das Verhören von Augenzeugen" (63). The next step in the semantic development was short, and the result was "aus dem Forschen der Gegenstand des Forschens, die Geschichte" (64). Finally, "bezeichnet [Geschichte] jede Art von 'Kunde'" (65).

10. Regarding Aristotle, see, for example, Wolfgang Kullmann, *Wissenschaft und Methode. Interpretationen zur Aristotelischen Theorie der Naturwissenschaft* (Berlin: De Gruyter, 2019), 197; *Aristoteles als Naturwissenschaftler* (Berlin: De Gruyter, 2014).

11. Zabarella, "De naturalis scientiae constitutione," 155.

12. John Herman Randall, *School of Padua and the Emergence of Modern Science* (Padvoa: Editrice Antenore, 1961).

On the Constitution of Natural Science

BIBLIOGRAPHY

Primary Sources

Zabarella, Giacomo. *De rebus naturalibus*. Vols. 1 and 2. Edited by José Manuel García Valverde. Leiden: Brill, 2016.

Zabarella, Jacobus. *Opera logica*. Cologne, 1597. Reprint, Hildesheim: Olms, 1966.

———. *Opera physica*. Edited by Marco Sgarbi. Reprint of *Commentarii in magni Aristotelis libros physicorum*. Frankfurt, 1602. Reprint, Verona: Aemme edizioni, 2009.

———. *De methodis, Liber de regressu*. Introduction by Cesare Vasoli. Bologna: Clueb, 1985.

Zabarella, Jacopo. *On Methods, i: Books I–II; ii: Books III–IV, On Regressus*. Edited and translated by John P. McCaskey. Cambridge, Mass.: Harvard University Press, 2013.

———. *Über die Methoden, De methodis. Über den Rückgang, De regressu*. Eingeleitet, übersetzt und mit kommentierenden Fussnoten versehen von Rudolf Schicker. München: Fink, 1995.

Zabarella, Jacques. *La nature de la logique*. Introduction, texte latin, traduction et notes par Dominique Bouillon. Paris: J. Vrin, 2009.

Secondary Sources

Bouillon, Dominique. *L'interprétation de Jacques Zabarella le Philosophe*. Paris: Garnier, 2009.

Landgren, Per. "Historia et Scientia: An Aristotelian Cognitive Structure of the Academic Disciplines." In *Early Modern Academic Culture*, edited by Bo Lindberg, 189–202. Stockholm: The Royal Swedish Academy of Letters, 2019.

Mikkeli, Heikki. *An Aristotelian Response to Renaissance Humanism. Jacopo Zabarella on the Nature of Arts and Sciences*. Helsinki: SHS, 1992.

Mikkeli, Heikki. "Jacopo Zabarella (1533–1589): The Structure and Method of Scientific Knowledge." In *Philosophers of the Renaissance*. edited by Paul Richard Blum and translated by Brian McNeil, 181–91. Washington, D.C.: The Catholic University of America Press, 2010.

Mikkeli, Heikki. "Giacomo Zabarella." In *The Stanford Encyclopedia of Philosophy*, edited by Edward N. Zalta (Spring 2018 edition). <https://plato.stanford.edu/archives/spr2018/entries/zabarella/>.

Palmieri, Paolo. "Science and Authority in Giacomo Zabarella." *History of Science* xlv (2007): 404–27.

Randall, John Herman. *School of Padua and the Emergence of Modern Science*. Padvoa: Editrice Antenore, 1961.

Sgarbi, Marco. "Jacopo Zabarella's Empiricism." In *The Aristotelian Tradition and the Rise of British Empiricism*, 53–77. Dordrecht: Springer, 2013.

JACOPO ZABARELLA

On the Constitution of
Natural Science

CHAPTER VI

The Definition and Division of Natural Science[13]

Since the whole nature of science depends on a characteristic subject and the subject of natural philosophy has been made known, it is easy to infer its definition from what has been said. Consequently, we say that natural philosophy is a contemplative science, which passes on complete knowledge of natural bodies as long as they have the principle of movement in themselves. However, complete knowledge of the subject, since that is the goal of each speculative science, consists of two things, as we have declared elsewhere:[14] that is, in knowledge of the subject's principles and accidents. Therefore, the purpose of natural science is nothing other than to learn the principles of natural bodies and their accidents through their causes. Out of this definition, we can understand the true division of the whole science in its principal parts, and, in dividing it, discover the errors of others.

I have heard that many primarily use the following definition. The natural philosopher, who is about to discuss natural bodies, ought to learn, especially, their principles, since the knowledge of the other things [i.e., the accidents] is dependent on the knowledge of the principles. Everyone who is going to track down knowledge of something ought to know, above all, the principles of it. Therefore, natural science is divided into two principal parts; the first one is about the principles of the natural bodies, and that [part] is contained in the eight books of physics; the second part, in which the natural bodies themselves are discussed, exhibits these principles. This part includes all the remaining books on nature, of which the primary one is the book *On the Heavens*. This division they pick out from the words of Aristotle himself. For in the beginning of his first book of *Physics*, he

---

13. Zabarella, *De rebus naturalibus*. These two chapters were translated by Per Landgren. Sincere thanks to Nigel Wilson for excellent support with the Latin as well as the English idiom.

14. For cross-references in these two chapters, see Zabarella, "De naturalis scientiae constitutione."

On the Constitution of Natural Science

says that he, in the first place, is about to discuss the principles of natural things, but in the beginning of *On the Heavens*, he asserts that now for the first time he is going to deal with a treatment of natural bodies. Therefore, they say that the eight books of *Physics* have no subject other than the principles of a natural body, with which a treatment on its common accidents ought to be connected, but, they continue, the natural body itself is the subject not in these but in the other, following books and that the treatment about this begins in the first book *On the Heavens*.

When I publicly began to expound philosophy, I found this view in various places quite widespread among contemporary philosophers, and also accepted and defended by them. However, I have never been able to approve of it since I consider it against reason and the teachings of *Posterior Analytics* by Aristotle. Consequently, I have always fought it decisively, but now it will be sufficient to say only a few words against it, since enough has been said by me in the logical works, and at the same time, I hear that the view now is abandoned by many who earlier were defenders of it but later came to a more correct view, about which I will soon say more. So, it seems not worth the effort to attack it at greater length. Accordingly, now discussing it briefly, we say that a subject cannot be discussed unless the principles or its accidents are discussed. For the whole of science deals with these two only. Therefore, it is against reason when it is said that in the prior part it deals with principles about the natural body but thereafter in the other books it deals with the natural body itself. But the treatment itself about principles is, in reality, a treatment about the natural body.

However, if we also make this concession to them, what shall we say about accidents? For about them they cannot use the same argument as they used about principles, since it is not necessary to discuss accidents of a thing before the thing itself is treated. Even more, it is totally against reason to undertake such a treatment since accidents by nature are secondary to the subject. We cannot come to a demonstration of them unless the subject is already known. Therefore, it is absurd that in the books about physics, the shared accidents of natural bodies are discussed first and thereafter, in other books, the natural bodies themselves.

Furthermore, Aristotle taught in the first book of *Posterior Analytics* that accidents specific to a genus ought not to be attributed to species but to the common genus itself; otherwise, sophistic knowledge is passed on.[15] And the accidents and principles, which are discussed in the books on physics, are common and relevant to every natural body. But in the books on heaven and in all the following books, the discussion is not about the natural body as a genus but separately about its every single species. Consequently, if Aristotle ascribes to them accidents, which are discussed in the books on physics, he passes on knowledge about natural accidents sophistically. But this argument is touched on by Averroes in his preface to the first book of the *Physics*.

Having, therefore, rejected this opinion, I believe that the common idea of Averroes and the Latins in the passage mentioned has to be accepted; they thought that the treatment of the natural body ought to be divided into two principal parts. For since it is proposed to study the natural body both in accordance with common sense, as long as a certain genus is wide open, and also in accordance with characteristic reasons for each species, and according to the didactic sequence, the genus is to be discussed earlier than the species.[16] Natural science should be divided in two parts: in a common part, which is about the genus itself and occupies the primary position in science, and the specific or particular part, in which the treatment will be about the individual species. The common part, then, is included in the eight books of Physics, in which Aristotle teaches these things, which together belong to the whole natural body. The other, later part comprises all other books on nature, which on account of the multitude and diversity of the species, are many and different. Their division and order will be clarified in the following [chapters]. Well then, there is no disagreement about the parts of this division, since all agree that there are two primary parts of

15. With "sophistic knowledge," Zabarella interprets Aristotle and means accidental knowledge, that is, sensual, experiential, and factual knowledge. See Jacobus Zabarella, "In duos Aristotelis libros posteriores analyticos commentarii," *Opera logica*, col. 646.

16. When Zabarella writes about didactic sequence or order of instruction, *ordo doctrinae* (De methodis, liber I, caput vi), his pragmatic rule is *ordo cognitionis*, order of knowledge, which is the order, *quo melius ac facilius discamus*, through which we learn more easily and better. Sometimes, it coincides with *ordo naturae*, the order of nature, which implies that genus is to be treated before species, as well as knowledge about principles before accidental/experiential knowledge. When he writes elsewhere about discovering new knowledge, *methodus stricte*, he displays his empiricism, since for us knowledge about species comes before genera, as well as accidental/experiential knowledge before knowledge about principles, since *omnis … nostra cognitio a sensu originem ducit* (De methodis, liber III, caput xix).

On the Constitution of Natural Science 277

this science; that one comprises the eight books on physics, and the other all the remaining books.

But in the whole argument for the division, there is a controversy. Some have said that the prior part ought to be about the principles of the natural body, but the posterior part about the natural bodies themselves. But we say, with Averroes and the Latins, that the prior part ought to be about the actual common genus as a natural body, and the posterior about its species. Averroes also mentioned this division in the beginning of his abridgement of the first book of *On the Heavens* and in the beginning of the first book of *Meteorology*. We see such a division of the art of logic by the same [author] in his preface to the first book of *Posterior Analytics*, and we have explained that in our logical works.

CHAPTER XLII

About the Completeness of Natural Science and Its Order

Now that the structure of the discipline and the order of all its parts thus have been clarified, it only remains to consider that someone could ask if the science of things natural, handed down by Aristotle, ought to be called complete or not complete. It seems to me, as I have said before, that it can be called both complete and not complete, since it is complete if we look upon the very form, that is the fabric and structure, but incomplete with regard to the subject-matter and the things considered. For there are many things in nature that Aristotle did not consider and many things that he did not know. However, if we should attain knowledge even of these things, we ought not, because of this, teach natural science in another order or another structure but only with Aristotle's order and structure remaining intact; we should say that natural science is rendered more complete as far as matter is concerned, not form. For many other things, especially about animals and plants, could be added that were not said by Aristotle, but it would be easy for anyone to annotate individual passages by the addition of details, within the order and structure of Aristotle, that were not changed and not weakened. As if we should say that Aristotle has not written any specific books on mines and minerals, so it was easy for Albert the Great, who wrote them, to add them to the books by Aristotle and locate them after the four books on meteorology, which we have said to be the right place.

278 JACOPO ZABARELLA

But besides, we can say that natural philosophy as written by Aristotle was complete even in regard to matter and things that have to be known and perfect in all its details, if not in reality, at least potentially. Seeing that it is reasonable, in general, to believe not only that much was passed over by Aristotle, since it was unknown to him, but many things that he knew were also left out by him, but he didn't want to write about them. Surely, no book or tract on the risibility of man has been written by Aristotle, or about the whinnying of the horse, or about other similar things. Nevertheless, the foundations and certain seeds were laid down by him, from which knowledge can emanate even about things he didn't write about. We can get help by what Aristotle taught us, to observe other things and be led to knowledge about them.

Therefore, I think it ought to be said about the books on natural philosophy by Aristotle what I usually have said about the works on geometry and arithmetic by Euclid. For there are many geometrical and arithmetical theorems that Euclid did not demonstrate but are demonstrated by others in explaining the works of Euclid himself. And we should not, because of this, call the geometry or arithmetic of Euclid unfinished and incomplete. For if Euclid had wanted to demonstrate everything that can be demonstrated about magnitudes or numbers, the volume would have grown to a measureless size, which easily could have averted the reader from the reading of it. Consequently, it was enough for him to demonstrate certain specific theorems from which demonstrations of many other theorems, on which he was silent, yes all, which could be thought out, can be derived. For all learned mathematicians know that there is not one geometrical theorem whose demonstration from Euclid's books, as a copious fountain, cannot easily be scooped. I think that was the reason why Euclid called his books "Elements," like fundamentals and principles, from which many others can be derived, in that very discipline as well as in other sciences and arts in which from time to time the use of mathematics is necessary. Hence, we can, yes, we even ought to say, that the books were written by Euclid with such great skill that in them, the discipline of mathematics is contained complete and whole, if not in reality, at least potentially. It seems that just the same ought to be said about the natural philosophy conveyed by Aristotle. For though he had taught what is most important about things of nature, he left out other things, about which we can be led to knowledge through the consideration of the things he wrote.

On the Constitution of Natural Science

Therefore, we can say that the natural philosophy written by Aristotle is complete even with regard to things that need to be known. For he transmits knowledge about everything that the human intellect can understand, either in reality, or at least potentially. This perhaps he himself wants to indicate at the end of the first chapter of the first book of meteorology, while he says that it remains to deal with animals and plants in general as well as in particular, since, when these are explained, the transmission of natural science as a whole is almost concluded. For he said "almost," because of the fourth book on meteorology and the books on mining, which he at that time had not spoken of, to indicate that he was not going to transmit a complete natural science in reality, but, nevertheless, a complete one potentially, as we have said.

It is obvious that the order of science as a whole is compositive. This has carefully been explained by us in the books *On Methods*. For there, we have said that progression of the whole discipline, with regard to the subject, is from more universals to less universals, from a natural body to the simple and to the mixed broadly conceived, from that [body] to the incomplete and to the complete, from that to the inanimate and the animate, from that to animals and plants, and finally to their species.[17] But since principles as well as accidents of the particulars should be considered in an orderly way, therefore, with regard to principles, progression is from the first and most remote principles to the nearer ones, and, finally, to the nearest ones to the natural species and from the simpler to composite. For internal principles of the natural body are, broadly speaking, more simple than internal principles of something mixed, as long as it is mixed, and they are simpler than internal principles of an animal, as long as it is an animal. This is the condition of the compositive order, and these are, on the whole, necessary to reach certain knowledge about things, as we have explained in the books referred to.

17. Even though the didactic sequence or order of instruction, *ordo doctrinae* (see note 16), for natural philosophy as a whole is compositive, and therefore should start from the principles (the subject or the natural thing or the thing in itself), Zabarella admits that *ordo naturae* is not single but manifold, which he has just exemplified, referring to, as I assume, *De methodis*, liber 1, caput 7. In what follows, he proposes some rules for an orderly instruction though, since the order should first of all make the learning process easier. *Ordo compositivus* starts from the principles, and *ordo resolutivus*, which suits the moral disciplines and the arts, starts with the *finis*, the end or goal, and ends with the principles.

18

MICHEL DE MONTAIGNE
(1533–1592)

Of Experience

PAUL RICHARD BLUM

INTRODUCTION

Among the thinkers of this anthology, Michel de Montaigne was the least connected to any institution. He was born in 1533 in a castle not far from Bordeaux in France and studied law in Bordeaux and Toulouse. After inheriting his parental castle, he withdrew for a while from any public office, dedicating his life to contemplation, book collecting, and writing. In search of medical treatment, he traveled through northern France, Switzerland, southern Germany, and Italy and published a *Travel Journal* about those experiences. His retreat was occasionally interrupted by terms as mayor of Bordeaux and one journey to Paris for political negotiations. He died at the castle of Montaigne in 1592.

Montaigne's major work was to be his *Essais*, first published in 1580 and subsequently expanded. The modern term of the literary genre "essay" stems from this work, meaning, originally, "attempt"—constantly trying to put thoughts into writing without regard for traditional and mandatory forms and styles. While it has become commonplace that the Renaissance humanists first and foremost cared for the human perspective in all endeavors

Of Experience   281

and theories, Montaigne radicalized that in writing a book that explicitly disregards the reader and focuses on the author's self; in the 1580 edition, he addresses the readers:

I have proposed unto my self no other than a familiar and private end: I have had no respect or consideration at all either to thy service, or to my glory.... I desire therein to be delineated in mine own genuine, simple, and ordinary fashion, without contention, art, or study; for it is my self I portray.... Thus, gentle Reader, my self am the groundwork of my book.[1]

It is a purposefully and paradoxically published private testimony of the author's thoughts, labors, and experiences. Indeed, the last chapter— book 3, chapter 13—bears the title "Of Experience." For the same reason, the author dispels all and any expectation of teaching, dogmatics, and manageable contents. Rather, the multifaceted reality of the world, opinions, and personhood is the topic of these approaches. It is of methodic importance that Montaigne, before publishing his masterpiece, provided for his father a translation of the *Theologia naturalis* of Raimundus Sabundus. Sabundus (died 1436), who worked in Toulouse, was influenced by his fellow countryman, the Catalan Raimundus Lullus, so that he published a book with the original title *Book of Nature or of Creatures*, in which he emphasized the human perspective on the world to the effect that the Bible, God's second book, acquired only secondary rank in philosophical theology. Therefore, later editions advertised it as "natural theology," thus introducing this very concept. Its introduction was deemed heretical. After making this book available in French, Montaigne wrote an extensive defense, "Apologie de Raimond de Sebonde," which became the largest chapter (book 2, chapter 12) in the *Essais*. Pretending to save the book from the suspicion of heresy, Montaigne confirms the frame of thinking: it is for humans to find their way to themselves and to the world, as all further insight is beyond human means.[2] Skepticism turns to fideism, so that religion is reduced to a pure matter of faith; the rest is introspection.

The concluding section of the *Essais*, as presented in the following excerpt, opens with the sober statement that to be human means to be illu-

---

1. Michel de Montaigne, *The Essayes Or Morall, Politike and Millitarie Discourses*, trans. John Florio (London: Edward Blount, 1603), fol. A6v.
2. Desan, *Montaigne*, 285–99; Blum, *Philosophy of Religion in the Renaissance*, 14–20.

sionary, and it closes with the prayer to enjoy old age with sanity. Montaigne musters his main inspirations: skepticism, stoicism, and hedonism. This is his legacy for the ages to come.

BIBLIOGRAPHY

Primary Sources

Montaigne, Michel de. *Les essais*. Edited by Jean Balsamo, Michel Magnien, and Catherine Magnien-Simonin. Paris: Gallimard, 2007.

———. *The Complete Essays*. Translated by M.A. Screech. London: Penguin Books, 1991.

———. *The Essayes Or Morall, Politike and Millitarie Discourses*. Translated by John Florio. London: Edward Blount, 1603.

———. *Apology for Raymond Sebond*. Translated by Roger Ariew and Marjorie Grene. Indianapolis, Ind.: Hackett, 2003.

Secondary Sources

Blum, Paul Richard. *Philosophy of Religion in the Renaissance*. Farnham: Ashgate, 2010.

Desan, Philippe. *Montaigne: A Life*. Princeton, N.J.: Princeton University Press, 2017.

———, ed. *The Oxford Handbook of Montaigne*. Oxford: Oxford University Press, 2016.

Fetz, Reto Luzius. "Michel de Montaigne (1533–1592): Philosophy as the Search for Self-Identity." In *Philosophers of the Renaissance*, edited by Paul Richard Blum and translated by Brian McNeil, 192–204. Washington, D.C.: The Catholic University of America Press, 2010.

Frigo, Alberto. "Montaigne's Gods." In *Inexcusabiles: Salvation and the Virtues of the Pagans in the Early Modern Period*, edited by Alberto Frigo, 15–32. Cham: Springer International Publishing, 2020.

Hartle, Ann. *Michel de Montaigne: Accidental Philosopher*. Cambridge: Cambridge University Press, 2003.

Langer, Ullrich, ed. *The Cambridge Companion to Montaigne*. Cambridge Companions to Philosophy. Cambridge: Cambridge University Press, 2005.

Of Experience

MICHEL DE MONTAIGNE
Of Experience[3]

Man is easily deceived. One may more easily go by the margins, where extremity serves as a boundary, as a stay, and as a guide, than by the midway, which is open and wide and more according to art than according to nature but therewithal less noble and with less commendation. The greatness of the mind is not so much to draw up and hale forward as to know how to range, direct, and circumscribe itself. It holds for great whatever is sufficient, and shows her[4] height in loving mean things better than eminent. There is nothing so goodly, so fair, and so lawful as to play the man well and duly, nor science so hard and difficult as to know how to live this life well. And of all the infirmities we have, the most savage is to despise our being.

Whoever will sequester or distract his mind, let him hardily do it, if he can, when his body is not well at ease, thereby to discharge it from that contagion. And otherwise on the contrary, so that she may assist and favor him and not refuse to partake of his natural pleasures and conjugally be pleased with them, thus adding, if she be wiser, moderation, lest through indiscretion, they might be confounded with displeasure. Intemperance is the plague of sensuality, and temperance is not its scourge but rather its seasoning. Eudoxus, who thereon established his chief felicity,[5] and his companions who raised the fame to so high a pitch by means of temperance, which in them was very singular and exemplary, favored it in its most gracious sweetness.

I enjoin my mind to behold both sorrow and voluptuousness with a look equally regulated—*Eodem enim vitio est effusio animi in laetitia, quo in dolore contractio.*[6] *As faulty is the enlarging of the mind in mirth, as the con-*

---

3. Montaigne, *The Essayes Or Morall, Politike and Millitarie Discourses*, book 3, chap. 13, end (661–64), edited by Jan Beran and Paul Richard Blum: spelling, punctuation, syntax, and expressions that are hard to understand have been modernized. The translation has been compared with Michel de Montaigne, *Les essais*, ed. Jean Balsamo, Michel Magnien, and Catherine Magnien-Simonin (Paris: Gallimard, 2007).

4. 'Mind' and 'soul' are feminine in early modern English.

5. Diogenes Laertius, *Vitae philosophorum*, VIII, 88.

6. Cicero, *Tusculanae Disputationes*, IV, 66.

tracting of it in grief—and equally constant, but the one merrily and the other severely, and insofar as she may bring unto it to be as careful to extinguish the one as diligent to extend the other. To have a perfect insight into good draws with it an absolute insight into evil. And sorrow has in its tender beginning something that is unavoidable and voluptuousness in its excessive end something that is evitable. Plato couples them together and would have it to be equally the office of fortitude to combat against sorrow and to fight against the immoderate and charming blandishments of sensuality.[7] They are two fountains; whoever draws from them—whence, when, and as much as he needs, be it a city, be it a man, be it a beast—is very happy. The first must be taken for medication and necessity and more sparingly, the second for thirst but not unto drunkenness. Pain, voluptuousness, love, and hate are the first passions a child feels; if reason approaches, and they apply themselves to it, that is virtue.

I have a dictionary severally and wholly to myself: I *pass the time* when it is foul and incommodious; when it is fair and good, I will *not pass* it: I run it over again and take hold of it. A man should run from the bad and settle himself in the good. This vulgar phrase of 'pastime' and 'to pass the time' represents the custom of those wise men who think to have no better account of their life than to *pass* it over and escape it, to *pass* it over and avoid it and, as much as in them lies, to ignore and avoid it as a thing of an irksome, tedious, and disdainful quality. But I know it to be otherwise and find it to be both praiseworthy and commodious, even in its last decay where I hold it. And nature has put the same into our hands, furnished with such and so favorable circumstances that if it presses and molests us or, if unprofitably, it escapes us, we must blame ourselves. *Stulti vita ingrata est, trepida est, tota in futurum fertur.*[8] *A fool life is all pleasant, all fearful, all fond of the future.* I therefore prepare and compose myself to forgo and lose it without grudging but as a thing that is losable, transitory, and by its own conditions not as troublesome and importunate. Nor beseems it a man not to be grieved when he dies, except for those who are such as to please themselves to live on. There is a kind of husbandry in knowing how to enjoy it; I enjoy it double to others. For the measure of enjoyment depends more or less on the application we lend it, especially at this instant

---

7. Plato, *Phaedo*, 60b.
8. Seneca, *Ad Lucilium Epistulae Morales*, 15, 9.

that I perceive mine to be so short in time I will extend it in weight. I will stay the promptitude of its flight by the promptitude of my holding fast to it and will by the vigor of usage recompense the haste of its fleeting. Accordingly, as the possession of life is shorter, I must endeavor to make it more profound and full.

Other men feel the sweetness of a contentment and prosperity. I feel it as well as they, but not in passing and gliding. Yet it should be studied, tasted, and ruminated, thereby to give thanks worthy of him who is pleased to grant the same to us. They enjoy other pleasures, as that of sleep, without knowing them. To the end that sleep should not dully and unfeelingly escape me and that I might better taste and be acquainted with it, I have heretofore found it good to be troubled and interrupted in it. I consult with myself about some contentment, which consultation I do not superficially run over but sound it considerately and apply my reason, which is now refractory, peevish, and distasted, to entertain and receive it. Do I find myself in some quiet mood? Is there any sensuality that tickles me? I do not suffer it to busy itself or dally about my senses but I associate my mind to it: not to engage or plunge itself therein, but therein to take delight; not to lose but therein to find itself. And for her part, I employ her to view herself in that prosperous state, to ponder and esteem the good fortune she has, and to amplify it. She measures how much she is beholden to God for that she is at rest with her conscience and free from other intestine passions, and has her body in her natural disposition: orderly and competently enjoying certain flattering and soft functions, with which it pleases him of his grace to recompense the griefs, wherewith his justice at his pleasure smites us. Oh how helpful is it to her to be so seated that wherever she casts her eyes, the heavens are calm around her. And no desire, no fear, or doubt troubles the air before her; there is no difficulty, either past or present or to come, over which her imagination passes not without offence. This consideration takes a great luster from the comparison of different conditions. Thus do I in a thousand shapes present to myself those whom either fortune or their own error does carry away and torment and those nearer to me who so negligently and incuriously receive their good fortune. They are men who indeed pass their time: they traverse the present and what they possess, thereby to serve their hopes with shadows and vain images, which fancy sets before them.

> *Morte obita quales fama est volitare figuras,*
> *Aut que sopitos deludunt somnia sensus.*[9]
> Such walking shapes we say, when men are dead,
> Dreams, whereby sleeping senses are misled.

Which hasten and prolong their flight according to how they are followed. The fruit and scope of their pursuit, is to pursue, as Alexander said, that the end of his labor was labor.[10]

> *Nil actum credens, cùm quid superesset agendum.*[11]
> Who thought that nought was done,
> When aught remain'd undone.

As for me then, I love my life and cherish it such as has pleased God to grant it to us. I desire not he should speak of the necessity of eating and drinking. And I would think to offend no less excusably in desiring it should it have redoubled. *Sapiens divitiarum naturalium quaesitor acerrimus.*[12] *A wise man is a most eager and earnest searcher of those things which are natural.* Nor that we should sustain ourselves by only putting a little of that drug into our mouth, by which Epimenides was wont to dispel hunger and yet maintained himself.[13] Nor that we should insensibly produce children at our fingers' ends or at our heels, but rather (speaking with reverence) that we might with pleasure and voluptuousness produce them both at our heels and fingers' ends. Nor that the body should be void of desire and without tickling delight. These are ungrateful and impious complaints. I cheerfully and thankfully and with a good heart accept what nature has created for me, am therewith well pleased, and am proud of it. Great wrong is offered to that great and all puissant Giver, to refuse his gift, which is so absolutely good, and disannul or disfigure it, since he made it perfectly good. *Omnia quae secundum naturam sunt, estimatione digna sunt.*[14] *All things that are according to nature are worthy to be esteemed.*

Of opinions of philosophy, I more willingly embrace those that are

---

9. Vergil, *Aeneis*, X, 641–42.

10. Flavius Arrianus, *De expeditione Alexandri Magni historiae* (Paris: Stephanus, 1575), 119F [V, 26].

11. Lucanus, *Pharsalia*, II, 657; also in Petrarca, *Carmina*, 36, 42.

12. Seneca, *Ad Lucilium Epistulae Morales*, 119, 5

13. Plutarch, *Septem sapientium convivium*, 157d.

14. Cicero, *De Senectute*, 71: "omnia autem, quae secundum naturam fiunt, sunt habenda in bonis."

Of Experience

the most solid, that is to say, such as are most human and most ours. My discourses are suitable to my manners, low and humble. Philosophy then brings forth a child, well pleasing me, when she betakes herself to her *quiddities* and *ergos*[15] to persuade us that it is a barbarous alliance to marry what is divine with that which is terrestrial, to wed reasonable with unreasonable, combine severe with indulgent, and couple honest with dishonest, and that voluptuousness is a brutish quality, unworthy of the taste of a wise man. The only pleasure he draws from the enjoying of a fair young bride is the delight of his conscience to perform an action according to order, as to put on his boots for a profitable riding. Oh that his followers had no more right, or nerves and marrow,[16] or juice, at the dismaidening of their wives than they have in his lessons.

That is not what Socrates, both his and our master, says. He values rightly as he ought corporal voluptuousness, but he prefers that of the mind as having more force, more constancy, facility, variety, and dignity.[17] This, according to him, goes not at all alone—he is not so fantastical—but only first. For him, temperance is a moderator and not an adversary of sensualities. Nature is a gentle guide, yet not more gentle than prudent and just. *Intrandum est in rerum naturam, et penitus, quid ea postulet, pervidendum.*[18] *We must enter into the nature of things and thoroughly see what she inwardly requires.* I quest after her track; we have confounded her with artificial traces. And that Academic and Peripatetic *summum bonum* or sovereign felicity, which is to live according to her rules, by this reason becomes difficult to be limited and hard to be expounded, and that of the Stoics, cousin-german to the other, which is to yield to nature.[19] Is it not an error to esteem some actions less worthy inasmuch as they are necessary? Yet, they shall never remove from my head that it is not a most convenient marriage to wed pleasure to necessity, with which (says an ancient writer) the gods do ever complot and consent.

---

15. "Quiddities" (a scholastic term for "essences") is an addition by Florio; "ergo" initiates the conclusion of a syllogism.

16. Florio translates French *nerf* as "or sinnewes, or pithe," obviously a two-for-one translation.

17. Plato, *Republic*, IX, 585d-e. Cf. Erasmus of Rotterdam, *Apophtegmata*, III on Socrates, sect. 76.

18. Cicero, *De finibus bonorum et malorum*, 5, 44.

19. Cicero, *De finibus bonorum et malorum*, 2, 34; Seneca, *Ad Lucilium Epistulae Morales*, 66, 41.

288   MICHEL DE MONTAIGNE

To what end do we dismember by a divorce a building framed with so mutual, coherent, and brotherly correspondence? Contrariwise, let us repair and renew the same by interchangeable offices so that the spirit may awake and quicken the dull heaviness of the body, and the body may stay the lightness of the spirit and settle and fix it. *Qui velut summum bonum, laudat anime naturam, et tanquam malum, naturam carnis accusat, profectò et animam carnaliter appetit, et carnem carnaliter*[20] *fugit, quoniam id vanitate sentit humana, non veritate divina,*[21] *He that praises the nature of the soul as his principal good and accuses the nature of the flesh as evil, assuredly he both carnally affects the soul and carnally eschews the flesh since he is of this mind not by divine verity but humane vanity.* There is no part or parcel unworthy of our care in that present, which God has bestowed upon us. We are accountable even for the least hair of it.[22] And it is no commission for sedation for any man to direct man according to his condition; it is express, natural, and principal. And the Creator has seriously and severely given it to us.

Only authority has force with men of common reach and understanding, and it is of more weight in a strange language. So here let us charge again. *Stultitiae proprium quis non dixerit, ignavè et contumaciter facere quae facienda sunt: et aliò corpus impellere, alio animum; distrahique inter diversissimos motus?*[23] *Who will not call it a property of folly to do slothfully and adversely what is to be done, and to drive the body one way and another way the mind, and oneself to be distracted by the most diverse motions?* Which the better to see, let someone tell you one day the amusements and imaginations that he puts into his own head and for which he diverts his thoughts from a good repast and bewails the hour he employs in feeding himself: you shall find there is nothing so unsavory in all the dishes of your table as is that goodly entertainment of his mind (it were often better for us to be found asleep than awake to that for what we wake), and you shall find that his discourses and intentions are not worth your meanest dish. Suppose they were the entrancements of Archimedes himself[24]—and what of that?

---

20. The English print has "incarnaliter" (noncarnally), but it translates as "carnaliter" (carnally).

21. Augustinus, *De civitate Dei*, XIV, 5.

22. Cf. Matthew 10:29–30; Luke 21:18.

23. Seneca, *Ad Lucilium Epistulae Morales*, 32.

24. Plutarch, *An seni respublica gerenda sit*, 5, reports that Archimedes resisted pleasures

Of Experience

I do not touch here, nor do I blend with, that rabble or rascality of men as we are, nor with that vanity of desires and cogitations that divert us. I only deal with those venerable minds that, through a fervency of devotion and earnestness of religion, are elevated to a constant and conscientious meditation of heavenly divine things. And I deal with those souls which by the violence of lively and vigor of a vehement hope, are preoccupied with the use of eternal soul-saving nourishment, that is, the final end, only stay, and last scope of Christian desires, the only constant delight and incorruptible pleasure. I deal with disdain to rely on our necessitous, fleeting, and ambiguous commodities; and I easily resign the care and use of sensual and temporal feeding to the body. It is a privileged study. Super-celestial opinions and under-terrestrial manners are things that among us I have ever seen to be of singular accord.

Aesop, that famous man, saw his master piss as he was walking: What (said he) must we not ... when we are running?[25] Let us husband time as well as we can; yet we shall employ much of it both idly and ill. As if our mind had not hours enough to do her business—without disassociating herself from the body—in that little space that she needs for her necessity. They will be exempted from them and escape man. It is mere folly: instead of transforming themselves into angels, they transmute themselves into beasts; in lieu of advancing, they abase themselves. Such transcending humors affright me as much as steep, high, and inaccessible places. And I find nothing so hard to be digested in Socrates' life as his ecstasies and communication with demons.[26] Nothing so humane in Plato as that for which they say he is called divine. And of our sciences those, which are raised and extolled for the highest, seem to me the most base and terrestrial. I find nothing so humble and mortal in Alexander's life as his conceits about his immortalization. Philotas by his answer quipped at him very pleasantly and wittily: he had by a letter congratulated Alexander and rejoiced that the Oracle of Jupiter Hammon had placed him amongst the gods; he answered that in respect and consideration of him, he was very

---

so much that when drawing, he had to be dragged away by his servants and then drew diagrams on his anointed body.

25. Maximus Planudes, "Aesopi vita," in Aesopus, *Aesopi Phrygis fabellae Graece & Latine, cum alijs opusculis* (Basel: Froben, 1524), 25–27.

26. Plutarch, *De genio Socratis*, sect. 10–11, puts Socrates's alleged *daemon* into doubt.

glad; yet there was some cause those men should be pitied that were to live with a man and obey him, who outwent others and would not be contented with the state and condition of a mortal man.[27]

> *Diis te minorem quòd geris, imperas.*[28]
> Since thou less than Gods
> Bear'st thee, thou rul'st with ods.

The quaint inscription, wherewith the Athenians honored the coming of Pompey into their City, agrees well and is conformable to my meaning.

> *D'autant es tu Dieu, comme*
> *Tu te recognois homme.*[29]
> So far a God thou mai'st accompted be
> As thou a man dost reacknowledge thee.

It is an absolute perfection and, as it were, divine for a man to know how to enjoy his being loyal. We seek other conditions because we understand not the use of ours, and go out of ourselves, forasmuch as we know not what is abiding there. We may long enough to get upon stilts, for while upon them yet we must go with our own legs. And while we sit upon the highest throne of the world, we sit upon our own tails. The best and most commendable lives, and that best please me, are (in my conceit) those that with order are fitted and with *decorum* are arranged to the common mold and humane model, but without wonder or extravagancy. Now old age has to be handled more tenderly. Let us recommend it to God, who is the protector of health and fountain of all wisdom, but merry and social:

> *Frui paratis et valido mihi*
> *Latoe dones, et precor integra*
> *Cum mente, nec turpem senectam,*
> *Degere, nec Cythara carentem.*[30]
> Apollo grant, enjoy in health I may
> That I have got; and with sound mind I pray
> Nor that I may with shame spend my old years,
> Nor wanting music to delight mine ears.

The end of the third and last book.

27. Quintus Curtius Rufus, *Historiae Alexandri Magni*, 6, 7, 30, and 9, 18.
28. Horace, *Carmina*, III, 6, 5.
29. Plutarch, *Pompey*, 27, 3.
30. Horace, *Carmina*, I, 31, 17. Apollo was the son of Latona.

19

FRANCESCO PATRIZI
(1529–1597)

On History

PAUL RICHARD BLUM

INTRODUCTION

Francesco Patrizi was one of the late Renaissance critics of Aristotelianism who combined humanist literary methods and Neoplatonic approaches in his philosophy of nature and of human affairs. He was born in 1529 on the island Cherso (today Cres) and died in Rome in 1597. Due to his origins in Dalmatia, now part of Croatia, he is also known as Frane Petrić. He traveled to many Mediterranean countries and islands and studied in Ingolstadt and Padua.[1] Besides classics and humanist interpretations of Aristotelianism, he also knew well the works of Marsilio Ficino and Giovanni Pico and corresponded with Bernardino Telesio. From 1556 through 1571, Patrizi served Venetian patricians before moving to Modena, and in 1577, he started teaching Platonic philosophy (a rarity at the time) in Ferrara until 1592, when he obtained the same position at the university Sapienza in Rome, which was independent of the church. His writings cover

---

1. On Padua, cf. chapters 10 and 17 on Pomponazzi and Zabarella, respectively, in this volume.

292   FRANCESCO PATRIZI

the philosophy of love, theory of language, including poetry and rhetoric, and—in his approach—the theory of history. He scrutinized the body of Aristotle's works (*Discussiones peripateticae*) and presented a new geometry before presenting his own philosophy of the natural universe (*Nova de universis philosophia*).

His philosophy of love emphasized the priority of the One from which all forms of love emanate. Inspired by Ficino's theory of love and of human knowledge, he emphasized the dynamics of love from the self to the other and back to the lover; hence, love is one manifestation of self-preservation that is to be seen in creation, in interhuman relationships, and in the preservation of nature. Patrizi extended the humanist model of poetry as imitating or reproducing nature to include producing marvelous things. Poetry imitates nature not by copying images but by being as creative as nature itself. In a similar vein, he wrote that rhetoric is not just sophistry but the art of creating meaning that can be shared. Speaking, he defines, is the human voice as articulate and signifying. This semiotics (in modern terminology) is the basis of communication and, consequently, not only artificial and not simply natural but both of them, as befits human intellect because speaking represents the state of mind about things themselves.

Patrizi's study of geometry is a reworking of Euclid's classic, which emphasizes the convergence of conceptual and real geometric proportions, a feature common to Neoplatonist philosophy of the Renaissance, and it had the enduring effect to advocate geometry as the lead discipline of all sciences. The critique of Aristotle operated by means of humanist philology, and it exposed Aristotle's indebtedness to Plato and his distortion of the original true philosophy (which incidentally debunked Aristotle's authority over logic and method). Among his efforts to restore ancient wisdom, Patrizi also re-edited the Chaldean Oracles, which had been introduced in the West by Gemistos Pletho,[2] and the *Elements of Theology* by Proclus. The "new" philosophy of the universe was marked by the introduction of four disciplines that claimed universality already in their titles with the Greek syllable *pan*—*panaugia, panarchia, panpsychia, pancos-*

2. See chapter 2 on Pletho.

mia: the universal light, power, mind, and cosmos. Light is the epitome of the all-pervading order in the world, which unfolds in the basic principles like essence, power, and operation; the soul is life and mind at the same time, in which the light and the power are realized so that the entire cosmos offers order, reality, and intelligibility. In this new philosophy, new approaches to known doctrines are included, for instance, a non-Aristotelian theory of space, mathematical theories, and an historical approach to philosophy.

The text that follows presents the third of ten dialogues on history. Patrizi departed from the humanist theory of history as a means to profiting knowledge from past masters and a means of rhetorical plausibility. He took the time dependence of human actions seriously, pointed out the difficulty of using the past as a guide for the present, and established the distinction between the memory of past events and the creation of a written history as a story. In the third dialogue, he evaluates the notion of memory between cosmic and human history.

BIBLIOGRAPHY

Primary Sources

Patrizi, Francesco. *De spacio physico et mathematico.* Edited by Hélène Védrine. Paris: Vrin, 1996.

———. *Della historia: diece dialoghi.* Venice: Arrivabene, 1560. Facsimile in Eckhard Kessler, ed., *Theoretiker humanistischer Geschichtsschreibung: Nachdruck exemplarischer Texte aus dem 16. Jahrhundert.* München: Fink, 1971, with an introduction and commentary.

———. *Della nuoua geometria Libri XV.* Ferrara: Baldini, 1587.

———. *Della poetica.* Edited by Danilo Aguzzi Barbagli. Firenze: Instituto nazionale di studi sul Rinascimento, 1969.

———. *Della retorica dieci dialoghi.* Venetia: Senese, 1562.

———. *Deset dijaloga o retorici / Della retorica dieci dialoghi.* Translated by Mate Maras. Istra kroz stoljeća, kolo 4, knj. 20. Pula: Čakavski sabor, 1983.

———. *Discussionum peripateticarum tomi IV, quibus Aristotelicae philosophiae universa historia atque dogmata cum veterum placitis collata ... declarantur ...* Basileae: Perna, 1581.

———. *Discussionum peripateticarum tomus quartus (Liber I–V).* Edited by Mihaela Girardi-Karšulin and Ivan Kapec. Zagreb: Institut za Filozofiju, 2012.

———. *Discussionum peripateticarum tomus secundus (Liber I–IV).* Edited by Luka Boršić. Zagreb: Institut za Filozofiju, 2013.

———. *La Città Felice*, October 12, 2000. http://web.archive.org/web/20001012120550/http://www.ecu.edu/medieval/cittafel.HTM.

———. *Lettere ed opuscoli inediti*. Edited by Danilo Aguzzi Barbagli. Firenze: Istituto nazionale di studi sul Rinascimento, 1975.

———. *Nova de universis philosophia = Nova sveopća filozofija* [Latin-Croatian]. Edited by Vladimir Filipović. Translated by Tomislav Ladan and Serafin Hrkač. Zagreb: Liber, 1979.

———. *Nova de universis philosophia: in qua Aristotelica methodo, non per motum, sed per lucem & lumina, ad primam causam ascenditur...* Ferrariae: Mammarellus, 1591.

———. *Sretan grad = La città felice*. In *Sretan Grad*, edited by Andrija Mutnjaković. Latin-Croatian, with Facsimile. Zagreb: DTP, 1993.

———. "The Happy City." In *Italian Renaissance Utopias: Doni, Patrizi, and Zuccolo*, translated by Antonio Donato, chap. 5. Cham: Palgrave Macmillan, 2019.

Secondary Sources

Castelli, Patrizia, ed. *Francesco Patrizi filosofo platonico nel crepuscolo del Rinascimento*. Firenze: Olschki, 2002.

Leinkauf, Thomas. "Francesco Patrizi (1529–1597): New Philosophies of History, Poetry, and the World." In *Philosophers of the Renaissance*, edited by Paul Richard Blum and translated by Brian McNeil, 205–18. Washington, D.C.: The Catholic University of America Press, 2010.

Nejeschleba, Tomáš, and Paul Richard Blum, eds. *Francesco Patrizi: Philosopher of the Renaissance*. Olomouc: Univerzita Palackého v Olomouci, 2014. http://www.renesancni-texty.upol.cz/soubory/publikace/Francesco_Patrizi_Conference_Proceedings.pdf.

Puliafito, Anna Laura. "L'uomo, gli animali, il linguaggio. Alcuni aspetti della riflessione patriziana su ragione, anima umana e anima dei bruti." In *The Animal Soul and the Human Mind: Renaissance Debates*, edited by Cecilia Muratori, 113–30. Bruniana & Campanelliana, Supplementi 35, Studi, 15. Pisa-Roma: Serra, 2013.

Vasoli, Cesare. *Francesco Patrizi da Cherso*. Roma: Bulzoni, 1989.

Online Resource

"Institut Za Filozofiju | Digitalna Baština | Frane Petrić." Accessed May 26, 2020. https://content.ifzg.hr/digitalnaBastina/digitalnaBastinaFranciscusPatricius.htm.

On History

FRANCESCO PATRIZI

On History[3]

THIRD DIALOGUE: IL CONTARINO,
OR, WHAT IS HISTORY?

Count Giorgio and Sir Paolo Contarini
and Francesco Patrizi

Francesco ill, visited by Venetian noblemen

During the long illness I suffered this last winter, there entered into my room to visit me one evening the brothers Count Giorgio and Sir Paolo Contarini, gentlemen of great kindness and importance.[4] They found me in profound thought. The Count approached the bed and asked, "What are you doing Sir Francesco, and how are you? Do you have a fever?" I raised my eyes to him and replied, "I'm studying, sir." "What are you studying," he asked, "as I do not see a book in front of you." "I read it quite well," I replied, "though it is invisible to you." "Might this book contain some *Elitropia*,"[5] said Sir Paolo smiling, "so then show us a bit, or tell us what it is." And they glanced suspiciously at one another with a little smile. I replied, "It is the book of my soul, given to me by God, which I carry by a belt and which never leaves my side." At this, the Count raised his brow rather as if I might be delirious; however, he asked, "What does this book say?" I replied, "It speaks of all things, for it was written by the hand of God." He still believed at that time that I was delirious, and he prompted me, in order to clarify, "So, what does your soul do with such a book?" "It studies there," I answered, "when it is not be kept from it, either due to physical harm or to some uncertainty, or when it remembers it. But the soul is mostly led astray by the senses."[6]

---

3. Francesco Patrizi, *Della historia: diece dialoghi*, translated by Cynthia Gladen and Paul Richard Blum (Venice: Arrivabene, 1560), fol. 12r–19r. Subheadings by the translators.

4. Paolo Contarini (1529–1585), a Venetian politician; see Gaetano Cozzi, "Contarini, Paolo," *Dizionario Biografico degli Italiani*, vol. 28 (1983), http://www.treccani.it/enciclopedia/paolo-contarini_(Dizionario-Biografico). Giorgio Contarini was Count of Jaffa (Ioppe; now Tel Aviv-Yafo); Petrus Iustinianus, *Rerum Venetarum ab urbe condita ad annum MDLXXV. historia* (Venetiis: Avantius, 1576), 222.

5. Heliotrope: Giovanni Boccaccio, *Decameron*, novella 8.3, writes that Calandrino is told that the "elitropia" will make whoever holds it invisible.

6. Nicola Cipani, *Liber mentalis: The Art of Memory and Rewriting*, in *Renaissance Rewritings*, ed. Helmut Pfeiffer et al. (Berlin: de Gruyter, 2017), 73–95.

"And you, my dear Count, what do you do with your book?" "I do not know," he replied, "Does my soul have such a book as well?" "Of course it does," I answered, "Yours, as well as Sir Paolo's, as well as do the souls of all men in the world." "I did not know this," said the Count, "I have never seen it, nor had it occurred to me that I might." "It is as I say," I answered. He then drew near me, took my arm, and touched my wrist and silently placed his hand on my forehead in order to feel the extent of the fever that must have been making me rave so. But he found my pulse calm and my forehead cool, and, astonished, he turned around and grabbed hold of Sir Paolo and said quietly: "He is free of fever, but surely he must be in a very melancholy mood and has come across some book and read it today." He then asked one of the servants whether that day or in recent days I had been given or they had seen a book in my hands. The servant replied that after I had taken ill in bed, I had not looked at nor had been given a book. Sir Paolo said then that they must see whether my mood was stable. At which both men approached the bed, sat down, and became quiet. They stayed that way for quite a while in order to see whether it was truly a mood and unwavering.

After a bit I said, "Sirs, you ought to look often at this book, for blessed you will be." "So then," said Sir Paolo, "is a specialized skill needed to understand what is written within the books of our souls and then to engage reading them?" "Everything in the world is written in them," I added, "just as in my own." "And what form do they take?" he asked. "In images, as they are in books from Japan and China, which are understood by letters, not by spoken words, which are different among them." "I don't understand you," he answered. "Each character," I explained, "in their books means something. Thus, it is an image of an idea that is written in the books of souls of all men, to make itself understood to people of all languages." "You have joined," said Sir Paolo then (in order to change the mood), "this nonsense of Plato, who dreamt up these tales of Ideas; so please think of something else." "Don't say that," I answered, "Dear Sir Paolo, for you ought to honor, revere, and admire Plato as a divine man and the images of God's wisdom as revealed in that marvelous man. Because otherwise God gets very angry with those who vilify good and wise men and equally with those who praise the wicked and the ignorant. Therefore, a good and wise man is a very blessed and divine thing, and the contrary is a guilty and ignorant man." At these words, the two cheered up quite a bit, and they seemed to believe that I might not be completely out of my mind, and they did not dare to return to the argument about the book of the soul. When I resumed suggesting to them that they might speak of looking at it and studying it, the Count then said, "Come now! Tell us about what you've been studying here by yourself that you might convince us to do the same."

The Inner Book and History

"That's wonderful," I replied. "I've been doing my research. I was attempting to understand what history is." "What?" said he, "Don't you have that in anyone else's books, rather than having to look at that of the soul?" "Whatever I find in other books, I also look for in the book of my soul. Many things I find in it as well, many I do not, and many others I find stated otherwise. Those that I do find there, I honor as being true, and those I do not find there, I regard as false; those that I find otherwise, I regard to be between true and false, uncertain and dubious." "How beautiful those must be," answered the Count, "but your speech is obscure." "Then I will speak clearly," I rejoined.

"All things that I find written in outside books, I compare to those that I have within the book of my own soul; many I find match, and many are different, while many others are partly the same and partly different; and it is these that I call uncertain and dubious to me. Then there are those things that I find outright contrary to what I think." Upon hearing this, the Count and Sir Paolo seemed to be caught between belief and disbelief, uncertain whether I was delirious or not. Then Sir Paolo said, "Those books, the ones you call being written by men, how are they different from the book written by God? And if he wrote it and gave the same book to all the souls of all men, wouldn't then all those 'outside' books be written in the same way, since they were all written using the paragon of the internal one?"

"I say to you, Sir Paolo," I answered, "the books of the soul have relief-letters and can be peeled back layer by layer, and studying in a way their anatomy one might arrive at their inner marrow. And because the soul has this book deep inside, it cannot be seen by those who do not see the soul, so that these men are endlessly looking outside themselves and never looking inside themselves; and as a result, it becomes impossible for them to know what they might have inside themselves: this divine writing from God. And then when these men set to writing, they write books about these things that they have seen in bodies outside of themselves. Then there are those who looking inwards see this book that I mentioned, but do not care for browsing in it and do not delve more deeply in it than the first or second layer. And from this stems the diversity of the external books. But there has never been a better anatomist nor anyone more well-read about this book than Plato. Such that whoever wishes to browse in his book of the soul, should read his books, and it will be perfectly revealed."

Both of them were astonished by the strength of the book and seemed convinced that I was not suffering a delusion, and therefore they desired to know more about what I had to say regarding history. Sir Paolo said, "Will you tell us what did you find in this book and what does it say about history?"

"I have found," I replied, "many contradictions as to the definitions of history one reads in the external books." "Such as?" he asked. "In Cicero," I answered, "that history is something that has been done, remote from the memory of our own time; and again that it is a narration of things that have been done." "In what consists your contradiction?" he asked. "In this," I said, "that this kind regards histories written of ancient things but not of things that happened this year, or in the last two years, such as the recent war in Rome, which is certainly not far from our present memory." "You speak the truth," he replied. "And when Cicero with great artifice flattered Lucceius[7] that he should write a history of things he did against Catilina, he did not ask him to distance himself from the memory of their times. And this is the truth. History, therefore, does not necessarily deal with ancient things," I responded, and that "the Chief Pontiff recorded in their annals things that occurred, good or adverse, year after year, to the Republic." "It's true what you say," said the Count, "therefore the first was not a good definition of history. But of this other one, what do you have to say?"

"About the other I have another doubt," I said, "namely, I read in my book, that I can make history of things that happen today." "But how so," asked Sir Paolo, "given that the present is not time?" "I see," I answered, "that what you say is true, as you are a philosopher, esteemed Sir Paolo. But

7. Cicero, *Familiares* V 12.

On History

299

further inside, I see that I can well do that with what has already happened to what is presently being done, but not with what is still being done. Ultimately, it always comes back to history being the thing that has already happened." "This is true," he answered.

I added: "Yet even further inside my image of history I see that one might also do it of future things." "Oh, that's quite impossible," said the Count, smiling. "That's not what I mean," I answered, "rather, it seems that the historian deals with the past as the prophet with the future. Isn't that so?" "Yes, it is," he replied. "Nevertheless, Moses was a prophet of the past, as were Epimenides of Knossos and as Aristotle knew him.[8] So, Isaiah and Jeremiah can be historians of the future." "Yes, but incorrectly so," argued he. "On the contrary, quite correctly," I countered, "more than others call a historian who writes of things far from himself and his times. Therefore, history is almost *isoria*, a glance done with one's eyes.[9] The prophet without doubt sees in a vision the things he predicts. And what is a truer and less fallible vision than that of a soul illuminated by God?" "This seems to be true," he said, "By the strength of your voice, but of course, it isn't like that, at its essence and according to common belief."

"We have not yet arrived at the essence," I answered, "but common belief does not make things and errs also in other things." "In what?" asked the Count. "Believing," I said, "that history is only concerned with the affairs of men." "And how might it be otherwise?" asked he. "It is certainly concerned with many things," I replied, "natural and supernatural." "What of nature?" he asked. "When Livy, or Thucydides, or any other writer," I continued, "describes a country, a mountain, a valley, a river, a port, or anything like that, aren't those natural things?" "Yes, they are," answered the Count. "And when they narrate for us the wonders, the omens, the miracles, and other such things, aren't they telling about supernatural things?" "Certainly," he said. "And thus," I suggested, "these are points of history, which no-one will deny." "Now, what you say is true," he replied, "I recognize that." "It isn't merely the common belief of men," I suggested, "that

8. Aristotle, *Rhetoric*, ed. J. H. Freese (Cambridge: Heinemann 1926), III, 17.10: "Epimenides the Cretan ... used to divine, not the future, but only things that were past but obscure." Moses was a prophet in reporting the origin of the world.

9. Ειοωρια—a mystical view. For "rimiramento" in mystical context, cf. Pietro da Poitiers. *Il giorno mistico ouero Dilucidatione dell'oratione e teologia mistica tradotto ... da fra Serafino da Borgogna* (Rome: Tinassi, 1675), vol. 2, 296; vol. 3, 293.

makes things what they are." "You speak very well," said he. "History can be made," I went on, "from all of these things, from what is seen, what is human, or whatever else. Indeed, whether they come from the future or from the past, they must merely be envisioned. Yes, and so from the future like the past things, as long as they are seen." "But only the visions of Prophets," said he. "That doesn't mean that they are not histories," I answered. "As you wish," replied Sir Paolo, "since it is thus written in your book."

Forms of Historical Record

"We have so far found out what history is made of," I continued, "but not yet what it *is*." "What else could it be," he answered, "other than a written account?" "What if it were a painting?" I asked. "A painting—how?" he responded. "Don't you Venetian gentlemen," I quickly asked, "have in the Hall of the Great Council, a painting of Alexander III and Barbarossa?"[10] "Yes, we do," he answered. "What else is that painting other than a history?" I asked. "What is carved in Rome upon the column of Trajan, and that of Antonino, and on the arches of Constantine and Severus, but histories of their victories and their triumphs?" "Without a doubt nothing other," he answered. "Not only, then," I continued, "is history written, but it is sculpted and painted; and these things are more properly history by being objects of vision." "What you say is true," said Sir Paolo, "but what then might history be?" I responded, "Tell me, Sir Paolo, why your Venetian ancestors had that history of Alexander painted in the Council Hall? You might know this, since you have been a Savio[11] and had access to the secrets counsels of the Republic." "This is not a matter of counsel," he answered with a smile, "anyone can know it. As I believe, it is so that for us and for posterity remains the memory of the pious and religious undertakings of our ancestors done for the Holy Church, and that the nobility when gathering there on every holiday has the religion and values of their ances-

10. In Venice, the Doge's Palace, Sala del Maggior Consiglio, is decorated with scenes of the strife between Pope Alexander III and Emperor Frederick Barbarossa in the twelfth century. Cf. Giorlamo Bardi, "Dichiaratione di tutte le istorie che si contengono ne i quadri posti nuovamente, nelle Sali di Scrutinio et del Gran Consiglio del Palagio Ducale della Serenissima Republica di Vinegia," appendix in *Delle cose notabili della città di Venetia libri II* (Venetia: Rampazetto, 1565), 35f.

11. Savio (wise) was the title of a member of the Venetian government.

On History

tors in front of their eyes." "Incidentally, the reliefs upon the arches and columns I was mentioning," I answered, "are they created in memory of the glorious deeds of the great princes?" "For this very same reason," he replied, "they are made."

"But those sculptures," I suggested, "the ones sculpted with words narrating some event, don't you also take them to be history?" "Certainly," he answered, "and maybe even more truly." "And why is that?" I asked. "Because," he answered, "these are truly narrations of things." "That means nothing," I declared. "And why nothing?" wondered the Count. "Because we have already said that history is memory, and not narration." "Fine," he replied, "but this description *is* memory." "But if memory can be made," I insisted, "without any narrating words, or with mere images of events, or with other material signs, or with various other things, in which way it perhaps had initially been written, what does it matter whether this history be in words rather than in any other manifestation, as long as it is memory?" "This you will find out," replied the Count. "But how was it written initially? And what was its origin?" "I will tell you," I answered.

Egypt and the History of Past and Future

Many times I have heard high ranking men of learning say that history had begun to be written in Egypt, not about what men did but about the rising and flooding of the Nile. For the people of Memphis placed in a place in the city a tall column called the Nilometer so that as from year to year the river rose and flooded the land all around, they marked the height of the water on the column. At the same time, they recorded the impact made by the rise on abundance or famine. Having diligently done so and observed for many years, they always knew in advance after the full rise what kind of year to hope for or fear, as the water rose to marks on the column that had been made and observed before.[12] These notations made on the column were nothing other than a memory of the effects of the water. On this paradigm they began writing about the deeds of illustrious men. However, others say that history was written in Egypt much earlier than these observations about the actions of Osiris, the most powerful of all the kings of the world. And that they did on columns. In the same manner, others wrote about the course of the skies, the number of years, the turn of two great years,[13] and more similar observations.

---

12. Diodorus Siculus, lib. 1, 36.

13. Great, or Perfect, Year: the return of all stars to their initial position; cf. Plato, *Timaeus* 39d.

302 FRANCESCO PATRIZI

Others say that the origin of history is even more ancient, and they say that Noah, as soon as the Flood ended, came out of the ark, wrote down in stone all that had happened, and then placed the stone on the plane of Miriadam in Armenia at the foot of Mount Gordiaeus, at the summit of which the ark came to rest.[14] Still others like to say that history was written many centuries before the Great Flood because many of the great early ancestors, whether due to Astrology or divine inspiration, foretold the destruction of the world, which they carved onto stones. That was done even by the children of Adam and that was, furthermore, the history recorded by the most ancient historians.

"It's wonderful to know this," said the Count. "Wonderful it is indeed," I said, "and wonderful the caution it gives." "What caution?" he asked. "That the earliest history written in the world was not written about the past, but about the future." "That is true," said Sir Paolo, "as it is true that the first to be written was the history you mentioned last." "And if it's true, as it is received as truth," I rejoined, "then we are not wrong to say first that history can also be written about the future." "One might say it for certain perfectly," he suggested, "being that that is true."

"Were I to believe something that you Sirs told me to believe," I answered, "I would willingly tell you. However, because of its greatness and newness, you could believe it to be a fable; but I value it highly and marvel at it." "And what is it?" asked the Count. "A long history," I said, "of the corruptions of the world and its renewals." "That's an enormous thing that you speak of," replied a smiling Sir Paolo. "I know well," I said, "that you are a follower of Aristotle and therefore you won't believe me. But I want to tell it to the Count." "Indeed, I want you to tell me," said he quickly, "as I am not so much an Aristotelian that I don't believe someone else. So please tell us, and we will hear you with good will." "Therefore, I will do it gladly," I said, "but I encourage you to remain attentive."

Antonio Marcello and the Hermit Hammun

"Friar Antonio Patrizi Marcello, who was the General of the order of the Franciscans for three times and bishop of Cittanova and Archbishop of

14. One of the presumed locations: Joannes Lucidus, *De emendationibus temporum ab orbe condito ad vsque hanc aetatem nostram* (Venetiis: Iunta, 1537), lib. 2, cap. 2, 17; Eleonora Caccia, "Il *De origine Orobiorum sive Cenomanorum* di Giangrisostomo Zanchi. Passati immaginari e interessi epigrafici nella Bergamo del primo Cinquecento" (PhD diss. 2014, Università di Studi di Bergamo, 2017), 82, https://aisberg.unibg.it/handle/10446/77105.

On History

Patras, was my grandfather's brother.[15] He was truly a man of deep knowledge and admirable eloquence. He told my father, from whom I heard it repeatedly, about going as a young man to visit the Holy Sepulcher in Jerusalem on a ship that through a storm was derailed to the Egyptian shore. There he came upon an Egyptian hermit of very ancient age and saintly life and very profound learning, called Hammun. The two then engaged in discussion, and the hermit began telling the friar about many marvelous things, both ancient and contemporary, about his land and its stories. Among them the best and most marvelous was this:

'Know, my son,' said the hermit, 'that our country has received many privileges from heaven above all others. For this reason it is fertile with all manner of fruit; it is salubrious with excellent air, and it has men of highest genius. In the past they discovered the most needed and most honored arts in the world and all the sciences. As a result, high-minded men came from your Europe and other places to learn our sciences. Those learned men here in Egypt remained the most ancient of all, since it was they who carried the memory of two instances of universal corruption and two of universal renaissance of the world body. In sum, Egypt, with the rare gifts and divine qualities that it has always had, is the temple of the whole world and image of heaven, since down to it the most excellent things have always come from above.' Marveling at this, Marcello asked him astonished, 'What about the two corruptions and two renaissances?' 'Yes,' said the Egyptian, 'it seems that you Europeans have always been children who don't know any white-haired scholarship.'[16] Beseeching the great man, Marcello asked to please tell what he meant and how the Egyptians have memory of so many and so stupendous things. 'Gladly,' he replied and began thus.

The Hermit Hammun's Story

You must know, my son, that the violent corruptions of men happen in many ways, but the principal ones are war, famine, pestilence, and earthquakes that annihilate

---

15. Cittanova, now Novigrad in Croatia; Patras in Greece was a titular bishopric of the Latin Church. Antonio Marcello was elected General of the Franciscans in 1517 and was Archbishop of Patras in 1520; see Lucas Wadding, *Annales Minorum*, vol. 16 (Rome: Bernabò, 1736), 50, n. xxix, 109, n. xxxv.

16. Almost verbatim from Plato, *Timaeus* 22b, in Marsilio Ficino's translation. Much of the following description of Egypt is appropriated from *Timaeus* 21a–25, the myth of Atlantis.

304   FRANCESCO PATRIZI

them. Beyond this, there are great and horrible floods and fires, especially when they occur all over the world. These things destroy not only humanity but also animals, plants, cities, arts, and entire countries. Similarly, the air through pestilence is very harmful; also because it is an element close to animals as they live within it and it disperses upon any solid thing that it encounters. It cannot cause damage to the world as much as water does, which is the enemy of all breathing creatures and able to do harm through its mobility. Due to this and its penetrating slenderness, fire is the most destructive force of all the others. Because of its qualities, fire is the most efficient among its companions, whereas land, because of its immobility, size and material quality, is like none of these other elements. But none of those mentioned causes general corruptions that is not moved by the heaven through the lights and the influence of the stars. Hence, it is more than true that the things of the lower world are occult means governed by the heavenly and even higher things. This means that even war is moved by celestial powers that heat and ignite the blood in people's hearts urging to offend others. It is clear that hunger and disease arise from the evil quality of the air infused from the lights above. Earthquakes and rifts in the ground come from the same. All this happens now here and now there, as the places on earth are assigned by the gods to certain sites in heaven and those to some stellar aspects and lights, and the lights to times, and the times to stellar revolutions. So that when the time of these lights has come, they cause the effects that I was talking about through the influxes brought by them on the earth. Therefore these assignments are very specific and the more the lights come together, the more frequently the famines, plagues, earthquakes and other things come, too, that are not the result of floods or fires. Those are universal and generated by several lights, which combine within larger times and therefore rarely descend to the destruction of the earth.

These global devastations happen to all things down here; they do not, however, destroy entire lineages of men nor of other things. This is for the following reason: the devastations come from the influxes and the lights in the heavens and, together with them, from the aspects, and the aspects are born of the revolutions of the planets and the firmament, and the planets follow divine intention, and they originate from the intelligible species of the first world, which is full of all things and founded in stability. Therefore, it is necessary that of all species only those individuals that are sufficient to preserve the corporeal world in conformity with the exemplar remain stable and imperishable. Everything else perishes that cannot remain alive with it. Now, when fire blaze brings destruction to the world, those who live near the sea and the great rivers are saved because the water protects them from the violent fire. On the other hand, when a flood washes people and

On History

things to the sea, those who live near high mountains are saved. This occasioned the Greeks to tell of Deucalion and Pyrrha who saved themselves in the mountains, thus making a fable, as they are wont to do, out of something true.

Well, in both cases, very few people remain afterward and everything around them was destroyed and annihilated; hence these people found themselves in a primal refuge in the forests, the coasts and mountains, dispersed here and there and living and suffering a savage, uncivil life deprived of all arts and learning. But growing eventually over time in numbers, distinct as families and from there in villages and then cities, instructed by the requirements for life, slowly they rediscovered the arts, learning and manners of a civilized life. This occurs with all catastrophic destruction that civilized life turns savage and brutish, and then the rough and sylvan life becomes mannered and civilized. It is for this reason that men of Europe and other places always seem new and children and do not have a longer memory than four or five thousand years back.

But we Egyptians do not fear this as we are protected from fires by the Nile and from floods because it almost never rains here. We have never lost, nor will we ever lose our arts, learning, or memories. This is why we alone are the most ancient among all people in the world and we carry the memories of infinite thousands of years. Even though the Romans from your Europe, the Arabs of Asia, and the Moors of Africa, as well as other peoples, have crossed our land with arms and fire and have destroyed many memories of ancient things, still there are many that remain and many of them are not buried.

I say to you, my son, that in the time of my grandfather, whose name was Sonchis, in the city the ancients called Sais, there lived a priest called Bitys.[17] As he was building a chapel, he found while digging the foundation a very beautiful ancient squared column carved with ancient sacred letters. As he uncovered them, since he was very learned, he found written there marvelous things about the destructions and renewals of the earth. Now listen to them carefully, my son, and admire and praise God the creator.

The Inscription on the Squared Column

This outstanding world-animal—visible image of the intelligible God, most beautiful and perfect in every part—in part it moves itself and in part it is moved by the creator God. This mutuality of movement is complete at that point when, with the

---

17. Sonchis of Saïs is mentioned in Plutarch, *Isis and Osiris*, chap. 10. Bitys, a prophet under King Ammon in Sais, is mentioned in Iamblichus, *De mysteriis* 8:5, Latin in Marsilio Ficino, *Opera omnia*, vol. 2, ed. Paul Oskar Kristeller ([Basel 1576] Torino: Bottega d'Erasmo, 1983), 1904.

306   FRANCESCO PATRIZI

destruction of everything, the Great Year of thirty-six millennia comes to an end. After that, when the chaos has paused for a thousand years and the earth was renewed from the start of the primal world and formed by the primal forms, the sky begins anew its revolution. When the Sun is at the beginning of Aries it revolves for nine millennia through the first three signs of the zodiac, which is its spring. For the next three seasons it is the same, and so in two parts in two signs. In this way each sign lasts three thousand years for every hundred degrees. The world does this infinite times within the infinite eternity of its maker. When it has run the first course of itself, it was from East to West. In the second course it is made revolve by God in the opposite direction. This is done out of necessity. For being always in the same stable manner, that befits only divine essences. But body is of the opposite manner. Now, the sky, being a body, cannot be without movement. But as far as it can, it moves in the same movement, which it reverses in itself. To do so always is not permitted except by him, the principle of any corporeal movement; and to move in two opposite circles is not allowed. It is also impious to say that the creator God moves it that way, and even more impious that there are two Gods of whom one moves this way and the other in the opposite way. Hence, it is necessary to say that one time it moves being set in motion by God, whence it receives new life and immortality. The other time, thus rejuvenated, it runs of itself in the contrary turn for infinite thousands of revolutions, that greatest of all things, moving on such small foot. On the completion of those revolutions, since this is the greatest above all other things, they make very great changes in us and in all things within it that cannot withstand the great and immediate alterations; and hence all things, animals, and people are destroyed. This upheaval is accompanied by many strange, new and marvelous events that are conform with the ending revolution. For example, when the revolt approaches the end, all animals, plants, and people stop at their present age when they are caught by the turn and no longer move toward old age but instead head toward childhood. Thus, those who are old, white-haired and wrinkled once again have dark hair and beards and smooth, unwrinkled faces. The mature ones shed their hair and become youths; the youths become children, and the children become babies. And so steadily, day and night they ebb until finally turned into tiniest beings they resolve into absolutely nothing. After this, chaos rests without form or movement, for a thousand years. During becoming pregnant from the divine world, as I have said, it returns with the beginning of the new turn to germinate. The people, plants and animals, which in the previous age had eventually been extinguished, are then the first to re-emerge from the earth, and from minors as they are born they will be, on the contrary, grown up.

These things, dear son, were written on three sides of the column, which I am

On History

relating. You see from this that this ancient sermon saying that men from the beginning of times were born from the earth, which is taken to be fabulous, is true.'

Thus, Marcello recounted that he was amazed and dumbfounded at the novelty and loftiness of Hammun's speech so that he stood beside himself quite a bit. Then he asked him, 'Now on the fourth side of the column, Father Hammun, what was written there?' Hammun replied,

There was, dear son, written nothing less marvelous and strange than what has already been told, and it was this: What was inscribed there was the memory of two completed revolutions, although the beginning of the first one did not exist. It was noted there that in the first one the Sun finished setting in the West. Following that as it began to rise in the second revolution, it went down in the East. In the third revolution, which is our own, it rises as we see it in the East and sets in the West. In this revolution, as in the other one that I was speaking of earlier, it was perhaps the ninetieth octave, God let the world move on its own, having himself moved it previously. After the current course, the world may not run anymore. This is because the matter that currently sustains it is weakened and used up in such a way that cannot sustain the forms without great discomfort. We men demonstrate this above all. But when the revolution is its completed at its own time, which perhaps is not so far away, God the creator will create new matter, and from it he will create a new world, new skies, new earth and new things. These will continue for another hundred new revolutions in the same manner as all those previous ones had run.

If we here in Egypt do not have a memory of it, do not hope, dear son, that any other nation of the world might have it. We here do have memory, I am telling you, that in the most ancient revolution the men were very tall such that with their feet standing upon the earth they could touch heaven with their heads, and they called themselves Emephim.[18] The men of the second period, smaller than those of the first, were tall above the clouds and were called Phthaim. Those of the third period were at the beginning equally of great stature, although much smaller than the Phthaim. We in Egypt called them Gigim, while you called them Giants. They lasted until the flood of Noah, living for hundreds and thousands of years, very healthy and of very tall stature. But after the flood, little by little they decayed, including knowledge and goodness. All of those things have come down in Egypt to very little. And I believe that it is like that for you.

18. Patrizi relies on the spurious histories of Annius of Viterbo: Anthony Grafton, *What Was History? The Art of History in Early Modern Europe* (Cambridge: Cambridge University Press, 2012), 140f.

308   FRANCESCO PATRIZI

I want to tell you, my son, and listen to me carefully, that toward the end of the second period, we found here in Egypt among us one of the Phtha, wise beyond measure above all other men on earth. So wise that he knew all the powers of stones, herbs, animals, of the heavens and stars, and he knew when these things were more powerful on things below and when less. In sum, he knew to work marvelous and strange things. This man foresaw the end of the revolution period in which he was living to be near, proven by the various animals which he killed and then shortly thereafter brought back to life; he prepared all the items needed on his return and let everything place together in a large vessel. He made sure with his letters and works that the universal destruction could not destroy his vessel and the things it contained; then he let carry himself many miles under the ground. When this man had killed himself (as he later recounted and also wrote it down) the end of the present revolution was imminent; he perished and ended in nothing. With the rebirth of the period, by the heavens' and his own virtue, this very same man came back to life just as he had been before.

Now, he was called Seth.[19] He foresaw the destruction of the lower world first by water, then by fire, and wrote down the memory of his first life, all of which I have described as part of the first and second periods, on two columns. One was made of metal so that it was protected from water, and the other was made of tiles so that fire could not destroy it. Then they were washed nine times in the waters of the Nile and carried up to the Mountains of the Moon[20] so that they might be a perpetual reminder of things both past and future. It predicted that the present period would shortly end as there was not enough matter left for something to sprout, but once God had reformed the entire body, a new world should grow anew. From these two columns, the ancient Egyptians received all of their own memories and they sculpted them upon the Pyramids and in marble with sacred letters, the one column that I described to you. And I will tell you something else: my grandfather, after seeing this, went to the Mountains of the Moon to see the columns of the wise Seth, and having seen them, he frequently recounted about it to me. This sermon, my son, so profound and sacred, take it back to your regions in Europe and tell it to men worthy of it so that Egyptians will be honored there, and glory will be rendered to God.

19. Cf. Flavius Josephus, *Antiquities of the Jews*, ed. William Whiston (Auburn: Beardsley, 1895), 1.67, who conflated Adam's and Eve's third son Seth with the Egyptian king Sesostris; there the two columns mentioned in the following sentences. Cf. Herodotus, *The Histories*, 2.102.

20. Now the Rwenzori Mountains, the legendary riverhead of the Nile; cf. Ptolemy, *Geographia*, IV, 8.

On History

"This sacred history, dear sirs, my Marcello brought back from the Holy Land, and he recounted it many times to my father, from whom I heard it many times, and now I am recounting it to you two so that it might do you good."

Objects of History

"What an excellent history you have told us, Patrizi," said the Count. "If that is history, it is worthy highest admiration. But what bearing does it bring to our own question?" "It brings to bear many things," I answered. "The first is this: Seth's was written about past things and those that were to come." "What you say is true," said the Count. "The second point is," I continued, "that history was being made from the very beginning of the world." "That is also true," he answered. "So that one may say it was the very first writing ever made." "It's true." "The third point," I added, "was that it was not written in letters, but carved with figures of things, which, as you know, the Egyptians held sacred." "This again is true." "And finally," I said, "it was nothing in truth but the memory of things." "Nothing else for sure." "We are able," I continued, "to extract from this for our purposes that history is nothing other than memory, whether written as we do to-day, or sculpted in figures, as has been described and all the other ancient ones in Egypt, or marked, such as was done on the column made at the Nile, or painted such as that of Alexander III." "It is really not otherwise," replied Sir Paolo. "Consequently," I went on, "such memories were the an-nals created by the Chief Pontiffs, as well as the books on Roman life left to us by Livy, and those on Greece by Thucydides." "Those are memories without error," he answered. "What about those left to us by Suetonius on the Caesars and Plutarch on illustrious men, what are they?" "Are they anything other than memories as well?" he responded. "It demonstrates rather," I suggested, "that up until now histories have truly been nothing other than memories." "Without error, nothing else."

"But memories—what are they about?" I continued. "What else," he replied, "than of human actions?" "But Theophrastrus who wrote about plants, and Aristotle, as you know, about animals" I said, "did they not make such memory?" "What you say is true," he replied, "but memory of what is that then?" "Now see," I said, "that I will attribute equal object to the universal term history by saying that it is a memory of things." "You

310 FRANCESCO PATRIZI

speak well," replied Sir Paolo, "but I wish that our conversation were now about the histories of humans, leaving aside all these other things."

"So then," I replied, "you are saying well that they are memories of human actions. Is that not what you are saying?" "Yes, I'm saying that for certain," he answered. "But here arises a doubt," I said, "slight in appearance but profoundly grave." "What is it?" I continued: "That many historians tell us that Augustus was a handsome young man, with shining eyes, and that he was calm and wise." "What does that matter?" he asked. "It matters," I answered, "because speaking in this way is not describing the actions of Augustus at all, but the disposition of his body and soul. And these things are in history, too, and are memory." "You are quite right," he answered, "so then what do we do?" "We focus, if you like," I said, "on the general term 'thing' and state that history is the memory of human things."

"Yes," he answered, "this is fine." "But don't you see a larger difficulty? What is it?" I asked. "That memory," he answered, "is only of things past and you claim that history is equally about future things." "That's quite a lot," I replied. "But let us look at it this way: Memory, which is a power of the soul, is it anything other than a conservatory of imaginations?" "It is nothing else," he replied. "And these imaginations," I continued, "are they anything other than images of things represented by the senses or otherwise to the soul, which in turn reshapes them in some manner? Don't our philosophers tell us this?" "They do," he answered. "Now tell me, these images and these imaginations, might they not come from future things? Might they be represented to the soul from dreams, omens, visions, divine inspirations, or some other ways?" "By this reasoning," he said, "it is demonstrated that memory can even be of future things." "Here we are, dear Sir," I continued, "memory and history can be had of things to come." "So it seems," he said.

"But for me there is still greater doubt about something else," I went on. "But what?" "That there are many forms of memory which perhaps are not history." "Which ones?" he asked. I replied: "They are those which are called memory that every man can create by himself." "What you say is true," the Count said now. "But these deal for the most part with things that concern people's own things and their relatives. And then there are those," I said, "he makes of past things, public and otherwise." "You are right," said the Count, "But what do you say if these are memoirs and per-

On History

haps commentaries?" "This is difficult to say," I replied, "since they are made privately. If I dare to tell you something strange, would you forgive me?" "Of course I'll forgive you," he said. "I wish to say," I began, "that even these are still histories." "And you say it with a trembling voice," said the Count. I answered, "I would never have said it without the promise of pardon, so strange does this opinion seem also to me." "Certainly it is strange," he replied, "So then would you say that memory means as much as history?" "Yes," I answered, "memory that is outside the soul, either written down, or in marble, or in another place." "For certain this is something new to say," he responded, "that history might just as well be a private memoir that anyone makes, as what is written about the affairs of great Princes and great Republics. Though now I regret to have said it," I went on, "since you much dislike it. But I'll remedy it for you right away." "In which way?" he asked. "In that," I answered, "we might consider history to be made only of great things, as you say, of great Princes and great Republics." "Oh, that we can do," he replied. "But even this," I added, "cannot be done on further thought." "Why is that?" he asked.

"Because history might be," answered Sir Paolo, "no less of this, namely, of a little Prince in a little Republic." "And incidentally," I suggested, "history might be done about a private person, since there are histories of the lives of some who were neither Princes nor men of Republics." "You speak truly," the Count said then, "but it will be best to separate that history, as we commonly understand it, from that of memoirs and commentaries." "Since it did not seem to us," I said, "that highness or lowness of the persons made a difference between them, let us see whether we can state something else." "And what might that be?" he asked. As we were about to continue the conversation, my doctor, Sir Leandro Zarotti[21] entered the room to check on my illness. And with his arrival, our discussion was interrupted. And then it was evening.

21. Mentioned as an outstanding physician in Bardi, *Delle cose notabili*, 200.

20

GIORDANO BRUNO
(1548–1600)

On the Infinite, Universe and Worlds

PAUL RICHARD BLUM

INTRODUCTION

Giordano Bruno was born Filippo Bruno in Nola (Campania, Italy) and studied in Naples, where he entered the convent of the Dominicans and assumed the name Giordano. After various incidents that showed his dissident mind in religious affairs, he started a life of a migrant scholar that led him through Rome, Northern Italy, Geneva (where he clashed with Calvinists), Toulouse, Paris, London, Oxford, and to several German universities (among others, Wittenberg and Helmstedt). While publishing some of his major works in Frankfurt, he accepted an invitation by a patrician from Venice. After attempts to teach in Padua, he was denounced to the Inquisition by his host in 1592 for heretical teachings; he was transferred to Rome, sentenced as an unrepentant heretic, and burned at the stake in 1600. His fame as a defiant unorthodox philosopher frequently overshadowed the core of his theories.

The introductory letter of the dialogue *On the Infinite, Universe and Worlds* (*De l'infinito, universo e mondi*), published in London in 1584, is a convenient summary of Bruno's thought.[1] He

---

1. I am indebted to Eugenio Canone for suggesting this text and further advice.

presents his work as a medicine of the mind able to heal readers from the fears that may arise from knowing that humans are finite beings in a finite world while longing for the infinite. The task of philosophy, he taught, is to free the human soul from illusions, such as the idea of some otherworldly individual life.

De l'infinito is divided into five dialogues with five interlocutors: *Filoteo* (the author's *alter ego*), *Elpino*, *Fracastorio* (a reminiscence of the Veronese physician and philosopher Girolamo Fracastoro, who died in 1553), *Burchio* (the personification of the pedantic Aristotelian), and *Albertino*, who enters the scene only in the final dialogue. After the dialogue *De la causa, principio et uno* (On cause, principle and one), also published in 1584, had presented Bruno's revision of metaphysics, *De l'infinito* outlines his cosmology of an infinite universe. While Bruno's ontology was inspired by pre-Socratic thinkers in cosmology, the author applies atomism to the unity of being as a whole, which he explains with the idea of the universal soul.

As in most of Bruno's writings, the explicit target of *De l'infinito* is Aristotle. Nevertheless, he remains indebted to Aristotelian concepts and terminology. Furthermore, one of Bruno's main critiques is directed against Christian theology and the Aristotelianism of medieval scholasticism. While *De l'infinito* deals specifically with cosmology, the author highlights the ethical implications of his interpretation of Copernican doctrine in terms of universal infinity. For him, Christian theology should reject the scholastic distinction between *absolute potency* (God) and *ordered potency* (creation) and declare the infinity of the universe, as the "infinite effect of the infinite cause." The cosmology of infinite worlds organized as interconnected and harmonic planetary systems is based on the principle of the conservation of all species.

As was customary at the time, the dedicatory epistle of *De l'infinito* expresses gratitude to the dedicatee of the work, the French ambassador Michel de Castelnau, and gives occasion to autobiographical remarks aimed above all at underlining the persecutions he suffered because of the novelty of his philosophy.

BIBLIOGRAPHY
Primary Sources

Bruno, Giordano. *On the Infinite, Universe, and Worlds*. In Dorothea Waley Singer, *Giordano Bruno, His Life and Thought*. New York: Schuman, 1950. Includes *De l'infinito Universo et Mondi*, translated into English by the author.

———. *Dialoghi italiani*. Edited by Giovanni Gentile and Giovanni Aquilecchia. Firenze, Sansoni, 1958.

———. *Opera latine conscripta*. Edited by Francesco Fiorentino et al. [Napoli; Firenze, 1879–1891]. Stuttgart-Bad Cannstatt: Frommann-Holzboog, 1962.

Secondary Sources

Blum, Paul Richard. *Giordano Bruno: An Introduction*. Translated by Peter Henneveld. Amsterdam: Rodopi, 2012.

———. *Giordano Bruno Teaches Aristotle*. Translated by Peter Henneveld. Nordhausen: Bautz, 2016.

———. "Giordano Bruno." *Internet Encyclopedia of Philosophy*, 2021. https://iep.utm.edu/bruno/.

Canone, Eugenio. "Giordano Bruno (1548–1600): Clarifying the Shadows of Ideas." In *Philosophers of the Renaissance*, edited by Paul Richard Blum and translated by Brian McNeil, 219–35. Washington, D.C.: The Catholic University of America Press, 2010.

Girelli, Lucia. *Bruno, Aristotele e la materia*. Bologna: Archetipo Libri, 2013.

Meroi, Fabrizio. "Bruno, Giordano." In *Encyclopedia of Renaissance Philosophy*, edited by Marco Sgarbi, 1–16. Cham: Springer International Publishing, 2019. https://doi.org/10.1007/978-3-319-02848-4_343-2.

Mertens, Manuel. *Magic and Memory in Giordano Bruno*. Leiden: Brill, 2018.

Rowland, Ingrid D. *Giordano Bruno: Philosopher/Heretic*. New York: Farrar, Straus and Giroux, 2008.

Saiber, Arielle. *Giordano Bruno and the Geometry of Language*. Aldershot: Ashgate, 2005.

Traversino, Massimiliano. *Diritto e teologia alle soglie dell'età moderna: Il problema della potentia Dei absoluta in Giordano Bruno*. Napoli: Editoriale scientifica, 2015.

Journal

Bruniana & Campanelliana, since 1995.

Online Resources

La biblioteca ideale di Giordano Bruno. L'opera e le fonti. Access to works and concordances. http://bibliotecaideale.filosofia.sns.it.

Bibliotheca Bruniana Electronica—The Complete Works of Giordano Bruno. Access to editions and secondary sources. https://warburg.sas.ac.uk/research/research-projects/giordano-bruno/download-page.

"Archivio Giordano Bruno—Studi e Materiali." http://www.iliesi.cnr.it/AGB/.
"Enciclopedia Bruniana e Campanelliana." http://www.iliesi.cnr.it/EBC/entrate
.php?en=EB.

GIORDANO BRUNO

On the Infinite, Universe and Worlds[2]

INTRODUCTORY EPISTLE

Addressed to the most illustrious Monsieur Michel de Castelnau, Seigneur de Mauvissière, de Concressault and de Joinville, Chevalier of the Order of the most Christian King, Privy Councillor, Captain of fifty men at arms, and Ambassador to Her most Serene Majesty the Queen of England.

If, O most illustrious Knight, I should have driven a plough, pastured a flock, cultivated an orchard, tailored a garment: none would regard me, few observe me, seldom a one reproves me; and I could easily satisfy all men. But since I would survey the field of Nature, care for the nourishment of the soul, foster the cultivation of talent, become as expert as Daedalus concerning the ways of the intellect; lo, one upon seeing me threatens me, who sees me attacks me, another having come close bites me, yet another having caught me would devour me; not one, nor few, they are many, indeed almost all. If you would know why, it is because I loathe the universality, I hate the vulgar herd, and in the multitude, I find no joy. One is that which enchants me: By her[3] power, I am free though subject, happy in sorrow, rich in poverty, and alive even in death. Through her virtue I envy not those who are slaves in freedom, who grieve in the midst of pleasures, who endure poverty in their wealth, and who die although they are alive. They carry their chains within them; their spirit contains her own hell that

---

2. For this anthology, we edited and amended the English translation by Dorothea Waley Singer: *Giordano Bruno, His Life and Thought* [includes *De l'infinito Universo et Mondi, English*]. The editing was provided by Andrew Olesh, Jr.

3. Bruno leaves open who or what this female "one" is: maybe wisdom, perhaps philosophy, but it could even reference Queen Elizabeth, to whom the addressee was the ambassador.

316 GIORDANO BRUNO

brings them low; within their soul is the disease that wastes them away; and within their mind the lethargy that brings death. They are without the generosity that would enfranchise, the longsuffering that exalts, the splendor that illumines, knowledge that bestows life. Therefore, I do not in weariness shun the arduous path, nor idly refrain my arm from the present task, nor retreat in despair from the enemy that confronts me, nor do I turn my dazzled eyes from the divine end. Yet, I am aware that I am mostly held to be a sophist, seeking rather to appear subtle than to reveal the truth; an ambitious fellow, diligent rather to support a new and false sect than to establish the ancient and true; an ensnarer of birds who pursues the splendor of fame by spreading forth the darkness of error; an unquiet spirit that would undermine the edifice of good discipline to establish the frame of perversity.

Wherefore, my Lord, may the heavenly powers scatter before me all those who unjustly hate me; may my God be ever gracious unto me; may all the rulers of our world be favorable to me; may the stars yield me seed for the field and soil for the seed so that the harvest of my labor may appear to the world useful and glorious and that souls may be awakened and the understanding of those in darkness be illuminated. For assuredly, I do not dissimulate; and if I err, I do so unwittingly, nor do I in speech or writing contend merely for victory, for I hold worldly repute and hollow success without truth, to be hateful to God as most vile and dishonorable. But I thus exhaust, vex and torment myself for love of true wisdom and zeal for true contemplation. This I shall make manifest by conclusive arguments, dependent on lively reasonings derived from regulated sense, instructed by phenomena that are not false; for these as trustworthy ambassadors emerge from things of Nature, rendering themselves present to those who seek them, obvious to those who gaze attentively upon them, clear to those who apprehend, certain and sure to those who understand. Thus, I present to you my contemplation concerning the infinite universe and innumerable worlds.[4]

---

4. Bruno's most appealing dedication to Mauvissière is reserved for the conclusion of the Arguments.

On the Infinite, Universe and Worlds 317

CONTENTS OF THE FIRST DIALOGUE

You find in the first Dialogue, FIRST, that the inconstancy of sense-perception demonstrates that sense is no source of certainty but can attain thereto only through comparison and reference from one sensible percept to another and from one sense to another, so that truth may be contained in diverse sources.

SECOND, the demonstration is begun of the infinity of the universe;[5] and the first argument is derived from the failure to limit the world by those whose fantasy would erect boundary walls around it.

THIRD, from the idea that it is unfitting to name the world finite and contained within itself, since this condition belongs only to immensity, will be drawn the second argument. Moreover, the third argument is based on the inconvenience and indeed impossibility of imagining the world to occupy no position. For inevitably it would follow that it was without being, since everything whether corporeal or incorporeal occupies corporeally or incorporeally some position.

The FOURTH argument is based on a demonstration or urgent question put forth by the Epicureans:

Moreover, suppose now that all space were created finite; if one were to run on to the end, to its furthest coasts, and throw a flying dart, would you have it that the dart, hurled with might and main, goes on to where it is sped, flying afar, or do you think that something can check and bar its way? ... For whether there be something to check it and bring about that it arrives not where it was sped, and does not itself plan the goal, or whether it fares forward, yet it does not set forth from the end.[6]

5. Bruno uses "universo" for the infinite universe. His word "mondo" is translated throughout as "world." Bruno uses "mondo" not only for our terrestrial globe but also for the universe as apprehended by our senses and as conceived by the Aristotelians. Thus, he speaks of our world (*questo mondo*)—including the stars that we see—occupying our space, bounded by the vault of heaven. For Bruno, this, together with innumerable other worlds—that is, other systems of heavenly bodies, each system occupying its own space—forms the one infinite universe (*universo*).

6. Lucretius, *De rerum natura*, I, 968–73, 977–79. Bruno quotes the Latin text. The English translations of this and all other passages from Lucretius are based on Dr. C. Bailey, *Lucretius on the Nature of Things* (Oxford: Clarendon Press, 1910). It will be noticed that Bruno does not here give the name of Lucretius. He has a few textual deviations from the received Latin text, which are noted by Gentile, *Dialoghi italiani* I, 271. Throughout his edition, Gentile cites parallel passages in the other works of Bruno.

318 GIORDANO BRUNO

FIFTH, Aristotle's definition of position is unsuited to primal, vast, universal space,[7] and it befits not to take the surface nearest and adjoining the content or other such foolishness, which would regard position as mathematical and not physical, not to mention that between the containing surface and the content which moves therein, there is always and inevitably an intermediate space which should rather be the position; and if we wish only to take the surface as space, we need to go seeking *ad infinitum* a finite position.

SIXTH, if we posit a finite world, it is impossible to escape acceptance of the void, if void is that which contains nothing.

SEVENTH, this space in which is our world would without it be a void, since where the world is not, there we must infer a void. Beyond our world then, one space is as another; therefore the actuality of one is also that of the other; wherefore too this actuality comes to action, for no actuality is eternally without action, and indeed it is eternally linked to action or rather is itself action, for in eternity there is no distinction between being and potential being.

EIGHTH, none of our sense-perceptions is opposed to the acceptance of infinity, since we cannot deny infinity merely because we do not sensibly perceive it; but since sense itself is included in infinity, and since reason confirms infinity; therefore, we must posit infinity. Moreover, if we consider well, sense presents to us an infinite universe. For we always see something contained within something else, and we never sense, either with our external or internal sense, something not contained within something else, or the like.

Last, before our eyes one thing is seen to bound another; air is as a well between the hills, and mountains between tracts of air, land bounds the sea and again sea bounds all lands; yet in truth there is nothing outside to limit the universe ... so far on every side spreads out huge room for things, free from limit in all directions everywhere.[8]

---

7. We translate Bruno's *loco* as "position" and *spacio* as "space," reflecting Bruno's interpretation that Aristotle wrongly reduces the Greek word χώρα to signify a space that occupies a definite position, whereas it should be used for the infinite immensity of physical space. Cf. *Physics*, IV 208a 28; 208b 1, 23, 34, etc.

8. Lucretius, *De rerum natura*, I, 984–88; 1006–1007. Quoted in Latin.

On the Infinite, Universe and Worlds

From the testimony of our sight then we should rather infer the infinite, since there is nothing that does not terminate in another, nor can we experience anything that terminates in itself.

NINTH, only verbally is it possible to deny infinite space, as is done by pertinacious fellows. For the rest of space, where the universe is not, which is called void, where indeed it is pretended that nothing exists, cannot be conceived as without the capacity to contain no less a magnitude than that which it does contain.

TENTH, since it is good that this world exists, no less good is the existence of each one of the infinity of other worlds.

ELEVENTH, the goodness of this world is not communicable to any other world whatsoever, just as my being cannot be communicated to the being of this or of that man.

TWELFTH, there is no reason or sense-perception which, since we accept an infinity undivided, utterly simple and all-embracing, will not permit also a corporeal and unfolded infinity.

THIRTEENTH, the space of this world that appears to us so immense is neither part nor whole in relation to the infinite, nor can it be patient of infinite activity; compared to such activity, indeed, that which can be comprehended by our imbecile minds is merely non-being. And to a certain objection it may be replied that we base our argument for infinity not on the dignity of space but on the dignity of the natures, since for the same reason that our space exists, so also should exist every other possible world; and their power of being is not actuated by our world's being, just as Elpino's power of being is not actuated by the existence of Fracastorio.

FOURTEENTH, if infinite active power actuates corporeal and dimensional being, this being must necessarily be infinite; otherwise, there would be derogation from the nature and dignity both of creator and of creation.

FIFTEENTH, the universe as vulgarly conceived cannot contain the perfection of all things, except in the sense that I contain the perfection of all my members, and every globe contains its entire contents. It is as if to say that everyone is rich who lacks nothing that he has.

SIXTEENTH, efficient infinity would be incomplete without the effect thereof, as we cannot conceive how such an effect should be only in itself. Furthermore, if such were or could be the effect, this in no way detracts from that which must appertain to every veritable effect, wherefore theologians name action *ad extra* or transitive in addition to imminent action, so that thus it is fitting that both one and the other be infinite.

SEVENTEENTH, to call the universe[9] boundless as we have done brings the mind to rest, while the contrary multiplies innumerable difficulties and inconveniences. Furthermore, we repeat what was said under headings two and three.

EIGHTEENTH, if the world be spherical, it has figure and boundary; and the boundary which is yet beyond this boundary and figure (though it may please you to term it nullity) also has figure so that the concavity of the latter is joined to the convexity of the former, since the beginning of this your nullity is a concavity completely indifferent to the convex surface of the world.

NINETEENTH, more is added to that which has been said under the second heading.

TWENTIETH, that which has been said under heading ten is repeated.

In the second part of this Dialogue, that which has already been shown concerning the passive power of the universe is demonstrated for the active power of the efficient cause, set forth with arguments of which the FIRST derives from the fact that divine power should not be idle; particularly positing the effect thereof outside the substance thereof (if indeed anything can be outside it), and that it is no less idle and invidious if it were to produce a finite effect than if it were to produce none.

The SECOND argument is practical, showing that the contrary view would deny divine goodness and greatness. While from our view, there follows no inconvenience whatsoever against whatever laws you will, nor against the matter of theology.

The THIRD argument is the converse of the twelfth of Part 1. And here is shown the distinction between the infinite whole and the completely infinite.

The FOURTH argument shows that no less from lack of will than from lack of power, omnipotence comes to be blamed for creating a finite world, the infinite agent acting on a finite subject.

---

9. Bruno here uses *mondo*, contrary to his usual convention. In the next argument and in the FIFTH of the SECOND PART, *mondo* denotes the Aristotelian conception.

The FIFTH argument demonstrates that if omnipotence does not make the world infinite, it is impotent to do so; and, if it does not have the power to create it infinite, then it must lack vigor to preserve it into eternity. And, if finite in one respect, it would be so in all, for every mode therein is something, and every thing and every mode are the same, the one as the other.

The SIXTH argument is the converse of the tenth of Part 1 and shows the reason why theologians defend the contrary view, not without expedient argument, and discourse of friendship between these learned divines and the learned philosophers.

The SEVENTH propounds the reasons that distinguish active power from diverse actions and discharges such argument. Further, it expounds infinite power intensively and extensively in more lofty fashion than has ever been done by the whole body of theologians.

The EIGHTH demonstrates that the motion of the infinity of worlds[10] is not the result of external motive force but of their own soul and that despite this there exists an infinite mover.

The NINTH shows how infinite motion may be intensively verified in each of the worlds. To this we should add that since each moving body at the same time moves itself and is moved, it follows necessarily that it may be seen in every point of the circle that it describes around its own center. And this objection we discharge on other occasions when it will be permissible to present the more elaborate doctrine.

CONTENTS OF THE SECOND DIALOGUE

The second Dialogue reaches the same conclusion. FIRST, four arguments are brought forward. The first shows that all the attributes of divinity are together as each one singly. The second demonstrates that our imagination should not be able to aspire beyond divine action. The third postulates the indifference of the distinction between divine intellect and divine action and demonstrates that divine intellect conceives the infinite no less than the finite. The fourth argument enquires, if the corporeal quality (the one perceptible to our senses) is endowed with infinite active

---

10. Here and subsequently, Bruno's *infiniti mondi* is best translated as "infinite number of worlds" or "infinity of worlds."

322   GIORDANO BRUNO

power; if so, what about all the quality that is in all the active and passive power?

SECOND, it is demonstrated that something corporeal cannot be terminated by something incorporeal, but either by a void or by a plenum, and in either case, beyond the world is a space which is ultimately no other than matter; this is indeed that same passive force whereby active force, neither grudging nor idle, is roused to activity. And the vanity is shown of Aristotle's argument concerning the incompatibility of dimensions.[11]

THIRD, the difference is taught between the world and the universe, because he who declares the universe 'infinite and one' necessarily distinguishes between these two terms.

FOURTH, there are brought forward contrary arguments that regard the universe as finite, wherein Elpino refers to all the sentences of Aristotle, and Philotheo examines them. Some are derived from the nature of simple, others from that of composite, bodies. And the vanity is shown of six arguments taken from the definition of motions which cannot be infinite and from other similar propositions which are without meaning, purpose or plausibility, as will be seen. For our arguments show forth more convincingly the reason for the differences and for the termination of motion. And so far as comports with the occasion and place, they demonstrate the true understanding of strong and of weak impulses. For, we shall show that an infinite body is in itself neither heavy nor light, and we shall demonstrate in what manner a finite body can or again cannot receive such variations. Thus will be made clear the vanity of Aristotle's arguments against those who posit an infinite world, when he supposes a center of circumference, maintaining that our earth attains to the center whether of a finite or of an infinite. Finally, there is no proposition, great or small, adduced by this philosopher in order to destroy the infinity of the world, either in the first book of his *De coelo et mundo*, or in the third book of his *Physica*, which is not adequately discussed.

CONTENTS OF THE THIRD DIALOGUE

In the third Dialogue there is FIRST denied that base illusion of the shape of the heavens, of their spheres and diversity. For the heaven is de-

---

11. *Physics,* IV, 2 209b *sqq.*

clared to be one general space, embracing the infinite worlds, though we do not deny that there are other, even infinite, 'heavens' using that word in another sense. For just as this earth has her own heaven, which is her own region, through which she moves and has her course, so the same may be said of each of the innumerable other worlds. The origin is shown of the illusion of so many deferent cycles so shaped as to have two external surfaces and one internal cavity, and of other prescriptions and medicines, which bring nausea and horror even to those who concoct and dispense them, not less than to the wretches who swallow them.

SECOND, we expound how both general motion and that of the above-mentioned eccentrics, and as many as may be referred to the aforesaid firmament are all pure illusion, deriving from the motion of the center of the earth along the ecliptic and from the four varieties of motion which the earth takes around her own center. Thus it is seen that the proper motion of each star results from the difference in position, which may be verified subjectively within the star as a body moving alone spontaneously through the field of space. This consideration makes it understood that all their arguments concerning the movable and the infinite motion are vain and based on ignorance of the motion of this our own globe.

THIRD, it will be propounded that there is no star that does not move as does our own and those others which being so near to us, let us sensibly know the differences in their orbits and in their motions: but those suns, bodies in which fire predominates, move differently to the earths in which water predominates; thus may be understood from where is derived the light diffused by stars, of which some glow of themselves and others by reflection.

FOURTH, it is shown how stars at vast distances from the sun can, no less than those near to it, participate in heat, and fresh proof is given of the opinion attributed to Epicurus, that one sun may suffice for an infinite universe.[12] Moreover, this explains the true difference between the stars that do and stars that do not scintillate.

FIFTH, the opinion of the Cusan is examined concerning the material and the habitability of other worlds and concerning the cause of light.

SIXTH, it is shown that although some bodies are luminous and hot of their own nature, yet it does not follow that the sun illuminates the sun

---

12. Cf. *Letter to Pythokles* in Diogenes Laertius, X.

324   GIORDANO BRUNO

and the earth illuminates herself, or that water illuminates itself. But light proceeds always from the opposed star; just as, when looking down from lofty eminences such as mountains, we sensibly perceive the whole sea illuminated; but were we on the sea, and occupying the same plane thereof, we should see no illumination save over a small region where the light of the sun and the light of the moon were opposed to us.

SEVENTH, we discourse concerning the vain notion of quintessences; and we declare that all sensible bodies are no other and composed of no different proximate or primal principles than those of our earth, nor have they other motion, either in straight lines or circles. All this is set forth with reasons attuned to the senses, while Fracastorio accommodates himself to the intelligence of Burchio. And it is shown clearly that there is no accident here which may not be expected also on those other worlds; just as if we consider well we must recognize that nothing there can be seen from here which cannot also be seen here from there. Consequently, that beautiful order and ladder of nature is but a charming dream, an old wives' tale.

EIGHTH, though the distinction between the elements be just, yet their order as commonly accepted is by no means perceptible to the senses or intelligible. According to Aristotle, the four elements are equally parts or members of this globe—unless we would say that water is in excess, wherefore with good cause the stars are named now water, now fire, both by true natural philosophers, and by prophets, divines and poets, who in this respect are spinning no tales nor forging metaphors, but allow other wiseacres to spin their tales and to babble. These worlds must be understood as heterogeneous bodies, animals, great globes in which earth is no heavier than the other elements. In them all particles move, changing their position and respective arrangement, just as the blood and other humors, spirits and smallest parts which ebb and flow are absorbed and again exhaled by us and other minor animals. In this connection a comparison is adduced showing that the earth is no heavier by virtue of the attraction of her mass toward her own center than is any other simple body of similar composition; that moreover the earth in herself is neither heavy, nor does she ascend or descend; and that it is water which unifies, and makes density, consistency and weight.

NINTH, since the famous order of the elements is seen to be vain, we

On the Infinite, Universe and Worlds 325

infer the concept of these sensible composite bodies which as so many animals and worlds are in that spacious field which is the air or the heaven, or the void, in which are all those worlds which contain animals and inhabitants no less than can our own earth, since those worlds have no less virtue nor a nature different from that of our earth.

TENTH, after it has been seen how the obstinate and the ignorant of evil disposition are accustomed to dispute, it will further be shown how disputes are wont to conclude. Although others are so wary that—without losing their composure, but with a sneer, a smile, and a certain discreet malice—they endeavor to conceal by these tricks of courteous disdain that which they have not succeeded in proving with reasons nor make themselves understand; they not only conceal their own patently obvious ignorance but cast it onto the back of their adversary. For they dispute not in order to find or even to seek Truth, but for victory, and to appear the more learned and strenuous upholders of a contrary opinion. Such persons should be avoided by all who have not a good breastplate of patience.

CONTENTS OF THE FOURTH DIALOGUE

First in this Dialogue is repeated that which has been said on other occasions concerning the infinity of worlds and how each one of them moves, and what is the configuration thereof.

Second, as in the second Dialogue, arguments against the infinite mass or size of the universe were refuted, after the vast effect of immense vigor and power had been demonstrated with many arguments in the first Dialogue; even so, the infinite multitude of worlds having been demonstrated in the third Dialogue, we now refute the numerous contrary arguments of Aristotle; though this word *world* has indeed one meaning when used by Aristotle and quite another when used by Democritus, Epicurus and others.

Aristotle, in arguments based on natural and impressed motion and on the nature of each which he formulates, holds that one Earth should move toward another. To refute these doctrines, FIRST, principles are established of no little importance for the elucidation of the true foundations of natural philosophy. SECOND, it is shown that however closely the surface of one Earth were contiguous with that of another, it would not happen

326 GIORDANO BRUNO

that parts of the one, that is to say, heterogeneous or dissimilar parts—I speak not of atoms nor of simple bodies—could move to the other Earth. Thereby the need is recognized to consider more carefully the nature of heaviness and of lightness.

THIRD, wherefore have these great bodies been disposed by nature at so great a distance one from another, instead of being placed nearer so that it would have been possible to pass from one to another? Thence, to a more profound vision it appears why worlds could not be placed as it were in the circumference of the ether; that is, they could not be adjoining unto a void which has neither power, virtue nor force, for it would then be impossible from one side to derive either life or light.

FOURTH, we consider in what respect local distance may or may not change the nature of a body. And why is it that if a stone be equidistant between two earths, it will either remain stably poised or if it does not do so, why it will move rather toward one than toward the other.

FIFTH, we consider how mistaken Aristotle was in holding the belief that between bodies, however distant, there is a force of heaviness or lightness attracting from one toward the other[13] from which proceeds the universal tendency to resist change of state (however lowly) from where arise flight and persecutions.

SIXTH, it is shown that movement in a straight line does not appertain to the nature of our earth or of other principal bodies, but rather to the parts of these bodies which, if not at too great a distance, move toward one another from the most diverse positions.

SEVENTH, it is argued from the behavior of comets that it is not true that a heavy body, however distant, suffers attraction or motion toward the body which contains it. This hypothesis indeed was based not on truly physical principles but on suppositions of Aristotle's philosophy, formulated by him from a consideration of those parts which are vapors and exhalations of our earth.[14]

EIGHTH, concerning another line of reasoning, it is shown that simple bodies of identical nature in innumerable diverse worlds have similar motion and how arithmetical diversity causes a difference of locality, each

---

13. Cf. *Physics*, IV, 4, 212a 25; 212b 30, etc.
14. Cf. *Physics*, IV, 208b I *sqq.*

On the Infinite, Universe and Worlds

part having its own center and being also referred to the common center which cannot be sought within the universe.

NINTH, it is established that bodies and their parts have no determined up or down, save in so far as the place of their conservation may be here or there.

TENTH, it is shown that motion is infinite and that a moving body tends toward infinity and to the formation of innumerable compositions but that heaviness or lightness do not therefore follow, nor infinite speed; and indeed, the motion of adjacent parts, inasmuch as they preserve their own being, cannot be infinite. Moreover, the attraction of parts to their own containing body can only take place within the region thereof.

CONTENTS OF THE FIFTH DIALOGUE

In the beginning of the fifth Dialogue is presented a learned person of a happier talent who, although educated in the contrary doctrine, yet by power to judge what he has heard and seen, can distinguish between two disciplines and can easily alter and correct his views. Those are described to whom Aristotle appears a miracle of nature, since they misinterpret him and, with little understanding, have an exalted opinion concerning him. Wherefore we should pity them, and flee from disputation with them, since against them it is only possible to lose.

Here Albertino, a fresh interlocutor, introduces twelve arguments which comprise every point against a plurality or multitude of worlds. The FIRST suggests that outside our own world we can appreciate neither position, time nor space, neither simple nor composite body. The SECOND asserts the oneness of the mover. The THIRD is based on the positions of mobile bodies; the FOURTH, on the distance of the horizons from the center. The FIFTH argues from the contiguity of the orbs of the worlds; the SIXTH from the triangular spaces which are caused by their contact. The SEVENTH maintains infinity in action (which does not exist) and supposes a determinate number which is not more reasonable than another. From the same reasoning, we can infer not merely as well but much more easily that the number of worlds is not determined but is infinite. The EIGHTH is based on the determination of natural bodies and on the passive force of bodies which does not correspond to divine efficiency and active power. But here we must consider that it is highly inconvenient to suppose the Supreme and Highest to be similar to a performer on the zither who cannot play in the absence of the instrument; he would be one who can do but does not because that what he can do cannot be done by him. This would posit an obvious contradiction which cannot be overlooked save by the most ignorant. The NINTH argument is based on urbane courtesy which lies in conversation. The TENTH avers that from the contiguity of one world with another must be deduced that the motion of one impedes that of the other. The ELEVENTH maintains that if this world is complete and perfect, it is impossible that one or more others should be added to it.

These are the doubts and motives whose solution involves only so much doctrine as will suffice to lay bare the intimate and radical errors of the current philosophy and the weight and force of our own. Here is the reason wherefore we must not fear that anything may disappear, or any particle veritably melt away or dissolve in space or suffer dismemberment by annihilation. Here too is the reason of the constant change of all things so that there exists no evil beyond escape, nor good which is unattainable, since throughout infinite space and throughout endless change all substance remains one and the same. From these reflections, if we apply ourselves attentively, we shall see that no strange happening can be dismissed by grief or by fear and that no good fortune can be advanced by pleasure or hope. Whereby we find the true path to true morality; we will be high minded, despising that which is esteemed by childish minds, and we shall certainly become greater than those whom the blind public adore, for we shall attain to true contemplation of the story of nature which is inscribed within ourselves and follow the divine laws which are engraved upon our hearts. We shall recognize that there is no distinction between flight from here to heaven and from heaven hither, nor between ascent from there hither and from here to there; nor yet is there descent between one and the other. We are not more circumferential to those others than they to us; they are not more central to us than we to them. Just as we tread our star and are contained in our heavens, so also are they.

Behold us therefore beyond reach of jealousy, liberated from vain anxiety and from foolish concern to covet from afar that great good which we possess close by and at hand. Behold us moreover freed from panic lest

On the Infinite, Universe and Worlds 329

others should fall upon us, rather than encouraged in the hope that we may fall upon them. Since the air which sustains our globe is as infinite as that which sustains theirs, and this free animal wanders through her own space and reaches her own destination as freely as do those others. When we have pondered and understood this, ah, how much further shall we be led to ponder and understand.

Thus, by means of this science we shall certainly attain to that good which by other sciences is sought in vain.

Here is the philosophy which sharpens the senses, satisfies the soul, enlarges the intellect and leads man to that true bliss to which he may attain, which consists in a certain balance, for it liberates him alike from the eager quest of pleasure and from the blind feeling of grief; it causes him to rejoice in the present and neither to fear nor to hope for the future. For the Providence or Fate or Lot which determines the vicissitudes of our individual life neither desires nor permits our knowledge of the one to exceed our ignorance of the other so that at first sight we are dubious and perplexed. But when we consider more profoundly the being and substance of that universe in which we are immutably set, we shall discover that neither we ourselves nor any substance suffers death; for, nothing is in fact diminished in its substance, but all things wandering through infinite space undergo change of aspect. And, since we are all subject to a perfect Power, we should not believe, suppose or hope otherwise, than that even as all issues from good, so too all is good, through good, toward good, from good, by good means, toward a good end. For a contrary view can be held only by one who considers merely the present moment, even as the beauty of a building is not manifest to one who sees but one small detail, as a stone, a cement affixed to it or half a partition wall, but is revealed to him who can view the whole and has understanding to appraise the proportions. We do not fear that, by the violence of some erring spirit or by the wrath of a thundering Jove, that which is accumulated in our world could become dispersed beyond this hollow sepulcher or cupola of the heavens, be shaken or scattered as dust beyond this starry mantle. In no other way could the nature of things be brought to nothing as to its substance than in appearance, as when the air which was compressed within the concavity of a bubble seems to one's own eyes to go forth into the void. For in the world as known to us, one thing succeeds ever to another thing, nor is there an ultimate depth from which as from the artificer's hand things flow to an inevitable nullity. There are no ends, boundaries, limits or walls which can defraud or deprive us of the infinite multitude of things. Therefore, the earth and the ocean thereof are fecund; therefore, the sun's blaze is everlasting so that eternally fuel is provided for the voracious fires, and moisture replenishes the attenuated seas. For from infinity is born an ever-fresh abundance of matter.

Thus, Democritus and Epicurus, who maintained that everything throughout infinity suffers renewal and restoration, understood these matters more truly than those who would at all costs maintain belief in the immutability of the universe, alleging a constant and unchanging number of particles of identical material that perpetually undergo transformation, one into another.

Make then your forecasts, my lords Astrologers, with your slavish physicians, by means of those astrolabes with which you seek to discern the fantastic nine moving spheres; in these you finally imprison your own minds so that you appear to me but as parrots in a cage, while I watch you dancing up and down, turning and hopping within those circles. We know that such a Supreme Ruler cannot have a seat so narrow, so miserable a throne, so straight a tribunal, so scant a court, so small and feeble a simulacrum that a phantasm can bring to birth, a dream shatter, a delusion restore, a chimera disperse, a calamity diminish, a misdeed abolish and a thought renew it again, so that indeed with a puff of air it were full to the brim and with a single gulp it were emptied. On the contrary, we recognize a noble image, a marvelous conception, a supreme figure, an exalted shadow, an infinite representation of the represented infinity, a spectacle worthy of the excellence and supremacy of Him who transcends understanding, comprehension or grasp. Thus is the excellence of God magnified and the greatness of his kingdom made manifest; he is glorified not in one, but in countless suns; not in a single earth, a single world, but in one-thousand thousands: I say, in an infinity of worlds.

Thus, not in vain is that power of the intellect which ever seeks and achieves the addition of space to space, mass to mass, unity to unity, number to number, by the science which discharges us from the fetters of a most narrow kingdom and promotes us to the freedom of a truly august realm, which frees us from an imagined poverty and adversity to the pos-

On the Infinite, Universe and Worlds

session of the myriad riches of so vast a space, of so worthy a field, of so many most cultivated worlds. This science does not permit that the arch of the horizon that our deluded vision imagines over the earth and that by our fantasy is feigned in the spacious ether, shall imprison our spirit under the custody of a Pluto or at the mercy of a Jove. We are spared the thought of so wealthy an owner and subsequently of so miserly, sordid and avaricious a donor. Nor need we accept nourishment from a nature so fecund and pregnant, and then so wretched, mean, and niggard in her fruit.

Very different are the worthy and honorable fruits which may be plucked from these trees, the precious and desirable harvests which may be reaped from the sowing of this seed. We will not recall these to mind that we may not excite the blind envy of our adversaries, but we leave them to the understanding and judgment of all who are able to comprehend and judge. These will easily build for themselves on the foundations we have given, the whole edifice of our philosophy whose parts indeed, if it shall please Him who governs and rules us and if the undertaking begun be not interrupted, we will reduce to the desired perfection. Then that which is inseminated in the Dialogues concerning *Cause, Principle and One* and has come to birth in these Dialogues on the *Infinite, Universe and Worlds* shall germinate in yet others, and in others shall grow and ripen, in yet other works shall enrich us with a precious harvest and shall satisfy us exceedingly. Then (having cleared out the tares, the darnels, and other accumulated weeds), we shall fill the stores of studious, and talented men with the best wheat that the soil we cultivate can produce.

Meanwhile (though I am sure it is unnecessary to commend him to you), I shall yet not omit as part of my duty truly to commend to you one whom you maintain among your court not as a man of whom you have need, but rather as a person who has need of you for many reasons you perceive. For, in having around you many who serve you, you differ in no wise from the common fold, bankers and merchants; but in maintaining one in some sort worthy to be advanced, defended and prospered, in this you have been (as you have indeed ever shown yourself) the peer of generous princes, of heroes and gods. These indeed have chosen such as you for the defense of their friends. And I would remind you, though such reminder is I know unnecessary, that when the end comes, you will be esteemed by the world and rewarded by God, not because you have won the love and respect of princes of the earth, however powerful, but rather for having loved, defended and cherished one man such as I have described. For those with fortune greater than yours can do nothing for you who exceed many among them in virtue, which will outlast all your trappings and tapestries. But your achievement for others may easily come to be inscribed in the book of eternity—either that which is seen on earth or that other which is believed to be in heaven. For that which you receive from others is a testimony to their virtue, but all that you do for others is the sign and clear indication of your own virtue.

Farewell.

21

FRANCISCO SUÁREZ
(1548–1617)

On Free-Will

SYDNEY PENNER

INTRODUCTION

Francisco Suárez was the foremost representative of the flourishing scholastic tradition centered in the Iberian peninsula. He was even designated the *doctor eximius* by Pope Paul V. Iberian scholasticism reached its peak in the Renaissance period, but its influence was felt around the world for centuries thereafter. Humanist ideas and practices, of course, had left their mark, including in Spain, by Suárez's time, and traces are found in his thought, which showed, for example, greater concern for original sources than earlier scholastics typically did.

Nonetheless, Suárez is obviously a scholastic in style and temperament, despite his chronological position. Aside from Aristotle, the authors with whom he most frequently engaged were paradigmatic scholastic authors such as Thomas Aquinas and John Duns Scotus. In fact, he claims always to be led by Aquinas. In keeping with his contemporaries' practice of commenting on Aquinas's *Summa theologiae* instead of Lombard's *Sentences*, most of Suárez's works are commentaries (in a broad sense) on the *Summa theologiae*. In that sense, his writings are certainly led by

334 FRANCISCO SUÁREZ

Aquinas. But the positions he defends are not always Aquinas's, including in some cases when he claims that they are. When addressing a question, Suárez will survey the full panoply of scholastic views: Thomist, Scotist, nominalist, and others. Sometimes, he settles on the Thomist answer, but sometimes he adopts other views. He also sometimes tries to chart a middle course. It is not without reason that he has often been called an eclectic philosopher.

Regardless which view Suárez finally adopts, he is almost without exception fair and judicious in his weighing of all the views. He almost never dismisses an alternative view quickly. This magisterial consideration leads to works of great length, but it is also precisely where Suárez's greatness as a philosopher is found. For concise articulations of overarching philosophical accounts of all reality, one should look elsewhere. For painstaking analysis and careful consideration of all the answers that have been given for specific questions, however, it is hard to find better than Suárez. In this sense, he is a philosopher's philosopher.

Suárez quickly became something of a father of Jesuit theology and philosophy. He was by no means the only prominent Jesuit voice; his rival Gabriel Vázquez (1549–1604) had considerable influence as well. But the influence of Suárez was pervasive in Jesuit writings for centuries after his death. His influence extended outside the Jesuit order, as well. Nearly every corner of Catholic scholarship was touched by his agenda and by his interpretations of Aquinas. Protestant universities, too, felt the force of Suárezian scholarship.

Suárez's best-known works, especially today, are his *Metaphysical Disputations* and *On Laws and God the Lawgiver*, but he also wrote several works contributing to the disputes raging in his day about how to understand human freedom next to divine foreknowledge, providence, and grace. These issues figured prominently in battles between Catholics and Protestants as well as battles within the ranks of both sides. On the Catholic side, the dispute reached its peak in the controversy *De auxiliis* between Dominicans and Jesuits. The papal tribunal convened to resolve the matter resulted in a stalemate.

No short excerpt from Suárez can do justice to his contributions to that debate. The attempts to defend the compatibility of human freewill and divine providence, without falling into one heresy or another, led to extraordinarily complex, subtle positions. But the following excerpt from *On Grace* provides a valuable glimpse of Suárez's position in this debate, including his defense of the famous understanding of freewill as requiring the freedom both to act and not to act once all the prerequisites of action have been posited. The excerpt exemplifies the careful analytical way in which Suárez proceeds, and it includes a taste of his extensive engagement with his predecessors and contemporaries.

To appreciate properly the extraordinary scope of Suárez's work, however, it should be kept in mind that this excerpt consists of a little more than one section of one of the six prolegomena to a work that fills four large volumes of his *Opera omnia*.[1]

BIBLIOGRAPHY

Primary Sources

Penner, Sydney. "Suárez in English Translation." Accessed June 17, 2021. http://sydneypenner.ca/SuarTr.shtml.

Suárez, Francisco. *On Efficient Causality:Metaphysical Disputations 17, 18, and 19.* Translated by Alfred J. Freddoso. New Haven, Conn.: Yale University Press, 1994.

———. *Opera Omnia.* Edited by M. André and C. Berton. 28 vols. Paris: Ludovicus Vivès, 1856–1878.

Secondary Sources

Bauer, Emmanuel J. "Francisco Suárez (1548–1617): Scholasticism after Humanism." In *Philosophers of the Renaissance*, edited by Paul Richard Blum, 236–55. Washington, D.C.: The Catholic University of America Press, 2010.

Maryks, Robert Aleksander, and Juan Antonio Senent de Frutos, eds. *Francisco Suárez (1548–1617): Jesuits and the Complexities of Modernity.* Leiden: Brill, 2019. Special issue, *Jesuit Studies* 22.

Mullaney, Thomas V. *Suárez on Human Freedom.* Baltimore: Carroll Press, 1950.

Penner, Sydney. "Free and Rational: Suárez on the Will." *Archiv für Geschichte der Philosophie* 95, no. 1 (2013): 1–35.

Schmutz, Jacob, and Sydney Penner. "Bibliography of Works on Francisco Suárez, 1850–Present." Accessed June 7, 2020. http://sydneypenner.ca/bib.shtml.

Schwartz, Daniel, ed. *Interpreting Suárez: Critical Essays.* Cambridge: Cambridge University Press, 2012.

---

1. The entirety of Suárez's *De gratia* can be found in vols. 7–10 of the *Opera omnia* (Paris: Vivès, 1857–58). The portion translated here is from vol. 7, 1–4, 10–16.

Scorraille, Raoul de. *François Suarez de la Compagnie de Jesus*. 2 vols. Paris: Lethielléux, 1912–13.

Shields, Christopher, and Daniel Schwartz. "Francisco Suárez." In *Stanford Encyclopedia of Philosophy*, edited by Edward N. Zalta. Accessed June 7, 2020. http://plato.stanford.edu/entries/suarez/.

FRANCISCO SUÀREZ

On Free-Will

DE GRATIA, PROLOGUE 1[2]

Chapter 1: On the Names 'Nature' and 'Freewill.'

Introduction: Freewill and Grace

1. Since free nature is the foundation of grace and grace is the perfection and health of nature, a discussion of grace presupposes some knowledge of such a nature. This is the reason why grace and nature or freewill[3] are usually conjoined not just in the same disputation but in the title of the whole work. Augustine, for example, wrote one book entitled *On Nature and Grace* and another one *On Grace and Freewill*. For this reason, therefore, it is necessary that in taking up this subject we first set out what we understand by the names "nature" and "freewill." For philosophers discuss nature in books examining Aristotle's *Physics* insofar as it is the principle of motion and rest. But at present we are not taking 'nature' that broadly but are taking it as it is said through antonomasia of intellectual or rational nature, which is the principle of the moral operations by which eternal happiness is secured or lost. Only intellectual nature is ordered to this end through grace. For this reason, Augustine said in *Against Julian* IV,

---

2. My thanks to Shane Duarte for valuable comments on an earlier version of this translation. Modern verse numbers are added to Bible references without flagging the additions. Likewise, in some places, terms left implicit in the Latin text are silently added to the English translation.

3. I take '*liberum arbitrium*' as a technical term naming the item under dispute. The equivalent term in contemporary philosophy might be 'freedom of the will,' though it has the disadvantage of already suggesting a theory as to which faculty would provide us with this freedom. I will translate '*liberum arbitrium*' with 'freewill' as a single word and reserve 'freedom of the will' for places where it is clear that it is the *will's* freedom that is being considered.

ch. 3, that only rational nature has the capacity for grace. But he is speaking about rational nature insofar as it includes intellectual nature, since angelic nature as well as human nature has the capacity for divine grace, since each is free.

"But grace," as Bernard says in *On Grace and Freewill*, "cannot be given except by God and cannot be received except by freewill," that is, by a free nature. For a free nature is required in order to achieve a supernatural end. But since human nature both is more familiar to us than angelic nature and is in need of grace under more headings and ways, we will always make our discussion about rational nature. But the doctrine could easily be applied proportionately to angelic nature. For it will not be difficult to realize where the basis of difference comes up and we will take care to indicate it. Moreover, we are not now talking about human nature as distinguished from the supposit nor about that more-than-human state that it obtains in the divine Word through the hypostatic union. For the former consideration of nature is metaphysical and in no way pertains to the present subject, whereas the consideration of the latter mystery is loftier, and we have pursued it in its proper place to the extent we are able. In the present place, then, we are considering human nature insofar as it is capable of grace in a created person, and insofar as grace is necessary for it to operate well and attain its end.

2. It should further be noted that grace perfects nature, especially insofar as it is the principle of human and free acts. Hence, the result is that freewill and grace are so joined together in disposition and function that they cannot be separated in discussion, as Augustine indicated well enough in saying: "If there is not the grace of God, how does Christ save the world? And if there is not freewill, how does he judge the world?" And in *Hypognosticon* III, ch. 11, he says: "Grace without freewill does not make a human being have a happy life and neither does freewill without grace." Bernard says in *On Grace and Freewill*: "Take away freewill and there is nothing to be saved; take away grace and there is nothing by which to be saved." Hence, the primary difficulty in this matter is situated in reconciling the necessity and efficacy of grace with freewill. Ignorance of this concordance has been the root and origin of almost all the errors that have been made in this matter. It is necessary, therefore, first to deal with what

338   FRANCISCO SUÁREZ

is signified by the names 'freedom' and 'freewill' before discussing the signification of 'grace.'

Three Kinds of Freedom

3. In the first place, a distinction needs to be made between three kinds of freedom. Hugh of Saint Victor makes the distinction this way in *Summa sententiarum* tr. 3, ch. 9: "For freedom is threefold: from necessity, from sin, and from suffering." But we number the members differently, for there is freedom from servitude, from coercion, and from necessity. Of these, only the third kind is the proper moral freedom necessary for human acts to deserve praise and reprimand, rewards and punishments. Hence, it alone deserves the name "freedom" strictly speaking.

For the others are called freedoms only insofar as they are opposed to some kind of necessity. For servitude brings in a kind of necessity of obeying, and for this reason the absence of servitude is called freedom in Romans 8:21: "the creature itself shall be freed from the servitude of corruption." Servitude, moreover, can be to sin or to punishment, and so the absence of guilt and the remission of punishments can be called a kind of freedom from sin or from servitude to sin, as in Romans 6:20–22: "For when you were servants of sin, you were free of justice … but now having been freed from sin and having been made servants of God, you have your fruit unto sanctification." And in 2 Corinthians 3:17: "where the Spirit of the Lord is, there is freedom." Hence, Augustine also said in *The City of God* IV, ch. 3: "the good man, even if he serves, at least if he serves another man, is free," namely, from sin; "but an evil man is a servant even if he reigns," namely, of sin. And in the same way he says in *The City of God* XIV, ch. 15, that the first man by sinning lost the freedom that he craved. For it was not freedom from necessity that he had craved, for he had that from the beginning and he had not lost it. But he desired freedom from subjection and this he lost, since he was made a servant of sin, punishment, and suffering, and he contracted a disordering of concupiscence and a battle of lust, which is a kind of penal servitude. Every absence of obligation or of debt—whether it arises from a law or from any other cause—is traced back to this signification. For thus a dispensation or exemption from a law is thought to be a kind of freedom. Hence, a privilege is also usually given

On Free-Will

the name "freedom," and someone for whom some debt is remitted is said to be freed from that debt.

But if someone were to consider the matter rightly, this entire freedom presupposes a proper freedom from necessity. For only a person who is free in acting has the capacity for proper servitude, guilt, punishment, command, or obligation. For this reason, just as a proper privation presupposes an aptitude, so also servitude and obligation presuppose a person apt for operating with indifference and without necessity. But since operations free from necessity can be under the right of another or under some burden and obligation, therefore the necessity of servitude and of obligation can exist in works along with freedom from necessity. Or, what comes to the same thing, someone can be deprived through law or servitude of the freedom that is contrary to them, and yet retain the proper freedom of works.

Coercion and Violence

4. What is coerced is almost the same thing as what is subject to the violent, for each goes against the internal appetite of the patient or of the one operating. But violent is said more generally of any motion contrary to appetite, whether elicited or innate, whereas [a motion] is properly called coerced when it is in conflict with an elicited and vital appetite, although sometimes those terms are confused. Two things, therefore, are required for coerced motion: that it comes to be or be endured of necessity, and that it be contrary to an internal affect. And thus coercion is a kind of necessity and adds something to it. Both are gathered from Aristotle, *Nicomachean Ethics* III, ch. 1, where he says: "the violent is from something extrinsic, without the patient contributing force," that is, while resisting in some way, as everyone explains it in accordance with what the same Aristotle says in *Eudemian Ethics* II, ch. 8. For if what is suffered is not resisted, the motion will not be violent even if it arises from something extrinsic. The coerced, therefore, insofar as it is such cannot be from something intrinsic. Otherwise, it would not be contrary to one's own inclination. But if it is from something extrinsic, it is by that fact necessary. For freedom from necessity is not found in undergoing but in acting, as I will prove below. For this reason, therefore, the coerced includes necessity, and what is not

free of coercion, insofar as it is such, cannot be exempt from necessity. But on account of other conditions the coerced is not interchangeable with the necessary. For there are many things that are necessary that are not contrary to internal appetite. In fact, necessary things often arise from internal appetite. For the same reason freedom that excludes necessity is more universal than freedom that is opposed to coercion alone. For every freedom from necessity is also exempt from coercion, but not the other way around, as is self-evident. For the love for God in the afterlife is free from coercion, yet not free from necessity.

5. Therefore, freedom from coercion alone only requires the absence of violence in such a way that a motion that is called free in this way is not contrary to internal appetite, whether or not it happens by necessity. But such a motion, assuming it is of the will, should be called voluntary rather than free. For these two properties in acts of the will are distinct and so they should also be distinguished by names, lest an ambiguity in words render the discussion uncertain. It is possible, therefore, for an act of a human being to be voluntary and thereby free from coercion that, nevertheless, is strictly speaking not free of necessity. One can see this in the love by which God loves himself and by which he produces the Holy Spirit and in the love with which the blessed love God, as well as in undeliberated acts of the will and in the affects of an appetite of someone who is sensing. The reason is sufficiently clear from what has been said, along with these additional points made by Aristotle and St. Thomas about the nature of the voluntary. For something is called voluntary that comes from an internal principle together with cognition. That whole nature can be found in an act even though it comes to be by necessity, since necessity alone excludes neither cognition nor conformity to an innate or elicited appetite. Here, also, is the source for that doctrine common among the theologians that force or coercion cannot be inflicted on the will in the case of elicited acts even if it can suffer necessity. For coercion excludes the voluntary, since it is directly opposed to that, but an act cannot be from the will and not be voluntary, since it cannot fail to be from an intrinsic principle together with cognition. Nor can it simultaneously be voluntary and coerced, since these two are opposed and involve an immediate contradiction. Necessity, however, does not involve that opposition to the voluntary, since necessity itself can be voluntary or conform to an internal appetite, as was said.

Two Clarifications

6. But two things should be noticed in this regarding the way of speaking, since they will be necessary for understanding the views of the Fathers. One is that coercion is of two kinds. One is coercion in a strict sense, which imposes an absolute and inevitable necessity against an internal affection. The other is coercion in a qualified sense, which is the kind that comes from punishments and fears. They do not introduce an absolute necessity but only a qualified necessity, namely, in order to avoid some disadvantage. The former, therefore, is the coercion that is entirely repugnant to an elicited act of the will, since the very fact that it is elicited makes it not coerced. But the latter kind of coercion is compatible with an absolute willing, in fact, even with freedom, since it does not introduce an absolute necessity. For this reason, although it is sometimes called coercion or violence, as is clear from Augustine, *Against Gaudentius* I, ch. 25, and Letter 48, it is not, strictly speaking and absolutely, coercion. Rather, it is a prohibition of doing some evil, as Augustine also said in *Against the Letters of Petilianus* II, ch. 83.

7. The other thing that should be noted is that sometimes a voluntary act is strictly necessary in such a way that the necessity itself is from something intrinsic and so it is conformed to the inclination and to the natural perfection of the will itself. In this case the act, although it is necessary, is voluntary in such a way that it can in no way be called coerced or violent, since it is in no way repugnant to an internal appetite. It is not repugnant either to an elicited appetite because the act, as it is being imagined, is voluntary, or to an innate appetite because the necessity itself is also not contrary to the will or to its innate inclination as it is being imagined. In this way the love for God in the blessed is necessary without any kind of coercion or violence. The affected appetites of someone sensing can also be placed in the same order for the same reason.

But sometimes a voluntary act can be necessary only from an extrinsic principle effecting or, as it were, impelling the will to act. In this case, although the act is voluntary and for that reason cannot be called absolutely coerced, nevertheless, since the necessity itself is not conformed to the natural condition and inclination of the will as a result of the fact that the necessity is only from an extrinsic principle, an act necessary in this way

340   FRANCISCO SUÁREZ

is sometimes wont to be called violent in some way, at least in a qualified sense. For it is contrary to a connatural mode and contrary to a certain innate appetite. And in this way the necessity put into the will in the case of acts that are free of themselves is customarily called a kind of coercion by the Fathers. Conversely, an act that is strictly free is usually called spontaneous and voluntary, at any rate perfectly so, and excluding the extrinsic necessity repugnant to the internal appetite or inclination of the will.

Freewill as a Faculty

8. Therefore, at present that is called free which is free from necessity. Moreover, it is customarily said both of the faculty operating without necessity and of the action itself. In the former way freewill is denominated, which is said to be *a faculty of the will and of reason*, at least when operating with indifference and with dominion over the action so that it is in one's hands either to will or not to will to exercise or to undergo the action. In *On the Merits and Forgiveness of Sins* II, ch. 18, Augustine said about this: "It is the decision of the will, which is freely turned to this or to that, and has its place among those natural goods which a human being can use well or badly." In this sense it is certain in the faith that human beings by their nature are free in this way or have some faculty free from necessity in their works, not only in their natural works but also their supernatural works. The Council of Trent clearly settles this in the Sixth Session (ch. 5 and canons 5 and 9). Augustine proves it thoroughly from Scripture and by arguments in *On Grace and Freewill,* and the moderns even more thoroughly when writing about this subject. We dealt with it more briefly in the beginning of Book I of *De auxilio.* But the erudite *Disputations* of Cardinal Bellarmine may especially be consulted in the whole controversy about grace and freewill along with the preface.

Free Acts

9. Hence the act which proceeds from this free faculty is also denominated free, but it must proceed from that faculty insofar as it is indifferent. For there is no lack of modern Catholics who deny that indifference or the absence of necessity is necessary for freedom of action, but say that the absence of coercion is enough. But this view was among Michael Baius's condemned assertions (assertions 39 and 41) and will be refuted ex-

On Free-Will   343

plicitly in Book III. Therefore, in order for an act to be truly free, it is not enough that it is voluntary or not coerced, but it must also not be strictly necessary, and, accordingly, it must proceed from a free power that retains its indifference and freedom and that in its very use and exercise it be allowed to operate with its free and undiminished power, so that it is in its hands to choose between contraries or contradictories, either to act or not to act. For in order for an act to be free it is necessary that it proceed from a free faculty insofar as it is free. But an act will not proceed from a free power insofar as it is such unless it has its faculty unencumbered with respect to either part, at least with respect to acting and to not acting. For of what advantage to the freedom of such an act is a power that has an innate indifference if that indifference is impeded in that use?

Therefore, assuming the distinction given between two kinds of necessity—one from an intrinsic principle through a natural determination of the power to one object, the other from an extrinsic principle through the impulse of some extrinsic agent—the former is repugnant not only to the act but also to the faculty of freewill. Therefore, it cannot happen that a power subjected to such necessity is free with respect to the same object, since that involves a contradiction, as is self-evident. But the latter necessity is not repugnant to a free faculty, as I assume for now and as I will prove a little later, but it is repugnant to free acts.

[...]⁴

Chapter 3: Whether a Power That After All the
Prerequisites for Acting Have Been Posited Can Both
Act and Not Act Is Rightly Described as Being Free

The Composed Sense and Divided Sense of 'Can'

1. One should know that it is usual to take that word "can" in the characterization [of a free power as "a power that after all the prerequisites for acting have been posited can both act and not act"] in two ways, namely, in a composed sense or in a divided sense. That is, either such that both acting and not acting are compatible with all those prerequisites, or such that with those prerequisites standing the power retains its complete freedom

---

4. This excerpt does not include chapter 2.

yet cannot use it for not acting except with the removal of some one of the stated prerequisites.

2. The first way of interpreting or restricting that characterization, then, is (if the word 'can' is taken in the composed sense) that it should be restricted to the prerequisites on the part of secondary causes—such as the intellect, the object, the imagination, and anything else that is similar— and it should not be extended to the prerequisites on the part of God. This is both [i] because a previous concurrence on the part of God is necessary, yet once it has been posited the will cannot both act and not act, but can only act, and also [ii] because the willing by which God wills freewill to operate is necessary for freewill to operate, and it is one of the prerequisites since it precedes the act itself and the determination of the created will. Once that willing by God has been posited, it does not remain possible for the created free will not to operate. It is necessary, therefore, to remove the prerequisites on the part of the first cause from that characterization.

[...]

3. The second way of restricting that characterization is so that if it is understood to include all prerequisites or necessary conditions, both on the part of God and on the part of the other causes, the word 'can' should be taken in the divided sense rather than the composed sense, with respect to each act of acting and not acting, which also are taken separately or individually. Thus the sense is that that power is free which still retains in itself the power not to act once all the prerequisites are posited, even though it is not possible for it to not act when all those prerequisites obtain. Rather, some one of those prerequisites must be removed in order for the free power to use its capacity for not acting. In a similar way when such a power does not act or does not will, it retains the capacity to act, and for that reason it is free, although it cannot conjoin that action or volition with precisely those prerequisites that concur in the case where it does not will, unless something that is absent is added and surpasses the order of nature or of causality.

[...]

Will Compared to Intellect

6. We can make both clear by comparing intellect and will. For intellect also has the capacity to act and not act, to believe and not believe, or to

On Free-Will

dissent and assent, and yet it is not formally free as the will is. It is necessary, then, to explain this difference in the definition of freewill. That cannot happen without the phrase "after all the prerequisites for acting have been posited." For we assume that freewill is neither multiple powers taken separately nor a collection of powers, but is one power alone that is the controller of its acts. But to be a capacity to do one thing and to do its opposite or to act and not to act applies not just to one power but to many, as was said about the intellect. It applies in its way even to the sensitive appetite, and much more to the will. Therefore, this capacity for either, taken in a general and imprecise way, does not explain the peculiar nature of this unique and simple power that is freewill, nor the proper nature through which it is constituted in the nature of a formally free power. In order to explain this kind of power, therefore, one rightly adds that it is a power that has the capacity to act and not to act after all the prerequisites for acting have been posited. For it is through this last phrase that one best explains the intrinsic force of a free power to elicit or sustain an act through its power alone and not just as the result of the absence of some condition necessary for acting or for not acting.

7. Hence, since this way of operating applies only to the will, it for that reason is formally free and is freewill. The intellect, however, does not have this intrinsic faculty indifferent in such a way that it can determine itself to act or to suspend that act or to determine itself to an opposite act. For if the truth of the object is evident and it is sufficiently proposed, the intellect gives assent by a natural necessity. But if it is not evident but only appears probable or credible, the intellect cannot determine itself except by the intercession of will (as is certain in the case of Christian faith and the same is true with proportion in human cases). Even in that case no intellect, once all the prerequisites for acting have been posited, can both act and not act, since one of the prerequisites for acting is that it be moved by the will. By positing such a motion it cannot fail to act, but if it is not posited then it necessarily does not act, not so much from a power for not acting but from an inability to act. But the will, once all the prerequisites for acting have been posited, just as it can act from an internal capacity for determining itself without the motion of another power, so also from the same internal capacity it can not act, by suspending its influence with its internal power and control. By the same capacity, it can also do something else

FRANCISCO SUÁREZ

or do a contrary thing, if on the part of the object a sufficient proposal of each option was made.

[...]

Characterization of Freewill Should Be Understood in Composed Sense

8. Second, from this we say that that characterization should be understood in the composed sense, just as it is understood by all the authors who touch on it. This is easily proven, because that something is able not to act in the divided sense once all the prerequisites for acting have been posited—that is, that it retain the capacity for not acting with the removal of some condition among the prerequisites—is not distinctive of a free power but applies to anything acting naturally. For the sun also illuminates in that way with all the prerequisites concurring, so that it is able not to illuminate if the windows are closed, and the eye sees an object that is imprinting a species but is ready to lack that vision if the species is removed. And the intellect itself that believes as long as it is moved by the will is able not to believe if the will either ceases to move it or inclines it to some contrary act. For it does not lose its power in first act that it has innately for either act when it is applied to believing by the will. Therefore, once all the prerequisites have been posited, the power not to believe or to dissent still exists in the divided sense. That, then, is not enough for a power to be formally free. Or it must be said that the intellect is a formally free power. But that is not true and is not granted by the mentioned authors. Therefore, in order to explain the formal freedom of the will through those words, it is necessary that they be taken in the composed sense.

9. The same argument can be taken from the will itself. For in the blessed state, the blessed do not love God freely but love him necessarily, since once the prerequisites for that love have been posited, they cannot not love in the composed sense, yet here also they retain the power not to love in the divided sense. For if the vision that is a prerequisite for that love were removed, the will would be able to cease from that love. [...]

10. Finally, reason establishes this part, since not just any power for acting and not acting suffices for freedom, but only that which results from an internal capacity and eminent power and control (as I showed in the previous chapter). On the other hand, to operate in such a way that once all the

On Free-Will   347

prerequisites for acting have been posited the faculty can only cease from operation in the divided sense—that is, by removing something from the prerequisites—is not to be able to cease by virtue of an internal power and control over the action. Therefore, it is not enough for freedom. The minor is proven: for in that case it would not cease in virtue of a power for not acting but in virtue of an inability to act, namely, because no cause has the strength to act without all the prerequisites for acting having been posited.

It is confirmed, for otherwise after the will begins to will once all the prerequisites have been posited, it could not spontaneously cease from the actual willing as long as the same prerequisites stand. It would be necessary that something be removed from the prerequisites in order to cease from that willing. But this is both contrary to experience and contrary to the use of freedom. Therefore.

[...]

Characterization Should Be Understood as
Applying to All Prerequisites of Action

12. I say, third: that characterization should be understood to be about all the prerequisites, whether on the part of God or on the part of other causes. Unless understood in that way, it is not sufficient for defining freedom, so that it can advance to a free act from a use of that freedom.

[...]

Thus explained, therefore, the assumption is proven specifically with respect to the prerequisite on the part of God that is taken out of the general characterization and is called the motion of God. For if that motion is one of the prerequisites and necessary without qualification for the will to operate and if once it is posited the power not to operate does not remain in the will except in the divided sense, then, once that prerequisite has been posited, the will is not in proximate potency for not acting but only in remote potency, since it is necessary that that motion first be removed by him who posited it. For the will itself cannot remove it, since just as it was not made by the will, so also it does not depend on the will except as on a receiving subject. The duration of a passion is not in the power of the receiving subject just as the passion's inception is not in its power, as was shown in ch. 2. Therefore, that power in the divided sense is not a power sufficient for free use, since there is no free use except by a proximate power, as I also proved. Therefore, the freedom not to act does not remain in a will moved in that way, and, consequently, neither is the acting itself free. For the same reason, as long as that motion is not given to the will, the will's power to act is only remote and on the receptive side. For it must first receive that motion, which is not in its active power but only in its receptive power. Therefore, then it is not in a free power to not act, but in necessity [to not act] and in an inability to act. Therefore, in order to save freedom even with respect to the previous prerequisite of divine motion, it is necessary (since it is also posited along with the other prerequisites) that the power for acting and not acting remain in the composed sense.

13. This is confirmed and explained by analogy to, for example, the power of writing that is in the hand. For it of itself is also the power not to write and yet is not free. For it can neither write without an action of the will nor can it in the composed sense not write when the motion of the will is posited, although remotely and in the divided sense it can (at least if the will removes its motion). Therefore, in a similar way if the will cannot will except when moved by God and with that motion posited cannot compose an absence of volition with that motion (although in the divided sense, that is, with that motion removed, it could not will), it is no more a free power than the moving power that is in the hand. It is similar with the intellect with respect to the power of assenting or dissenting through faith. For it is not formally free in this, since it can neither assent except when moved by the will nor can it in the composed sense fail to assent when it is moved by the will, but only in the divided sense, which division (if I may speak in this way) is not in its active power. Therefore, if the will of a human being is related to the prior motion of God in such a way that it cannot will without that motion and once that motion is posited it cannot not will except in the divided sense (which is not in its active power), then surely the will is no more free than the intellect. For it cannot itself actively remove the motion of God just as it cannot produce it. For what difference does it make that one motion is from a created will and another from an uncreated will? Surely the latter blocks freedom more, since the motion of an uncreated will is more efficacious, deeper, and has more of a direct influx into the effect.

[...]

15. [...] Therefore, in order to save true freedom the composed sense is universally and without exception necessary with respect to everything

that is properly a prerequisite for acting, whether on the part of secondary causes or on the part of God.

Response to Objection Concerning God's Concurrence

16. In response to the foundation of the contrary view, we deny the first part concerning the prior concurrence. For a simultaneous one suffices, which as it is given in the thing itself is not among the prerequisites for willing but is a concomitant. With that the use of freedom is involved. But insofar as it is only in first act, it is among the prerequisites. Nevertheless, when in that state it is posited or offered on the part of God, it can at the same time be composed with the absence of the act for which the offered concurrence in the first act is presupposed.

The same thing should be said about the other part concerning the will of God. For we concede that some willing of God is prior to the human being's volition, and yet we say that at the same time not to act and to act can be composed with that willing, since it is not necessary for there to be an absolute willing that such an act occur and be posited in reality, as Soto rightly says in *On Nature and Grace* I, ch. 16. Rather, a willing that includes some condition—namely, a willing concurring with the freewill of a human being to this or that act if he himself wills to cooperate, which always remains in his hand and in his power—is sufficient. For this reason the important theologians rightly said that although the will of God precede from eternity, nevertheless, its volition as it is determined to willing to concur with a created will to such an act is not a preceding willing but a concomitant one. But this concomitance seems to consist in the object of that divine will, by which it wills to concur with a human will. For it does not will the act of the human will without qualification and absolutely through that volition, but wills it as co-effecting with the human will and, as it were, under the condition "if the human will itself wills to cooperate." For this reason such a willing by God cannot perform anything through itself alone nor before the created will simultaneously brings about the effect. And thus it is easily understood how those two wills are simultaneously conjoined to the same action. For the divine will is prepared, as it were, from eternity and has its power applied to co-acting with the human will. Hence, when in the temporal order the human will through its freedom is conjoined to the divine will, they together bring about the effect.

22

TOMMASO CAMPANELLA
(1568–1639)

Soul, Intellect, and Body

ELISABETH BLUM

INTRODUCTION

Tommaso Campanella can be read as the last of the Renaissance philosophers since he embraced the anthropocentric perspective of the humanists, Neoplatonic metaphysics, and the tools of secular Aristotelianism; on the other hand, through his works, he paved the way to philosophy based on human reason, as advocated by Francis Bacon, René Descartes, and Galileo Galilei. He was born in 1568 in Stilo, Calabria (southern Italy, part of the Spanish Empire). His father was a poor cobbler. Baptized Giovan Domenico, he took on the name Tommaso when he entered the Dominican Order, where he obtained his education.

He was impressed early on by the works of the natural philosophers Bernardino Telesio, Giambattista Della Porta, and Galileo. In 1594, he was denounced to the Inquisition and condemned as a heretic. After his release, he joined a conspiracy against the Spanish government and was arrested in November 1599; he spent life in various prisons until 1626. In 1634, he fled to France and was protected by King Louis XIII and Cardinal Richelieu. He died in 1639. Before and after his incarceration, but notably

Soul, Intellect, and Body

while also in prison, Campanella wrote, and frequently rewrote, his numerous books. While imprisoned in Rome, he might have encountered Giordano Bruno, whose philosophy greatly influenced his own thought.

Campanella's philosophy covers philosophy of nature and metaphysics, epistemology, as well as the humanities, politics, religion, and natural theology. He wrote in conventional treatises, a utopia (*The City of the Sun* being his best-known work)—both in Latin and Italian—and philosophical poems with commentaries. The philosophy of nature proclaims that sense is present in all things as the common condition for things to be observed, understood, and meaningful. This was inspired by Bernardino Telesio, whom Campanella admired and defended against criticism. The universal principle of all things that is present in all of Campanella's works is the triad of power, wisdom, and love (termed primalities): transferred from Christian theology of the Trinity to every being, these primalities explain the structure of reality, the relation and hierarchy of things, as well as the ability of the human mind to understand the truth. In his *The City of the Sun*, the magistrates Power, Wisdom, and Love, under the guidance of the Metaphysic, govern society regarding order, education, and community. Religion is, therefore, a natural feature in all animate beings and the power of the human mind. Hence, religion is not, as argued by Machiavelli, whom Campanella repeatedly attacks, a ruse that is subservient to politics. In his *Ateismo trionfato* (*Atheism conquered*), Campanella compares various religions and cults in order to show that rationality is in harmony with the divine revelation, which is best fulfilled in Christianity. In several works he advocated for the cooperation of worldly powers (like Spain or France) with the leader of the Christian world, the Pope. In 1616, Campanella (still in prison) was the only philosopher to defend Galileo, who was under attack for his Copernican astronomy. Although he disagreed with the astronomer's mathematical method, he defended the new approach to abolish the scholastic linkage of Aristotelian physics with biblical revelation, thus claiming "freedom to philosophize."

We chose the following excerpts from book 4 of Campanella's *De homine* (On Man), a theological work, because they are representative of his thought in various important ways. They show his penchant toward naturalism as well as his endeavor to reconcile his philosophy with the fundamental teachings of Christian theology; his critical stance toward the

352 TOMMASO CAMPANELLA

scholastic reading of Aristotle and his own metaphysical assumptions (panpsychism, the trinitarian structure of all existing things) are also evident. We see an original evaluation of the soul and mind, where rationality is a common trait of all animals, abstract thought is just imperfect sensation, and knowledge of the universal is the vague beginning of real knowledge, which is of the individual. The excellence of man is still asserted, obviously not based on the exclusive possession of a rational soul but rather on a separate mind with a direct connection to the divine.

BIBLIOGRAPHY

Primary Sources

Campanella, Tommaso. *A Defense of Galileo, the Mathematician from Florence.* Translated by Richard J. Blackwell. Notre Dame, Ind.: University of Notre Dame Press, 1994.

———. *Atheismus triumphatus. L'ateismo trionfato, overo riconoscimento filosofico della religione universale contra l'antichristianesmo macchiavellesco.* Edited by Germana Ernst. 2 vols. Pisa: Scuola normale superiore, 2004.

———. *Compendio di filosofia della natura.* Edited by Germana Ernst and Paolo Ponzio. Santarcangelo di Romagna: Rusconi, 1999.

———. *De homine.* Edited and translated by Romano Amerio. Inediti Theologicorum liber IV. Roma: Centro internazionale di studi umanistici, 1960.

———. *Del senso delle cose e della magia.* Edited by Germana Ernst. Bari: Laterza, 2007.

———. *Economica. Questioni economiche.* Edited and translated by Germana Ernst. Pisa: Serra, 2016.

———. *Ethica. Quaestiones super ethicam.* Edited by Germana Ernst. Pisa: Edizioni della Normale, 2011.

———. *Inediti theologicorum.* Edited by Romano Amerio et al. Firenze: Vallecchi; Centro internazionale di studi umanistici, 1949ff.

———. *La città del sole: Dialogo poetico. The City of the Sun: A Poetical Dialogue.* Translated by Daniel J. Donno. Berkeley: University of California Press, 1981.

———. *La città del sole (Nuova edizione).* Edited by Luigi Firpo, Germana Ernst, and Laura Salvetti Firpo. Bari: Laterza, 1997.

———. *Metafisica: Universalis Philosophiae seu Metaphysicarum rerum iuxta propria dogmata. Liber I.* Translated by Paolo Ponzio. Bari: Levante, 1994.

———. *Opera latina Francofurti impressa annis 1617–1630.* Edited by Luigi Firpo. 2 vols. Torino: Bottega d'Erasmo, 1975.

———. [*Philosophia realis.*] *Disputationum in quatuor partes suae Philosophiae realis libri quatuor.* [...] *Suorum operum tomus II* [...] *Physiol., Ethica, Politica, Oeconomica, cum quaest.* Parisiis: Houssaye, 1637.

———. *Selected Philosophical Poems*. Edited and translated by Sherry Roush. English and Italian. Pisa: Serra, 2011.

———. *Selected Philosophical Poems of Tommaso Campanella. A Bilingual Edition*. Translated by Sherry Roush. Chicago: University of Chicago Press, 2011.

Secondary Literature

Ernst, Germana. "Tommaso Campanella." In *The Stanford Encyclopedia of Philosophy*, edited by Edward N. Zalta (Fall 2014). Stanford, Calif.: Metaphysics Research Lab, Stanford University, 2014. https://plato.stanford.edu/archives/fall2014/entries/campanella/.

———. "Tommaso Campanella (1568–1639). The Revolution of Knowledge from the Prison." In *Philosophers of the Renaissance*, edited by Paul Richard Blum, and translated by Brian McNeil 256–74. Washington, D.C: The Catholic University of America Press, 2010.

———. *Tommaso Campanella: The Book and the Body of Nature*. Dordrecht: Springer, 2010.

Firpo, Luigi. *I processi di Tommaso Campanella*. Edited by Eugenio Canone. Roma: Salerno, 1998.

Headley, John M. *Tommaso Campanella and the Transformation of the World*. E-Book, Original 1997. Princeton, N.J.: Princeton University Press, 2019.

Ricci, Saverio. *Campanella. Apocalisse e governo universale*. Roma: Salerno, 2018.

Roush, Sherry. *Hermes' Lyre: Italian Poetic Self-Commentary from Dante to Tommaso Campanella*. Toronto Italian Studies. Toronto: University of Toronto Press, 2002.

Journal

Bruniana & Campanelliana since 1995.

Online Resource

"Archivio Tommaso Campanella." Accessed February 24, 2020. Digitized texts and material. http://www.iliesi.cnr.it/ATC/.

354   TOMMASO CAMPANELLA

TOMMASO CAMPANELLA

Soul, Intellect, and Body[1]

THE SOUL, AND FIRST ABOUT THE SENSITIVE
SOUL AND ITS FUNCTIONS

*In the plants there is a sensitive soul, nor does the vegetative soul lack that
same sensitive faculty. The vegetative, irascible, appetitive, and motive faculties
altogether arise from the primalities.[2] The sense and corporeal spirit is just a
single one, but the exterior sensory recipients and functions of that spirit are
multiple. Not so, however, the temperament or form of the sensory recipients,
nor are there several organs of the inner sense. Instead, all are functions of one
and the same spirit: for instance, memory is anticipated sensation and passion
that, like a scar, renews the remembrance of an object by another similar object;
the imaginative faculty is the conjunction and dissection of past sensations, and
the making up of new ones in analogy to these; reason is also a sensation concerning the similar; Aristotle's "intellection" is a long-distance sense, or tenuous
sensation that cannot attain the impression of particulars. Further follow some
inquiries on the human soul according to our philosophy.*

In *Questions on Physics*[3] we have shown that the sensitive and the vegetative soul are one and the same, and that plants do sense the useful or
harmful nourishment, absorbing the first and rejecting the latter. They
could not be nourished without a sense of touch or without a sense of taste.
They lack the other sense organs that are affected by objects from a long

---

1. Tommaso Campanella, *De homine*, ed. and trans. Romano Amerio. Inediti Theologicorum IV (Roma: Centro internazionale di studi umanistici, 1960), 24–34, 76–88. This
excerpt translated by Elisabeth Blum. Paragraphs in italics are summaries by Campanella.
The overall heading is ours. We refrain from providing citations for references in the text,
which would exceed the purpose of the anthology.

2. *Primalitates* (primalities) is a term coined by Campanella for the universal fundamental principles of all being, Power, Wisdom, and Love. From the inner dynamics of the
Divine Trinity, they are infused into all created things as the indispensable conditions for
their being what they are: in order to exist, a thing must have the power to be itself, must
know itself, and love this power and knowledge.

3. *Quaestiones physiologicae* is part 2 of Campanella's *Philosophia realis*, Paris 1637; the
quaestiones LIII–LVIII, 495–563, deal with the human soul. The same issues, referring to
the same sources, had already been treated in his *Philosophia realis*, 1623, in *Opera latina*,
1975, vol. 2, pt. 1, 161–98.

Soul, Intellect, and Body

distance, since they are fed by the sap of the earth and do not need motion for seeking or fleeing, as they are defended by their own hardness.

For the mobile animals, however, it is obvious that the digestion and distribution of nourishment cannot be achieved without sense: neither the distinction of what must be excreted from what is useful, nor the extraction of the latter and expulsion of the former, to which the vegetative soul is also stimulated by the bile, as if it felt the spur and angrily ejected the excrements together with the bile.

As to the veneric sense, nobody can deny that we cannot attribute to a senseless soul either the distinction of the beautiful from what is not beautiful, or the care for that immortality, which is obtained through the works of Venus. Moreover, obviously mere imagination can move the sex organ, and well-conceived fear can depress its erection—not a feat for a senseless soul! Therefore, Galen was wrong in believing that the appetitive soul was deprived of sense. We argued against him there, with the support of St. Ambrose's authority.

We also said that the irascible soul is highly sensible, since we are immediately incensed by the awareness of contempt, while not urged towards revenge by blows inflicted unwittingly, or by our father. To recognize contempt is, indeed, the task for a soul well-endowed with imagination. Moreover, striving for realms and governing them belongs to the rational soul, while Galen erroneously attributes it to a senseless irascible soul.

Indeed, we reduce all the so-called potencies of the soul to these three (vegetative, irascible, and sensitive), since the *appetitive* that Aristotle added belongs to the vegetative, the *locomotive* belongs to the sensitive and to the irascible, while the *intellective* belongs either to the sensitive, or to the mind that comes from beyond. Every faculty, however, relates to the three primalities, either to power, or to wisdom, or to love; and as these three constitute the sensitive soul, all its potencies can be reduced to them. Motion, namely, is power; all cognition is wisdom; every appetite of the sentient soul is an act of the innate love.

We have also said that the exterior sense has different sense organs, while the sentient soul is but one. Otherwise it could not compare the objects of one sense organ with those of the others and notice their differences and agreements. Indeed, sight and hearing would be separate like me and you. If you perceived the color of some object, and I the sound, neither

I nor you would be able to make a judgement about the underlying object of either, while it is evident that the sentient soul immediately compares and judges all those subjects. To this end, in fact, the Aristotelians (with the exception of Themistius) assumed a common sense.

Thus, in all sense organs it is one and the same soul, and since it is corporeal, it is extended along the nerves. Where there is discontinuity, however, no judgement can be made. Therefore, we do not feel when our clothing or our hair is cut—not even if our bones are cut, because they are dense and have little sensitivity, and the soul does not extend there. But owing to the connection with the brain the teeth are more ready to feel.

Moreover, as Augustine says, if we observe something attentively, we close one eye, so that the sentient soul may flow entirely into the other one, and when we listen attentively, we scarcely see those who pass by us, because almost the entire spirit concurs at the ears. This is also why we use sleep, for sleep is the assembly of the spirit at the head. Thus, the spirit retires from the eyes inwards, so that even the open eyes of sleepers do not see. This would not happen if the sense were the form of the sense organ, which could not remove itself thence. This also shows us that the sentient spirit is corporeal.

Furthermore, consider swoon, when the spirit withdraws inwards and leaves the outer parts without sense and motion and by cold water is recalled outwards to the service of the body. This could not happen if the soul were the form of the body, since the form does not withdraw from that, of which it is form. The form of the ship does not retire from the outside to the inside of the ship, as the sailor does.

Moreover, if the nerves are blocked by liquid, there is no movement, because the spirit cannot pass. Therefore, the moving spirit is corporeal. Also, the fetid odors of some trees can kill a man, because they condense and weigh down the spirit and displace it from its symmetry—however without damaging in any way that complexion of the brain, which Galen held to be the sentient soul. The same is evident in cases of extreme joy, when somebody dies of joy, while Aristotle's form, or Galen's complexion are in no way damaged. It is caused by the impetuous outward-flowing of the spirit towards the thing that gives it unhoped for joy and, consequently, its suffocating in the narrow passages of the nerves. And hemlock kills

Soul, Intellect, and Body

a man just by the dense vapor that blocks the cells and the passages of the spirits.

Thence Galen concludes against Plato that the soul is mortal, though he is not entirely right. For also the other, immortal soul had to be acknowledged, which cannot govern the body without the spirit, and therefore departs when the body is killed.

From all this it is obvious that the corporeal spirit is the sentient soul, as we have already stated in the previous book, following Ambrose, Lactantius, Augustine, Origen, and the Mosaic Law, and that the sentient spirit is one, while the organs are many. Even if we do not see with our hearing, this does not mean that the spirit of hearing is not also that of sight. As a man writes with a pen and digs with a hoe, not with a pen, he will not, for all that, be a different man, but the actions will be different. Suppose there were in the hearing organ a crystalline body and a transparent cornea for the light to enter and that the spirit was in the crystalline body, then there would be sight also in the ear.

We have shown that the sentient spirit is one and the same not just in the outer sense organs, but also in the inner compartments, since memory, phantasy, and estimation or sensitive discourse are all operations of the same spirit. For it is evident that people who have a very thin spirit are of weak memory, but of easy comprehension. For what is thin suffers easily. Sensation, indeed, is produced by a foregoing suffering. Thence the dense-spirited are stupid. The past sensation, however, does not remain, since a thin spirit evaporates easily towards the congenial heavens before communicating with the oncoming spirit, which is continuously, like a flame from oil, produced from the blood, as St. Ambrose and the very nature of things confirm. Memory, in fact, is anticipated sensation. Reminiscence is the stimulation of a sensation by a new one that is similar according to any of the ten terms of comparison. For instance, when I see a ship, I remember the shipwreck I had suffered when sailing, and vomit again. Hence it is evident that the anticipated, and the stimulated, and the present passion are one and the same.

Imagination or phantasy, on the other hand, is the fiction of new passions or emotions over and above the past ones: either by combining and separating those, as when I imagine a golden mountain by connecting the impression of gold with that of a mountain, both of which we preserve like scars in our mind; or by making up new instances along the lines the former ones, as when we invent other worlds out of this world. Indeed, it is certainly the same spirit that senses an object and that elaborates upon it and that revisits its own passions. Thence at times, when awake, we imagine something so intensely that we also seem to see it. The same happens when we are asleep. Therefore, it is not a different soul that imagines or that senses, but it is the operation that differs. The one, in fact, is dealing with objects that are already impressed in the spirit, the other with present objects, while they are being impressed.

As to the estimative faculty that perceives in sensual things the things that are not sensual (e.g., when the lamb, seeing the wolf, through estimation at once with him sees also the hostility), it is not something different from the sentient soul, but rather a certain sensual discourse, which leads from the object to its operations, passions, and relations. Therefore, we posit the reasoning faculty to be one with the sentient, since no thing is sensed entirely, and yet it is known entirely. Thus, when we are just a little touched by fire, we estimate the entire very hot fire, as well. And the same is true for the beasts, since from one stalk of fodder the horse knows the entire fodder.

Sense is therefore also discourse or furnished with discourse. Sense, namely, is not merely the passion, but judgement of the passion, and withal of the object by which we are affected. Hence Aristotle's *universal intellection* is the same as the sense that suffers an impact also at a distance. For when we see something from a distance, we say that something is moving, but from close by that it is a man, and closest that it is Peter, since then we sense all sensual differences that cannot move us from far off in the same way as from close by. But when Aristotle demonstrates that the intellect differs from the sense because it is about the universal, while sense is about the individual, he is misleading. For the intellect also senses individuals and the sense the universal. Hence the Aristotelian intellect belongs typically to children and beasts, who do not distinguish singularly. Thus, such children call all women "mother," and a dog barks at everybody as enemies in a universal way, until, close by, it recognizes its owner. Cognition in a universal way is imperfect. Therefore, Thomas did not attribute it to God but instead the cognition of individuals up to the smallest particulars of

Soul, Intellect, and Body

their nature. The Platonic universal we will treat separately: this belongs to another, more divine soul.

Nor is the power to understand a different one from the sentient, because a vehement sensible impact destroys it, but not a vehement intelligible impact. Understanding, namely, is the cognition of a distant object, and of what is in common; and while it sees what is in common from afar, it will see much more something that is present and particular. Sensation, in turn, concerns the present object: hence it is destroyed by fire, which imposes a greater passion than the sense can tolerate. Therefore, the sense must not be compared with the intellect, unless you compare a slight sensible with a mighty intelligible. Thus, in fact, he who senses the smallest particulars, senses the greater, for the smallest sensible things are greater, if considered as intelligible things.

From all this it is evident that memory is anticipated sensation, reminiscence is sensation renewed by the similar, phantasy is a coupling and dissecting of sensations, and discourse is sensing the similar within the similar, as, for instance, from the notion of bone I come to sense the nature of stone, and such is reason, as well. As for intellect, it is a feeble sense of similar things insofar as they are one, because it does not capture the singularities by which they differ. Therefore, the operations that Aristotle ascribed to different souls belong to one. Nor are there different souls, because one of these operations is proper to one species and not found in others. For the organs of the operations are not the same, and the finesse or density of spirit is not the same. A dense one, indeed, scarcely senses, but it retains for a long time, though only the strong impressions, and it lacks discourse, because it does not revisit its motions and does not pass over from these to others. A fine spirit senses easily, but does not retain, because it evaporates, and it lacks discourse, because the motion is disrupted by its evaporating. One of medium density apprehends and remembers well and is good in discourse, especially if it is pure and unstained by soot. The excessively fine spirits succumb to raving, the excessively dense ones to stupidity. And since one and the same man lacks or surfeits in these respects according to time and circumstances—as a child, youth, or elder, in health or in disease—it is evident that these are the properties of one soul, which is not a different one, or to be divided, because in some souls some of these properties are not to be found. On this point see *Ques-*

360   TOMMASO CAMPANELLA

tions on Physics. Now it remains to see whether, besides the sensitive spirit, there is, in man, some other kind of soul, and by which reasons it may be ascertained.

THE INTELLECTIVE SOUL

Beyond the corporeal sentient soul that he has in common with the beasts, there is in man a mind that is infused by God. It is not intermingled with matter, nor its immersed form. Its proper operation is the contemplation of God and religion. It joins a thoroughly formed body that is endowed with sense, to which it is united not accidentally, but substantially. None of the arguments are valid that deny this truth, which is established by other, most convincing arguments, ignored by the Aristotelians. Furthermore, man is not merely soul, but also mind, spirit, and body, though the mind uses the latter two as its organs and can perform all the operations of the sentient soul and bring them to perfection. This is, what all the church fathers, and Moses, and the apostles teach, if they are interpreted correctly.

The human mind is not a body, nor does it become a body, when it cognizes a body, even though according to the Aristotelian dogma it appears to be informed by matter and corporeality. Instead it is an incorporeal life that is united with the corporeal spirit, and through that with the entire body. It is neither a quality of the body, nor is it divisible in and for itself, or accidentally, according to the division of the body, as the white color and the spirit are. Rather it is entirely in the entire body, and in every single part in a totality that is not quantitative, but essential and virtual. Therefore, it is not a form, unless in a very broad understanding of the term, and not rooted within the body, but independent from it. How this works can hardly be understood, however one might try to explain it. Nonetheless it moves by accident in accordance with the movement of that whole body.

Even the Aristotelians have taught that the soul is not a body. Rather, as Alexander of Aphrodisias says, like in a heavy body heaviness is its form, but not a body, thus the soul is *of* a body, but not a body itself. Yet this assertion is self-contradictory. For they say that the soul is not a body because it cognizes bodies, since the receiving ought to lack the nature of what it receives. However, as every intellection occurs by a passion and reception of the intelligible object in the intellect, it would follow that, if the intellect itself were the form of a body, it would not receive any form of corporeality, which it thinks, unless it is one and the same with that of the body, of which itself is the form. Indeed, the body of which it is the form would impede the reception, like a red-tinted pupil does not perceive whiteness otherwise than changed into redness, as they themselves say. Therefore, the intelligent substance ought to be mingled with the body, and not an act of the body, as Aristotle concludes, referring to Anaxagoras, in book 3 *On the Soul*.

Empedocles inquired how the intellect could receive corporeal forms, if it is not a body itself. Even though the similar is cognized by the similar, and in cognizing the intellect becomes similar with the cognizable object, it would, however, not become similar, unless it were of a similar nature. The Aristotelians reply that it is similar potentially, but not actually, just as the pupil potentially resembles the colors. But if that were so, then the intellect that were actually cognizing bodies ought to become a body itself, like the pupil, which becomes colored when it actually receives a color. This they counter by saying that it receives a body intentionally, but not really. However, since this intention is not irreal like a chimera, but real (called an intention only for not being strongly impressed, just like the colors of the rainbow in a cloud that are real, but not permanent, are for this reason called intentional), it would follow that the soul was informed by bodies really, which is false: for then it would be prime matter. This is accepted by Theophilus, Marianus, and other Aristotelians, who teach that the soul is prime matter, because it can become everything. And David of Dinant says that even God is prime matter, if he is the first of all intellects. See, what blasphemous idiocies, once they have swallowed Aristotle's teaching that knowledge is a passion, and that the soul is informed by the things known. But more on this topic later.

However, such reasoning is not conclusive—that the soul is incorporeal, if it conceives of all bodies: because it conceives of all substances and beings, it does not follow that it is neither substance nor being, and because it conceives of all forms, it does not follow that it is, therefore, not a form. I would even say that not all bodies are understood, but only those that are in some way dissimilar to it, since the similar is not affected by the similar. Thus, as Aristotle also testifies, the touch senses warmth and coldness, while it is warm itself; but it does not feel a heat that is equal or inferior in degree to its own. For we do not suffer from what is of equal, or of less force than our own, but from a major one. Thence, the feverish person does not feel the warmth of the physician, which is less than his own, nor any other equal heat, but a greater one, e.g. that of fire. Likewise, if the soul is a body, it will not feel a corporeality similar to its own, but a greater one. And even the animated corporeal spirit does not feel the air, which is similar to it (except through discourse), while it feels all the bodies that are more dissimilar. Besides, if cognition is suffering from an agent object, and if a body does not act through itself, but through its form, it is neither sensed by itself, nor understood, unless by discourse. Also, as the pupil, being visible, nonetheless sees such objects that are dissimilar from itself, but not the similar ones, in that same way the intellect would relate to its objects. A mirror, as well, represents all bodies—even itself, if it is reflected in another mirror—but not the air. Therefore, from the soul reflecting upon itself and perceiving bodies, it does not follow that it is not a body itself. Indeed, since it cannot be affected, except by things with which it shares a common nature, it would necessarily have to be counted in the genus of bodies, as Empedocles said, unless one takes knowledge to be something different from passion. In fact, by communality of nature the soul would understand the intelligences and incorporeal things more easily than the body, if it were not a body. Or, if one preferred that it should in no way resemble its objects, then the angel would not know the angels, with whom it is of the same nature, while it would know the bodies better, of which there is passion, and not information, but a judgment about the thing that affects or incites us. We will come to this in its proper place.

We must investigate yet another reason why the soul is not a body. We say, as St. Ambrose said, that the soul is life, and the cause of life in the living. The body as such, however, is not life, otherwise each body would be life. Likewise, the body as such is not hot, or fire, for then each body would be fire. Therefore, the body is enlivened by life and heated by heat. But you might say that a certain body is the life of other bodies, as for instance the fire or the spirit that is fiery. Then I would say that it is not life insofar as it is body, but insofar as it is fire, for it is hot insofar as it is fire. Thence it would only be life insofar as it is hot, i.e. rather enlivened, and then such life would be heat. Thus, even admitting that the corporeal spirit were the soul, it still would not be life insofar as it is corporeal, but insofar as it is

Soul, Intellect, and Body

hot, or rather not even insofar as it is hot, but insofar as it is sensitive, powerful, and appetitive. Consequently, being a soul would not depend on corporeality, nor on a quality of the body insofar as it is corporeal, but on the primalities, which are Power, Wisdom, and Love.

However, you might say: in *Metaphysics* we had proved that the body, as well, consists of the natural Power, Wisdom, and Love. That is right, however not in an active, but in a passive way: the power of the body as such is receptive; the sense as such is made for receiving and passive; the appetite in it, by which it longs for the forms like the female for the male, is also receptive. But the Power, Wisdom, and Love of the soul are active. Thus, the mind proceeds from one thing it has cognized to infinite other things, since, unlike the body, it is not restrained by such reception, but working on multiplying.

Indeed, if the soul were a body, then the bigger the bodies and the bulkier the things, the more soul they would have or be. Instead it is well known that those who are more corpulent are more stupid and less capable of love and of sense. Hence no soul, insofar as it is knowing and willing, is a body. Yet there, where the primalities are imprinted in corporeality, it can be a body, as is evident in the animal spirit. However, since it is proved that beyond the animal spirit, we have another far more divine kind of soul, it follows that this latter is incorporeal. This, too, is evident, since a body does not extend itself beyond its limits, save through some quality, as the fire does through heat and light. However, a quality that depends on the body cannot become infinite and extend at whatever it does not affront directly. Thence the light of the sun does not illuminate our hemisphere by night, because it does not affront it directly, nor can it extend itself beyond the limit of the sky. Whereas the soul considers both hemispheres and transfers itself to any place where it is not, and beyond, without end, up to the divine and incorporeal beings. Even though it is in the body, it still is something more divine.

Furthermore, I say that, while the soul is in the spirit as the light is in the air, it is not, for all that, extended quantitatively. For otherwise the intellect would remain in whatever part of the body were cut off, as the white color does in any part of the snow. Even if a part of the soul should remain in both parts of some animal that had been cut asunder, this happens because its soul is the corporeal spirit, which is inside the nerve tissue and

364   TOMMASO CAMPANELLA

cannot evaporate immediately. So it moves, until it escapes out of the narrow nerves. Hence, where the nerves are narrow, as in the tails of lizards and in the heart, the animal movement remains for a longer while. But not, as the Aristotelian prattle will have it, because the souls that had been potentially two had become actually two. Apart from begging the question in stating that "they became two, because they could become two," such a division does not confer actual being, but rather corrupts it. In the case of trees, however, where there is much narrowness, and a dense spirit, and where the parts are not determined, but rather can be multiplied, the spirit remains after they are divided, so that they can become two trees—that is, two souls as well as two bodies. Even in human beings some part of the animal spirit remains for a while there, where the fibers are most narrow, as revealed by some movement and tremor. But the intellect does not remain. Hence, it is not extended, like the white color, nor a corporeal part, like the spirit.

Therefore, when we say that the mind is in the spirit and in the body like the light is in the air, we still do not hold it to be extended, but just declare its independence. Which is why Ambrose, who had said this in his book *On the Good Death*, taught afterwards in *On Human Dignity* that the soul which is installed by God should properly be called mind, while the spirit should be called soul, and that the entire mind is in the entire body and in any part of it entirely. Augustine, as well, follows this view in *On Trinity*. But how this can be no man can understand, especially if it is supposed to be a form, which is, furthermore, neither a complexion, nor an external quality, nor a figure. For all these forms are entirely in the whole, but not entirely in the part, as it is evident in all things. Therefore, I am amazed how the Scholastic thinkers can teach in accordance with Augustine and Ambrose that the mind is entirely in any part, while those are in fact both denying that it is a form. Ambrose even teaches expressly against Aristotle in a letter and in the book *On Isaak*, stating that it is not an entelechy. And the Scholastics say: like God is entirely in the world as a whole and entirely in any part, in the same way the soul is in the body. But it is certain that God is not the form of the world, nor is the angel the form of the heavenly sphere. On the other hand, however, they say that the mind is the form of the body. This cannot be claimed, unless they use the term *form* equivocally, in the sense of an active force that works in some things in a certain way, as it does not in others (as it was assumed in the Council of Vienne against Averroes). Hence, Caietan responds to Scotus's arguments concerning this point, saying that the soul does not move—neither *per se*, nor *per accidens*—with the movement of a part, but only with the movement of the whole, in which it is in a defined way, as all the intelligences are. But all the intelligences, indeed, behave in this way, because they do not inform, while whatever is the form of a body moves with any of its movements. Not to mention how Aristotle in book 2 *On the Soul* and Alexander of Aphrodisias teach expressly that the act perishes together with its subject, suffers everything along with it, and cannot be separated, while some parts of the soul can be separated, just because they are not the acts of any body.

As to St. Thomas, he says that of such forms that regard the whole and the parts equally, the whole is in the whole, and part in the parts. Thus, the form of water is divided with the division of water, and that of whiteness with the cutting asunder a white thing, because owing to homogeneity the form regards all the parts equally. And even though these forms are not divisible quantitatively *per se*, yet, with the division of the subject they are divided *per accidens*. Such forms, instead, which do not regard the whole and the parts equally, because the whole is heterogeneous, are not divided with the division of a part. Thus, also the soul, which informs an organic body that is differentiated in its parts and regards *per se* the whole, the parts, however, in reference to the whole: it is not divided *per accidens*, nor does it move, when one finger is moving (even though it is entirely in every part), but only when the whole is moving. But this doctrine is unintelligible. For if the parts have different forms, since they have different figures, colors, and complexions, as it is evident in animals, it follows that they cannot be informed by a partial form alone, but only by the form of the whole, which belongs to it in its totality, embraces soul and body, and in its unity relates to the idea. Such is both, humanity and "*guitareity*," i.e. the form of a guitar. But such a form of the whole cannot be found entirely in every single part, not even in homogeneous things.

In what way the soul, which is the form of a part, namely of the body alone, could be entirely in any single part, nobody can explain. However, when Caietan discusses this, he posits a principle, making a threefold distinction between forms: such that regard the whole and the parts equally, such that regard to them in different ways, however in the first place

366 TOMMASO CAMPANELLA

the whole, and such which fall in between. But the second class makes no sense, namely that the form should regard in different ways the parts and the whole, which are of different forms, and yet be entirely in every part, which is of a different order of being. And at the same time this is in contradiction to the first class, for if the entire essence of the form of water is in every single part of water, because it equally regards the whole and to the parts, then the essence of the soul, which does not regard them equally, could not be entirely in every single part. And experience tells us the same: the entire soul does not appear to be in one part, as does the entire essence of water in every single particle. This means that for Caietan the opposite would follow from the opposite. Furthermore, when they teach that the entire essence of whiteness is in any single part, but not so its accidental power, nor its quantity, whereas the essence of the soul is in any single part in its entire totality, and not just in a virtual or quantitative one, they fail to convince, because as to the power of vision it is nowhere but in the eye, and as to other powers elsewhere: firstly because heterogeneity presupposes rather a diversity of forms than a totality of the form in any single part, and secondly because if the soul is indivisible, all its powers are united, and thus wherever the soul might be concerning its essence, there it would also be concerning its powers.

Therefore, it is giving in to the authority, not to the reasoning, when I concede that the mind is entirely in any single part in an essential totality, which is not quantitative either *per se*, or *per accidens*, and I add that it is similarly there, as they say, in a virtual and potential totality. If it does not see, except through the eye, this does not mean that its visual power is not in the whole. For it would also see, if the eye were in the ears, and likewise in the breast, as Augustine and Pliny tell about the headless monsters. Thus, the other parts lack the organ rather than the power for sight, like when we are inside a house we do not see, except through the windows— not because the power is lacking, but because without[4] a window in a dark wall the mind does not sense. The same is true for the bone, since the mind senses through the spirit that is joined to it, which in the bone is absent,

---

4. Our conjecture: the word "without" (lat. *sine*) ought to be inserted here to save the sense, since the literary translation ("a window in a dark wall does not sense") obviously contradicts the intended demonstration; that this sentence is corrupted was pointed out in one of the source manuscripts.

Soul, Intellect, and Body

or only feeble. Whereas a nude soul is at the same time seeing, hearing, touching, understanding, and everything else, as St. Bernhard and Augustine state more than once. More on this point later.

Thus, the soul is in this double way entirely in any single part and entirely in the whole, as the Saints say, and I can understand this without difficulty as long as the soul is not supposed to be a form. Whereas the conclusion that it is a form can be understood in this sense: that it is, however, not rooted in matter in the Aristotelian way, but in itself subsistent and intelligent, and that it is *called* the form of a heterogeneous organism for being its life-giving force, as St. Ambrose says, and its ruler and inmate, according to Chrysostom in his 14th *Homily on Genesis*, and thus is the life of this one individual and not the life of that other one (hence called *form* against Averroes, so that it is not believed to be only one in all). But Chrysostom teaches in his book *Against the Nameless* that we cannot understand in which manner the entire soul can be both in the whole and in every single part (even though he does not hold that it is a form) just as we cannot understand, he says, how God is in the world. And indeed, he is talking to the point and worth to be heard by everybody.

A certain kind of example, however, might be given imagining a mirror that was broken in many parts with the same entire image appearing in each single fragment. The broken mirror would stand for the heterogeneous body, whereas an intact mirror with one image only in the whole would represent the homogeneous body which, like the water, has only one form. But ours is still a rather faulty analogy, since the images in the fragments would differ as to their number, and because in addition there would not be simultaneously in all fragments just the one and total image.

LIST OF CONTRIBUTORS

ELISABETH BLUM is Reseacher at Palacký University Olomouc (Czech Republic) and specializes in Renaissance philosophy. Among others she translated Giordano Bruno's *Spaccio de la bestia trionfante* into German. Her most recent book is *Perspectives on Giordano Bruno* (2018)

PAUL RICHARD BLUM is T.J. Higgins, S.J., Chair in Philosophy, emeritus, at Loyola University Maryland, Baltimore, and researcher at Palacký University Olomouc, Czech Republic. He has published on Renaissance philosophy, early modern scholasticism, and philosophical anthropology.

EVA DEL SOLDATO is Associate Professor of Italian Studies at the University of Pennsylvania. She specializes in the early modern reception of the Platonic and Aristotelian traditions. Among her most recent publications is *Early Modern Aristotle. On the Making and Unmaking of Authority* (2020).

GÜNTER FRANK is Professor of Philosophy at Karlsruhe Institute of Technology and Director oft he „European Melanchthon-Academy" at Bretten (Baden-Württemberg). Among his recent publications is *Topic als Methode der Dogmatik – Antike – Mittelalter – Frühe Neuzeit* (2017).

ROBERT GOULDING is associate professor of liberal studies and history of science at the University of Notre Dame. He specializes in Renaissance science, and the scientific culture of the universities. Among his recent publications is *Defending Hypatia: Ramus, Savile, and the Renaissance Rediscovery of Mathematical History.*

GREGORY GRAYBILL is an Anglican pastor in Iowa. He is a Fulbright scholar and has a D.Phil in Theology from the University of Oxford, with a specialization in the Reformation.

370   *Contributors*

MARK JURDJEVIC is Professor of History at York University in Toronto. He studies the political culture of the Italian Renaissance. Among his most recent publications are *Machiavelli: Political, Historical, and Literary Writings* and *Florentine Political Writings from Petrarch to Machiavelli* (both 2019).

TIMOTHY KIRCHER is H. Curt '56 and Patricia S. '57 Hege Professor of History at Guilford College. He specializes in Renaissance humanism. Among his most recent publications is *Before Enlightenment: Play and Illusion in Renaissance Humanism* (2021).

PER LANDGREN, FLS, PH.D. (HISTORY OF SCIENCE), PH.LIC. (LATIN) is an associate member of History Faculty at the University of Oxford and practices conceptul research in early modern and modern intellectual history.

JOZEF MATULA was Assistant Professor at the Department of Philosophy at Palacký University in the Czech Republic (1997-2021). Since January 2021 he has been working for the Gallery of Icons in Žilina (Slovakia). He specializes in Medieval and Renaissance philosophy, history of tolerance and Byzantine art. Among his most recent publications are *Leone Ebreo: Renaissance Dialogue between Love and Wisdom* (2020, in Slovak).

JOHN MONFASANI is a Distinguished Research Professor at The University at Albany, State University of New York. He specializes in Renaissance humanism. Among his most recent publications is *Vindicatio Aristotelis. Two Texts by George of Trebizond in the Plato-Aristotle Controversy of the Fifteenth Century* (2021).

TOMÁŠ NEJESCHLEBA is Professor of Philosophy at Palacký University in Olomouc, Czech Republic. He focuses on the History of Medieval and Renaissance philosophy and published articles and books on St. Bonaventure, Giovanni Pico della Mirandola, Pietro Pomponazzi, Francesco Patrizi, Johannes Jessenius, and Valerian Magni.

SYDNEY PENNER is a Senior Lecturer in Philosophy at Asbury University. He specializes in early modern scholastic philosophy, especially that of Francisco Suárez. Recent publications include "Making Use of the Testimonies: Suárez and Grotius on Natural Law" and "Suárez on Substantial Forms: A Heroic Last Stand?"

VICTOR M. SALAS is Associate Professor of Philosophy at Sacred Heart Major Seminary (Detroit). His research focuses on medieval and late scholastic metaphysics. He has been the editor of many volumes devoted to scholastic thought, the most recent being Brill's *A Companion to Francisco Suárez* (2015).

Contributors

JAMES G. SNYDER is an Associate Professor of Philosophy and Dean in the Office of Academic Affairs at Marist College. His research focuses primarily on Renaissance Platonism.

DETLEF THIEL, free philosopher at Wiesbaden, Germany, had lectureships in philosophy (Trier University; Wiesbaden University of Applied Sciences); co-editor of *Collected Works* of Salomo Friedlaender/Mynona (33 vols. so far). Books on Jacques Derrida (1990), Plato (1993), and *Maßnahmen des Erscheinens. Friedlaender/Mynona im Gespräch mit Schelling, Husserl, Benjamin und Derrida* (2012).

INDEX

Addante, Luca, 262
Aeschylus, 117
Aesopus, 289
Agrippa von Nettesheim, Heinrich
  Cornelius, 6, 8, 187-201
Ahriman, 48
Al Ghazzali, 151
Albert the Great, 94, 165, 167, 277
Alberti, Leon Battista, 4, 8, 102–17
Albertini, Tamara, 138
Alberto of Carpi, 165
Albizzi, Maso degli, 173
Aleksander, Jason, 98
Alexander Milesius, 148
Alexander of Aphrodisias, 69, 157, 360, 365
Alfonso of Aragon, King, 82
Allen, Michael J. B., 120, 138
Ambrose, 92, 94, 95, 355, 357, 362, 364, 367
Amerio, Romano, 352, 354
Ammonius Saccas, 35
Anaxagoras, 151, 200, 361
Andersson, D. C., 205
Anfossi, Maria, 84
Annius of Viterbo, 307
Anselm of Canterbury, 94
anthropocentrism, 83, 350
anthropology, 8, 224
Antoninus, Emperor, 54
Apellicon of Teos, 253
Apuleius, 109, 189
Aquilecchia, Giovanni, 314
Arabic, 10, 11, 13, 190, 196
Archimedes, 53, 239, 288
architecture, 102, 188, 233
Argyropoulos, John, 37

Ariew, Roger, 282
Aristides, 110
Aristippus, 150, 260
Aristotle, passim
Aristotelianism, 4, 7, 68, 156, 158, 159, 291,
  313, 350
Arvanitis, Phillip, 9
astronomy, 188, 351
Athanassiadi, Polymnia, 37, 38
atoms, 146, 326
Atticus, 34
Augustine, 53, 78, 91, 92, 94, 95, 97, 195,
  199, 228, 288, 336, 337, 338, 341, 342, 356,
  357, 364, 366, 367
Austin, Amy M., 12
Averroes, 157, 161, 164, 165, 168, 195, 200,
  239, 276, 277, 365, 367
Avicenna, 59, 151, 160, 165

Baccilieri, Tiberio, 9
Bacon, Francis, 6, 188, 263, 350
Badia, Lola, 12
Bailey, C., 317
Baius, Michael, 342
Baker, Patrick, 83, 85, 86
Balsamo, Jean, 282, 283
Barbagli, Danilo Aguzzi, 293, 294
Bardi, Giorlamo, 300
Baruch, 200
Basil, 50, 78, 92, 95
Bauer, Emmanuel J., 335
Bausi, Francesco, 172
Bede the Venerable, 94
Bellarmine, Robert, 342
Beran, Jan, 191, 283

373

Index

Bernard of Clairvaux, 94, 337, 367
Bertolini, Lucia, 104, 105
Besomi, Ottavio, 84
Bessarion, Basil, 4, 5, 8, 38, 50, 51, 52, 67-81
Bihlmaier, Sandra, 225
Biondi, Albano, 119
Bird, H. W., 190, 196
Black, Crofton, 120
Black, Robert, 170, 172
Blackwell, Richard J., 352
Blum, Elisabeth, 350, 354
Blum, Paul Richard, 3, 9, 10, 13, 36, 38, 82,
    85, 98, 157, 158, 159, 187, 190, 202, 203,
    262, 270, 280, 281, 282, 283, 291, 294, 295,
    312, 314
Boccaccio, Giovanni, 103, 295
Bock, Gisela, 172
Boenke, Michaela, 104, 264
Boethius, 72, 78, 83, 94
Böhme, Jakob, 9
Boiadjiev, Tzotcho, 38
Bonaventura, 94, 97
Bond, H. Lawrence, 98
Bondì, Roberto, 264
Bonner, Anthony, 12, 13
Boršić, Luka, 293
Boschetto, Luca, 104
Bouillon, Dominique, 273
Bowersock, Glen W., 85
Boyle, Robert, 6
Brisson, Luc, 35, 36, 38
Bruni, Leornardo, 82
Bruno, Giordano, 7, 8, 12, 189, 190, 312–
    32, 351
Burckhardt, Jacob, 102, 104
Bydén, Börje, 38
Byzantines, 4, 5, 34-38, 50, 69, 71

Caccia, Eleonora, 302
Caesar, 112, 149
Caietan, Thomas de Vio, 365, 366
Cain, 193
Cambridge Platonists, 138
Camillo Renato, 188, 190
Camillus, 110

Campanella, Tommaso, 8, 263, 350–67
Camporeale, Salvatore I., 83, 85, 86
Cannarsa, Maria Luisa, 104
Canone, Eugenio, 312, 314, 353
Cardini, Roberto, 105
Cartei, Stefano, 83, 84
Casini, Lorenzo, 205
Cassiodorus, 209
Cassirer, Ernst, 9, 84, 157, 159, 167, 204
Castelli, Patrizia, 294
Castelnau, Michel de, 313, 315
Cato, 86
Celenza, Christopher S., 2, 83, 85, 86
Ceron, Annalisa, 104
Chaldaean Oracles, 34–48
Chaldeans, 4, 292
Charles, King, 174
Charlet, Jean-Louis, 70
chastity, 21
Chrysippus, 192
Chrysostom, 367
Church, 77
Church, doctors of the, 52
Cicero, 53, 104, 111, 112, 117, 194, 195, 196,
    197, 224, 230, 239, 242, 256, 259, 283, 286,
    287, 298
Cipani, Nicola, 295
Clement VII, pope, 170
coercion, 338-342
Concordia, 118
Constantine, Peter, 172
Constantinople, 34, 96
Contarini, Gasparo, 157, 158, 295
Contarini, Paolo, 295
Conti, Daniele, 190
Cook, Brendan, 84
Copenhaver, Brian, 52, 84, 120
Copernicus, Nicolaus, 7
Correard, Correard, 189, 190
Corrias, Gian Matteo, 85
Corsaro, A., 172
Cortese, Paul, 9
Cosentino, P., 172
cosmographer, 96-100, 193
Cozzi, Gaetano, 295

Index

creation, 13, 14, 19, 21, 29, 31, 42, 51, 54, 86, 124, 126, 139, 143, 153, 154, 161, 179, 198, 232, 236, 301, 317, 344, 349, 354
Cutinelli-Rèndina, Emmanuele, 172
Cynics, 150
Cyprian, 92, 94
Cyril of Alexandria, 50, 78
Cyrus, 48

D'Aprile, Adrien, 9
Dambergs, Yanis, 13
Daniel, 199
David, 124, 199
David of Dinant, 361
De Angelis, Simone, 225
De Franco, Luigi, 262, 264, 265
De Keyser, Jeroen, 70
De Panizza Lorch, Maristella, 85
Del Soldato, Eva, 52, 67, 70
Della Porta, Giambattista, 350
demiurge, 41, 46, 47
Democritus, 143, 191, 200, 256, 325, 330
demons, 43, 45, 133, 190, 289
Demosthenes, 53, 192
Desan, Philippe, 281, 282
Descartes, René, 3, 7, 203, 263, 264, 350
devil, 16, 120, 121, 122, 127, 132, 193, 217, 230
Didymus of Alexandria, 256
Diodorus, 256, 301
Diogenes, 191, 200
Diogenes Laertius, 283, 323
Dionysius the Areopagite, 95, 145
divine beauty, 145, 146
divine love, 145, 148
Dominic, saint, 89, 90, 91, 94
Donation of Constantine, 82, 83, 85
Donato, Antonio, 294
Donno, Daniel J., 352
Dougherty, Michael, 120
Duclow, Donald F., 98
Dunn, Catherine M., 243

Eber, Paul, 224
Elizabeth, Queen, 315
Empedocles, 144, 200, 361, 362
empiricism, 2, 263, 272, 276

Enlightenment, 2, 3
entelechy, 72, 364
Epictetus, 72
Epicureans, 146, 317
Epicurus, 50, 68, 104, 137, 150, 260, 323, 325, 330
Epimenides, 286, 299
Erasmus of Rotterdam, 8, 202, 287
Erasthenes, 53
Ernst, Germana, 352, 353
ethics, 8, 34, 82, 188, 202, 203, 233, 271
Euclid, 254, 256, 258, 278, 292
Eudoxus, 283
Eugene IV, Pope, 82
Euripides, 112, 192
Eusebius of Caesarea, 50
Ezekiel, 199

Fabius, 238, 239
Fachard, Denis, 172
faith, 5, 10, 15, 27, 28, 33, 69, 74, 75, 78, 81, 84, 125, 127, 133, 139, 157, 158, 196, 200, 201, 254, 281, 342, 345, 348
Fantazzi, Charles, 204, 205
Farmer, Stephen, 119, 120
fate, 40, 59, 79, 177, 329
Fetz, Reto Luzius, 282
Ficino, Marsilio, 4, 5, 8, 37, 69, 70, 120, 136–55, 188, 189, 190, 194, 197, 291, 292, 303, 305
fideism, 6, 157, 158, 281
Filelfo, Francesco, 37
Filipović, Vladimir, 294
Fiorentino, Francesco, 314
Firpo, Laura Salvetti, 352
Firpo, Luigi, 352, 353
first mover, 60-65
Flavius Arrianus, 286
Flavius Josephus, 308
Florence, 4, 6, 102, 105, 118, 120, 169–85, 352
Florence, Council of, 4, 34, 67
Florio, John, 281, 282, 287
fortune, 4, 103–15, 149, 212, 213, 285, 328, 332
Fracastoro, Girolamo, 9, 313

Index

Frank, Günter, 223, 225, 226
Freddoso, Alfred J., 335
free will, 8, 51, 82, 83, 131, 197, 333–49
frenzy, 114, 137, 143, 144, 145, 146, 147, 148, 188
Frigo, Alberto, 282

Galen, 263, 355, 356, 357
Galileo Galilei, 7, 53, 350, 351, 352
Gambino, Susanna, 105
Garin, Eugenio, 85, 119, 120
Gehenna, 132, 134
generation, 56, 57, 58, 59, 60, 193
Gentile, Giovanni, 314, 317
George of Trebizond, 4, 5, 8, 38, 49-66, 67, 68, 69, 70, 71, 75, 77, 78
George, E., 205
Gilbert, Allan, 172
Gilbert, Neal Ward, 243
Giles of Rome, 94
Girardi-Karšulin, Mihaela, 293
Girelli, Lucia, 314
Gladen, Cynthia, 295
God: dignities, 30; essence, 18: existence, 14; omnipotent, 54, 320, 321; perfections, 20; second god, 40, 42, 47, 55, 56, trinity, 26, 30, unity, 23, 30
Gottlieb, Carolus, 225, 226
Goulding, Robert, 240, 243
Gouveia, Antonio de, 259
grace, 335-337, 342, 349
Grafton, Anthony, 102, 105, 307
Gratian, 94
Graybill, Gregory, 223, 226
Grayson, Cecil, 103, 104, 116
Grazzini, F., 172
Gregory, 78, 92
Gregory Nazianzen, 95
Grendler, Paul F., 270
Grene, Marjorie, 282
Guerlac, Rita, 204
Guidi, Andrea, 172
Gutas, Dimitri, 190, 196

Hanegraaff, Wouter, 190
Hankins, James, 52, 71, 159, 172

Hannibal, 238
happiness, 4, 60, 103, 107–12, 119, 127, 128, 129, 130, 137, 149–55, 194, 336
harmony, 41, 42, 95, 114, 144-148, 351
Hartle, Ann, 282
Haselbach, Brigitte, 99
Hay, William Henry, 157, 159, 167
Headley, John M., 353
hedonism, 50, 51, 282
Heracles, 230
Heraclitus, 137, 144, 191
heresy, 50, 157, 167, 193, 281, 334
Herillus the Sceptic, 150
Hermes [Mercurius] Trismegistus, 137, 144
hermeticism, 188
Herodotus, 308
Hesiod, 103
Hieatt, A. Kent, 85
Hieronymus, 199
Hilary, 92, 94
Hill, Benjamin, 2
Hippocrates, 112
history, 291-311
Hladký, Vojtěch, 38
Holy Ghost, 22, 29–32, 199, 200
Homer, 53, 111, 112, 116, 248
Hopkins, Jasper, 96, 98, 99
Horace, 166, 260, 290
Horomazes, 48
Hotson, Howard, 270
Hrkač, Serafin, 294
Huarte, Juan, 203
Hugh of Saint Victor, 338

Iamblichus, 194, 305
idolatry, 56, 59, 66, 128, 209
idols, 56, 127, 128
Ignatius of Loyola, 203
immortality of the soul, 5, 43, 110, 130, 136-138, 151, 157–160, 167, 225, 239, 257, 262, 306, 355, 357
infinity of the universe, 313, 317
intellect, 40-48, 66, 94, 99, 101, 137, 141, 149–54, 158, 159, 162–67, 199, 228, 231–39, 255, 263, 279, 292, 315, 321, 329, 330, 344–48, 358, 359–64

intellective soul, 159, 160–67
intelligences, 56, 62, 113, 142, 165, 167, 362, 365
Isaiah, 127, 199, 201, 236, 299
iynges, 47
Izbicki, Thomas M., 98

Jeremiah, 199, 299
Jerome, 92, 94, 95, 199, 256
Jesuit Order, 8, 334, 335
Jews, 10, 308
Joannes Lucidus, 302
John Cassian, 94
John Chrysostom, 50, 92, 95, 367
John Damascene, 95
John Duns Scotus, 94, 166, 333, 365
John Scotus Eriugena, 97
John the Baptist, 87, 89, 199
John, Saint, 130, 199
Johnston, Mark D., 12
Jurdjevic, Mark, 169, 171, 172, 173

Kabbalah, 188
Kane, Kevin, 9, 203
Kapec, Ivan, 293
Keen, Ralph, 225, 226
Kennedy, Leonard A., 9, 242
Kessler [Keßler], Eckhard, 84, 293
Kircher, Timothy, 102, 103, 105
Kraye, Jill, 156, 159
Kristeller, Paul Oskar, 9, 84, 138, 156, 157, 159, 167, 189, 194, 204
Kuhn, Heinrich C., 171, 172
Kullmann, Wolfgang, 272
Kusukawa, Sachiko, 225, 243

La Boétie, Étienne de, 8
Lactantius, 92, 94, 357
Ladan, Tomislav, 294
Lagarde, Bernardette, 37, 59
Lagerlund, Henrik, 2
Lalla, Sebastian, 242
Landgren, Per, 270, 273, 274
Langer, Ullrich, 282
Leibniz, Gottfried Wilhelm Leibniz, 12, 139

Leinkauf, Thomas, 294
Leo X, pope, 170
Leonardo da Vinci, 9
Leonello d'Este, 102, 105
Liber de Causis, 161
Licinius, 196
light, 2, 27, 32, 33, 41, 45, 54, 79, 80, 87, 97, 99, 100, 114, 117, 119, 129, 132, 140, 141, 142, 144, 148, 153, 193, 196, 198-200, 218, 222, 226, 227, 230, 232–34, 238, 239, 244, 249, 256, 268, 293, 323, 324, 326, 357, 363, 364
Limbrick, Elaine, 190, 197
Linacre, Thomas, 202
Llull, Ramón [Ramon Lull, Raymond Lull, Raimundus Lullus], 3, 4, 8, 10-33, 281
Lo Monaco, Francesco, 84
Locke, John, 263
logic, 11, 12, 49, 71, 82, 84, 91, 93, 188, 202, 240, 246, 251–55, 257, 258, 270-277, 292
Lohr, Charles H., 13
Louis XII of France, King, 177
Louis XIII, King, 350
love, 21, 22
Lucanus, 286
Lucian, 109
Lucretius, 104, 116, 317, 318
Ludovico of Milan, Duke, 177
Lullism, 12, 188, 193
Luther, Martin, 84, 223, 224
Lycurgus, 105, 185

Machiavelli, Niccolò, 5, 8, 169–86, 351
MacIlmaine, Roland, 243
Magi, 35, 36, 39
magic, 6, 35, 120, 187, 188, 190, 314
Magnien, Michel, 282, 283
Magnien-Simonin, Catherine, 282, 283
Maltese, Enrico Valdo, 37
Manilius Probus, 116
Maras, Mate, 293
Marcelli, N., 172
Marcello, Antonio, 302, 303
Marchand, Jean-Jacques, 172
Marianus, 361

Mariev, Sergei, 70, 71
Marolda, Paolo, 105
Marsico, Clementina, 84, 85
Martelli, Mario, 172
Martial, 109, 111, 117
Martin V, Pope, 82
martyrs, 87, 88, 133
Maryks, Robert Aleksander, 335
Masi, Giorgio, 172
Matheeussen, Constantinus, 205
mathematics, 73, 163, 167, 168, 188, 241,
   242, 254–58, 271, 278
Matula, Jozef, 34, 36
Maximus Planudes, 289
McCaskey, John P., 273
McCormick, John P., 171, 173
McLaughlin, Martin, 105
Medici, Cosimo de', 174–77
Medici, family, 170
Medici, Giovanni de', 170
Medici, Giulio de', 170
Medici, Lorenzo de', 149, 169–85
Meerhoff, Kees, 243
Melanchthon, Philipp, 6, 7, 8, 223–39
Melera-Morettini, Matteo, 172
Meroi, Fabrizio, 314
Mertens, Manuel, 314
metaphysics, 6, 36, 82, 84, 91, 92, 161, 163,
   167, 168, 188, 242, 254, 271, 313, 350, 351
method, 3, 6, 7, 8, 11, 12, 72, 74, 93, 109, 197,
   241–53, 272, 276, 292, 351
Michael of Ephesos, 165, 167, 168
Michele Mercati, 139
Mikkeli, Heikki, 273
Milo of Crotona, 150
miracles, 87-91, 158, 200
mirror, 5, 97, 98, 100, 101, 227, 246, 362, 367
Mithra, 48
Mithridates, 111
Mocchi, Giuliana, 264
Mohammed, 50, 51
Mohler, Ludwig, 51, 52, 70
Molinari, Jonathan, 38
Momus, 74, 104, 190
Monfasani, John, 4, 38, 49, 51, 52, 70, 71,
   72, 77, 78, 85

Montaigne, Michel de, 7, 8, 11, 116, 189,
   280–90
Montevecchi, Alessandro, 172
More, Thomas, 8, 202, 203
Morison, Richard, 202, 203, 204, 205
Moses, 199, 253, 254, 299, 360
Mullaney, Thomas V., 335
Müller-Jahncke, Wolf-Dieter, 190
Murphy, James J., 242
Muses, 147, 148, 149
music, 95, 137, 146, 147, 148, 188, 290
Muslims, 10, 11
Mutnjaković, Andrija, 294
mysteries, 11, 36, 148, 191

Najemy, John M., 170, 173
natural theology, 3, 11, 281, 351
Nauta, Lodi, 84, 85
Nejeschleba, Tomáš, 118, 120, 156, 294
Neoplatonism, 4, 137, 188, 201, 254, 291,
   350
Nestor, 117
Newlands, Carole E., 242
Nicholas of Cusa [Cusanus], 4, 8, 12, 56,
   82, 85, 96–101, 323
Nicholas V, Pope, 49, 82
Nifo, Agostino, 9
nobility, 13, 20, 27, 90, 178, 188, 203, 207,
   210, 262, 300
Numenius, 34, 55
Nürnberger, Richard, 225

occult sciences, 6, 187, 189, 304
Odysseus, 131
Olesh, Andrew, 315
Omodeo, Pietro Daniel, 264
Ong, W. J., 240, 242, 243
Ophites, 193
oracles, 4, 35–42, 48, 195, 199, 206, 289, 292
Ordine, Nuccio, 189, 190
Origen, 357
Orpheus, 36, 148
Ottaviani, Alessandro, 264
Ottoman Empire, 4
Ovid, 122, 230

Index

pagan wisdom, 4, 75, 77, 78

Palmieri, Paolo, 273

Paracelsus, 9

paradise, 42, 90, 130

Partridge, Christopher, 6, 190

passions, 44, 127, 133, 203, 204, 284, 358

Patrizi, Francesco, 7, 8, 37, 291–311

Paul V, Pope, 333

Paul, Saint, 89, 90, 92, 93, 122, 125, 145

Pearson, Caspar, 102, 105

Pedullà, Gabriele, 173

Pellissier, Pierre Augustin, 37

Penner, Sydney, 333, 335

Peregrino Agli, 143

Perfetti, Stefano, 158, 159

Perion, Joachim de, 259

Perosa, Alessandro, 84

Persia, 48

Persian mystics, 35

Peter Lombard, 94

Peter of Verona (St. Peter Martyr), 88

Peter, Apostle, 90, 130, 165

Petrarca, Francesco, 5, 8, 104, 117, 173, 286

Petrus Iustinianus, 295

Phrinis, 79

Piano, Natasha, 173

Pico della Mirandola, Gianfrancesco, 118, 119, 130, 197

Pico della Mirandola, Giovanni, 4, 5, 8, 37, 38, 118-135, 189, 291

Pietro da Poitiers, 299

piety, 44, 56, 59, 75, 84, 200, 254

Pine, Martin L., 157, 159

Plastina, Sandra, 264

Plato, 4, 5, 34-38, 48-81, 98, 111, 117, 136-139, 143-151, 157, 166, 167, 185, 193-97, 234, 254-58, 260, 284, 287, 289, 292, 296, 298, 301, 303, 357

Plato-Aristotle controversy, 51, 69

Platonism, 5, 38, 50, 55, 57, 59, 60, 63, 67, 68, 69, 71, 120, 136, 137, 151, 200, 233, 236, 255

Plautus, 109, 114, 116

pleasure, 19, 20, 71, 82, 84, 87, 109, 113, 119, 122, 128, 129, 133, 143, 146, 150, 153, 212, 214, 222, 285, 286, 287, 289, 328, 329

Pletho, Georgios Gemistos, 4, 5, 8, 34–48, 50, 51, 59, 69, 292

Pliny, 104, 111, 366

Plotinus, 5, 34, 35, 98, 136, 138

Plutarch, 34, 36, 48, 198, 286, 288, 289, 290, 305, 309

Pocock, J. G. A., 173

Poel, Marc van der, 190, 192

poetry, 102, 103, 137, 147, 148, 149, 188, 238, 241, 292

Pompey, 112, 290

Pomponazzi, Pietro, 5, 6, 7, 8, 69, 70, 156-68, 291

Pontani, Anna, 52

Ponzio, Paolo, 352

Porphyrius, 194

primalities, 351, 354, 355, 363

prime matter, 54, 79, 361

Proclus, 34, 138, 254, 256, 257, 258, 292

prophecy, 89, 148

providence, 54, 79, 233, 329, 334

Psellos, Michael, 35, 36, 37, 38

Ptolemy, 50, 53, 308

Puliafito, Anna Laura, 294

Pupo, Spartaco, 264

Pyrrho, 191, 197

Pythagoras, 36, 137, 144, 255, 256, 257

Pythagoreans, 36, 42, 48, 148, 188, 197, 254, 255, 257, 258

quintessences, 324

Quintus Curtius Rufus, 290

Raimondi, Francesco Paolo, 157, 159

Ramus, Petrus [Pierre de la Ramé], 6, 7, 8, 9, 240-261

Randall, John Herman, 9, 84, 157, 159, 167, 204, 272, 273

rationalism, 2

Ray, Meredith K., 171, 172

Rees, Valery, 139

Regoliosi, Mariangela, 85, 104, 105

Reiss, Timothy J., 243

religion, 5, 27, 39, 69, 71, 74–78, 80, 86, 87, 188, 204, 215, 281, 289, 300, 351, 360

Remigius of Auxerre, 94

Index

resurrection, 17
Reuchlin, Johannes, 223
revelation, 2, 4, 5, 11, 73, 123, 139, 157, 188, 224, 351
rhetoric, 4, 49, 82, 84, 188, 192, 241, 258, 292
Ricci, Saverio, 353
Richelieu, Cardinal, 350
Robichaud, Denis J.-J., 138
Roush, Sherry, 353
Rowland, Ingrid D., 314
Rubini, Rocco, 4
Ruffinus, 199

Sabundus, Raimundus, 11, 281
sages, 36, 42, 48
Saiber, Arielle, 314
saints, 78, 87, 121, 123, 126, 127, 130
Salas, Victor M., 118
Salatowsky, Sacha, 225
Sallust, 86
Salutati, Coluccio, 8
salvation, 6, 27, 36, 52, 53, 78, 125, 139, 191, 196
Sanchez, Francisco, 189, 197
Santanach, Joan, 12
Satan, 121, 134
Savonarola, Girolamo, 118, 119
scepticism, 6, 7, 189, 197, 282
Schenkel, Peter Michael, 84
Schicker, Rudolf, 273
Schmitt, Charles B., 52, 270
Schmutz, Jacob, 335
scholasticism, 1–4, 8, 50, 68, 83, 85, 138, 203, 313, 333, 335, 364
Schulz, Peter, 38, 71
Schwartz, Daniel, 335, 336
Scipio, 112, 239
Scorraille, Raoul de, 336
Screech, M. A., 282
Sellberg, Erland, 243
Seneca, 284, 286, 287, 288
Senent de Frutos, Juan Antonio, 335
Sergio, Emilio, 264
Sextus Empiricus, 72

Sgarbi, Marco, 273
Shakespeare, William, 7, 203
Sharratt, P., 243
Shields, Christopher, 336
Sices, David, 172
sign, 97
Simplicius, 69, 72
Singer, Dorothea Waley, 314
Siniossoglou, Niketas, 38
Sirri, Raffaele, 265
Skinner, Quentin, 172, 173
Snell, Bruno, 272
Snyder, James G., 9, 136, 139, 270
Socrates, 116, 144, 145, 148, 195, 200, 250, 258, 287, 289
Soderini, Piero, 170
Soler, Albert, 12
Solomon, 199, 217, 239
Soto, Domingo de, 349
soul, 42–44, 46, 54, 62, 72, 119, 137, 208, 212, 213, 216, 222, 224, 228, 354, 355, 361, 362, 363
Sowerby, Tracey A., 204, 205
space, 140, 256, 293, 317, 318, 319, 322, 323, 327-330, 331
Spicker, Paul, 205
Spruit, Leen, 265
Stausberg, Michael, 38
Steuco, Agostino, 37
Stiening, Gideon, 225
Stoicism, 6, 34, 104, 158, 203, 256
Stoics, 150, 287
Stoppelli, Pasquale, 172
Strabo, 166
Strazzoni, Andrea, 187, 190
Suárez, Francisco, 8, 333–49
Suetonius, 309
Suhrawardi, 35
Sulla, 198
superstition, 148, 200
Sylvester, Pope, 83

Talon, Omer, 242, 243, 259
Tambrun, Brigitte, 38
Tambrun-Krasker, Brigitte, 35, 36, 37

Index

Tardieu, Michel, 35
Tateo, Francesco, 105
Telesio, Bernardino, 7, 8, 262–69, 291, 350, 351
Terence, 109, 115
Thamus, 193
Themistius, 356
Themistocles, 238
Theodore Gaza, 50, 68, 72, 166
Theophilus, 361
Theophrastus, 190, 192, 196, 258, 309
Theutus, 193
Thiel, Detlef, 96, 98, 99
Thinking Machines, 11, 13
Thomas Aquinas, 3, 4, 50, 56, 82–95, 138, 157, 195, 196, 333, 334, 365
Thomas Becket, 88
Thomas, Apostle, 89
Thomson, Douglas F. S., 190, 197
Thucydides, 299, 309
Timon, 74
Timotheus, 79
Tobriner, Alice, 204
Tobriner, Marian Leona, 204, 205
transcendentals, 84
Traversari, Ambrogio, 117
Traversino, Massimiliano, 314
Trinity, 8, 26-33, 36, 51, 54, 62, 351, 354
Trinkaus, Charles Edward, 85

utopia, 351

Valdés, Juan de, 262
Valentinianus, Ammianus Marcellinus, 196
Valerius Maximus, 196
Valla, Lorenzo, 4, 8, 9, 82-95
Valverde, José Manuel García, 156, 157, 159, 271, 273

Varotti, Carlo, 172
Vasoli, Cesare, 105, 273, 294
Vázquez, Gabriel, 334
vicissitudes, 112, 329
Victor, Sextus Aurelius, 190
Vimercato, Francesco, 70
Virgil, 53, 89, 111, 199
Viroli, Maurizio, 172
virtue, 41
virtues, 19, 23, 41, 88–91, 106, 108, 124, 127, 144, 150, 151, 200, 201, 207, 212, 218, 246, 257, 269
Vitoria, Francisco de, 9
Vives, Juan Luis, 6, 8, 9, 202–22
void, 318, 319, 325, 326, 329

Wadding, Lucas, 303
Waddington, Charles, 240, 243
Wallace, William A., 7, 270
Watson, Foster, 205
Wels, Volkhard, 226
Wilson, Catherine, 139
Wilson, Nigel, 274
wisdom, 1, 2, 4, 7, 11-33, 36, 68, 73, 76, 78, 88, 119, 144, 145, 198-206, 216, 218, 222, 226, 227, 228, 233, 236, 260, 261, 263-269, 290, 315, 316, 351, 355
Woodhouse, Christopher Montague, 35, 39, 59
worship, 56

Xenocrates, 255
Xenophon, 230

Zabarella, Jacopo, 7, 8, 270–79, 291
Zeno, 258, 260
Zippel, Gianni, 85
zodiac, 58, 306
Zoroaster, 35-39, 43, 48

Philosophy in the Renaissance: An Anthology was designed in Arno Pro and composed by Kachergis Book Design of Pittsboro, North Carolina. It was printed on 55-pound Natural Offset and bound by Maple Press, York, Pennsylvania.